DYSTOPIAN DISCORD

Cold War Politics and Cambodian Communism

B.D. MOWELL, Ph.D.

UNG
UNIVERSITY *of*
NORTH GEORGIA
UNIVERSITY PRESS

Copyright © 2025 by B.D. Mowell.

All rights reserved. No part of this book may be reproduced in whole or in part without written permission from the publisher, except by reviewers who may quote brief excerpts in connections with a review in newspaper, magazine, or electronic publications; nor may any part of this book be reproduced, used for AI training, stored in a retrieval system, or transmitted in any form or by any means electronic, mechanical, photocopying, recording, or other, without the written permission from the publisher.

Published by:
University of North Georgia Press
Dahlonega, Georgia

Front cover image photographer is unknown, public domain.
Back cover image photographed by Wikimedia Commons user "Sgroey", CC BY 4.0.
Cover and book design by Corey Parson.

ISBN: 978-1-959203-13-1

CONTENT WARNING:
 Some of the photos and illustrations in the appendix depict extreme cruelty and violence. The images may be disturbing and are not suitable for children or for individuals sensitive to such material. **Discretion is strongly advised.**
 The author and publisher considered omitting certain content, including images. However, it is imperative that the world understand and remember the horrific nature and scale of the crimes perpetrated by the Khmer Rouge against the Cambodian people. Today, in many countries, particularly among younger generations, there is little awareness of this dark stain on humanity, due in part to misinformation. While the atrocities of the Pol Pot regime were being carried out, communist apologists denied their existence, dismissing such reports as Western Cold War propaganda. In the many years since the overthrow of the Khmer Rouge, far-left revisionists have sought to downplay, obscure, or justify many of the regime's brutal, dystopian actions.
 The historical record of the Khmer Rouge and their callous, sociopathic conduct is clear and incontrovertible. It is essential to confront these stark realities in order to recognize the nature of the regime and the depths of evil humanity can inflict even on the most innocent and vulnerable. It is equally crucial to understand the existential threat posed by radical, iconoclastic utopian ideologies and totalitarian regimes. We must acknowledge and heed the bitter lessons history provides. Communism is not benign.

Dedication

As a young adult, I had a murky and ever-evolving notion of my future options and what might be the best career or intellectual paths to explore. Like many students pursuing higher education, I found it somewhat daunting to identify mentors and role models who could dispense professional and educational guidance. Fortunately, one of the strengths of a cafeteria-style curriculum within U.S. higher education is that students can take courses from a diverse range of academic disciplines and that address myriad topics and perspectives reflecting nearly the totality of human knowledge. This educational sampling process ultimately enables many of us to find paths best suited to our interests and capabilities.

We have all taken courses that for whatever reason, we did not connect with intellectually or otherwise. Fortunately, many courses and the perspectives and knowledge they impart are impactful and aid us in some way along our respective paths. More importantly, many people in our lives are impactful in that they take an interest in us as individuals and in some way(s) contribute to our personal and professional evolution and the paths we ultimately take. I consider myself fortunate to have had many excellent professors who were not just experts in their respective fields and effective at imparting knowledge and enthusiasm to students, but who also had a particular impact upon my journey. My career as a professor reflects that over the course of my education at various universities I was able to find mentors and role models in the form of knowledgeable, patient, and consummate professionals who helped me in various ways with regard to the academic world. I dedicate this book to some of these remarkable, kind and giving souls. Thank you for helping me along the trail!

Florida Atlantic University
Dr. Jay Mendell – for being a kind and wise mentor, friend and role model
Dr. Arthur Sementelli – for teaching a nearly hopeless case how to use statistics in research

Florida International University
Dr. Eduardo Gamarra – for many insightful classes and useful dissertation guidance
Dr. Markus Thiel – for helping forge one of my academic specialties (international organizations) and for guidance and patience as my Ph.D./dissertation committee chair
Dr. Zion Zohar – for being an excellent professor and role model

Harvard University Extension/Summer College
Dr. Tom Nichols – for likely the most interesting class out of 10 college/university degrees

University of Georgia
Dr. Diane Napier – for your unwavering kindness, patience and mentorship as Ed.D./dissertation committee chair and for enduring me as your teaching assistant : -)

University of Miami
Ambassador Ambler Moss – for being a role model as a professor and consummate public servant

Table of Contents

Foreword	vii
Acknowledgments	xi
Introduction	xiii
Chapter 1: Antecedents and Genesis of Cambodian Communism	1
Chapter 2: Political Dynamic of the Early Independence Era	29
Chapter 3: Onset of Cambodian Civil War	57
Chapter 4: Expanding Civil War and Vietnamese Involvement	91
Chapter 5: The Dystopian Khmer Rouge Regime, 1975–1979	129
Chapter 6: The Khmer Rouge Genocide	157
Chapter 7: The Rump State and Vietnamese Occupation, 1979–1991	185
Chapter 8: Post-Cold War Cambodia	209
Appendix: Photo Gallery	235
Select Chronology	263
List of Abbreviations	275
Index	277
About the Author	289

Foreword

Except for a few well-known tourist attractions, or what was learned from news coverage and popular culture representations of the Vietnam War, people who are not native to the region know very little about Southeast Asia, and perhaps the most opaque and little-understood of the countries in mainland Southeast Asia is Cambodia. Beyond the ancient temples of Angkor Wat, Cambodia is *une terre inconnue* to most Westerners. Cambodia's role in the communist movement in Southeast Asia is even more shrouded in mystery, particularly the role played by the Khmer Rouge, who brought a reign of terror upon the country that resulted in the deaths of millions and the destruction of Cambodian society from which the country is yet to emerge.

Much of this lack of knowledge and understanding, especially regarding the period after World War II to the present, stems from Western misunderstanding of communism and how it is affected by history and culture. This is reflected in the Western obsession with Domino Theory. The latter was a Cold War policy that posited the view that a communist government in one nation would quickly lead to communist takeovers in neighboring states, each falling like a row of dominoes. As a young army officer preparing for my first tour in Vietnam in 1967–68, I was lectured frequently on our reason for being in Vietnam, and the Domino Theory was always at the center of such lectures. I was in Vietnam for less than two months when I learned from my Vietnamese counterparts that historically and culturally, there was no way that the various nations of Southeast Asia would ever be able to work together in the fashion described by the Domino Theory. This was especially true where China was involved. Going back centuries, there was too much historical and cultural baggage for such a collaboration. The war between communist Vietnam and the communist Khmer Rouge, who controlled Cambodia, and the 1979 invasion of communist Vietnam by communist China are but two examples that illustrate why a monolithic communist Southeast Asia is improbable.

Dystopian Discord: Cold War Politics and Cambodian Communism is an exhaustively researched and documented study of how the Khmer Rouge style of communist rule in Cambodia was distinct from other Asian communist countries. Cambodia's unique culture and history, vis-à-vis not just its neighbors but the wider world, sheds some light on the atrocities committed by the Khmer Rouge. Using information taken from declassified intelligence documents in addition to historical works, B.D. Mowell, an academic and author with decades of experience, pulls the veil that has hidden the truth behind the disastrous reign of Pol Pot (born Saloth Sar) and his murderous Khmer Rouge for decades. It helps to explain how the son of a prosperous farmer, who was educated at some of Cambodia's most prestigious schools, and who studied at the *École Française de Radioelectricité* on a full scholarship, and who was a school teacher, could become one of the most brutal despots in modern history. While Pol Pot was ideologically a Maoist, he was mainly a Khmer ethnonationalist.

During Pol Pot's rise to power, he was aided by Viet Cong militia and North Vietnamese military forces in his battle against the Cambodian government controlled by Lon Nol. He had been head of the resistance to the royal government of King Norodom Sihanouk until Lon Nol ousted Sihanouk. After the latter development, the Khmer Rouge and the King joined forces to oppose the U.S.-supported Cambodian government.

Despite shifting alliances, however, the Khmer Rouge movement was always unique in its nativist views. After the North Vietnamese defeated the South Vietnamese forces and united Vietnam under communist rule, immediate conflict arose between Cambodia and Vietnam, no surprise to those who were aware of the long and contentious history between the Vietnamese and the Khmer.

This book presents a scholarly examination of Cold War Cambodia. While *Dystopian Discord* is primarily targeted toward academic audiences, it is a journey well worth taking for the general public as well. And not just for

FOREWORD

the enlightenment of the Cambodian situation. At the end, you will have a better understanding of how the world works.

It is probably Pollyannish to think that if American decision-makers in the 1950s had possessed a better understanding of the cultural and historical factors at play in Southeast Asia, the history of our involvement in the region would have been different. But it is a nice thing to contemplate.

Charles Ray
Former U.S. Ambassador to Cambodia (2002–2005)

Acknowledgments

A debt of gratitude is owed to many people who aided in this book coming to fruition. The entire staff at University of North Georgia Press was phenomenal and I could not have asked for a better or more professional experience with a publisher: many thanks to Director BJ Robinson, Managing Editor Corey Parson, Assistant Managing Editor Ariana Adams, and Marketing and Content Manager Nicole Clifton. Gratitude is also extended to the many academic colleagues and subject matter experts who contributed feedback to the project and manuscript and to Ambassador Charles Ray for contributing the Foreword. Lastly, my thanks are extended to my wife Kim and stepson Neill for putting up with me during the several years devoted to researching and writing the book.

Introduction

The rhetoric associated with communist movements as well as many commonly held external perceptions of communism as an ideology (e.g., the shared goal of radical socioeconomic reform as a centripetal force) and how it manifested in the geopolitical arena can sharply contrast with political reality. Naive notions of workers across the world from widely diverse national, cultural, and political backgrounds uniting under the common goal of a utopian socio-political and economic vision in reality did not generally succeed in supplanting existing ethnocentric and nationalistic attitudes or rivalries. In a few instances (e.g., the Tito regime in Yugoslavia), some communist regimes invested sustained effort to suppress traditional ethnic and territorial rivalries internally and may have experienced some measure of success temporarily. However, the latter was more an exception than the rule as animosity and violent conflict driven by racial or cultural divisions or territoriality were common realities in many communist regimes.

The discord characteristic of communist regimes was not merely internal in nature. Despite any overarching ideological commonalities, the enduring presence of nationalism, cultural/ethnic rivalries, xenophobia, existing international disputes (e.g., boundary demarcation, conflicting historical claims over territory), or some combination of the latter facilitated strife, including military conflict between many communist states. Just as some western nations such as Greece and Turkey were ostensibly allies yet succumbed to such pressures and devolved into conflict, so too did many communist states. An additional catalyst driving strife among communist states was an often-substantive difference in the interpretation of communist doctrine. A fundamental example of the latter appears in the early Cold War polarization of communist bloc nations into those aligned with the Soviet Union and its emphasis upon industrialization and urban issues versus those regimes allied with China and its emphasis upon agricultural and rural issues and China's ostensible commitment to advancing the spread of communism internationally.

Similarly, just as the circumstances of countries with democratic or capitalist systems are not monolithic, such dynamics also exist in the nature of communist regimes. Thus, oversimplified visions of a unified West facing a unified communist bloc during the Cold War belie the complex political realities that existed among states in both camps. Among communist states, some ideologies and regimes were more radical and iconoclastic than others; some states were more inclined than others to engage in atrocities, such as ethnic/political cleansing or other forms of brutality and human rights violations; and some states were more prone than others through either regime belligerence or other circumstances to devolve into internal or intrastate conflict.

The Khmer Rouge regime provides an excellent case study of a dysfunctional, dystopian, and bellicose state. Communist doctrine in general can be characterized as a radical, naive ideology that was among the chief sources of human conflict and misery in the 20th century. However, the militant, sadistic, iconoclastic, and anarchical strain of communism implemented by the Khmer Rouge facilitated among the most Orwellian and catastrophic societal experiments undertaken by any communist regime or, indeed, any civilization in human history. A substantial body of literature has deservedly examined the Khmer Rouge regime in terms of its bizarre and radical ideology, its gross ineptitude, and its systemic normalization and embrace of widespread atrocities and human rights violations.

However, less attention has been paid to the Khmer Rouge as a case study in both (1) internal conflict and (2) the discord and geopolitical wrangling that existed between many communist movements (ideologies) and communist states during the Cold War. The Khmer Rouge regime was virulently xenophobic and nationalistic in nature, characteristics that have not been conventionally associated with communism in the literature but which have frequently been present at least to some degree in many communist regimes. These attributes motivated the Khmer Rouge to see ethnic and cultural minorities within Cambodia as enemies which they targeted for persecution and eradication. Additionally, the animosity toward outsiders and interest in forcefully settling traditional rivalries with neighboring states/ethnicities empowered the regime to undertake reckless and aggressive actions toward its neighbors, particularly communist Vietnam, which ultimately led to war between the communist states and the demise of the Khmer Rouge government.

This book presents an analysis of the Khmer Rouge movement in general, juxtaposed against the nationalistic and xenophobic nature of the Cambodian communist movement and its leadership. The revolutionaries who followed Pol Pot were not merely advocates of a radical social, political, and economic metamorphosis through communism and the national restructuring it would facilitate. Significantly, they also sought to reassert the dominance of ethnic Khmers within their own country, a process that potentially included the ouster or eradication of certain minority groups within Cambodia. Additionally, the Khmer Rouge also sought to reestablish Cambodian (ethnic Khmer) control over many of the adjacent countries' territories to which the ethnic Khmer population had historical claims and that they perceived to have been rightfully theirs.

A clear distinction cannot necessarily be made between the groups the Khmer Rouge deemed to be their domestic enemies and those they regarded as foreign enemies, as such categories often overlapped. For example, the Khmer Rouge hated and distrusted the Vietnamese and Thai minorities living in Cambodia, regarding them as outsiders whose loyalties were potentially aligned with neighboring states that had historically been rivals of Cambodia and the Khmer people. The targets of their revolutionary zeal were not only political opponents and class enemies in the conventional ideological perspective of communist revolutionaries or those who otherwise stood in the way of their radical and sinister societal vision. The Khmer Rouge strain of communism was a hyper-nationalist movement and, upon coming to power, it targeted most populations that were not ethnically Khmer living as minorities in what the regime deemed as rightly Khmer territory. Also, the non-Khmer populations in certain border areas of neighboring states were targeted for attack and expulsion, ethnicities such as the Vietnamese that had been traditional rivals.

Levels of Analysis

In seeking to understand the conduct of states and the many different influences that impact state actions, it can be useful to categorize factors/theories into distinct levels of analysis. Such analysis can lend insight concerning state conduct within the international arena and suggest possible causal factors. While variations exist, customarily three-to-four main levels of analysis are considered within International Relations (IR): (1) the individual level, which examines how the psychology, political perspectives, and socio-cultural mores and actions of individuals (e.g., leaders) can impact state characteristics; (2) the state or domestic level, which examines the influences of internal factors, such as culture, public opinion, nationalism, societal ethnocentrism/xenophobia, or government type; (3) international factors at the interstate/bilateral or regional level, which include considerations related to diplomatic relations, territorial/boundary issues, reciprocal trade/interaction, etc.; and (4) international factors at the global level, which would include such considerations as Cold War politics, international terrorism, or impacts from imperialism and colonial control. Some IR scholars combine the third and fourth categories under the broader umbrella of "international" considerations. In seeking to correlate causes of war to levels of analysis from a realist perspective, Waltz attributed human nature as the cause at the individual level, socio-political factors at the state/domestic level, and structural anarchy (the lack of international government/order) at international levels.[1] It would be difficult to attribute the Khmer Rouge regime and its conduct/conflicts to a single level of analysis. Considerations relative to the individual level, state/domestic level, and international—interstate/regional as well as global—level all combined to some degree for the discordant nature of the movement to manifest. Accordingly, any attempt to understand the Khmer Rouge must acknowledge the relevance of each level.

Scholars cannot discount the importance that Pol Pot and other individual actors in senior leadership roles within the Khmer Rouge movement had upon forging their radical, xenophobic, and belligerent path. Many of the future revolutionaries' formative years that molded their socio-political outlook occurred amid a climate of both mounting anti-colonial turmoil and internal rivalry between ethnic Khmers and minorities, helping to facilitate xenophobic outlooks toward westerners as well as regional rivals and non-Khmer ethnicities living in Cambodia. Examples of Pol Pot's virulent racism are discernible in public comments, including an infamous 1978 Cambodian radio pronouncement concerning a political revolt among communists in eastern Cambodia, in which the dictator blamed the Vietnamese and advocated for the extermination of the entire Vietnamese population in order to purify Cambodia. Many senior leaders of the Khmer Rouge also appear to have been driven by a desire to reclaim former Khmer territory, portions of which belonged to Laos, Thailand, and Vietnam, and this agenda helped facilitate a belligerent, confrontational policy toward all three nations. Additionally, the militant interpretation of communism—typified by a reckless, naive approach to agrarian collectivization and utopianism—that came to characterize the Khmer Rouge regime resulted in part from individual leaders' experiences. For example, Pol Pot's youthful observations (and, most likely, misinterpretations) of agricultural collectivization in Tito's Yugoslavia, as discussed in Chapter 5, and later observations of the early stage (though not the end results) of China's disastrous Cultural Revolution.

State/domestic-level considerations, such as nationalism and ethnocentric or xenophobic national attitudes, also factored heavily in the emergence of the communist variant that emerged in Cambodia. For example, various leftist factions, including what would eventually become the Khmer Rouge, were among the diverse elements in Cambodia agitating for independence in the mid-20th century. Unlike many other states that underwent socialist revolutions, Cambodian communism developed in tandem with nationalism. This pattern was not entirely unprecedented, as the communist movements that manifested in many developing nations sometimes possessed at least some element of nationalism/ethnocentrism, but Cambodia's strain of nationalism was especially pronounced. Ethnic Khmers within the Cambodian communist movement were also increasingly resentful of minority elements that held leadership roles in the burgeoning communist movement—including ethnic Chinese and, in particular, ethnic Vietnamese—from whom Pol Pot and his supporters would eventually wrest control as the early manifestations of Cambodian communism evolved. Long-standing, historical conflicts existed between the Khmer people and neighboring populations, including a history of Khmer subjugation by those they deemed as regional competitors, such as China and Vietnam. The ethnic factions within early Cambodian communism likely served to exacerbate xenophobic tendencies and hostilities on the part of the ethnic Khmers within the country's burgeoning communist movement.

Scholars can undertake an analysis of international factors via a two-fold approach of examining influences at the interstate or regional level and, more broadly, those at the global level. The interstate and regional dynamic of Cambodia produced a discordant political dynamic and helped shape the bellicose and distrustful attitudes of Khmer Rouge leadership. This dynamic included these overlapping considerations: (1) disputed territory and other specific manifestations of bilateral conflict, (2) deep-seated historical rivalries inexorably linked with (3) culturally ingrained national/ethnic animosities toward neighboring states, and (4) uncertainty as to the shifting balance of power (and a desire held by multiple countries to be the regional hegemon) among the states of Indochina all combined to place many of the region's communist movements in competition. Specifically, such interstate/regional considerations permeated the mindset of Khmer Rouge leadership and helped steer the communist polities of Cambodia and Vietnam on a path of political and military confrontation, despite their ostensible ideological kinship within the communist world.

International/transnational considerations that superseded the state-to-state or regional dynamic also served as significant factors in the discordant and inimical nature of the Khmer Rouge regime. Substantive disputes over what should be the communist doctrine and agenda resulted in the Cold War-era world not merely being divided into an east-west polarity but also split into dichotomous communist bloc factions which were as, or more, averse toward each other, as both factions were hostile toward democracy or capitalism. While an exhaustive analysis of the Chinese-Soviet rift is beyond the scope of this discussion, these developments were of primary importance:

1. Following the death of Stalin, the USSR eventually adopted more comparatively moderate geopolitical stances, including a posture of coexistence with the west. Concerned with the eruption of open conflict—possibly even including nuclear war with the west—the post-Stalin Soviet leadership developed a more limited and guarded interest in advancing the spread of revolutionary movements globally. Beijing regarded the later policy moderations as betrayals of communist principles.

INTRODUCTION

2. China and the USSR frequently had conflicting national agendas, such as Moscow's increasingly close relations with India, a major Chinese rival.
3. China sought to modify many precepts of what it deemed "European communism," adapting doctrine and practice more toward what Beijing viewed as the agrarian realities of developing nations.
4. In part, the rift also reflected the personal disdain the leaders held for each other, as Mao had a better relationship and was more ideologically aligned with Stalin than with Khrushchev. Mao regarded the Khrushchev regime as weak, as evidenced, for example, in both de-Stalinization efforts which publicly condemned former communist policies and the increased resistance on the part of some states—such as Hungary and Yugoslavia—to Soviet control over elements of the Eastern European communist bloc. Conversely, Khrushchev regarded Mao as unintelligent, reckless, and out of touch with many geopolitical realities, such as the danger of provoking war—including a nuclear exchange with the west.

Beginning in the 1950s and for the next several decades, both China and the USSR saw themselves as the legitimate standard bearer of communism internationally. This competition to lead the global movement played out in many areas of the developing world, as both China and the USSR sought to exert influence over communist states and movements in the form of military and material aid, political guidance, and on-site advisors. The rivalry for the hearts and minds of international revolutionaries as well as the desire for hegemony within the international communist movement and geographical areas in which both countries sought influence occasionally led the two powers to support different competing factions within the same country/conflict—e.g., Chinese support for a mujahedeen guerilla faction during the Afghan-Soviet War.[2]

As explored in this book, the growing distrust, deteriorating relations, and, ultimately, the war between Cambodia and Vietnam can be regarded as a proxy conflict, with China supporting the Khmer Rouge regime and the Soviet Union supporting Hanoi. Following the toppling of Pol Pot's regime by Soviet-backed Vietnamese forces in 1979, the Khmer Rouge established a rump state and waged a guerrilla resistance campaign for many years from remote areas in Cambodia's rugged and forested north and west with the ongoing support of the Chinese government. Though not the sole causal factor, the sustained Cold War-era strife between China and the USSR in addition to the factionalized nature of international communism helped to escalate the conflict between Cambodia and Vietnam to the point of a proxy war between the major communist powers.

International Relations Theory

Attributing the inimical nature of the Khmer Rouge to a single level of analysis is difficult; equally problematic is explaining the circumstances and their causes using a single theory. Scholars have described attempting to frame the complex and conflict-prone Southeast Asian region within IR theoretical paradigms as "notoriously problematic."[3] Within international relations and security/conflict studies, a multitude of theoretical frameworks have been formulated through attempts to explain and contextualize various phenomena. The diverse range of theories address myriad international developments from many different, often conflicting, perspectives, and new paradigms or variations derived from existing theories emerge regularly. For example, the largely discredited primordialism perspective—often associated with classical realism and which would presuppose a normative pattern wherein different groups would compete for, and come into conflict over, territory and resources within most regions, including Indochina—lies in stark contrast with a more nuanced constructivist analysis of *how* ethnic relations/conflicts evolved due to a complex set of circumstances.[4]

While not all theoretical perspectives are equally valid or apply to all international issues, often the same international issue can be juxtaposed against multiple theories, with each potentially able to offer legitimate insight and interpretation through its lens. Several fundamental theories of international relations—including realism/neorealism, liberal theory/idealism (by way of the absence of its precepts), constructivism, and Marxist/conflict theory—potentially have applicability, though perhaps not to equal degrees, in seeking to explain the tumultuous circumstances and conflicts of the Khmer Rouge. The following presents brief explorations of the potential applicability of several major IR theories to the analysis of the discordant nature of the Khmer Rouge. Particular attention is paid to realist and neorealist concepts, as they provide a useful framework for understanding the phenomenon.

INTRODUCTION

(Neo)Realism

The fundamental concepts of classical realism contend that sovereign states are the dominant actors in an anarchical (decentralized and unstructured) international arena and propose that states act rationally in their own self-interest, competing with other states in the pursuit of additional power or to maintain existing power. Realists perceive state behavior as being largely driven by the conditions/structures within the international system; thus, if those structures are understood, the behavior of states as rational actors, including actions related to conflict, should be predictable.[5] An implication of classical realism is that states fitting the model may be more inclined toward belligerence and the use of military force rather than pursuing non-confrontational resolutions (e.g., mediation) or less overt forms of leverage, such as diplomacy or bargaining. While certain other IR theories may also have relevance, realism and many derivatives of the realist school of thought are clearly useful in attempting to explain the Khmer Rouge dynamic. Various strands and sub-theories of realist thought are applicable to the focus of study and deserve at least brief exploration, including neorealism, offensive and defensive realism, balancing, hegemonic stability theory, and power transition theory, for example. The potential relevance of other major theoretical perspectives—liberalism/idealism, constructivism/structuralism, Marxism, and the English School—within international relations concerning the bellicose nature of the Khmer Rouge is also briefly explored, though a comprehensive analysis and application of each theoretical perspective within IR transcends the scope of this study.

Neorealism (also known as structural realism), a modern adaptation of traditional realist thought, partly bridges the gap between realism and liberalism/idealism and between historical conditions within the international system (classical realism) and those of the contemporary, globalized world. Neorealism shares many perspectives with classical realism, including an emphasis upon the drive of states to obtain power. Both perspectives also view states as existing in an international system devoid of significant structure or authority. In explaining this lack of order within the international sphere, Kenneth Waltz states that "among men as among states, anarchy, or the absence of government, is associated with the occurrence of violence."[6] Within such anarchical systems, states engage in zero-sum competition wherein the actions of one state to increase its security will concomitantly decrease the security of others.[7] One of several key distinctions between classical realism and neorealism—being central to the focus of this research—is the cause of war. Classical realists see war as a reflection of negative aspects of human nature (e.g., greed, ambition, jealousy, suspicion, aggression) and as being something essentially natural and to be expected. For example, the lingering mistrust and animosity following centuries of traditional rivalry between ethnic Khmers and ethnic Vietnamese could be expected to erupt in war or, more specifically, to result in the most recent manifestation of a centuries-old cycle of repeated conflicts between the populations.

In contrast, rather than directly blaming an inherently competitive and belligerent human nature, neorealists attribute war primarily to flawed or entirely absent anarchical international systems that are incapable of providing global or regional order and that tend to promote interstate competition and conflict. Peace and stability, or the absence thereof, would depend upon the structure of the international system—which, according to realists, is largely a reflection of how power is divided among the most important state actors globally or within a region.[8] Exploring this neorealist concept of "balancing" (balance of power theory) among competitor states, Morgan notes that:

> a state may enhance its power to achieve balance in various ways—by undertaking arms buildups or improvements, joining an alliance, or helping others (terrorists, guerillas, third-party states) hostile to a government considered too powerful... A state can also fight to weaken other states, using war to redistribute power. Another possibility for maintaining a fairly even power distribution is to have a balancer. For example, if two states are vying to attain a dominant position and one gets close to achieving superiority, an important third party moves to support the weaker side to preserve the balance.[9]

Neorealist concepts related to balancing clearly apply to aspects of the Khmer Rouge phenomenon and its geopolitical machinations. Following the U.S.-Vietnamese War, Vietnam had emerged as not only the most powerful state militarily within Indochina but also the regional standard-bearer of communism. Not wishing to remain subordinate in the shadow

INTRODUCTION

of Vietnam, Cambodia's historical rival, the Khmer Rouge may have been further incentivized to mobilize military manpower—at least, what meager resources were at its disposal—and initiate efforts intended to undermine or intimidate Vietnam (as well as non-communist rival Thailand). The naive Khmer Rouge ambition to be the regional hegemon or, at least, an effective rival/counter to its competitor states for that distinction certainly helped facilitate Cambodia's alliance with China.

Also a product of the neorealist school of thought, power transition theory contends that the likelihood of war increases when either a regionally or globally dominant state or a state with hegemonic ambitions is challenged by a dissatisfied up-and-coming competitor state.[10] Potential challengers may seek the creation of a new power dynamic, as they do not regard themselves as being in an adequate position in the current order and, believing they can defeat the dominant state, are not content to remain in a subordinate position.[11] It could be argued that both Cambodia and Vietnam saw themselves as the dominant state in Indochina—or both at least aspired to this status—thus, this power dynamic and the desire of both states to assert their position within the region was one of several factors that brought them into conflict. Even outside the political maneuvering of nations to establish dominance within the region, power transition theory is still potentially relevant in the form of the dichotomous Cold War dynamic between China and the USSR in which Moscow, long the standard bearer for global communism, was being aggressively challenged by a strengthening China for influence and power in many political arenas and world regions—including Southeast Asia.[12] In many regions, this competition for power and influence played out in an overtly adversarial fashion, including the Cambodia-Vietnam proxy war in which Hanoi had Soviet backing and the Khmer Rouge regime had Chinese support.

Hegemonic stability theory provides another example of an international structural dynamic that could help explain the actions of the Khmer Rouge regime. The theory argues that a global or regional hegemon can provide peace and stability in that the clearly dominant state, either through benevolence or, perhaps more likely, coercion, and via the acquiescence of weaker states within the region to the dominant power can facilitate a greater degree of political and economic stability within areas under its sway. The hegemon will have little incentive to impose its will militarily as the mere possibility of it exercising that option would allow it to obtain its objectives and other states would be deferential to the hegemon's authority as they would understand they could not successfully oppose the dominant state in military conflict.[13]

While France was arguably the hegemon in Indochina in the early 20th century (depending on how the British presence is assessed), the end of the colonial era in effect created a regional power vacuum, with no single post-colonial state economically, politically, or militarily dominant in the region. Following France's departure, several other world powers, including China, the Soviet Union, and the United States, sought to replace its influence within the region, but none were fully successful. While not all IR scholars agree with the premise, the theory posits that, if the presence of a strongly dominant hegemon can provide stability from which all states in the region can benefit, then the decline or collapse of that dominant power can likewise facilitate regional disorder, even war.[14] IR theorist John Mearshimer argues that such regional vacuums can motivate states to compete with each other for power and dominance in order to become the hegemon, thus destabilizing the region and potentially setting the stage for armed conflict. The circumstances of post-colonial Indochina exemplify many elements of hegemonic stability theory with some states in the region assuming—at least to some degree—competitive and, in some instances, aggressively confrontational postures toward others.[15]

In mid-20th century Indochina, no regionally dominant state hegemon or strong intergovernmental organization existed that could maintain stability and help defuse regional conflict. Despite the fact that Cambodia, Laos, and Vietnam were all communist states by 1975, no monolithic, unified international communist structure existed to ameliorate conflicts between the countries. In fact, a sharply divided international communist system, polarized into two antagonistic blocs, exacerbated the already contentious Cambodian-Vietnamese relationship and helped facilitate war between them. From the neorealistic perspective, the international and regional political dynamic in general and the international communist system in particular were anarchical rather than conducive to stability in either the region or bilateral Cambodia-Vietnam relations. Thus, these dynamics failed to empower the nations/region in overcoming historical cycles of rivalry and conflict. However, many IR scholars discount the value of strong international systems, including hegemonic systems, as vehicles for peace and stability. For example, Keohane and Nye note that systemic constraints against war appear to be more effective at the macro level in limiting use of force by major/superpowers, with war remaining a more common occurrence in (sub)regional rivalries and among smaller states.[16]

Theories related to balancing and hegemonic stability illustrate the plurality of models that exist within neorealism. This diverse and sometimes conflicting range of neorealist theories can be organized into two basic divisions: defensive realism and offensive realism. Defensive realism derives in part from suppositions related to the security dilemma within IR, which, in short, postulates that states' actions to enhance their own security/power can potentially trigger comparable actions on the part of other (rival) states. This potentiality—combined with uncertainty about other states' intentions—can lead to escalation and conflict. Defensive realism is also based partly upon the neorealist-derived balance of power theory, which contends that, as the power and influence of one state grows, other states in the region—particularly competitors—will seek to enhance their own power/influence to counteract that growing influence. Cold War-era Indochina can be said to exemplify the balance of power theory, as China sought to offset Soviet influence in communist Vietnam by cultivating an alliance with neighboring Cambodia. Both paradigms that contributed to the formulation of defensive realism as a theory (the security dilemma and balance of power theory) view anarchical conditions—e.g., lack of central order/governance—within the international arena as the catalyst for conflict: states view expansion and power acquisition as the means to obtain security and stability.

Offensive realism, also derived from the neorealist tradition, asserts that the absence of international/regional order and stability—an issue of greater concern in some areas of the world (e.g., Cold War-era Southeast Asia) than others—and the associated likelihood of conflict, incentivizes states to maximize their power as a survival strategy. Power is not pursued for its own sake nor due to an innately belligerent nature but as a means of providing security and continuity for the state in an uncertain world/region. Offense is perceived to be the best defense and best guarantor of state survival. Whereas classical realism would interpret the aggression of states as reflecting baser elements of human nature—e.g., greed, pride, distrust—offensive realism (and neorealism more broadly) would interpret such conduct as a never-ending quest for security facilitated by the absence of stability and central authority within the international system.[17] Acquisition of territory and resources and the buildup of military force all contribute to strength and thus increase the likelihood of national survival. Establishing dominance as a regional hegemon or preventing a traditional competitor state from doing so—via aggression if necessary— is a logical outcome driven by the goal to survive as a state, according to this paradigm. Mearsheimer, one of the key figures within the neorealist tradition, asserts that states will pursue expansion and power acquisition if the benefits (in added security) of such actions outweigh the perceived risk and cost.[18]

Liberal Theory/Idealism

While many strands of liberal theory, also known as idealism, exist, it is difficult to see how the international dynamic it envisions would be directly relevant to the discordant circumstances of the Khmer Rouge. It is additionally challenging to see how such elements could have been present to effectively mitigate the regime's destructive conduct. The cornerstones of liberal theory related to state conduct within the international arena stipulate that (1) the international system is not necessarily anarchical and can facilitate cooperation among states and create some degree of centralized order; (2) states can advance their own interests without zero-sum competition; (3) non-state actors, such as non-governmental and intergovernmental organizations or multinational corporations, can rival the influence of state actors and elicit positive change within the international system, including facilitating peace and stability (neoliberal institutionalism); and (4) ethical and moral principles can be shared globally and can serve as important drivers of state conduct within the international system, overriding more intrinsic traditional motivators of state conduct such as acquisition of power. Liberal and neoliberal theory stress the importance of economic, social, and political institutions as drivers of state interactions and emphasize that stable, effective political and legal institutions domestically and internationally can promote peace and stability.[19] Liberal and neoliberal perspectives within IR also regard state action as reflecting complex domestic institutions and interests and, consequently, the conduct of states within the international dynamic can

INTRODUCTION

be as diverse as their constituent populations—meaning not all will adhere to models seeking to predict foreign policy, conflict, or other behavior.[20]

If any applicability to this study is to be found with regard to the (neo) liberal framework, it is via the absence of many of the tenets and prerequisite conditions, permitting more realist models of state conduct to prevail. The nature of the Khmer Rouge, that is, its internal chaos and bellicose relations with multiple neighboring states, serve as excellent case studies to refute the liberal/idealist school of thought as a universal norm within the international dynamic and to illustrate what circumstances can manifest outside the orderly, civilized, and perhaps overly optimistic (if admirable) vision of the liberal/idealist paradigm within IR. Neorealist criticisms of the liberal school assert that the international system remains largely devoid of substantive structure/order, states remain concerned with their own vested interests, and state power (e.g., military and economic capability) remains key to the influence and security of the state within the international system.[21] Non-state actors, such as Intergovernmental Organizations (IGOs) or Non-Governmental Organizations (NGOs), have not always had an influential presence in all world regions (e.g., Cold War era Indochina), and where they do exist, neorealist critics contend that their influence may be overstated as they wield only as much influence as states permit. Such critiques of liberal theory appear valid with regard to the circumstances of the Khmer Rouge.

At most, it can be said that some of the principles of the liberal/idealist school can be witnessed in the downfall and distant aftermath of the Khmer Rouge. While other factors likely weighed more heavily in the decision (border security, regional stability, Pol Pot's repeated military provocations, etc.), Vietnam officially justified its 1978 invasion of Cambodia principally on humanitarian grounds, citing the need to end the Khmer Rouge genocide—a justification in line with (neo)liberal theory (e.g., Just War Theory) that establishes morality and human rights as justification for armed conflict between states. Although the international order or any shared global moral standard failed to prevent or mitigate its nefarious, violent conduct decades after the regime was toppled, an international judicial structure aided in efforts to hold some Khmer Rouge leaders accountable to standards of international law. Though, as discussed in Chapter 8, even this attempt to obtain justice largely fell short of expectation. It might also be argued that Indochina's long history of conflict, competition, and discord, along with the Khmer Rouge's conduct, exemplify the realist paradigm. However, these dynamics eventually helped facilitate a transition toward liberal institutionalism and greater regional stability evident today in the Association of Southeast Asian Nations (ASEAN), for example.

Constructivism

Whereas realist and liberal/idealist traditions within IR describe existing conditions in the international dynamic, constructivism as a theory endeavors to explain why the circumstances of state behavior and the international system came into existence. Constructivism does so by considering a diverse range of factors, including cultural, economic, ideological, and sociological considerations—not merely perceptions of immutable norms related to power or security, for example. In a sense, constructivism can be regarded as a type of social theory which seeks to explain international relations/conflict via a methodologically flexible and holistic approach. Nye and Welch succinctly note that constructivists "believe that leaders and other people are motivated not only by material interests, but also by their sense of identity, morality, and what their society or culture considers appropriate."[22]

Constructivist theory differs from realism/neorealism in that it does recognize anarchy (lack of structure/governance) within the international dynamic but does not necessarily regard this anarchical presence as inherently bad, for example, as a facilitator of zero-sum competition among states for power or survival. The anarchy within the international system can vary in nature from peaceful or benign to competitive or belligerent.[23] Alexander Wendt, one of the founders of constructivism as a school of thought within IR, contends that states are not necessarily at the mercy of any inherent circumstances within the international order and that they can choose to remain in an unstructured, competitive, anarchical international system, or they can opt to create or modify systems in order to move in the direction of international cooperation and increased stability. Wendt famously summed up this perspective, in which states are in control of shaping their own structural conditions within the international arena, by stating that "anarchy is what states make of it."[24] Constructivists also differ from the realist tradition in that they do not regard state actions as the product of simple cost-benefit (risk-reward) calculations but via complex combinations of identities, norms, and values.[25]

INTRODUCTION

An application of constructivist precepts to the Khmer Rouge phenomenon potentially allows for a more nuanced and diverse explanatory model to be developed than may be the case with using only (neo)realist concepts. For instance, at least some incentive on the part of the Khmer Rouge in the persecution of non-Khmer minorities and the regime's aggression toward neighboring states may not have been derived by desire for power or other tangible benefit but via societal/cultural traits, such as endemic ethnocentrism and xenophobia and the desire for revenge following centuries of cyclical conflict. At minimum, the regime advanced such rhetoric in an effort to solicit support among the ethnic Khmer population.

Marxist/Conflict Theories

Many of the core concepts of Marxist theory that attempt to explain state behavior and the international dynamic are similar in naïveté and wishful thinking to elements of liberal/idealist paradigms in IR, in that they crafted a vision of how they wanted the world to be rather than how it (and human nature) exists in reality. For example, Marxist theories of international relations predicted humanity would transcend war when all states embraced communism, yet this theory could not reconcile the latter prediction with the frequent armed conflicts between communist states (as well as intrastate conflicts between communist factions) in the 20th century. Such armed conflicts include, for example, Vietnam's invasion of Cambodia, the Vietnam-China border war, Sino-Soviet hostilities, China-Mongolia border strife, etc. The Marxist paradigm within IR also incorrectly predicted that capitalist nations would increasingly devolve into cycles of war with each other, and Marxist IR perspectives were unable to explain the decades-long era of peace, stability, and cooperation experienced by most western nations following WWII.[26] Marxist-Leninist perspectives contended that such perpetual conflict among capitalist nations would stem from their inherently expansionistic and imperialistic nature and the associated competition for resources and markets.[27] While such an explanatory model could potentially be applied to the colonial era (including the circumstances of Indochina under western control), by the mid-20th century, capitalism, democracy, and the international relations of western nations had matured beyond the application of many dated Marxist tenets. Such flawed and outmoded suppositions explain why

Marxist theory has declined in influence within IR as a means of explaining state behavior and the international dynamic.

However, certain elements of Marxist theory do perhaps offer insight into the interstate conflicts that characterized the Khmer Rouge regime. Similar to realist thought, Marxist theory regards people—and, in turn, states—as self-interested and prone to compete for resources or power, particularly if there may be inequitable distribution. Borders between ethnic Khmer, Thai, and Vietnamese, for example, had changed repeatedly over previous centuries, reflecting cycles of competition between the groups. By the 20th century, much of what had once been Cambodian territory was lost to neighboring populations, and, due to conflicting historically based claims of ownership, territorial/boundary disputes existed among several states in the region. Although few commercially coveted resources existed in the disputed borderlands (and what resources that did exist in some areas, including timber, would have proven difficult to utilize due to accessibility and transport infrastructure), the potential value of resources in the disputed areas were conceivably a consideration. Pol Pot and other Khmer Rouge leaders may have been partly incentivized to reclaim what were once Khmer lands to sustain a growing population and its agricultural needs and to potentially help alleviate the country's poverty via (re)settlement and developing some of the disputed territory. The paradigm, along with realist principles, can also potentially address regional power imbalance as a contributing factor in that the Pol Pot regime may have sought to counter real or perceived increases in the regional military or political influence of Vietnam, for example.

Marxist theories (those focused on explaining internal societal conflict) might also offer insight in attempting to understand certain aspects of the internal upheavals and human rights violations associated with the Khmer Rouge. Marxist logic contends that societies characterized by class divisions are prone to internal conflict as eventually the exploited and alienated working class will overthrow the elite-controlled government to facilitate a more equitable distribution of wealth and resources. While the Khmer Rouge did not disclose certain intentions during their assent to power, once they seized control of the Cambodian government, the revolutionary hatred they harbored toward groups perceived to be class enemies or obstacles to their radical vision became immediately clear. However, the Marxist model cannot sufficiently explain all of the violence and persecution directed against

INTRODUCTION

many segments of Cambodian society. The Khmer Rouge perpetrated atrocities, including large-scale killings against non-Khmer minorities in Cambodia—many of whom were impoverished peasants and who could not be construed as members or supporters of the traditional ruling elite or as supporters of western capitalists. As discussed in Chapter 8, debate exists as to whether such actions constituted ethnic cleansing, targeting segments of the population based upon their culture or race or, alternatively, whether the Khmer Rouge undertook "political cleansing/purges" of segments of Cambodian society they deemed most likely to oppose their radical vision—an ideological targeting of victims that often, though not always, correlated to ethnic/cultural minorities.

The English School and the Pluralistic Approach of this Study

As evidenced in the preceding examples, many IR theories can potentially lend analytical insight to the same phenomenon, including the discordant nature of the Khmer Rouge. The English School of international relations shares some perspectives with many of the major international relations theories. Like realism, which it is often compared to, the English School does not discount state sovereignty and regards the international system as essentially anarchical and prone to conflict. Certain concepts within the English School also align with many constructivist precepts, such as social inquiry/theory, as a means of understanding the complex international dynamic.[28] To a great degree, the English School can be perceived as an integrative paradigm that seeks to bridge many of the gaps between other, often conflicting, theories within IR. In fact, if realism can be regarded as one antipode of IR theory, characterized by a pessimistic view of international competition for power, and liberal/idealist theory as the antithesis, characterized by an overly optimistic appraisal of an increasingly cooperative and stable international dynamic, the English School lies between the two, offering a more nuanced and complex analysis of the world.[29] Adherents of the English School contend that to adequately understand international phenomena, they must be studied and interpreted from multiple perspectives rather than through one theoretical lens. Thus, the English School generally seeks not to compete with or replace other theories within IR but to add to the diversity and seek connections between other perspectives.[30] Some scholars suggest that, given the pluralistic approach to theory and methodology, the English School offers potential as a grand theory within international relations.[31]

In seeking to understand international phenomena, such as the conduct of state actors, the methodological approach of the English School is also more subjective and interdisciplinary in nature and less dependent upon statistical analysis than that of many other IR theories. IR theorist Anne-Marie Slaughter concisely encapsulates the nature of the English School compared to other traditions, explaining that it "does not seek to create testable hypotheses about state behavior as the other theories do."[32] She elaborates that "instead, its goals are more similar to those of a historian: detailed observation and rich interpretation is favored over general explanatory models ... English School writers hold historical understandings to be critical to the study of world politics."[33] Given the parameters of this book in seeking to broadly explore both the domestic and international discord associated with the Khmer Rouge, the flexibility of the English School lends itself well as a model. Slaughter additionally states:

> It is not enough simply to know the balance of power in the international system, as the realists would have it. We must also know what preceded that system, how the states involved came to be where they are ... and what might threaten or motivate them in the future. Domestic politics are also important, as are norms and ideologies.[34]

Building upon the latter concepts within the English School, an interesting concept forwarded by Hedley Bull proposes that one key to regional/world stability and reduction in the frequency of war is "ideological homogeneity" in which populations from diverse nationalities, cultures, and ethnicities have a common political outlook.[35] While some world regions might serve as a case study in support of peace and stability through ideological homogeneity (or at least political similarity)—such as post-WWII Western Europe—such regions would be the exception rather than the rule. Certainly, 20th century Cambodia and Indochina would serve as a better example of heterogeneity in political ideology and many other aspects of the human condition.

While some relevance to the Khmer Rouge phenomenon can potentially be found in various theoretical paradigms, no single theory or level of analysis is adequate to address the totality of Cambodian communism, the conduct of Pol Pot's communist faction or regime, or the influences that served as drivers. Of the major theories within IR, realist and particularly neorealist models appear to be closer in relevance, but even with regard to the latter, they alone as theoretical frameworks may not be sufficient. It has been suggested that none of the major theoretical traditions by themselves (realism, liberalism, etc.) are sufficient to adequately explain state conduct in response to conditions present within the complex international dynamic or the interplay between domestic and international considerations which, combined, serve to drive state behavior.[36]

Rather than limiting the exploration of the Khmer Rouge to one explanatory model, this analysis utilizes a holistic, qualitative historical approach reflecting Hedley Bull and the English School of international relations, which does not require the author or readers to explore phenomenon from a single, narrow vantage point but instead permits analysis and interpretation. A diverse range of hundreds of primary and secondary sources, including archival documents, were utilized in this research. Primary sources include declassified and publicly released intelligence documents from government sources (e.g., U.S. Central Intelligence Agency archives), previously classified intelligence and diplomatic documents made public via WikiLeaks, and original journalistic and government research. Secondary sources include English- and foreign-language scholarship within the large body of academic literature, government documents, and reputable journalistic analyses. Over a five-year period, information was obtained, analyzed, and integrated to provide an updated analysis of the Khmer Rouge phenomenon, with a particular focus on examining the characteristics and causal factors of the regime's discordant actions both domestically and internationally.

Organization

The first chapters of the book establish a historical and socio-political foundation for understanding the Khmer Rouge phenomenon and the circumstances that enabled the movement to expand in power and influence. Chapter 1 explores the antecedents of the Khmer Rouge movement and the reality that the emergence of communism in Cambodia was not a simple process with a single point of origin. A complex range of both domestic and international/geopolitical factors in the 20th century, as well as historical precursors and ethno-cultural considerations, combined to contribute to the emergence of what initially were several distinct and competing strands of communism within Cambodia. Chapter 1 focuses primarily upon examining the key historical foundations critical to understanding the evolution of Cambodian communism and subsequent Cold War-era developments within the country.

Chapter 2 provides an analysis of the domestic and international political dynamic of Cambodia's early independence era. Communism in Cambodia was never purely a domestic phenomenon. Particularly in the earliest phases of its evolution, it reflected the political agendas and machinations of external sources of influence, particularly those of neighboring Vietnam. The Vietnam-U.S. War (known regionally as the Second Indochina War) and the geopolitical dynamic associated with Hanoi and its relations with the newly independent Cambodian government factored heavily in the development of communism in the latter country and the emergence and growth of Pol Pot's faction within the movement. The chapter explores the critical period following independence and the initial decline and eventual resurgence of Cambodian communism.

Chapter 3 examines the onset, nature, and ramifications of the Cambodian Civil War, including the improving fortunes of the communist movement. By the late 1960s, North Vietnamese and Viet Cong forces routinely used Cambodian territory to attack South Vietnam. The deteriorating security situation and subsequent U.S. decision to bomb areas of eastern Cambodia served to destabilize the country politically and help fuel the growth of opposition elements, including the Khmer Rouge insurgency. Sihanouk, in an effort to keep the broader Indochina conflicts out of Cambodia, had pursued a policy of pseudo-neutrality in which his government, while officially neutral, essentially collaborated in supplying Vietnamese communist forces and permitted their use of Cambodian territory.

Chapter 4 provides insight into the short-lived (1970–1975) Khmer Republic and the communist insurgency within Cambodia. Following his removal by conservative elements and political rivals, former Cambodian ruler Norodom Sihanouk, from political exile in China, formed an alliance with the Khmer Rouge, marking a turning point in the movement's gradual political shift away from Vietnamese and Soviet alignment and toward an association with China amid an intensifying climate of Cambodian nationalism. The new government of U.S.-backed Lon Nol sought to expel Vietnamese troops operating in Cambodia and also stirred nationalistic and xenophobic sentiment and undertook pogroms against Vietnamese minorities living in the newly proclaimed Khmer Republic. The increasingly authoritarian regime also transitioned away from previous assertions of Cambodian neutrality, assuming an anti-communist stance and aligning itself with the U.S., which propped up the government with substantial foreign and military aid. Internal support for the regime steadily eroded as Cambodian support grew for the insurrectionist coalition, including communist factions. Cambodian communist groups became increasingly unified under Pol Pot's Khmer Rouge faction, which was supported by supplies, training, and troops from communist Vietnam as well as aid from China. Always distrustful of Vietnam, the Khmer Rouge feared Hanoi's desire to create a regional federation in which Cambodia would be subservient, though Pol Pot maintained a cordial attitude until the end of the Civil War in order to continue receiving aid from Hanoi.

The second section of the book addresses the bellicose, dystopian, and violent nature of the Khmer Rouge regime, its conflict with Vietnam that ultimately resulted in Pol Pot's ouster, and the long-lasting impact the Khmer Rouge had on Cambodia. Chapter 5 explores the ideological influences upon the Khmer Rouge regime and many of its radical policies. Most of the dystopian regime's actions related to the iconoclastic restructuring of society were rooted in communist concepts such as the Soviet model of "war communism." The chapter dispels attempts to justify certain Khmer Rouge actions such as the brutal forced expulsion of urban populations into slave labor camps. Various aspects of the international relations (isolationism) of the regime amid the backdrop of Cold War politics are also examined.

Chapter 6 discusses the horrific nature and scale of the Khmer Rouge Genocide, which occurred in three distinct phases and tended to target certain groups to a greater degree. Attempts to undertake forensic analysis and to estimate the number of lives claimed by the regime are examined. Attention is given to the silence of the international community, including some elements which attempted to deny or minimize the nature and scope of the atrocities being perpetrated. Characteristics of the discordant, isolationist foreign relations of the regime are further examined, including its feigned political neutrality and increasingly belligerent actions toward neighboring states including Vietnam.

Chapter 7 examines the Vietnamese invasion and occupation and the creation of the Khmer Rouge rump state that waged a prolonged guerilla campaign for some two decades. Sporadic eruptions of border fighting between the Khmer Rouge and Vietnam continued through 1978 when, in December following repeated border provocations and incidents of Khmer Rouge attacks upon ethnic Vietnamese within Cambodia or just across the border with Vietnam, Hanoi launched a Soviet-endorsed full-scale invasion of Cambodia, quickly seizing the capital and most of the country's territory. The pro-Vietnamese People's Republic of Cambodia was established in early 1979, though with Chinese (and U.S.) backing, the Khmer Rouge established a rump state and continued to wage a guerilla campaign against Vietnam and their Cambodian allies from remote, mountainous strongholds. The conflict ceased to be purely a proxy war between the two external communist superpowers in 1979 when fighting (albeit limited) briefly erupted along the Chinese-Vietnamese border. For the next decade, direct conflict sporadically reignited either over territorial disputes or via direct Chinese military efforts to support Pol Pot's guerilla campaign, ending in 1989 when Hanoi withdrew its military forces from Cambodia.

Chapter 8 explores the circumstances of post-Cold War Cambodia, the long-term impact of the Khmer Rouge, and the largely unsuccessful attempts to bring Pol Pot and other Khmer Rouge leaders to justice. After initially signing a 1991 treaty to end the guerilla war, surrender their arms, and participate in upcoming national elections, the Khmer Rouge resumed fighting the following year and refused to recognize the election and new government, which included the restoration of Sihanouk as a constitutional monarch. Disillusionment, defections, and internal leadership struggles weakened the remnants of the Khmer Rouge throughout the late 1990s, eventually leading to the capture of many of the group's remaining leaders, including Pol Pot who died in custody before his war crimes trial concluded. Due to the stigma associated with Khmer Rouge atrocities, far-left revisionists have sought to disavow the regime's history, asserting that it was not a legitimate manifestation of communist doctrine. While relative stability has been achieved in the post-Cold War era, Cambodia has not fully overcome the long-term legacy of conflict.

INTRODUCTION

Endnotes

1. Kenneth Waltz, *Man, the State and War: A Theoretical Analysis – Anniversary Edition* (New York: Columbia University Press, 2018).
2. A. Hilali, "China's Response to the Soviet Invasion of Afghanistan," *Central Asian Survey*, 20(3), 2001, pp. 323–351.
3. L. Quayle, *Southeast Asia and the English School of International Relations: A Region-Theory Dialogue* (New York: Palgrave, 2013).
4. S. McHale, "Ethnicity, Vioence and Khmer-Vietnamese Relations: The Significance of the Lower Mekong Delta," *The Journal of Asian Studies*, 72(2), 2013, pp. 367–390.
5. Bill McSweeney, *Security, Identity and Interests: A Sociology of International Relations* (Cambridge, UK: Cambridge University Press, 1999).
6. K. Waltz, "Anarchic Orders and Balances of Power," in *Neorealism and Its Critics*, ed. R. Keohane, (New York: Columbia University Press, 1986), p. 98.
7. M. Levinger, *Conflict Analysis: Understanding Causes, Unlocking Solutions* (Washington, DC: United States Institute of Peace, 2013).
8. Patrick Morgan, International Security: Problems and Solutions (Washington D.C.: CQ Press, 2006).
9. Ibid, pp. 44.
10. M. Bussmann and J. Oneal, "Do Hegemons Distribute Private Goods?: A Test of Power-Transition Theory," *Journal of Conflict Resolution*, 51(1), 2007, pp. 88–111.
11. E. Matthews and R. Callaway, *International Relations Theory: A Primer* (New York: Oxford University Press, 2017).
12. W. Kim and S. Gates, "Power Transition Theory and the Rise of China," *Social Media + Society*, 18(3), 2015; A. Goldstein, "Great Expectations: Interpreting China's Arrival," *International Security*, 22(3), 1997, pp. 36–73.
13. Matthews and Callaway, 2017.
14. D. Snidal, "The limits of Hegemonic Stability Theory," *International Organization*, 39(4), 1985, pp. 579–614.
15. J. Mearsheimer, *The Tragedy of Great Power Politics* (New York: W.W. Norton, 2001).
16. R. Keohane and J. Nye, *Power and Interdependence* (New York: Longman, 2011).

17. O. Israeli, *International Relations Theory of War* (Santa Barbara, CA: Praeger, 2019).
18. J. Mearsheimer, *The Tragedy of Great Power Politics* (New York: W.W. Norton, 2001).
19. M. Levinger, *Conflict Analysis: Understanding Causes, Unlocking Solutions* (Washington, DC: United States Institute of Peace, 2013).
20. W. Wagner, W. Werner and M. Onderco, "Rouges, Pariahs, Outlaws: Theorizing Deviance in International Relations" in *Deviance in International Relations: 'Rogue States' and International Security*, eds. W. Wagner, W. Werner and M. Onderco (New York: Palgrave-Macmillan, 2014).
21. D. Geller and J. Singer, *Nations at War: A Scientific Study of International Conflict* (Cambridge, UK: Cambridge University Press, 2000).
22. J. Nye and D. Welch, *Understanding Global Conflict and Cooperation* (New York: Pearson, 2016), p. 9.
23. Ibid.
24. A. Wendt, "Anarchy is What States Make of It", *International Organization*, 46(2), 1992.
25. W. Wagner, W. Werner and M. Onderco, "Rouges, Pariahs, Outlaws: Theorizing Deviance in International Relations" in *Deviance in International Relations: 'Rogue States' and International Security*, eds. W. Wagner, W. Werner and M. Onderco (New York: Palgrave-Macmillan, 2014).
26. J. Nye and D. Welch, *Understanding Global Conflict and Cooperation* (New York: Pearson, 2016).
27. Daniel Geller and David Singer, *Nations at War: A Scientific Study of International Conflict* (Cambridge, UK: Cambridge University Press, 1998).
28. B. Buzan, *From International to World Society?: English School Theory and the Social Structure of Globalisation* (Cambridge, UK: Cambridge University Press, 2013).
29. M. Wight, "Western Values in International Relations," in *Diplomatic Investigations: Essays in the Theory of International Politics* (London: Allen & Unwin, 1966).
30. L. Quayle, *Southeast Asia and the English School of International*

31. Barry Buzan, *From International to World Society?: English School Theory and the Social Structure of Globalization* (Cambridge, UK: Cambridge University Press, 2006).
32. A. Slaugter, "International Relations: Principal Theories," in *The Max Planck Encyclopedia of Public International Law*, ed. R. Wolfrum (Oxford, UK: Oxford University Press, 2013), pp. 29–33.
33. Ibid.
34. Ibid.
35. H. Bull, *The Anarchical Society: A Study in World Politics* (New York: Columbia University Press, 2012).
36. Thomas Risse-Kappen, "What Have We Learned?" in *Bringing Transnational Relations Back In: Non-State Actors, Domestic Structures and International Institutions*, ed. Thomas Risse-Kappen (Cambridge, UK: Cambridge University Press, 1997).

Relations (New York: Palgrave, 2013).

Antecedents and Genesis of Cambodian Communism

To adequately understand the 20th century political dynamic of Cambodia, including the manifestation of its radical and dystopian communist movement and subsequent Cold War-era geopolitics, more contemporary developments must be juxtaposed against the backdrop of circumstances from antiquity through the colonial era. The ethnic identity and civilizational achievements of the early Khmer people as well as their long history of interactions and competition with other neighboring populations in Indochina factored heavily into 20th century Cambodian politics, including the evolution of communist ideology and policies under Pol Pot and the Khmer Rouge. This analysis begins with the earliest origins of the Khmer people within the region, which not only provides differentiation between the people of contemporary Cambodia and neighboring cultures but also serves as a source of Cambodian cultural pride and nationalism as well as xenophobia, societal attributes which intensified rather than diminished under the Khmer Rouge strain of communism.

Pre-Colonial Cambodia

The Khmer people are the ethnic majority in Cambodia, today comprising approximately 97% of the country's population–though as discussed in Chapter 6, their numerical dominance was not quite so pronounced until minority targeting during the communist era. In this work, the term *Khmer* is used in reference to this prevalent ethnic/cultural group, a term which is distinct, for example, from the *Khmer Rouge* (literally "Red Khmer") which originally referred to the Cambodian communist movement in general and eventually came to refer specifically to the communist faction dominated by Pol Pot, or the term *Khmer Issarak* ("Free Khmers"), a reference to a mid-20th century partisan movement among the Khmer people which sought to end colonial rule. Considering that contemporary Cambodia is essentially a nation-state, the term *Khmer* is used synonymously with the term *Cambodians* in reference to a specific ethnicity or nation.

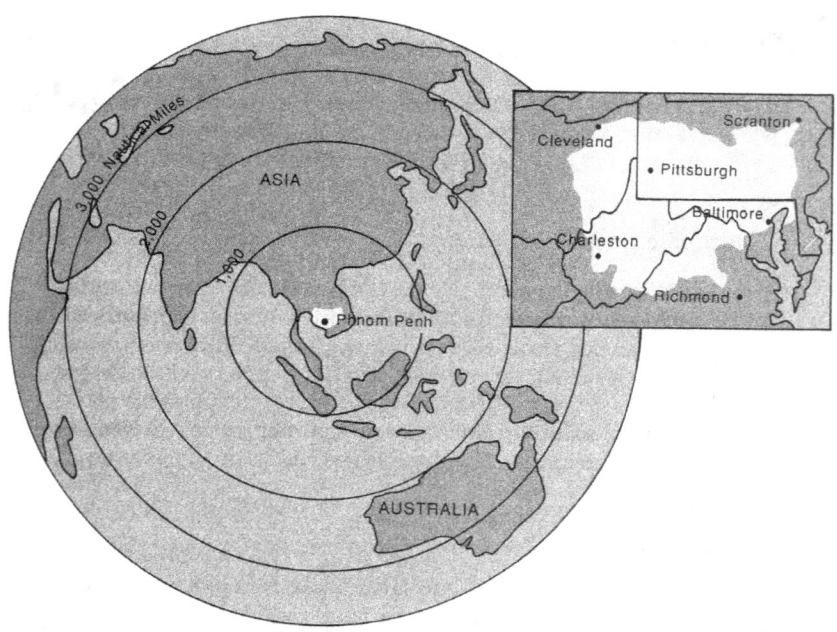

Map 1: Cambodia and its Relative Size and Location

Much of the Khmer people's earliest history remains shrouded in mystery and subject to debate. Many historians and anthropologists believe successive waves of various populations from different areas of the Asian continent traversed through and settled in Southeast Asia at various points in the prehistoric era. Some scholars contend that the ancestors of the Khmer emigrated eastward from the Indian subcontinent several thousand years ago.[1] Others have suggested that Khmer ancestors migrated via riverine routes from what would today be southeastern China prior to the 1st century CE. Whatever their original hearth area or migration route, the consensus of opinion is that the ancient ancestors of the Khmer likely arrived in the interior of Indochina and began to establish themselves as a successful culture and as the dominant group within the area prior to the arrival of Laotian, Thai, or Vietnamese populations, all of which would eventually emerge as long-term regional rivals to the Khmer and Cambodia.

Given the degree of rivalry that would eventually be present between the groups, it is interesting to note that the ancient ancestors of the Khmer are thought to have been ethnically and linguistically related to the ancient forebearers of the Vietnamese.[2] However, as centuries and millennia passed, they diverged culturally, often due to the influences of other civilizations, principally India in the case of the Khmer and China for the Vietnamese. Upon their ingress into the Mekong Delta region, the ancient Khmer intermingled with pre-existing populations that had developed advanced irrigation, metal-working, and other technological skills the Khmer adopted and continued to refine. In part due to the embrace and adaptation of successful practices and technologies of other peoples, including the adoption of a Sanskrit-based written alphabet, irrigation technology, and other innovations from India, the initially disunited Khmer people became a unified kingdom and were en route to becoming a highly accomplished civilization and significant regional power by the 9th century CE.[3] Chandler asserts that ancient India's many positive cultural contributions to the emerging Khmer state were especially important and transformative in the development of Khmer civilization and power:

> During the first 500 years or so . . . (of the first millennium) India provided Cambodia with a writing system, a pantheon, meters for poetry, a language to write it in, a vocabulary of hierarchies–not the same as a caste system, Buddhism, the idea of universal kingship, and new ways of looking at politics, sociology, architecture, iconography, astronomy and aesthetics. Without India, Angkor would never have been built, yet . . . Indian influence in Cambodia was not imposed by colonization or by force (and) . . . Indianization never produced the identity crisis among Cambodians that Chinese colonization and cultural imperialism produced among the Vietnamese.[4]

Initially, the Khmer in Indochina appear to have been organized into smaller, quasi-independent states that were culturally similar but also often at war with each other. Brief periods of unification for some smaller Khmer states existed and often reflected the success and demise of specific warlords, reverting to smaller autonomous states upon the death or overthrow of the conquering leader. The first significant, unified Khmer state was the Angkor Kingdom, established in 802 CE when King Jayavarman II proclaimed himself ruler of all Khmer people, establishing his capital at the archaeologically famous Angkor site. The earliest written accounts of military campaigns and international relations of the Khmer as a people reflect that the early Angkor Kingdom sought to establish hegemony within Indochina, waging war with the Vietnamese to the east as well as such smaller entities as the Champa, a culturally distinct group that had immigrated to the Indochina Peninsula from Malaysia.[5]

By the 12th century, Khmer civilization was thriving, attaining significant accomplishments in agriculture and architecture (e.g., Angkor Wat), establishing extensive and far-reaching trade routes, and expanding to control large areas of the Indochina Peninsula—far beyond the present-day borders of Cambodia, including much of present-day Laos, Thailand, and Vietnam. By the 14th century, Angkor, the capital which also bore the name of the unified state, was possibly the largest city in the world with a population approaching 1 million.[6] For several centuries, the Khmer remained the dominant military power within the region and, reflecting this status, they became to an extent economically reliant (e.g., spoils, tribute) upon warfare with adjacent cultures including the Vietnamese.[7]

However, after reaching its zenith territorially and otherwise in the early 13th century, Khmer power and influence began a prolonged period of slow decline, due in part to intensifying warfare with regional competitors. Ongoing conflicts with neighboring powers progressively undermined the once-important trade routes which linked Cambodia to the outside world and previously contributed to its wealth and power. Cambodia was surrounded by increasingly powerful competitor states. It experienced pressure from the Thais to the west and the Vietnamese from the east, both of which demanded tribute and seized progressively larger amounts of what had originally been Khmer/Cambodian territory, eventually reducing it to a vassal state with a puppet monarchy by the 18th century.[8] Explaining the process of progressive Khmer decline in the face of competition from rivals, Brinkley states:

> Cambodia's neighbors were quick to seize upon this weakness. The Siamese (Thailand) to the west and Vietnamese to the east began taking

ANTECEDENTS AND GENESIS OF CAMBODIAN COMMUNISM

bites out of the state, beginning in the 1500s and 1600s. Meantime, the Vietnamese migrated southward until they outnumbered Cambodians in the southern delta region. Over time, they became the de facto rulers . . . Over the years the Khmer allied themselves with either Thai or Vietnamese rulers, whichever they thought could serve as protectors against the other neighbor's aggression . . . Cambodian leaders acquired a new character trait: an overwhelming sense of dependency.[9]

The decline of early Cambodia may also have been partly attributable to chronic labor shortages due to such warring rival states as Thailand, which enslaved large numbers of ethnic Khmer laborers following military forays and subsequently removed them from Cambodian territory to toil in the victors' lands.[10] Khmer/Cambodian decline was also physical and technological in nature. The once-dominant civilization that built the architectural wonder Angkor Wat eventually ceased undertaking such projects and over time lost the ability to do so. A leading theory posits that this decline started with the damage and eventual abandonment of Angkor Wat and other cities and infrastructure due to a prolonged period of heavy monsoons and catastrophic flooding in the early 15th century.[11] (See Map 6: Cambodian Flood Plains in Chapter 4.) Other theories have suggested that decimations stemming from plague, prolonged crop failures, intensifying warfare, or a combination of such factors were responsible. Perhaps even more significant than declining urban or transport infrastructure was that, as Khmer civilization continued its retreat, the extensive irrigation system fell into a state of disrepair and disuse. This loss substantially reduced agricultural output, including rice production, which represented an essential food staple. As the result of a combination of such factors, the Khmer heartland is thought to have undergone a period of prolonged demographic decline, further weakening the Khmer people in the face of competition from regional rivals.

The by-now more advanced, wealthy, and powerful Kingdom of Vietnam began a brief period of direct administration over what remained of Cambodia in the first decades of the 19th century. Ethnic Vietnamese also began to resettle primarily into portions of what is now eastern Cambodia. By this period, the Vietnamese and certain other neighboring cultures (e.g., Thais) had come to regard Cambodia as a stagnant backwater with an ignorant and uncivilized population, a condescending attitude which would later be shared by the French during the European colonization era.[12] The contempt which outsiders showed Cambodian/Khmer culture and their subjugation at the hands of outsiders were realities not lost upon the Cambodian people or their leaders. Such circumstances would have significant impact on the 20th century Cambodian national psyche and factor into the decolonization struggle and nationalistic, ethnocentric, and xenophobic ethos of the Khmer Rouge communist movement.

French Colonial Encroachment

In a sense, it is misleading to describe Cambodia's colonial era as having begun with the French. Through territorial conquest and direct or indirect rule, Cambodia had already fallen under Vietnamese or Thai tutelage long before the onset of European encroachment into Southeast Asia. However, throughout much of the latter 19th century, the British and French competed to carve out territories in the region, with Britain ultimately in control of Myanmar and Malaya and France with Vietnam, Cambodia, and Laos by the end of the century. While other pretexts may have been offered by the new powers, such as bestowing Christianity or other vestiges of western civilization to less developed areas or that their military presence merely provided for the safety of their missionaries, merchants, and other western citizens in the region, the European powers' motives were to seize the natural resources of the territories they usurped and add those areas to their global network of colonial possessions.

The first phase of French involvement in Indochina entailed a limited number of Jesuit missionaries arriving along the coast of what is now Vietnam beginning in the 17th century. As the number and presence of French missionaries and traders grew in Vietnam, Paris cited the missionaries' safety and continued work as a pretext for increased military and political intervention. This shift happened in stages, beginning with the siege and capture of Saigon in 1859.[13] Having conquered present-day Vietnam by the late 19th century, the French then turned west, acquiring territories associated with present-day Cambodia and Laos from Thailand (Siam). In 1887 all the territories under French control were brought under the same administrative structure as a federation of protectorates and colonies, which became collectively known as French Indochina. The French frequently modified the interior boundaries of their Indochinese territories, including reapportioning areas that were historically associated with Cambodia—an area never deemed important economically or otherwise by Paris—to regional rival Vietnam, the focal point of French economic activity within the region.[14]

Cambodia did not initially see the French as a conquering enemy. In fact, after having lost territory to neighboring Vietnam and Thailand and consequently falling under the alternating control of both, Cambodian leadership initially viewed the French as a means of regaining some self-determination and keeping their regional competitors at bay. In 1863 Cambodia's King Norodom, seeing France as the lesser of several foreign threats, signed a treaty with Paris. France deployed troops and established protectorate status over Cambodia. Perhaps seeing no other realistic alternative to end his country's position as a perpetually threatened and subjugated vassal state, Cambodia's King Norodom acquiesced to the French presence, but he was increasingly relegated to figurehead status, with Paris assuming greater control. Having failed in efforts to impede French expansion in Indochina, Thailand, one of the last independent states in the region, eventually acceded and formally recognized French suzerainty over Cambodia four years later.[15]

For the French, Cambodia possessed less commercial value than Vietnam, but it was geographically significant in multiple respects. The French viewed Cambodia as a buffer between their Indochina territories and British-aligned Thailand. The territory which comprised the original French Protectorate of Cambodia was a small remnant (essentially the southeastern one-third of present-day Cambodia) of what had been Cambodian territory at the zenith of the Khmer Empire. However, Paris saw Cambodia as a staging area for further territorial acquisition in the region. As an element of a broader and ongoing annexation of Thai-controlled lands on the Indochina Peninsula, the French seized the territory that now constitutes western Cambodia (i.e., areas around and west of the large Tonle Sap Lake) from Thailand in a brief 1906–07 war, citing a disputed boundary as justification for the incursion.[16]

Economically, Cambodia fared little better under the French than it had as a Vietnamese or Thai vassal state. In exchange for French assurances of protection against Thailand and Vietnam, Cambodia granted Paris mineral and timber rights, and the new power began extracting the country's natural resources. Life remained unchanged for the majority of the Khmer population which continued to subsist in the same state of abject poverty as had existed for centuries. Foreign interests controlled most sources of Cambodia's export economy and retained the profits, with agricultural exports largely managed by remote Chinese or Vietnamese merchants from Saigon and Phenom Penh while the rubber plantations established in the 1920s remained under French control.[17] To offset the expenses incurred in administering the Cambodian protectorate, France also levied heavy taxes, often accompanied by promises of providing services such as building schools, which went largely unfulfilled—e.g., after more than 70 years of colonial oversight, France established Cambodia's first high school in 1935, and it was mainly for children of the royal family or used to train others from privileged backgrounds to serve as bureaucrats in the French colonial administration.[18]

While French infiltration had served the primary intended purpose of ending Thai and Vietnamese dominance, Cambodia's autonomy was not secured through the arrangement. Although the French were initially content to exploit Cambodia economically, their controlling influence soon evolved into direct political intervention as well. This pattern emerged in the 1870s with many French demands for reform that were appropriate and beneficial, including their insistence on the abolition of slavery, requiring the monarchy to renounce claims of direct ownership of all lands in the country, and requiring at least partial reform of widespread government corruption on the part of Cambodian leaders.[19] Following short-lived and unsuccessful demonstrations against French rule in the 1880s, the colonial government asserted its authority over the Cambodian monarchy, stripping it of most remaining power, including the ability to appoint or dismiss officials.[20] Adding insult to injury related to the latter development, many Cambodians were alienated by the reality that those tasked with administration of French colonial rule in their country were often ethnic Vietnamese, Chinese, or Thai, the regional historic rivals of the ethnic Khmer majority.

Evolution of Political Agitation in Modern Cambodia

In the latter 19th and early 20th centuries, nationalist, anti-colonial, and anti-western/European sentiment in Cambodia grew amid an emerging groundswell of similar developments in many other parts of Asia. For example, by the 1920s the Indian National Congress was a major political force, able to galvanize significant local support in calling for British decolonization in South Asia. Throughout much of the Mideast in the post-WWI era, the unrealized western promises of autonomy following the Ottoman Empire's defeat fueled nationalist agendas among Arab populations. Nascent independence movements also began to gain strength in Southeast Asia, often utilizing older movements in India and elsewhere as models. While little, if any, direct communication occurred between Cambodian nationalists and independence movements in other parts of the continent during this era, the mere knowledge that elsewhere in Asia far-reaching and strengthening resistance to European rule existed helped to embolden Cambodians in their burgeoning efforts to secure self-determination.

Communist movements, often combined with nationalistic and anti-colonial elements, also began to coalesce in other Asian states, some of which would impact the genesis of communism in Indochina. Although small numbers of Indochinese communist leaders including Ho Chi Minh had received training in the Soviet Union, in the first decades of its existence Soviet leadership was preoccupied with internal affairs rather than exporting revolution, and Moscow remained indifferent to the establishment of Indochinese communist cells in the pre-war era. Not until the Cold War era would any significant Soviet involvement in Southeast Asia manifest. However, the communist movements in nearby China and Vietnam would eventually begin to diffuse to Cambodia (and Laos) via its Chinese and Vietnamese minorities. The Chinese Communist Party was founded in 1921 and, within six years, became locked in a prolonged civil war resulting in its 1949 seizure of power, inspiring communist insurgencies in other areas of Asia. The first Cambodian-based Chinese Communist Party cell was organized among ethnic Chinese minority communities in 1930, but the group remained small and ineffectual and did not attract support among the ethnic Khmer majority.[21]

Of greater future significance for Cambodia, the first known instance of communist activism in its territory was on the part of ethnic Vietnamese minorities in the 1920s, spreading quickly to Cambodia shortly after the founding of the first small communist cells in Vietnam the same decade.[22] The theoretically transnational but Vietnamese-dominated Indochinese Communist Party was founded by Ho Chi Minh in 1930 through merging smaller regional communist groups.[23] The latter action had been called for in 1929 by the Soviet government and international communist leadership, as they viewed a unified regional party for all of Indochina as a stronger entity which would presumably be better able to coordinate political efforts and resist French colonialism than a loosely aligned network of independently led national parties. Furthermore, the Soviets concluded that as the largest numbers of communists within the Indochina region were ethnic Vietnamese, it was logical that they assume the mantle of leadership for the new Indochinese Communist Party.[24] The hierarchical diffusion of communist movements in different regions of Indochina originated chiefly through the efforts of Vietnamese revolutionaries rather than those from China or the Soviet Union.

The Communist International movement, better known as the Comintern, was established in Moscow shortly after the Bolshevik Revolution with the goal of advancing the communist cause internationally. The Soviet-dominated Comintern was aware of the long conflicted history between various ethnicities in Indochina, including the ancient rivalry between Cambodia and Vietnam. The European proponents of a Vietnamese-led unified regional communist effort in Indochina appeared to have assumed the national and ethnic rivalries so prevalent in the region's history would be largely superseded by a common embrace of communist doctrine and a bond forged through the shared struggle against capitalism and imperialism, regarded as the primary enemies of all Southeast Asian populations. The Comintern may have also assumed that increasing levels of interaction, cooperation, and codependency among Indochina's ethnic groups under the communist banner would help the various nationalities put historical rivalries and cultural mistrust aside. In the case of the Cambodia-Vietnam dynamic, such optimistic assumptions proved to be incorrect.

The earliest manifestations of indigenous communism (established/led by ethnically Khmer Cambodians as opposed to ethnic/cultural minorities residing in the country) among Cambodians can be attributed to the climate of far-left political agitation present at the seat of France's colonial empire. France was one of Europe's hotbeds of Marxist political activism by the turn of the century, with Paris its focal point. Within many of its colonies abroad, including Cambodia, the French government and local colonial authorities selected small numbers of promising students among indigenous populations to live in France and obtain university educations or other training with the goal of preparing natives to serve colonial administrations locally more effectively in various roles/professions. Many of these young students—lonely, culturally alienated, and removed from any other support systems—were easy targets for recruitment and became involved in communist movements. To many in Europe or the developing world in the early-mid-20th century, communism was the wave of the future, and many of the students from colonial possessions also identified with communism's strong anti-imperialism message. Several young Cambodian nationalists who would form the first generation of that nation's indigenous communist leaders became indoctrinated as communists during their educational stints in France. This generation included Saloth Sar who, after living in Paris for three years to study radio-electricity (unsuccessfully), returned home sans degree but committed to ending French rule and establishing a communist regime in Cambodia.[25] The political pseudonym adopted by this young revolutionary and future dictator was Pol Pot.

Such a pattern of communism spreading from the seat of European colonial power to its dependencies and protectorates was not unique to French Indochina as similar developments occurred elsewhere, such as the Indonesian Communist Party emerging out of the Dutch Communist Party in the 1920s.[26] In fact such a hierarchical, top-down pattern of communist cells spreading to the colonial world was often by deliberate design. Just as communist ideological strategy saw an elite cadre of indoctrinated revolutionaries organizing the proletariat to oppose capitalism and undertake class warfare in western nations, so too did the Comintern and national communist leadership in many countries envision communism's spread to the colonial world, bypassing Marx's prerequisite step of industrialization. Proponents of a borderless, transnational approach to spreading communism advocated peasant revolts in colonies as a means of globally striking against their common enemies—capitalism and imperialism.[27] Many such early 20th century revolutionaries, including Ho Chi Minh, saw international boundaries as irrelevant since, in their minds, the entire world was divided into just two categories: workers, as opposed to the people, and institutions which conspired to exploit and oppress them.[28] It should be stressed that Ho Chi Minh and many others in the original transnational communist vanguard did in fact exhibit nationalist tendencies later in their revolutionary careers, a political reality which contributed to and exacerbated conflicts with neighboring states, which in Ho's case included Cambodia.

Colonial governments, including the French, actively repressed any movements exhibiting anti-imperialist or nationalist tendencies throughout the early 20th century, which included the nascent communist movements in Indochina. Through arresting the members of the then-small communist cells in Cambodia and Laos, the radical left had been almost totally quelled by 1935 and substantially weakened in its hearth area of Vietnam.[29] However, nearly as quickly as existing communist supporters could be detained, new ones were recruited due in part to intensifying anti-French/colonial sentiment which the revolutionaries exploited. By 1940, sufficient strength had been regained to enable communist party leadership to organize a new round of uprisings against French rule. These uprisings resulted in the widespread arrest and execution of many communist leaders, with others—including Ho Chi Minh—having previously fled to the relative safety of communist-controlled territory in nearby China.[30] Though efforts would continue to combat the spread of communism among Indochina's population, the radical left would remain a primary source of declining colonial authority in much of the region, as would a new set of geopolitical circumstances emerging from the east. The expansionist policies of Japan in the 1930s and '40s would ultimately help to further erode the control France and other European colonial powers exerted over their Asian territories and hasten the maturation of independence movements.

Impacts of World War II

The WWII era ushered in new manifestations of external powers maneuvering for control in Cambodia and Southeast Asia. French colonial forces in Cambodia had been militarily weakened by prolonged efforts to quell internal dissention, being cut off from supplies and reinforcements due to WWII and due to a failed attempt from Thailand to militarily seize long-disputed territories in western Cambodia in what became known as the 1940–41 Franco-Thai War. Japan invaded French Indochina in September 1940, beginning with Vietnam, followed by Cambodia and Laos the following year. While officially neutral, the government and military leadership of independent Thailand had been friendly to Japan. Endeavoring to foster further goodwill with the Thai government while simultaneously undermining European colonialism, Tokyo directed the collaborationist Vichy French colonial regime to cede Cambodia's disputed western territories to Thailand, and approximately one-third of Cambodia's land area was forfeited.[31]

Japan's primary interests in Indochina were to cut off potential supply routes to beleaguered China and exploit the region's resources for its war effort. As the area had been under the control of the newly created Vichy government in France—a regime actively collaborating with Japan's ally Germany—Japan maintained control of military and foreign affairs but allowed the Vichy colonial regime to retain some elements of internal administrative authority, including control of police and a small light infantry force used multiple times during Japanese occupation to quell nationalist demonstrations.[32] Paradoxically, Japan somewhat successfully promoted anti-French and anti-European/colonial sentiment among Cambodian populations and other occupied nations of Southeast Asia. At the same time it tolerated the continued, albeit limited, presence of Vichy colonial administration. Japan regarded the cultivation of anti-European attitudes as a precursor to Cambodia and other occupied lands' viewing the Japanese in a favorable light as liberators. The Japanese hoped many of their recently "liberated" Asian subjects would embrace the new hierarchical order and accept the Japanese as more suitable colonial masters within the framework of Tokyo's "Greater East Asia Co-Prosperity Sphere" propaganda.[33]

A revival of nationalism and anti-French/colonial sentiment had already begun to strengthen by the time Cambodia's King Sisowath Monivong died in 1941. In a controversial instance of continued French efforts to control Cambodian politics, the Vichy colonial government denied right of succession to the deceased monarch's apparent heirs in the powerful Sisowath family and instead designated a new king, Norodom Sihanouk from another prominent house. The move was designed to pit politically influential Cambodian families against each other and install an impressionable and ill-prepared 19-year-old king who would presumably be easier to control and would perhaps be loyal to the colonial government out of gratitude for his accession. French expectations that Sihanouk would function as a figurehead and compliant tool for their continued control would soon prove to be misplaced as, by the end of WWII, the young king was demonstrating defiance to French wishes and a strong, nationalistic will of his own. The French also facilitated Vietnamese immigration into traditionally Khmer territory; by 1944, 250,000–300,000 ethnic Vietnamese lived in Cambodia, further complicating the internal political dynamic, and helping set the stage for ethnic conflict.[34] Cambodians were especially incensed that French policies favoring Vietnamese settlement had reduced ethnic Khmers to minority status in the Mekong Delta region, an area traditionally claimed by Cambodia but which Paris would cede to Vietnam in 1949, a primary causal factor in later Cambodian-Vietnamese strife.[35]

The final year of WWII was politically significant for Cambodia. Increasingly desperate for allies and labor, Japanese forces seized direct control of Cambodia and other areas of French Indochina from the Vichy administration and disarmed remaining French colonial forces in March of that year, hoping local populations would rally to the Japanese cause.[36] Japan's actions were also motivated by the accelerating pace of Germany's impending demise and the associated concern that the Vichy French administration might abruptly switch sides in the war effort.[37] Three days after the removal of the last vestiges of French colonial authority and acting upon Japan's instructions, the former figurehead monarchs of Cambodia, Laos, and Vietnam declared full independence from France. While such actions never cultivated any significant support for Japan among local populations, they did help fuel the flames of nationalism and anti-colonial sentiment. Cambodia's King Sihanouk sought to further bolster and legitimize his country's cultural heritage and, seeing the opportunity to do so, followed the declaration of independence with decrees reinstating the traditional Khmer alphabet and calendar.[38]

By 1945 the Japanese government was also actively supporting the fledgling Khmer Issarak ("Free Khmer") guerilla movement which opposed French control in favor of Cambodian independence. Initially, the Khmer Issarak partisan movement was a loosely organized coalition of predominantly far-left groups that advocated guerilla-style insurrection as a means of securing independence. Soon after its formation, the Khmer Issarak movement had established close ties with the larger and better organized Viet Minh (short for *Viet Nam Doc Lap Dong Minh Hoi* or "Revolutionary League for Vietnamese Independence") pro-independence communist movement in Vietnam. In its infancy, Vietnamese communism underwent several reorganizations and name-changes, being renamed *Viet Minh* during WWII, and organized as a national coalition of various groups resisting both French colonial and Japanese control, with independence given priority over class war.[39] By war's end, the Viet Minh had established operations in Cambodia and began recruiting for their cause. Their activities were not restricted to areas with significant Vietnamese populations, and they largely treated the Khmer Issarak and other Cambodians as subordinates. The relationship between communist cells in Cambodia and Vietnam would evolve to have profound impacts not only upon communism's evolution in Cambodia but also upon the adversarial geopolitical dynamic that would eventually emerge between the two countries.[40]

Post-War Transitions and Expanding Vietnamese Influence

The end of WWII facilitated the return of French colonial rule and the new French government's concomitant nullification of the declarations of independence issued by Cambodia, Laos, and Vietnam. The French, British, and Indian troops that marched into Cambodia at war's end arrested many of the newly declared state's leaders, including the self-proclaimed premier Son Ngoc Thanh, charging them as Axis collaborators, which in turn triggered demonstrations and widespread unrest and bolstered popular support for nationalist guerillas.[41] Paris retained King Sihanouk both to provide continuity and placate Cambodia's population, and perhaps more importantly because he adroitly swore allegiance to France and temporarily ceased any pro-independence rhetoric—actions which permanently undermined Sihanouk's credibility in the eyes of many Cambodian nationalists.[42] While the King's government was granted latitude in administrating Cambodia's internal affairs, French colonial authorities proceeded to arrest many political activists and crack down on independence movements to reassert their authority.[43] Public sentiment for the Cambodian nationalist cause grew rapidly in the post-war period, as did support for the Khmer Issarak partisan insurrection which escalated in many areas of Cambodia and would soon receive increased organizational support and other assistance from communist guerillas in neighboring Vietnam.

By 1947, the communist insurgents in Cambodia, Laos, and Vietnam had forged ties through the Vietnamese communist leaders who had become the dominant influence among Indochina's burgeoning far-left revolutionaries. By the late 1940s, increased Chinese aid combined with accrued practical experience contributed to the Viet Minh evolving as a potent fighting force; they, in turn, sought to lend aid to the revolutions in neighboring territories.[44] The Vietnamese assisted in training Cambodian and Laotian guerillas both militarily and politically. Vietnamese communist partisans commonly crossed the border into Cambodia and Laos, either as trainers or even to directly engage colonial forces. Weapons and other supplies necessary to keep the fledgling Cambodian communist movement afloat regularly moved across the border. A declassified Central Intelligence Agency (CIA) report summarized the increasing degree to which the Viet Minh had become involved in the Cambodian communist insurrection by the turn of the decade:

> The Viet Minh stepped up their efforts to direct events in Cambodia. First, they created special teams staffed by Vietnamese "familiar with Cambodia" to promote the development of a political base. Second, they sent "volunteer" military units to campaign with the pro-Viet Minh rebels. And third, they set up a Central Office of Cambodia in the southwestern province of Kampot. The Central Office was put under the Foreign Affairs Section of the "Southern Department," then the main Viet Minh controlling authority for southern Vietnam. The number of Vietnamese cadres and "volunteers" at first numbered in the low hundreds . . . never to exceed 2,500.[45]

Ho Chi Minh and the Viet Minh leadership were more sensitive to the centuries of animosity, conflict, and distrust between Cambodia and Vietnam than was the Comintern. Since the fall of the ancient Angkor Kingdom, Cambodia had been regarded as a pawn over which Vietnam and Thailand battled for control, and both nations had long demonstrated scornful and dismissive attitudes toward Cambodia—a reality not lost upon the ethnic Khmer population.[46] Justifications of Cambodian animosity toward Vietnam were not entirely confined to events of the distant past. As mentioned previously, Paris encouraged the settlement of ethnic Vietnamese in Cambodia and favored them in appointments within the colonial bureaucracy. Also, to enhance the agricultural capacity of its Vietnamese colony—the northern areas of which did not have an abundance of arable land—the French colonial government reapportioned the fertile Mekong Delta region to Vietnam in 1949, despite the territory having been considered Cambodian for centuries.[47] Sensitive to such realities and in an effort to avoid further complicating their already complex relationship with Cambodia, the Viet Minh made deliberate effort to conceal their involvement in Cambodia's revolution by using front organizations, fictionalized

ANTECEDENTS AND GENESIS OF CAMBODIAN COMMUNISM

leaders with Cambodian names, and by requiring Viet Minh advisors stationed there to adopt Cambodian names.[48]

The Vietnamese realized that such efforts could at best only provide a short-term solution to the precarious relationship. Eager to cultivate more grassroots support, in the summer of 1950 the Viet Minh organized several military and political schools in guerilla-held areas of southwestern Cambodia to recruit and train larger numbers of ethnically Khmer Cambodians as communist revolutionaries, and by the fall, they had nearly 300 students in training.[49] Such efforts on the part of the Viet Minh were not purely magnanimous in nature, as having established bases which could be used as staging areas and sanctuaries and storing sources of food and other supplies just across the border in Cambodia and Laos was seen as logistically useful in an intensifying campaign against French forces in Vietnam.[50] Considerable work needed to be done if responsibility of the Cambodian revolution was to be shifted increasingly toward the ethnic Cambodians. For example, in 1950, French intelligence estimated that less than 50 ethnically Khmer Cambodians and approximately 1,000 ethnic Vietnamese minorities living in Cambodia were members of the communist party.[51]

The latter statistic indicates that most of the increasingly potent Khmer Issarak guerila forces active in Cambodia up to that point were anti-colonialists and nationalists but not primarily communists. A 1949 analysis undertaken by the French colonial authorities estimated that at that time there were around 11,000 Khmer Issarak insurgents active across Cambodia.[52] The limited support for the communist cause among Khmer Issarak insurgents and ethnic Cambodians in general and strategies to address the latter was the primary focus of a 1950 border meeting between Vietnamese and Cambodian communist leaders. The consensus was that the elite and middle classes overwhelmingly favored an independent but democratic and politically moderate Cambodia and the agrarian peasant class was too rooted in traditional values to embrace communism. Most of the population was to a great degree nationalist but too traditional, ignorant, and intransigent to be ideologically recruited for proletarian revolution.[53] One potential strategy discussed to aid in growing the ethnic Cambodian support for communism was to form an independent Cambodian communist party ostensibly divorced from Vietnamese control. In a late meeting in 1950 with Viet Minh leadership in Moscow, Joseph Stalin expressed support for such a strategy and Ho Chi Minh is thought to have concurred, setting the stage for an emerging autonomous Cambodian communist movement.[54]

The Indochinese Communist Party Congress, in only the second such gathering since 1935, convened in February 1951 at the Viet Minh's mountain headquarters and, as one of its first acts, officially modified the organization's name to the "Vietnamese Workers' Party."[55] The action was undertaken as a gesture to ethnic-Khmer and ethnic-Laotian party leaders in support of their political autonomy and to signal the end of Vietnamese communist political dominance and insurgencies in those nations. The Congress facilitated communist party creation in Cambodia and Laos, but secret directives from within Vietnamese party leadership advocated that the Viet Minh retain control of the new parties to a great degree:

> Fine print in the directive's later clauses showed that the new parties would be less than fully independent. One clause stated that the Vietnamese Party reserved the right to supervise its "brothers." Another indicated that Vietnam had set up bureaus "to assist the revolutionary movement" in Cambodia and Laos. A third stated that "if conditions permit," the three national parties would eventually merge (again). The theme of merger also appeared in the . . . party platform, published in March 1951. The plank stated that Vietnam sought eventually to bring about a "federation of states of Vietnam, Cambodia and Laos, if the three peoples so desire."[56]

Efforts on the part of the Viet Minh to directly control communist politics in Cambodia and elsewhere in Indochina eventually led to internal political strife within the movement. Cambodian communists would ultimately fracture into distinct factions. The far-left nationalists who resented Vietnamese dominance and prioritized Cambodian self-determination were the majority and evolved into the Khmer Rouge movement led by Pol Pot. The term *Khmer Rouge* (Red Khmers) had originally been used by the Sihanouk government to refer to all Cambodian communists, but eventually the term came to refer to a particular strand within the movement, led by Pol Pot and Maoist in its ideological orientation. The minority communist faction that remained under the direction of Vietnam and Ho Chi Minh became widely known in Cambodia as the *Khmer Viet Minh*, a term of

ANTECEDENTS AND GENESIS OF CAMBODIAN COMMUNISM

derision intended by other Cambodians to mock them for their perceived foreign allegiance to a historical enemy.⁵⁷

The Rising and Declining Fortunes of Early Cambodian Communism

The Cambodian Communist Party initially developed along bifurcated, parallel lines, each with a distinct source of foreign influence. As noted, one strand was to form among the small cadres of Cambodian students sent to France on scholarship wherein many became infatuated with communist ideals. While these political seeds may have been planted in the minds of individuals even earlier, the first core groups of Cambodian students who became indoctrinated communists and sought to bring Marxist revolution to their homeland were organized abroad in the 1940s–50s. Many of the Cambodian communist students' leaders first became activists in the French Communist Party before taking control of the nearly 200-member Khmer Students Association in Paris and transforming it into a far-left revolutionary group.⁵⁸ After returning to Cambodia, the student revolutionaries would become integrated with Vietnamese-trained revolutionaries, usually drawn from the peasant class, with which no previous interaction existed.⁵⁹ In addition to being better educated in general, the Khmer student revolutionaries had often received extensive formal training in communist doctrine and political strategies from the French party and/or the Comintern and, as a result, quickly assumed leadership roles in the Cambodian cells. This was the case with Pol Pot and many others among the Paris students, including Khieu Samphan, Ieng Sary, and Son Sen, ultimately Prime Minister/General Secretary of the Communist Party, Foreign Minister, and Head of Party Security/Secret Police in the Pol Pot regime, respectively.

It should again be emphasized that the Khmer Issarak movement was not a communist organization itself but a diverse coalition of pro-independence factions, only some elements of which were far left politically. Illustrating this reality, in the wake of earlier Viet Minh efforts to control the Khmer Issarak rebellion, many elements of the Issaraks viewed Vietnamese influence with heightened distrust, with some Issarak factions even occasionally cooperating with the French in their efforts to combat the Viet Minh.⁶⁰ At the time of the first nationwide congress of Khmer Issarak groups in April 1950, approximately one-third of its leadership and delegates were communists, most of whom were directly or indirectly under the control of Vietnam.[61] Reflecting the increasingly polarized nature of the pro-independence rebellion, many non-communist Issaraks received varying levels of assistance from the Thai government and occasionally used Thai territory as a base of operations.[62] It is worth noting that a small communist faction within Cambodia at the time was affiliated with the fledgling Thailand Communist Party (as opposed to the Viet Minh) which sought to overthrow the Thai government. While still a political minority, the prominence of communists among the Khmer Issarak and the power and influence they wielded within the independence struggle had expanded significantly in recent years and would continue to do so through 1953.

As of 1950, ethnic Khmers remained a minority among the ranks of communist cells with most communist revolutionaries drawn from the ranks of ethnic minorities living in Cambodia. The presence of communist cells was strongest in areas inhabited by the approximately 500,000 ethnic Vietnamese of Cambodia and, secondarily, areas populated by its 400,000 ethnic Chinese, with revolutionaries from both groups initially placed under the authority of the Viet Minh, though the ethnic Chinese had originally sought to be aligned with their brethren to the north.[63] The continuing dominance of non-Khmer ethnicities as most communist leaders and fighters further fueled the distrust many Cambodians held toward the communist movement, and many viewed the communists as pawns manipulated by the Vietnamese in a veiled effort to reestablish control over Cambodia and its people.

The Cambodian rebellion expanded considerably by early 1953, with King Sihanouk claiming that nearly two-thirds of Cambodian territory had been occupied by communist forces in a March letter to France's president. The claim greatly exaggerated the degree of communist control over Cambodian territory and was almost certainly a deliberate calculation by Sihanouk to worry Paris and goad the colonial power into taking more steps toward an increasingly independent non-communist Cambodian government. Sihanouk's efforts at manipulating the French were bolstered by a gloomy assessment of the senior French military commander in Cambodia in whose view the military situation was untenable and who suggested an independent Cambodian regime aligned politically and economically with France was the most feasible strategy for countering the communist threat.[64]

ANTECEDENTS AND GENESIS OF CAMBODIAN COMMUNISM

The communist factions, which were now attracting increased numbers of ethnic Khmers, constituted the best-armed and most militarily potent elements within the Khmer Issarak coalition, and fears concerning the strength of the insurgency's communist elements—as well as Vietnamese influence—were not totally without merit, as reflected in U.S. intelligence assessments of their numbers, composition, and organization:

> The communists'... military strength (as estimated by French authorities) carried at about 7,000 in early 1953. The Liberation Army had three categories of troops: main forces, local forces, and guerilla/militia. The main forces, some thousand strong, were well-armed with a heavy leavening of Vietnamese "volunteers." The local forces had about 3,000 well-armed troops, a mixture of Cambodians and Vietnamese. The lightly armed guerilla-militias, 3,000 strong, were largely Cambodians. Vietnamese commanded most of the bigger units. Those headed by Cambodians had Vietnamese advisors.[65]

By the standards of many contemporary conflicts, a fighting force of some 7,000 seems modest. However, the latter number is more significant when juxtaposed against a national population of just 4.4 million (estimate as of November 1953) and the size of other forces in Cambodia at the time.[66] While precise numbers do not exist, it is likely that by early to mid-1953 communist revolutionaries comprised the majority of armed, trained fighters within the Khmer Issarak guerilla confederation. The communist guerillas' numbers were also substantial in comparison to Cambodian military forces, which only numbered approximately 13,000 as of 1952.[67] Also, with most French military capabilities abroad invested in escalating colonial conflicts elsewhere—principally Vietnam and increasingly in Algeria and Morocco—the numbers of French troops present in Cambodia were modest. The prevalent French colonial military practice after 1949 was to train and commission Cambodian officers to lead ethnic Cambodian troops, and by 1953 only small numbers of French military personnel were deployed in Cambodia, primarily trainers, advisers, and other specialists.[68]

Throughout the early 1950s, the Cambodian sovereignty movement continued to gain ground politically. France in effect granted semi-autonomous status in 1949 but retained control over foreign policy and defense. In 1950 the United States and most other western nations extended diplomatic recognition, as did two Asian countries, South Korea and Thailand.[69] King Sihanouk staged what was essentially a bloodless coup in June 1952, dismissed the cabinet and National Assembly, assumed direct rule and personal control over domestic security forces, and promised full sovereignty from French control within three years.[70] Additionally, Sihanouk declared martial law, but rather than reviling him as a despot or usurper, many Cambodians—particularly the peasant class with which the communists had failed to make significant inroads—at that time regarded him as a national hero and the standard bearer of Cambodian nationalism in the effort to end French rule.[71]

In June 1953 Sihanouk announced what he described to the press as a pleasure trip to France and multiple other foreign destinations. In reality, the trip was a carefully calculated effort to embarrass and outwit the French government via a public, international media campaign to lobby for Cambodian sovereignty using his royal status as King. After being admonished by the French government for openly demanding Cambodian autonomy, Sihanouk proceeded over the next several weeks to travel to the United States, Canada, and Japan in what he described as a "royal crusade for independence."[72] He received no more encouragement internationally than he had gotten in Paris, with the U.S. Secretary of State John Foster Dulles warning that Cambodian independence without French protection would lead to the country being taken over by communists and urging Sihanouk to work more cooperatively with France.[73] The King's defiant reaction to Washington's rebuff was to give an interview to *The New York Times* in which he ominously warned that unless moderate, pro-independence Cambodians were able to realize their dream of sovereignty, they would increasingly turn away from him and more moderate political outlets in Cambodia to the Viet Minh-led communist insurgents and seize independence by force.[74]

The political climate of Cambodia was such that if Sihanouk could not facilitate full independence, popular support could shift from him as the front runner of the independence movement to his chief rival, Son Ngoc Thanh, leader of the non-communist factions of the Khmer Issarak.[75] While his public scare tactics and international lobbying campaign had some impact in that the French government renewed talks with Cambodia's representatives in Paris, Sihanouk achieved little in the way of tangible results stemming from his "royal crusade" tour. However, Sihanouk did realize his efforts on the world stage garnered considerable international publicity, which he hoped could still lead to political leverage if sustained, certainly if the attention helped increase fears related to communism's advance in the region.

France's efforts to quell the communist insurgency in Vietnam were going badly, and they were also increasingly entangled in efforts to curb communist/Viet Minh activity in neighboring Laos.[76] A succession of French governments in the early 1950s refused to directly address the unravelling Indochina territories due to a climate of prolonged crisis, allowing matters to progressively worsen through inaction.[77] Sihanouk sought to use the latter realities to his advantage by continuing to portray an independent Cambodian state with himself as its leader as the solution to France's security concerns in Cambodia. In June he went into a brief self-imposed exile in Thailand and announced he would not return until the French granted full sovereignty and revisited his rhetoric regarding the ominous outcomes that would result from continued French intransigence. The Thai government had not been informed of his plans to exile himself in Bangkok or use their territory to continue his political agitation and, embarrassed and angered by this development, forbade him from engaging in politics while there, facilitating his return to Cambodia a mere seven days later.[78] The latter tactic having been ineffective, Sihanouk then revisited a strategy he had first undertaken one year earlier: directing the security forces under his authority to combat what had been described as radicalism and sources of foreign influence within the country. The approach was calculated to make him appear as a strong leader to his people; perhaps equal in importance was his calculation to curry favor with France and implant an impression with Paris that as the head of a sovereign Cambodia, he was capable of effective anti-communist strategies.

Sihanouk's political maneuvering was increasingly successful in some respects as 1953 progressed. Importantly, he not only prevented the erosion of his influence and standing among the Cambodian people but also, by maintaining a public and aggressive pro-sovereignty stance, Sihanouk solidified his internal credibility as the country's chief advocate for statehood. While many international leaders and media outlets found his international appeals clumsy and unstatesmanlike (e.g., an article in the *Washington Post* written several years later addressing Sihanouk's machinations described him as "absurd," "crazy," and "infuriating"[79]), to many Cambodians he appeared as a strong leader and determined advocate, as evidenced in large-scale pro-Sihanouk demonstrations that occurred in many parts of the country.[80] In continuing to assume the mantle of leadership in pursuit of sovereignty, Sihanouk undermined the nascent communist movement at a critical juncture by robbing them of their primary political issue, which was the claim that only communists could end French colonial rule in Cambodia through ongoing armed revolutionary struggle. While he would collaborate with the Khmer Rouge in later years, at this juncture Sihanouk championed constitutional democracy and actively denounced communism, earning him frequent condemnation through communist radio broadcasts and other organs.[81]

In addition, the gradual progression in French concessions throughout the 1950s, including the attainment of domestic rule and semi-autonomous status, were to a great degree derived from Sihanouk's efforts. Increasingly, many Cambodians viewed Sihanouk as successful in obtaining concessions from France and moving Cambodia closer to autonomy through political wrangling, whereas the Vietnamese communist efforts on behalf of their own nation were inching toward sovereignty at a slow pace and only via bloody and prolonged military struggle.[82] Following more French political concessions over subsequent months, in October 1953 Sihanouk proclaimed Cambodia's independence, which went unchallenged by Paris. The attainment of independence dealt indigenous (Khmer) communists in Cambodia a blow from which they would not recover for many years. Additionally in one of its first acts, the government would take an aggressive stance toward expelling Viet Minh forces from Cambodian territory, reflecting resurgent nationalist sentiment that would continue to make its presence felt for decades. Significantly, at the 1954 Geneva conference convened to finalize the French peace settlement in Indochina, Sihanouk dealt another setback to communism through his refusal to accept initial Soviet demands that an independent Cambodia be partitioned into two states, one communist and one non-communist as was done in Vietnam.[83]

Endnotes

1. Joel Brinkley, *Cambodia's Curse: The Modern History of a Troubled Land* (New York: Thames and Hudson, 2003).
2. Michael Coe, *Angkor and the Khmer Civilization* (New York: Thames and Hudson, 2003).
3. Brinkley, 2012.
4. David Chandler, *A History of Cambodia: Fourth Edition* (Boulder, CO: Westview Press, 2008), pp. 16–17.
5. Chandler, 2008.
6. Brinkley, 2012.
7. K. Hall, "Economic History of Early Southeast Asia," in *The Cambridge History of Southeast Asia*, ed. N. Tarling (London: Cambridge University Press, 1993).
8. J. Tully, *A Short History of Cambodia: From Empire to Survival* (Sydney, Australia: Allen & Unwin, 2006).
9. Brinkley, 2012 pp. 22–23.
10. D. Seekins, 1987.
11. S. Lovgren, "How Water Built and Destroyed This Powerful Empire," *National Geographic*, April 5, 2017.
12. Brinkley, 2012.
13. R. Ross, *Cambodia: A Country Study* (Washington, D.C.: Federal Research Division, Library of Congress, 1990).
14. CQ Researcher, "Cambodia: A Nation in Turmoil," http://library.cqpress.com/cqresearcher/document.php?id=cqresrre1985040500 Accessed June 27, 2018.
15. Ross, 1990.
16. J. Corfield, *The History of Cambodia* (Santa Barbara, CA: Greenwood Press, 2009).
17. D. Chandler, *Brother Number One: A Political Biography of Pol Pot* (Boulder, CO: Westview Press, 1999).
18. J. Brinkley, 2012.
19. J. Brinkley, 2012.
20. D. Chandler, 1999.
21. B. Kiernan, *How Pol Pot Came to Power: Colonialism, Nationalism, and Communism in Cambodia, 1930–1975* (New Haven, CT: Yale University Press, 2004).

22. Kiernan, 2004.
23. R. Smith, "The Foundation of the Indochinese Communist Party, 1929–1930," *Modern Asian Studies*, 32(4) 1998.
24. S. Morris, *Why Vietnam Invaded Cambodia: Political Culture and the Causes of War* (Stanford, CA: Stanford University Press, 1999).
25. D. Chandler, 1999.
26. R. Smith and B. Williams (eds.), *Communist Indochina* (New York: Routledge, 2013).
27. Ibid.
28. H. Minh, *Ho Chi Minh: Selected Writings 1920–1969* (Honolulu: University Press of the Pacific, 2001).
29. Morris, 1999.
30. Morris, 1999.
31. Barend Jan Terwiel, *Thailand's Political History: From the 13th century to recent times* – Kindle Edition (Bankok, Thailand: River Books, 2012).
32. GlobalSecurity.org, *Cambodia: Japanese Occupation, 1940–1945*, https://www.globalsecurity.org/military/world/cambodia/history-japan.htm Accessed June 2, 2018.
33. W. Swan, "Japan's Intentions for its Great East Asian Co-Prosperity Sphere as Indicated in its Policy Plans for Thailand," *Journal of Southeast Asian Studies*, 27(1) 1996.
34. V. Thompson and R. Adloff, "Cambodia Moves Toward Independence," *Far Eastern Survey*, 22(9) 1953.
35. S. McHale, "Ethnicity, Violence and Khmer-Vietnamese Relations: The Significance of the Lower Mekong Delta, 1757–1954," *The Journal of Asian Studies*, 72(2) 2013.
36. H. Sasagawa, "Japan's Involvement in Cambodia During World War II," in *Vietnam-Indochina-Japan Relations during the Second World War: Documents and Interpretations*, eds. S. Masaya, N. Van Khanh, and B. Lockhart (Tokyo: Waseda Institute of Asia-Pacific Studies, 2017).
37. Central Intelligence Agency, "Intelligence Report: Communism and Cambodia," (May 1972) https://www.cia.gov/library/readingroom/docs/esau-54.pdf Accessed June 20, 2018.
38. M. Woollacott, "King Norodom Sihanouk: Cambodian Monarch who Offered the Prospect of Continuity, but Subverted the Growth of

ANTECEDENTS AND GENESIS OF CAMBODIAN COMMUNISM

Democracy," *The Guardian*, October 15, 2012.
39. R. Cima, *Vietnam: A Country Study* (Washington, D.C.: Federal Research Division, Library of Congress, 1989).
40. McHale, 2013.
41. CIA, May 1972.
42. Ibid.
43. Sasagawa, 2017, 74.
44. D. Chandler, *The Tragedy of Cambodian History: Politics, War, and Revolution since 1945* (New Haven, CT: Yale University Press, 1991).
45. CIA, May 1972, p. 2.
46. Brinkley, 2012.
47. Brinkley, 2012.
48. CIA, May 1972.
49. CIA, May 1972.
50. Chandler, 1991.
51. Chandler, 1991, p. 48.
52. A. Dommen, *The Indochinese Experience of the French and the Americans: Nationalism and Communism in Cambodia, Laos, and Vietnam* (Bloomington, IN: Indiana University Press, 2002).
53. Chandler, 1991.
54. CIA, May 1972.
55. CIA, May 1972.
56. CIA, May 1972.
57. CIA, May 1972.
58. GlobalSecurity.org, "1949–1956 – The Paris Student Group," https://www.globalsecurity.org/military/world/cambodia/history-rouge-2.htm Accessed July 30, 2018.
59. Brinkley, 2012.
60. CIA, May 1972.
61. GlobalSecurity.org, "1945–1960 – The Cambodian Left: The Early Phases," https://www.globalsecurity.org/military/world/cambodia/history-rouge-1.htm Accessed June 15, 2018.
62. D. Chandler, "Khmer Issarak (Free Khmer)," in *Southeast Asia: A Historical Encyclopedia, from Angkor Wat to East Timor, Volume 1*, ed. O. Gin (Santa Barbara, CA: ABC_CLIO, 2004), pp. 725–726.
63. CIA, May 1972.

64. Chandler, 1991, pp. 68–69.
65. CIA, May 1972, 12–13.
66. G. Siampos, "The Population of Cambodia 1945–1980," *The Milbank Memorial Fund Quarterly*, 48(3) July 1970, 317–353.
67. J. Grant, *Cambodia: The Widening War in Indochina* (New York: Washington Square Press 1971).
68. S. Hoadley, *Soldiers and Politics in Southeast Asia: Civil-Military Relations in Comparative Perspective, 1933–1975* (New York: Routledge, 2017).
69. F. Munson, *Area Handbook for Cambodia* (Washington DC: US Government Printing Office, 1968).
70. M. Vachon, "How King Sihanouk Brought French Rule to a Peaceful End," *The Cambodia Daily*, November 11, 2013.
71. E. Becker, "Sihanouk and the Saga of the Khmer Rouge," *The Washington Post*, January 28, 1979.
72. K. So, "Cambodian Information Center: The Road to Khmer Independence," http://www.cambodia.org/facts/?page=independence Accessed August 5, 2018.
73. Chandler, 1991, pp. 67–68.
74. Ibid.
75. Munson, 1968.
76. Dommen, 2002.
77. P. Brocheux and D. Hemery, *Indochina: An Ambiguous Colonization, 1858–1954* (Oakland, CA: University of California Press, 2011).
78. M. Osborne, *Sihanouk: Prince of Light, Prince of Darkness* (Honolulu, HI: University of Hawaii Press, 1994).
79. Warren Unna, "Sihanouk's 'Absurdity' Serves Cambodia Well," *The Washington Post*, November 23, 1963.
80. R. Smith, *Communist Indochina* (New York: Routledge, 2012).
81. Thompson and Adloff, 1953.
82. CIA, May 1972.
83. Unna, 1963.

Political Dynamic of the Early Independence Era

Any attempt to examine the Khmer Rouge's discordant internal and geopolitical circumstances must be juxtaposed within the broader Indochina region's historical and political circumstances, the late colonial era's geopolitical dynamic, and the Cold War. Many developments in the years leading up to and immediately following Cambodian independence were inexorably linked to external or otherwise broader events that would help shape the ideology and the violent, xenophobic agenda of Cambodian communism and its leaders. For example, the territorial disputes—particularly the 1949 reassignment of the traditionally Cambodian Mekong Delta region to Vietnamese control—and other festering historical conflicts between the Khmer and Vietnamese helped escalate the frequency and severity of ethnic violence and instill growing distrust, resentment, and hatred in members of both groups, with each blaming the other and (deservedly) the French for the worsening climate.[1]

Casting partial blame on Paris for growing ethnic tensions in Indochina is justified, as many French colonial administration policies indeed helped to revive and exacerbate long-standing animosities among historical rivals within the region. Paris, in effect, structured its territories in Indochina as a federation of ethnic enclaves. In theory, inhabitants were free to relocate within French Indochina for economic or other purposes, but the French primarily facilitated the immigration of ethnic Vietnamese and Chinese, as both groups were perceived by Paris to be more industrious, more compliant with French authority, or more useful as civil servants than other ethnicities, such as the Khmer.[2] Table 1 illustrates the degree to which ethnic Vietnamese settled Cambodia during the French colonial era, with most clustering in certain parts of historically Khmer territory, including Phnom Penh and further south in the Mekong Delta region.

Colonial-era economic and demographic favoritism supported by stereotyping the perceived virtues and inadequacies of various ethnicities was not lost upon the groups often dismissed as lacking in some respect, including the Khmer and Lao. Both of these groups came to resent their dismissive treatment and the increased presence of other groups within their territories. The French colonial government's tendency to pit ethnic groups against each other (via a "divide and conquer" strategy) within their sphere of Indochina to maintain control was a significant and sustained source of ethnic tension in the period and helped facilitate the rise of ethnic-based nationalism in French Indochina. As militant strains of nationalism and xenophobia manifested in parts of the region, populations that had once been privileged minorities, such as the Vietnamese in Cambodia, found themselves increasingly on the outside politically and otherwise.[3] By the 1950s, for example, ethnic distrust and animosity superseded any ideological kinship that might have previously existed between the nascent Cambodian communist movement and the Viet Minh.

Table 1: Progression of Ethnic Vietnamese Settlement of Cambodia in French Colonial Era

Year	Vietnamese Population Estimate	Cambodian Population Estimate
1874	4,452 (0.6%)	746,424
1911	79,050 (5.8%)	1,360,188
1921	140,225 (7.0%)	2,000,000
1936	191,000 (6.4%)	3,000,000[4]
1950	319,596 (7.8%)	4,073,967[5]

*Population data between 1874–1936 obtained from Goscha (2009). Data from 1950 obtained from Poole (1974).

Geopolitics and Indochina

The issue of France's colonies and their self-determination was politically divisive for the country. Many French leaders supported decolonization in at least some of France's overseas possessions. Western attitudes from the 19th century and earlier which favored colonial and western-centric attitudes, such as the mission to "civilize" and bring order, had begun to erode in the interwar period and further gave way to less nationalistic perspectives stemming from the fight against Axis aggression/expansion and the subsequent founding of the UN in 1945. Indeed, as a reflection of growing global attitudes favoring decolonization and self-determination, many French reformers emerged among the ranks of political and military leaders, diplomats, the intelligentsia, and the general public who advocated for either elevating the status of many French colonies to near-equal political footing with the seat of power or, alternatively, granting full autonomy.[6] However, colonial policy was politically divisive, and by the fall of 1946, the provisional French government (Fourth Republic) and many national leaders, including Charles de Gaulle, expressed public commitment for retaining overseas possessions. French leaders who supported retaining the country's colonies did so for various reasons, often in combination. Considerations included maintaining national prestige and international influence; the desire to retain the colonial network's resources to aid in rebuilding the post-WWII economy; the anti-communist agenda that began to emerge in the aftermath of WWII; and, to some extent linked with the latter, an interest in furthering Catholicism/Christianity abroad.[7]

Opinions varied internationally as to the best solution for a stable post-Japan Indochina, with the policies of many nations, including the U.S., evolving as geopolitical circumstances shifted. United States President Franklin Delano Roosevelt recognized the importance of the region in terms of its natural resource base, strategic position adjacent to critical trade routes, and its potential as a market for U.S./western exports. However, Roosevelt did not support retaining the traditional colonial system perpetuated by many European powers and, in particular, did not think that France, amid growing anti-colonial sentiment in many of its possessions and after having been weakened by the devastation of WWII, could serve as a source of stability in Asia or other world regions.[8] He originally favored ending colonial control and creating an interim international trusteeship that would facilitate a transition toward independence for Southeast Asian dependencies.[9] Chiang Kai-Shek's nationalist China, which Roosevelt anticipated would defeat its own communist insurrection following WWII, would serve as the source of regional stability in eastern Asia rather than the European powers. When Roosevelt formally proposed such an arrangement, it received initial support from the Soviets and nationalist China but not Britain and France, both of which at the time sought to restore their respective colonial networks at war's end. Disagreements within the U.S. and strained relations with Chiang over various other political and military matters during the remainder of WWII, combined with pressure from European allies, eventually led Roosevelt to accept the resumption of colonial rule in Indochina as well as other regions.[10] The reversal in U.S. policy concerning French colonialism also reflected an American desire for French military participation in the Pacific theater following Germany's defeat. The policy favoring renewed colonial control was largely continued by subsequent U.S. administrations and helped set the stage for anti-colonial conflicts in future years.

Several external powers, including China and the USSR, ultimately consented to the 1946 return of French troops/authority to its colonies in Indochina. Nationalist China regarded the European powers as more capable of quelling the nascent communist movements within the region (as opposed to such smaller, autonomous states as an independent Cambodia), and Chiang's government also recognized it would need the support of western nations in its own intensifying civil war against communist revolutionaries. Soviet acquiescence to renewed French presence reflected political realities, such as the Free French government under de Gaulle establishing favorable relations with Moscow upon signing a mutual cooperation pact in 1944. The governments continued cordial ties in the early years of the Fourth Republic largely out of joint concern for an Anglo-centric post-war international dynamic dominated by the U.S. and Britain.

Return of Colonial Authority

Due to Japanese actions in the dismantling of Vichy French authority in the last months of WWII, Paris needed to reestablish an administrative and military presence within Indochina. Reflecting the absence of any remaining French authority within the region and the enfeebled state of France at the end of the war, the summer 1945 Potsdam Conference established that nationalist China would accept the surrender of Japanese forces, preserve order, and seek to pacify areas of northern Indochina (north of the 16th parallel) while the British would do likewise in the south. At war's end in September, the approximately 200,000-strong Chinese 1st Army was dispatched into northern Indochina and (initially with the blessing of the U.S.) continued the detention of Vichy French POWs interred by the Japanese in the final phase of the war.[11] Not only had the Vichy French forces initially collaborated with the Japanese but also the practical concern on the part of both China and the U.S. was that liberated French forces would attempt to reassert control over colonial administrative roles and facilities and, in doing so, antagonize pro-independence elements of the local populations. During WWII, the U.S. had maintained positive relations with Ho Chi Minh and the Viet Minh forces, with the latter even receiving American aid in exchange for collaborative wartime actions, such as safeguarding downed American pilots and undertaking guerrilla operations against the Japanese.[12] However, the influx of foreign military forces at the end of WWII undermined Ho Chi Minh and the Viet Minh's position.

Conversely, British forces assuming control from the defeated Japanese in southern Indochina (Cambodia and southern Vietnam) promptly released and rearmed French POWs, facilitating their reoccupation of colonial administrative buildings and other properties en route to reasserting French authority.[13] Even before the arrival of additional French forces from Europe, widespread anti-colonial demonstrations and fighting had erupted in Cambodia and southern Vietnam by October 1945 and subsequently spread to northern areas of French Indochina following the withdrawal of China, which had eventually acquiesced to Paris. French forces were aided in the escalating fighting against the Viet Minh by British and Indian troops as well as by many former Japanese POWs rearmed by the British and placed under their command. The Viet Minh also recruited small numbers of former Japanese soldiers, many of whom were perhaps sympathetic to the anti-western/colonial attitudes of Ho's forces, to fight against the French and help train recruits. Britain and ultimately—in a reversal of their initial positions—China and the U.S. regarded the restoration of French colonial control as preferable to a Viet Minh communist regime in Vietnam that seemed poised to spread to Cambodia and Laos.

The First Indochina War (and the Regional Political Dynamic)

Many historians perceive the First Indochina War as officially beginning in 1946 when the French initiated large-scale military campaigns to seize the Viet Minh-held city of Haiphong, Vietnam in November, followed by heavy fighting to eject the communist forces from Hanoi the following month.

Scholars sometimes characterize this conflict as being specific to Vietnam, as most of the troop deployments, fighting, and casualties were concentrated in the latter, specifically North Vietnam. However, the First Indochina War was, in reality, a broader effort throughout the region to end French control, following the refusal of Paris to fully accept declarations of autonomy on the part of Cambodia, Laos, and Vietnam in 1945. The war was among the first of many anti-colonial conflicts that would help define the first decades of the post-WWII era internationally. Like the Second Indochina War (known as the Vietnam War in the U.S.), the First Indochina War was, in effect, a proxy war, and it transcended its geographical confines, symbolizing the broader Cold War conflict between the western world and communism.

Initially, the post-WWII French government underestimated the scope and intensity of attitudes favoring autonomy and naively assumed it could pacify the independence movements throughout its territories in Indochina. An ill-conceived and vaguely-defined power sharing proposal had tentatively been explored between the French and Viet Minh in which Paris would ostensibly govern its Indochina territories jointly with representatives of nationalist groups, but the compromise proved unworkable in Vietnam and was abandoned in 1946.[14] The failure of the latter attempt at a political solution marked a turning point in the conflict in that both the French government and pro-autonomy elements (specifically the Viet Minh) within French Indochina became increasingly intransigent and unwilling to compromise in their respective positions as fighting intensified. The paradoxical determination of Paris to retain its overseas possessions amid a climate of mounting nationalism and anti-French sentiment throughout the region made prospects for a peaceful compromise nearly impossible. By 1947, the French strategy of prioritizing the capture and retention of urban centers had largely driven the Viet Minh forces of Vietnam and the Khmer Issarak forces of Cambodia into the countryside from which they would wage guerrilla campaigns, a state of affairs that came to characterize the First and Second Indochina Wars as well as other conflicts within the region.

Certain developments related to the First Indochina War would have significant impact upon the evolution of Cambodian communism and the domestic and international conduct of the Pol Pot regime. While a small and ineffectual communist presence (as discussed in Chapter 1) existed in Cambodia prior to the First Indochina War, the first functional communist presence was an outgrowth of Cambodian resistance to renewed French rule. The Khmer Issarak movement was founded in 1945 as a coalition of nationalist political elements determined to resist French domination. Within two years, the Viet Minh sought political control over the Cambodian resistance movement, facilitating the fracturing of the Khmer Issarak into two distinct factions: those willing to accept Vietnamese leadership under the umbrella of the Indochina Communist Party—which became known as Khmer Viet Minh—and the traditional ethnic Khmer nationalists who rejected Vietnamese tutelage. Viet Minh efforts to build support for their influence and communism in general within Cambodia met with little success initially due to a combination of reasons: Cambodia was a low priority for Vietnamese communists; ethnic Khmers were generally not receptive to collaborating with or being led by the Vietnamese; and Cambodia's King Sihanouk undermined any potential communist appeal by making his own demands for concessions, ultimately including autonomy from the French.[15]

Whereas French pacification efforts failed in Vietnam, they met with at least partial success in Cambodia and Laos. In Cambodia's case, the January 1946 Modus Vivendi Agreement established Cambodian control over most domestic institutions while permitting France to retain an advisory role in domestic affairs and retain complete authority over international affairs and defense. Incidents of (usually rural) violence directed against the French continued to increase throughout 1946–47, though such incidents were generally sporadic and uncoordinated due to the disorganized nature of the Khmer Issarak at the time.[16] Armed resistance from the Khmer Issarak's non-communist elements began to decline in 1947 due to several developments, including the return of the southwestern provinces Battambang and Siem Reap from Thailand stemming from French and U.S. pressure; declining support for the Issarak—many of whom had been based across the Thai border—on the part of a new government in Bangkok; and an amnesty offered to Issarak fighters by the Cambodian government.[17] Although Paris retained control over economic and defense matters, Cambodia's quasi-autonomous status was expanded further in 1950 when the French granted approval for the government to establish diplomatic missions, which brought prompt recognition by Britain, the U.S., and other western nations.[18]

King Sihanouk was not satisfied with Cambodia's semi-autonomous status and continuation of French tutelage. In particular, he regarded full sovereignty as a necessary course of action to prevent the First Indochina War from spilling into Cambodia, potentially facilitating Vietnamese (Viet Minh) and/or communist domination.[19] Sihanouk's concerns were in part driven by the reality that, by the early 1950s, Vietnamese communists had almost completely co-opted the leadership of the remaining Issarak independence movement in Cambodia, and Viet Minh fighters had crossed the border to establish bases of operation in Cambodia to support their ongoing campaign against the French. Sihanouk had deprived Cambodia's nascent communist movement of their chief political issue by successfully extracting increasingly substantive French concessions, weakening France's direct control enough that the King announced in October 1953 that full sovereignty had been attained. Correctly asserting the communist presence within Cambodia was largely under the influence of the Vietnamese and that the latter had deployed forces within Cambodian territory, the King further undermined communism within the country by deploying the Royal Khmer Army in engagements intended to eject the Khmer Viet Minh in December.[20] The latter action prompted an incursion into northeastern Cambodia by Vietnamese forces, establishing a new theater and new layer of complexity to the First Indochina War and leaving the Vietnamese in control of much of northeastern Cambodia by the time the Geneva Conference opened.[21]

The eventual arrival of additional French military personnel and firepower, facilitated initially by the British Navy, brought urban areas throughout most of French Indochina under control relatively quickly. However, the resistance campaigns undertaken by nationalist guerrilla forces throughout the region, particularly the Viet Minh, led to escalation. The deployment of increasing numbers of troops along with naval and air support enabled French forces to exact a heavy toll on organized resistance and win a number of military engagements (e.g., the French victory at the January 1951 Battle of Vinh Yen, enabled largely by air support), yet it only served to prolong and intensify the conflict rather than facilitate victory for Paris. As in the subsequent Second Indochina War, large segments of the population of French Indochina were unsympathetic to communism and actively resisted its advance. The latter added a dynamic of internal discord to the war, with significant segments of the Indochina population that might have otherwise opposed the French regarding Paris as the lesser of two evils, the greater threat being the establishment of communist (Viet Minh) control. In Cambodia, Laos, and particularly Vietnam, the French-approved indigenous military forces actively engaged communist militants, making the First Indochina War in part a civil war.

While the precise number of casualties incurred during the First Indochina War is difficult to ascertain, particularly for statistics specific to Cambodia and Laos, estimates reveal the war to have been a major conflict. Up to 300,000 or more Viet Minh fighters and their allies are thought to have died, with a small percentage of that total having been killed in operations against French forces in Cambodia or Laos.[22] French historian Michel Bordin concluded that 112,032 members of French Union forces died in the conflict.[23] The latter figure includes fatalities among soldiers who were French nationals as well as colonial African troops, members of the French Foreign Legion, and the indigenous military forces of the French-approved regimes in Cambodia, Laos, and Vietnam. Both figures are specific to military fatalities and do not include civilian deaths, which are widely believed to be comparable to or even greater than the total number of military fatalities. The First Indochina War had also proven to be costly for a country rebuilding from the devastation of WWII, and, by its final year, the U.S. was subsidizing most of France's military expenditures in the conflict.

The 1954 Geneva Conference

Due to anti-colonial insurrections (primarily directed at the British or French, both of which had initially attempted to reassert control over their colonial possessions) or other political strife, the years in the aftermath of WWII were characterized by escalating destabilization and military conflicts in many world regions. By the 1950s, such instability and conflict had become increasingly widespread in several sub-regions of Asia, with the looming potential for further deterioration. An international conference was convened in Geneva in May 1954 with the goal of formulating plans for peace and stability in two areas of particular concern: the Korean Peninsula and French Indochina. While the conference achieved nothing of value related to Korea, the wrangling of attendees over the disposition of French Indochina at the talks provides an insightful case study in Cold War-era diplomacy. More importantly, in failing to sufficiently resolve the existing conflicts within Indochina, the Geneva Conference set the stage for much of the war and strife that would occur within the region in subsequent years.

Participants related to the Indochina talks included Cambodia, Laos, (communist/Viet Minh) North Vietnam, (non-communist) South Vietnam, and five external powers: Britain, China, France, the U.S., and the USSR. The U.S.-led western agenda chiefly entailed curtailing the spread of communism and the expanding international influence of China and the Soviet Union. The western nations were not a united front, and varied agendas (e.g., anti-communist hawks as opposed to those open to negotiation and compromise with far-left elements) also existed internally among the delegates of some states in attendance, including the U.S. delegation. U.S. Secretary of State, John Foster Dulles undertook a balancing act of maintaining willingness to negotiate and pursue a diplomatic settlement while simultaneously threatening the communist bloc with greater degrees of U.S./western intervention within the region, potentially including the establishment of military bases or other forms of direct action. Many conservatives in the U.S. and other western nations advocated a hardline stance of no compromise with communists and subsequently vilified Dulles and his allies in the negotiations for even coming to the table with Moscow, Beijing, and the Viet Minh, and, in particular, for conceding to the division of Vietnam and the creation of a communist state in the north.[24]

In the months leading up to the Geneva Conference, Viet Minh incursions into both Cambodia and Laos increased substantially, as did communist guerrilla activity already present in both countries. The latter developments, coupled with increased Soviet and Chinese interest in the region, and perhaps more importantly the Viet Minh victory over the French at Dien Bien Phu and deteriorating colonial control were intended by the communist bloc to allow them to negotiate from a position of strength at the conference and force concessions from the west. Some significant western concessions were indeed obtained, including the withdrawal of all French military forces, recognition of full independence (in the case of Cambodia and Laos, reaffirmation of autonomy) of former French possessions, and the agreement to not establish western military bases or other direct military presence in the countries. The political alignment of Cambodia and Laos was of paramount importance and one of the earliest issues that threatened to derail the talks.[25] The governments of Cambodia and Laos also largely acceded to North Vietnamese demands that they both pursue positions of neutrality in the geopolitical conflict between western and communist bloc nations, though Cambodia asserted that, as a sovereign state, it had the inherent right to determine its own political alignments and solicit assistance from any nations of its choosing. As one element of the tenuous commitment to neutrality, both nations also agreed to prohibit the establishment of foreign military bases within their territory.

The communist bloc had indeed undertaken the Geneva talks from a position of regional strength as they hoped. In addition to communist control over northern Vietnam (and pockets of presence in the south), as of spring 1954 nearly half of Cambodia and a comparably large portion of Laos were either under the control of communist Vietnamese forces that had crossed the borders via direct incursions or that of Viet Minh-trained far-left indigenous guerrillas.[26] The Cambodian and Laos militaries and the remaining French forces experienced limited success in stemming the advancing tide of communist forces in Indochina in the preceding months. However, despite the latter military reality and the backing and encouragement of Moscow and Beijing, the communist Vietnamese actually achieved few of their original objectives from the Geneva Conference.[27] Although they controlled approximately two-thirds of Vietnam at the time of the conference, the Viet Minh eventually acquiesced to the roughly equal division of the country at the 17th parallel, as they regarded this split as a temporary division of Vietnam that could be reversed by elections the Accords called for in 1956, elections that the Vietnamese communists believed they would win and thus would facilitate the reunification of the country under their control. The Viet Minh also agreed to cease hostilities, withdraw their military forces from Cambodia and Laos, refrain from interference in the internal political affairs of both nations.

Communist demands that the areas of Cambodia and Laos under their control at the start of the talks be formally partitioned into communist and non-communist territories—driven by the need of the communist forces to "regroup," similar to how Vietnam would be divided at the 17th parallel—were initially rejected by the non-communist governments of Cambodia and Laos as well as the western nations in attendance.[28] Much to the disappointment of the Indochinese communists, neither Moscow nor Beijing pressed the matter of division or otherwise stood in steadfast support of Hanoi's more ambitious agenda at the conference.[29] The noncommunist delegates contended that indigenous communist forces in Cambodia and Laos were small in number, had overstated their strength, and that communist-held territory in both countries was principally the result of incursion on the part of Viet Minh troops; thus, formal territorial division was not justified.[30] After initial recalcitrance at the beginning of the talks, both China and the Soviet Union largely acceded.

China's failure to support the communist agenda at the negotiations can be attributed to multiple factors. In the Korean conflict's aftermath, China began pursuing policies of coexistence, diplomatic engagement, and political compromise, when possible, with the west. Specifically, China was concerned the ongoing conflicts in French Indochina could result in broader U.S./western military intervention similar to the Korean conflict, and Foreign Minister Zhou Enlai was willing to pursue diplomatic avenues and make concessions to avoid such an outcome.[31] Perhaps more importantly, Beijing viewed Indochina as its geopolitical domain and desired to check the expanding influence of the Vietnamese communists within the region. Thus, the Chinese pressured the Viet Minh to accept terms that, in effect, weakened Hanoi's position, including Vietnamese military withdrawal from Cambodia and Laos and the abandonment of initial demands to partition the two countries. Until the 1954 Geneva Accords, China had been the primary source of foreign support for the Viet Minh, but the latter felt betrayed by their former ally in Geneva, and the conference marked the start of deteriorating relations between the countries. This deterioration ultimately culminated in Beijing backing the Khmer Rouge in Cambodia as a regional counterweight to Hanoi's influence.

Soviet motives for tepid support of the Viet Minh at the talks were varied: a desire for improved relations between the communist bloc and the west in general; a desire to curry favor with the French government that Moscow hoped would reject the European Defense Community and oppose a rearmed West Germany; and a prioritization of Soviet interests elsewhere (e.g., Europe) rather than Southeast Asia.[32] Ultimately, neither Moscow nor Beijing wanted to risk derailing the Geneva peace negotiations or trigger an escalation or broader western intervention in the French Indochina conflict by advocating too forcefully on behalf of communist factions. A declassified CIA analysis provides a cogent summary of the outcome relative to Cambodia and the inability of the Vietnamese to elicit Chinese and Soviet backing in Geneva:

> The Vietminh at Geneva decided to give up on Cambodia. The communists agreed to withdraw all Vietminh troops from Cambodian soil within 90 days after the Accords were signed. Sihanouk's delegation signed them on July 21, 1954, having gotten virtually everything it demanded.... The Vietminh thereupon set about salvaging as much as they could of their Cambodian structure. That is, they shipped cadres and sympathizers to North Vietnam, leaving behind a few Party members to mind the store... The number of Cambodian nationals who went to North Vietnam in 1954 was... probably fewer than 3,000 (but were)... nonetheless important, since they form the leadership of Cambodian communism.[33]

Cambodia's nascent communist movement felt betrayed and dejected by the Geneva Conference's developments. Just as the communist and non-communist leadership in Vietnam had been represented separately in Geneva, the Viet Minh and their Khmer and Laotian revolutionary counterparts had initially insisted that, given the territory controlled by leftist forces in Cambodia and Laos, dual representation for both the governments and the communist factions in each nation was necessary. Representatives of communist forces in Cambodia and Laos had travelled to Geneva in hope of being given status as delegations at the talks, to advocate for separate spheres of territorial control in the countries, among other things, with Cambodian communists referring to their proposed territory as Khmerland. Delegations representing the Cambodian and Laotian governments backed by the western nations in attendance refused proposals for separate communist delegations for the countries and, in the case of Cambodia, ultimately succeeded in rejecting demands related to territorial partition. Exploring the magnitude of this setback to the communists in Cambodia, Short asserts that:

> Failure to carve out a communist-administered region to serve as a base for Khmerland on the model of North Vietnam... dealt the Cambodian communists a death blow. (The latter)... could argue

as much as they wished that Cambodia was an integral part of the Indochinese battlefield; that stable resistance bases existed in 36 of Cambodia's 98 districts; that... 800,000 people and 40% of the country's territory was under communist control; and that therefore Khmerland should enjoy the same rights as North Vietnam... (but), the fact that they held no clearly defined "liberated zone" meant that their claims and their presence were ignored.[34]

The Geneva Conference of 1954 is perhaps best known for facilitating ceasefire agreements in Cambodia, Laos, and Vietnam and ostensibly settling the independence struggles against French rule in what would later become known as the First Indochina War. However, the Accords would continue to have significant impacts for many years throughout the region. In neighboring Laos, the royalist government ultimately agreed to integrate the communist Pathet Lao ("Lao Nation") forces in the governing coalition and to temporarily recognize their administrative control over portions of the country to permit the regrouping of their forces pending a final political agreement. Indigenous communist forces in Laos had already established a separate parallel government four years earlier with the assistance of Vietnamese communists, who later used the territories of Laos and Cambodia in efforts to infiltrate and undermine the non-communist South Vietnamese regime. The 1954 Geneva Accords had afforded the communists in Laos status and legitimacy by giving them de facto control of two provinces and, perhaps more importantly, political inclusion in the national government. They also benefited substantially from the direct support of neighboring North Vietnamese communists whose involvement in Laos was not curtailed by the Accords—though the agreement in theory prohibited using the territory of Laos or Cambodia for Viet Minh incursions into South Vietnam, no real capacity existed to monitor or enforce the latter terms.[35] A prolonged civil war soon reignited between Laotian communist and government forces. The strength of the communists in Laos and the scope of territory under their control would continue to expand in coming years, ultimately resulting in a communist regime aligned with Hanoi and at odds with Cambodia's non-communist government.

It has been suggested that the North Vietnamese at least initially attempted to abide by the terms of the Geneva Accords, as it was in their vested interests (e.g., increased stability with the region and optimistic prospects for a desirable final outcome) at the time the agreement was forged.[36] The Accords had brought about the withdrawal of French troops from the North, temporarily prohibited the deployment of any other foreign troops in Vietnam, and called for elections within two years on to address reunification and which government the country would adopt—elections the North initially thought it would win. However, following the abandonment of election plans in the South and emboldened by what had essentially been a French military capitulation two years earlier, the North Vietnamese and communist insurgents in the South resorted once more to an armed insurrection, one that would become inexorably intertwined with the political fortunes of neighboring Cambodia and Laos. The Geneva Accords did little to impede communism or provide more than a brief respite from war in Indochina. The Accords facilitated the creation of communist-led North Vietnam, did not prevent the latter from undermining the self-determination of the non-communist South or interfering in neighboring states, and the Accords empowered the communist movement in Laos, which would eventually seize power with assistance from Vietnamese communists.

Among the radical movements of French Indochina, the communists of Cambodia benefited the least from the terms reached in Geneva. By October 1954, French forces and most Viet Minh forces had been withdrawn from Cambodian soil as well as from neighboring Laos, as agreed in Geneva. The terms of the Accords called for elections to seat democratically elected governments in each of the former French territories. Upon failing to revise the constitution, which forbade the monarch from simultaneously holding or seeking elected political office, King Sihanouk abdicated in March 1955 and installed his father Norodom Suramarit on the Cambodian throne. Sihanouk, who assumed the title Prince, set about building a political coalition and national party primarily composed of conservative and anti-communist elements—ironically named the "Popular Socialist Community" (Sangkum Reastr Niyum)—apparently behind the goal of pulling some support from politically disaffected elements that might otherwise have supported the left.[37] Most of Cambodia's right/nationalists and much of the country's center unified around the former king, who was widely respected for his leadership in attaining autonomy, and his coalition won 83% of the popular vote and all seats in the National Assembly in the September elections.[38] The enfeebled remnants of Cambodian communists organized a political wing named the Pracheachon ("People's") Group to participate in the elections but only obtained 4% of the vote—mostly from Chinese and Vietnamese minorities—and failed to obtain a legislative seat.[39] Significantly, Sihanouk regarded his national popularity and the decisive election as a mandate, and he began to move his government in an increasingly autocratic direction over the next 15 years of his rule. Addressing this progression, Chandler explains that:

> Sihanouk felt he had obtained a mandate to govern Cambodia as he saw fit. The subsequent eclipse of the (left) . . . gave him the impression, encouraged by many foreign visitors and by his entourage that his crusade had been not only successful but also astute and that the suffusion of Cambodia the state by Sihanouk the man was a salutary political development. A consequence of this, especially evident in the 1960s, was that Sihanouk felt no obligation to be at peace with (regional rivals) . . . or grant freedom of action to people he disliked.[40]

Rebuilding Cambodian Communism

As illustrated in the following section, Cambodian communism evolved via several transformative stages. Between the 1920s and 1940s, a small, decentralized presence of communist supporters existed but was primarily confined to members of Cambodia's ethnic Chinese and Vietnamese minorities and influenced from abroad by communist movements in the latter countries. In the 1940s–50s, small cadres of Cambodian students who had been awarded scholarships to study abroad in France were recruited and indoctrinated by the French Communist Party, becoming known as the "Paris Group." When Vietnamese control over Cambodia's communist movement waned in the aftermath of the Geneva Accords and the withdrawal of Viet Minh forces from Cambodian territory, many members of the educated and politically trained "Paris Group" assumed leadership roles, facilitating the first truly Khmer-led communist presence in Cambodia. Factions and dissention within Cambodian communism continued to exist and were further complicated by external geopolitics, including the Cold War dynamic and Sino-Soviet split. For example, the Cambodian communists who fled to North Vietnam following the Geneva Conference tended to identify with their Vietnamese counterparts and Vietnam's patrons in the

USSR, whereas most (though not all) ethnic Khmer communists inside Cambodia in the 1960s began to gravitate toward Pol Pot's faction.

Evolution of Communist Organizations in Cambodia Through the Khmer Rouge

Communist Party of China (c. 1921–present) – Founded in China in 1921, had likely established a modest, disorganized presence among Cambodia's ethnic Chinese minority by early to mid-1920s. Perhaps the first presence of communist ideology within Cambodia among the ethnic Chinese minority.

Indochinese Communist Party (1930–1945) – Founded, controlled, and almost entirely composed of ethnic Vietnamese, yet ostensibly functioned as the official regional communist organ. The first ICP cell within Cambodia may have been formed as early as 1930 via ethnic Vietnamese emigres working in Cambodian rubber plantations.[41]

Viet Minh – Translated as "League of Independence for Vietnam," the organization was founded in 1941 originally as a coalition of various groups organized to fight for Vietnamese independence. The Viet Minh was dominated by communists and became the Communist Party of Vietnam following the dissolution of the ICP in 1945. Functioned as the de facto leadership of communist insurgents in neighboring Cambodia and Laos for many years and heavily impacted the path of communism and domestic politics in both.

Khmer Issarak – While not a communist organization itself, Cambodia's Khmer Issarak ("Free/Independent Khmer") was founded in 1945 as a diverse political coalition of various pro-independence, anti-French groups, each with its own leadership. A minority of far-left groups were included in the coalition, including communists.

Khmer Viet Minh – A derisive term given to the group by Cambodian leader Norodom Sihanouk for far-left members of the Khmer Issarak to disparage their connection with and support of communist forces in neighboring—and historical rival—Vietnam. Following the 1954 Geneva Conference and associated withdrawal of Vietnamese forces from Cambodia, several thousand ethnic Khmer communists chose to withdraw from Cambodia with their Vietnamese allies, further weakening the influence of communism in Cambodia at the time and, in effect, creating a foreign-based faction of Cambodian communists that would ultimately compete with Pol Pot's faction for leadership.

The "Paris Group" (1940s–c. 1960) – Cambodian students selected to study abroad in France who became recruited, indoctrinated, and trained by the French Communist Party. Many members eventually assumed leadership roles in communist movements/regimes in Cambodia, though initially the students had little connection to the peasant-based and Vietnamese-led communist movement in their country. The "Paris Group" and the Vietnamese/peasant factions would ultimately become rivals for the leadership of Cambodian communism. Members were drawn from the ranks of the Khmer Students' Association (KSA, 1949–1956) and, following a French government ban of the latter, its successor organization, the Khmer Students' Union (KSU, 1956–60).[42]

Kampuchean People's Revolutionary Party/KPRP (1951–1960) – Arguably more of an umbrella organization for the Cambodian far-left than a single party with a unified message, the KPRP marked a turning point in which the country's radical left was led and organized primarily by ethnic Khmers rather than external sources. Diverse views existed within the KPRP, including pro- and anti-Vietnam/Viet Minh attitudes and doctrinal positions aligned with China's rural, agrarian emphasis as opposed to the more traditional urban-centric Marxist-Leninist focus reflecting the Soviet Union and European communism.

Pracheachon Group (1955–1972) – Arguably the first Khmer-led communist group organized as a political party, the Pracheachon was the political wing established as a front of the KPRP by those Cambodian communists who had not fled to Vietnam. The party was organized to run in national elections beginning in 1955 and never experienced political success, due to both lack of popular support and harassment by the Cambodian government.

Workers' Party of Kampuchea (1960–1966) – Renamed, reorganized successor of the KPRP.

Communist Party of Kampuchea/CPK (1966–1981) – Renamed, re-organized successor—essentially the Pol Pot communist faction—of the Worker's Party of Kampuchea and its predecessor, the KPRP.

Khmer Rouge – Term given to the CPK by Cambodian leader Norodom Sihanouk, meaning "Red (communist) Khmers." Originally an umbrella term for all Cambodian communists, "Khmer Rouge" came to refer to a specific faction of radicals led by Pol Pot.*43

Among the era's most prominent leaders of the Pracheachon and Cambodian communism was Hou Youn. Having completed a law degree in France, Youn was one of the best educated members of the Paris Group and a leading intellectual among the ranks of the country's far left in the 1950s–60s. Despite the poor performance of the Pracheachon in national elections, Sihanouk sought to appoint representatives from the far left to his government, either out of a desire to consolidate support for his regime across a broad spectrum of Cambodian society (Youn was both part-Chinese ethnically as well as a leader of the far left, and Sihanouk at different times sought to build support among both groups) or perhaps merely to more closely monitor the activities of potential political rivals. Youn, while also often critical of Sihanouk's policies, publicly proposed a far-left collaboration with Sihanouk's regime, a politically practical attitude not shared by all communist leaders. As a result of these circumstances, Youn was invited into Sihanouk's governing Sanghum Party in 1958 and held several cabinet positions, including Minister of the Interior, before ultimately being elected to the national legislature in 1966.[44]

The political successes and national profile Youn attained in the early independence era was the exception rather than the norm among the country's far left leadership. Pol Pot returned to Cambodia without a degree in 1953 after four years of study in France. He and many other members of the Paris Group joined the socialist-oriented KPRP and began to assume leadership roles. During this period, Pol Pot adopted his revolutionary pseudonym while supporting himself as a teacher and conducting public life as Saloth Sar. By 1960, Pol Pot, with the support of like-minded revolutionaries,

---

* It should be noted that complexities exist with the dates of existence and even the naming of some organizations. For example, the Pol Pot regime engaged in revisionist tendencies, such as rewriting the dates for the founding/existence of certain groups including the KPRP, which the Khmer Rouge claimed was first established several years later (post-Geneva)—possibly to disavow any connection to the Vietnamese. Also, examples exist of reviving the names of previous organizations (perhaps in pursuit of legitimacy) despite having little-to-no actual ties to the original organization and, in turn, obfuscating the years of existence of the group.

had transformed an organization he initially regarded as disorganized and unfocused into an overtly Marxist-Leninist group with a more defined and hierarchical leadership structure. One of Pol Pot's chief mentors within the Cambodian communist movement was Tou Samouth (Achar Sok), the KPRP cofounder and leader of its urban, Vietnam/Soviet-aligned wing, whose disappearance in 1962—either at the hands of Sihanouk's security forces or (perhaps more likely) Pol Pot, who viewed Samouth as a personal and ideological rival—helped facilitate Pol Pot's rise within the party.[45] The following year, Pol Pot was elected General Secretary of the Workers' Party of Kampuchea (renamed the Communist Party of Kampuchea three years later), a position he would hold until 1981, two years after being deposed as dictator. However, the Sihanouk regime's communist crackdowns, beginning in 1963 and intensifying in subsequent years, eventually forced the nascent organization underground, with Pol Pot and other leaders operating from remote, heavily forested areas in northern Cambodia.

Several other Paris Group members played key roles in defining the direction of Cambodian communism and positioning the movement in conflict with Vietnamese and Soviet models. Ieng Sary—who would later serve as Foreign Minister and Deputy Prime Minister in the Khmer Rouge regime—and Pol Pot joined the French Communist Party, which provided many members of the Cambodian Student Group with extensive training, including travel to other communist states. During a 1951 trip to a communist youth gathering in East Germany, both met Cambodian peasants who had been operating under the leadership of the Viet Minh and concluded the ethnic Khmer revolutionaries were influenced too heavily by Cambodia's traditional rival. This and other experiences led Ieng Sary and many other members of the Student Group to advocate for a more disciplined and distinctly Cambodian communist organization, led by ethnic Khmers. Others, including Khieu Samphan (Chair of the State Presidium in the Khmer Rouge regime) and Hou Yuon—both earning doctorates in law and accordingly among the best educated members of the Paris Group—helped frame the doctrinal development of Cambodian communism. For example, Yuon's 1955 dissertation emphasized the central role of agrarian peasants in the path to development, discounting the traditional Marxist prerequisite stages of industrialization and urbanization.[46] Samphan's 1959 dissertation stressed the need for Cambodia to become economically self-sufficient rather than continuing its dependency upon foreign trade and western nations, which he asserted led to the exploitation of the country (see the discussion of Marxist theory in the Introduction).[47]

Vietnam Training its own Khmer Revolutionaries

At the same time some members of the Paris Group and their ethnic-Khmer supporters sought to forge a uniquely Cambodian path to communism, many other Cambodians continued to align with the Vietnamese and accept their tutelage and support. Following the Geneva Conference and subsequent withdrawal of Vietnamese forces from Cambodian soil, North Vietnam undertook several parallel initiatives in an effort to train ethnic Khmers to become effective communist guerillas. The largest group, composed of around 1,200 Cambodians as of 1955, was situated in a camp south of Hanoi under the auspices of the Ministry of Foreign Affairs, but with a Khmer leadership committee headed by Son Ngoc Minh (Achar Mean), one of the cofounders of the KPRP.[48] As exemplified by Minh, whose father was ethnic Khmer but mother was Vietnamese, many of the Cambodian revolutionaries who were receptive to alignment with Vietnam were connected to the Vietnamese by either marriage or ancestry. In addition to the camp established specifically for training ethnic Khmer revolutionaries, several hundred Cambodians who had crossed into North Vietnam joined that nation's army in segregated companies attached to Vietnamese army regiments, with the understanding that at some point they would return to Cambodia as trained fighters to advance communism in their homeland.[49] Also, some tribal populations (e.g., the Jarai whose territory extended from South Vietnam into Cambodia) in Cambodia's remote northeastern areas near the border of South Vietnam were receptive to communist indoctrination and received training and support from the North Vietnamese government.[50]

Aside from public pronouncements of support for the Pracheachon Group in its early electoral efforts in Cambodia—which might partially explain the latter's lack of political success in attracting ethnic Khmer voters—North Vietnam had little substantive linkage to the small Khmer-led communist movement in Cambodia in the late 1950s. The latter reflected several political realities: (1) Hanoi's realization that the remaining Cambodian communist movement was small, disorganized, and ineffectual—as the majority of the original ethnic Khmer communists fled to exile in Vietnam in the wake of Geneva; (2) at the time, Cambodian communism/revolution was a low priority, with needs in North Vietnam, followed by South Vietnam and Laos, taking precedence in that order; and (3) the North Vietnamese government initially attempted to cultivate favorable relations with the Sihanouk regime and thus did not want to be overtly linked to elements of his political opposition within Cambodia.[51] Interestingly, a far more substantial—if complex and surreptitious—interrelationship existed between Vietnamese revolutionaries and Cambodia's ethnic Vietnamese minority, as encapsulated in a declassified intelligence report released by the CIA:

> The (Vietnamese) communists were less discreet in their dealings with Cambodia's half million Vietnamese. Over the years the (Vietnamese) minority had become more sympathetic to the communist cause, and by the late 1950s included several thousand Lao Dong Party members, some of whom had come from South Vietnam after Geneva. The Vietnamese Party structure in Cambodia was correspondingly complex. It had the normal committees, chapters and cells... In places with thick Vietnamese populations the Party exercised de facto though secret control... However, the Vietnamese communists did their best to placate Sihanouk.[52]

The newly independent state of Cambodia initially attempted to pursue a path of neutrality to avoid regional and global (Cold War) entanglements. Though neutral in principle, the Sihanouk administration's foreign policy was to a large degree driven by a desire for security in the face of Cambodia's traditional rivals, Vietnam and China, as well as by a desire to facilitate economic development; both objectives necessitated pursuit of foreign aid, initially derived primarily from the west. During the first decade of independence (1953–1963), the U.S. was the principle foreign aid donor, providing some $97 million in military assistance and over $265 million in economic aid, substantial amounts given the population of only some 6 million at the time.[53] In addition to financing various economic and social welfare projects, U.S. aid subsidized a large portion of the country's 30,000-man military forces' salaries, as well as their equipment.[54] France was also a significant source of military aid to Cambodia in this period through the transfer of military equipment and supplies left behind after independence—combined with later supplementary deliveries—and the presence of several hundred French military trainers and advisors.[55]

Cambodia established formal diplomatic relations with both North and South Vietnam, but both governments failed to respect Cambodian sovereignty and neutrality and interfered in Cambodian affairs in different respects. Both North Vietnamese troops and communist insurgents in the South continued to use Cambodian territory and even establish bases in the country, despite pledging in the 1954 Geneva Accords to withdraw and respect Cambodian sovereignty. As the conflict in Vietnam escalated, South Vietnamese forces also entered Cambodian territory to strike communist forces, using the neighboring state as a base of operations. In 1959, the governments of South Vietnam and Thailand (possibly with the advanced knowledge and complicity of U.S. intelligence) supported a failed plot on the part of several right-wing Cambodian leaders to overthrow the Sihanouk regime. They targeted the regime in part due to ongoing territorial and other disputes with both countries and also due to the perception that Sihanouk was soft on communism and largely ineffectual in addressing the growing threat it posed within the region.[56] The failed plot was among the first major developments leading to soured relations between the Sihanouk regime, the U.S., and its proxy South Vietnam.

With the expanding power of Viet Cong insurgents in South Vietnam, Sihanouk began to question whether the Cambodian relationship with the U.S./west would sufficiently guarantee Cambodian security, and the regime began to consider ties with major communist powers.[57] Relations with the USSR and China in the early independence era proved to be fluid and evolving, eventually reflecting the polarizing complexities of the Sino-Soviet rivalry. Sihanouk established diplomatic relations with, and made an official state visit to, the Soviet Union in 1956, followed by a series of agreements related to cultural, educational, and research collaborations the following year. Relations with Moscow remained cordial in the first years of Cambodian independence, with the Soviets publicly praising Cambodia's role as a leader among nonaligned nations. However, the relationship's depth was limited and gradually deteriorated as Sihanouk and other Cambodian leaders became increasingly aware of the threat posed to the government by communist influences in general, specifically the threat posed by Soviet-aligned North Vietnam and Viet Cong insurgents. Diplomatic relations were established with China in 1958, as Sihanouk recognized the potential China offered as a future ally and hedge against the influence of the Vietnamese and other regional rivals. The bilateral relationship with Beijing would evolve slowly, and barriers to trust and substantive cooperation existed, including Sihanouk's somewhat justified concerns regarding the influence of Beijing over Cambodia's sizable Chinese minority. Even in the initial absence of meaningful linkages to either major communist power, Cambodia's mere establishment of diplomatic ties with Beijing and Moscow against the advice of the west instilled concern and suspicion in the U.S., which was being increasingly drawn into the escalating Second Indochina War.

Map 2: Cambodia and Neighboring States

Endnotes

1. S. McHale, "Violence, and Khmer-Vietnamese Relations: The Significance of the Lower Mekong Delta, 1757–1954," *The Journal of Asian Studies*, 72(2), 2013, pp. 367–390.
2. Christopher Goscha, "Widening the Colonial Encounter: Asian Connections Inside French Indochina During the Interwar Period," *Modern Asian Studies*, 43(5) 2009, pp. 1189–1228.
3. Goscha 2009.
4. Adapted from Goscha, 2009.
5. Peter Poole, "The Vietnamese in Cambodia and Thailand: Their Role in Interstate Relations," *Asian Survey*, 14(4) 1974, pp. 325–337.
6. Jessica Pearson, "Introduction: Globalizing the History of French Decolonization," *French Politics, Culture & Society*, 38(2) 2020, pp. 1–8.
7. R.E.M. Irving, *The First Indochina War: French and American Policy 1945–54* (London, UK: C. Helm, 1975).
8. Walter LaFeber, "Roosevelt, Churchill, and Indochina: 1942–45," *The American Historical Review*, 80(5) 1975, pp. 1277–1295.
9. Gary Hess, "Franklin Roosevelt and Indochina," *The Journal of American History*, 59(2) 1972, pp. 353–368.
10. LaFeber 1975.
11. Lorenz Luthi, *Cold Wars: Asia, the Middle East, Europe* (Cambridge, UK: Cambridge University Press, 2020).
12. Goscha 2009.
13. John Springhall, "Kicking Out the Vietminh: How Britain Allowed France to Reoccupy South Indochina, 1945–46," *Journal of Contemporary History*, 40(2) 2005, pp. 115–130.
14. Arthur Dommen, *The Indochina Experience of the French and the Americans: Nationalism and Communism in Cambodia, Laos and Vietnam* (Bloomington, IN: Indiana University Press, 2001).
15. Central Intelligence Agency, "Intelligence Report: Communism and Cambodia," (February 1972) https://www.cia.gov/readingroom/document/5077054e993247d4d82b6aa9 Accessed March 17, 2022.
16. David Chandler, *The Tragedy of Cambodian History: Politics, War and Revolution Since 1945* (New Haven CT: Yale University Press, 1991).
17. David Chandler, *A History of Cambodia* (Boulder, CO: Westview Press, 2008).

18. Chandler 1991.
19. Elizabeth Becker, *When the War was Over: Cambodia and the Khmer Rouge Revolution* (New York: Public Affairs, 1998).
20. CIA, February 1972.
21. Ibid.
22. Bethany Lacina and Nils Gleditsch, "Monitoring Trends in Global Combat: A New Dataset of Battle Deaths," *European Journal of Population*, 21(2) 2005, 145–166.
23. Michel Bodin, *Dictionnaire de la Guerre d' Indochine, 1945–1954* (Paris: Economica, 2004).
24. Robert Randle, *Geneva 1954: The Settlement of the Indochinese War* (Princeton, NJ: Princeton University Press, 2016).
25. Alec Holcombe, "Dien Bien Phu and Geneva, 1954" in *Mass Mobilization in the Democratic Republic of Vietnam, 1945–1960* (Honolulu, HI: University of Hawaii Press, 2020).
26. David Chandler, *The Tragedy of Cambodian History: Politics, War and Revolution Since 1945* (New Haven, CT: Yale University Press, 1991).
27. George Modeleski, "The Vietminh Complex" in *Communism and Revolution: The Strategic Uses of Political Violence*, Cyril Black ed. (Princeton NJ, Princeton University Press, 2015), p. 211.
28. Warren Unna, "Sihanouk's 'Absurdity' Serves Cambodia Well," *The Washington Post*, November 23, 1963.
29. Unna, 1963.
30. William Rust, *Eisenhower and Cambodia: Diplomacy, Covert Action and the Origins of the Second Indochina War* (Lexington, KY: University Press of Kentucky, 2016).
31. Zhai Qiang, "China and the Geneva Conference of 1954," *The China Quarterly*, No. 129 March 1992, pp. 103–122.
32. Ibid.
33. CIA, February 1972, p. 19.
34. Philip Short, *Pol Pot: Anatomy of a Nightmare* (New York: Henry Holt, 2005), p. 103.
35. Patit Paban Mishra, "From Geneva to Geneva: A Discourse on Geopolitical Dimensions of Conflict in Laos: 1954–1962," *Journal of International Studies*, 1(7), January 2020, pp. 103–118; Arthur Dommen, *Laos: Keystone of Indochina* (New York: Routledge, 2018).

36. Pierre Asselin, The Democratic Republic of Vietnam and the 1954 Geneva Conference: A Revisionist Critique," *Cold War History*, 11(2) 2011, pp. 155–195.
37. Russell Ross, *Cambodia: A Country Study* (Washington D.C.: Federal Research Division – Library of Congress, 1990).
38. Ibid.
39. CIA, February 1972.
40. David Chandler, *A History of Cambodia* (Boulder, CO: Westview Press, 2008), p. 228.
41. Ben Kiernan, "Origins of Khmer Communism," *Southeast Asian Affairs*, 1981, pp. 160–180.
42. Ananda Naidu, "Origins of Khmer Communism," *Proceedings of the Indian History Congress*, Vol. 60, 1999, pp. 960–965.
43. David P. Chandler, "Revising the Past in Democratic Kampuchea: When Was the Birthday of the Party?" *Pacific Affairs,* 56(2) 1983, pp. 288–300.
44. CIA, February 1972.
45. Kiernan 1981.
46. D. Seekins, "Historical Setting," in *Cambodia: A Country Study*, ed. R. Ross (Washington: GPO for the Library of Congress, 1990).
47. Ibid.
48. CIA, February 1972.
49. Ibid.
50. Ibid.
51. Ibid.
52. CIA, February 1972, pp. 29–30; The Lao Dong Party is a naming/translation variation for the Workers' Party of Vietnam (the Vietnamese successor organization of the regional Indochinese Communist Party), subsequently renamed the Communist Party of Vietnam in 1976.
53. Central Intelligence Agency, "Intelligence Memorandum: Communist Military Aid to Cambodia, 1963–66", (May 1967). Accessed January, 2022.
54. Central Intelligence Agency, "Intelligence Memorandum: Cambodia—Economic Effects of U.S. Aid Withdrawal," (December 19, 1963). Accessed January, 2022.

55. CIA, 1967.
56. John Prados, Lost Crusader: The Secret Wars of CIA Director William Colby (New York: Oxford University Press, 2003); The Sihanouk regime had made overtures to socialist political elements in Cambodia and in 1958 normalized diplomatic relations with China.
57. CIA, 1967.

Onset of Cambodian Civil War

3

The political dynamic of Indochina's nations has been inexorably interconnected throughout much of history, to the point that conflict or other instability does not tend to remain confined to one state. The latter reality is exemplified by the Second Indochina War (known as the Vietnam War in the U.S.) which began as a conflict largely specific to Vietnam but ultimately engulfed much of the region, including Cambodia. A declassified U.S. intelligence report issued early in the Second Indochina War levied much of the blame for the post-independence regional instability and political turmoil on France, noting that traditional political and cultural institutions within the region eroded following nearly a century of colonial control without the development of any viable successor traditions or unifying institutions supported by the local tradition-steeped populations.[1]

Some variant of the Cambodian Civil War may have occurred even in the absence of instability and armed conflict in Vietnam. However, without the spillover from the neighboring Vietnamese conflict and the associated Cold War dynamic in which proxies were cultivated and armed by external powers, the Cambodian Civil War might have at least been more modest in scope and intensity and may have been more likely to have a negotiated peace. Specifically, without escalation in the Vietnam conflict (e.g., the direct intervention of Vietnamese communists) and the associated Cold War security dynamic, it is less likely communist insurgents in either Cambodia or Laos could have emerged as potent adversaries to their respective governments in the comparatively brief period following independence.

The Vietnam conflict's escalation was not the sole consideration in the advancing fortunes of Cambodian communism or the country's march toward civil war. The Sihanouk regime underestimated the threat posed by the far left, in part because Cambodia's small communist movement was regarded as less of a threat than traditional state rivals or external interference from the U.S. While there were periods of relatively mild, generally localized communist supression, through much of the 1960s, Sihanouk largely tried to co-opt leftist leaders by including many of them in the government (e.g., Hou Yuon as Minister of Commerce and Industry and Hu Nim as Undersecretary of State) or otherwise permitting them to assume public roles as teachers, professors, or in other traditional capacities, hoping their integration into the mainstream would moderate their political views while diluting the budding communist movement's leadership.[2] Sihanouk also found the socialists politically useful in that he often played the left and right against each other to obfuscate and partly deflect criticism of his own regime.[3] By the time the government awoke to the threat, bowed to conservative pressure to take action, and attempted to crack down on the burgeoning communist movement, the communists had grown sufficiently in strength to compete for public attention and support and to undertake armed insurrection.

The Second Indochina War – Origins

The terms of the 1954 Geneva Conference, which recognized the autonomy and neutrality of Cambodia and Laos and temporarily divided Vietnam, were intended to facilitate peace within the region. However, by the following year, the hastily assembled framework for regional stability was unravelling. One of the key elements of the Accords was the plan to conduct elections in both North and South Vietnam in 1956 to potentially facilitate the reunification of Vietnam under a single, unified government democratically elected by the majority. However, nationalist Ngo Dinh Diem, Prime Minister of the non-communist French Union "State of Vietnam" organized in the South as well as the U.S. and other western governments attempting to support that regime, were justifiably concerned that a reunified Vietnam would fall under the dominance of Vietnamese communists. Communist organizers had been making inroads in disseminating their message and gaining support particularly among the peasant class, which comprised the majority of population on both sides of the 17th Parallel. A 1954 U.S. intelligence report estimated the population of North Vietnam at approximately 14.1 million and South Vietnam at 10.4 million, adding further concern that the South's non-communist political agenda could not prevail in a combined plebiscite of all voters in both countries.[4] In July 1955, Diem announced the reunification vote's cancellation in the South on the grounds that the communist North could not be trusted to conduct a fair election. Three months later, a rigged referendum—in which Diem claimed to have won over 98% of the vote against electoral opponent and former French endorsed Emperor and Head of State, Bao Dai—established him as the first president of the newly established Republic of Vietnam.[5] Similar margins of victory were won by communists in various "elections" conducted in the North, conveying that neither regime actually embraced democracy.

A breakdown in effective international relations and discourse, beyond merely the failure of the Geneva Accords, contributed to the deteriorating political climate. Not only were North and South Vietnam at loggerheads but also other nations, rather than brokering communication and compromise, became polarized in aligning themselves either in support of or opposition to one of the regimes. At one stage, the political dynamic of Vietnam resembled the paradoxical China-Taiwan dynamic in which two governments in two distinct geographical locales simultaneously claimed to be the legitimate government of the same state. In the final years of French tutelage, the Democratic Republic of Vietnam in the North and the State of Vietnam (commonly referred to as Free Vietnam in this era) in the South had, since 1945 and 1949, respectively claimed to be the legitimate government of the entirety of Vietnam. Beginning in 1950 and reflecting Cold War politics, members of the international community began to select which competing claim to recognize and exclusively align with one of the two regimes: China and the Soviet Union recognized the North, while the U.S. and Britain recognized the South. Such "one Vietnam" diplomatic policies by their very nature profoundly hindered, if not outright severed, discourse with the other non-recognized Vietnamese regime, impeding opportunities for external approaches, including the potential for mediation.

When Diem proclaimed a permanent split through the autonomous Republic of Vietnam's creation in 1955, his government dropped claims to any territory or control north of the 17th Parallel. Ho Chi Minh's government viewed the Diem regime and efforts to permanently carve off a separate state as illegitimate and, in effect, the North maintained its claim as the sole legitimate government of all Vietnamese. Beginning in late 1955, western nations, including the U.S., withdrew their diplomatic presence in North Vietnam. Foreign aid provision also reflected the polarization within the international community, as what had already been modest western developmental or humanitarian aid to the North ceased yet, together with military aid, increased exponentially to the South. Throughout the 1950s, military and other assistance from the USSR and China expanded rapidly in the North. Concerned with the potential for escalation, the Soviet government proposed a permanent two-state solution with both North and South Vietnam being admitted to the UN in 1957, but the proposal was not embraced in North Vietnam or by western nations.

Different events can potentially be cited as the starting point for the Second Indochina War (again, known as the Vietnam War in the U.S.) and, accordingly, difference of opinion exists as to what year marked the start of the war. In 1954–1955, Vietnam was partitioned into two states and, amid scattered low-intensity violence, a large-scale population shift occurred in which as many as 1 million fled the communist controlled North and approximately 150,000 people—primarily former Viet Minh guerillas and their families—relocated from the South.[6] In early 1956, Diem authorized a purge of communist activists and political opponents in the South. In April, U.S. military advisors took over the responsibility of training South Vietnam's military from the French. In December, the North Vietnamese government formally authorized a communist insurgency in the South over the objections of China and the USSR, neither of which supported escalation at the time. By the following year, Vietcong insurgents initiated bombing/terror campaigns in the South, attacking the country's political and economic elites as well as the U.S. military presence. In March 1959, Ho Chi Min's government officially declared a state of war with the goal of reunifying Vietnam under communist control.

In the early emergence of Vietnam's conflict, the Cambodian government sought to stay out of the fray, adopting a formal position of neutrality in its foreign policy in January 1957.[7] Partly to better reflect an image of neutrality, and partly out of consternation with the corruption, infighting, and incompetence witnessed among centrist and right-wing lawmakers since attaining independence, Sihanouk endeavored to broaden his political base by integrating the Cambodian left through bureaucratic appointments and advancing a small number of hand-picked leftists into the National Assembly.[8] Thus began Sihanouk's delicate balancing act of attempting to shift between the center, left, and right when the nation's and/or his own political interests might benefit. Some communists, including many that had been among the ranks of the Khmer Issarak guerillas who fought for Cambodia's independence, initially thought armed struggle might, in turn, be the path to achieving a communist state in Cambodia. However, most communist Issarak faded away once independence was achieved, regarding the latter as their primary goal. Also, government overtures to the left, combined with a lack of support for socialism/communism among the citizenry and the absence of a foreign patron, directed Cambodia's nascent communist movement—including Pol Pot's militant faction—away from the path of armed revolution; instead, it moved toward a period principally characterized by "political struggle" (e.g., propaganda, recruitment, establishment of political cadres/cells) through the mid-1960s.[9]

Regional Escalation and Cambodian Realignment

Historical disputes lingered between Cambodia and the newly proclaimed South Vietnam, principally related to territorial/boundary issues. After failing to have the international community convene an international conference to address his grievances with neighboring South Vietnam, Sihanouk began to use Cambodia's neutral status in a new approach to hedge his security. He was concerned the U.S./west, the primary backers of South Vietnam's regime, might not be able to sufficiently address Cambodia's needs and concerns in the event of Cambodian conflict with Saigon or in the event of escalating conflict with communist insurgents aided by the North. As a hedge for his own regime's stability and the security of Cambodia, the politically fluid and non-ideological Sihanouk began actively soliciting aid from, and better ties with, the international communist bloc, particularly China and the Soviet Union. The November 1963 overthrow and assassination of South Vietnam strongman Ngo Dinh Diem, which occurred with the advanced knowledge and at least tacit consent of the U.S. government, rattled Sihanouk. Though not sympathetic to Diem, Sihanouk feared South Vietnam's ability to defeat the communists may have been diminished by the coup, and his concerns related to possible U.S. interference in Cambodian affairs were understandably heightened.[10] Shortly after the overthrow of the Diem regime, Sihanouk officially renounced U.S. aid and, following further deterioration in relations, formally severed diplomatic ties with the U.S. by 1965.

The U.S. had been the single largest source of military and foreign aid to Cambodia since its independence. However, Sihanouk had become increasingly dissatisfied with aspects of the U.S. aid arrangement. In particular, he was opposed to certain strings attached—such as Cambodia's being prohibited from accepting communist bloc military aid—which ran afoul of his scheme to hedge the country's neutrality and its geopolitical value within the region by leveraging additional assistance from a more diverse range of donor states.[11] The termination of all U.S. aid in 1963 appears to have been an abrupt, emotional, and ill-conceived strategy on Sihanouk's part, and, although both angry with and distrustful of Washington, he may not have intended for relations with his chief financial benefactor to deteriorate as far or as rapidly.[12] Inadequate understanding of the U.S. aid package's terms, which Sihanouk rejected, may also have been a factor, as Cambodian negotiators indicated they desired existing U.S. aid to continue for the next six months, during which time new aid terms could be negotiated—apparently unaware the existing aid agreement could not be extended after Cambodia issued notice of formal termination to Washington.[13]

Sihanouk's impetuous break with U.S. aid necessitated his pursuit of communist bloc states to offset the loss. Significant volumes of military and economic aid had been provided by the communist bloc to North Vietnam between 1955–64, amounts which increased considerably as the war in Vietnam intensified in subsequent years (see Table 2). While not realistically expecting aid comparable to the amounts provided to Hanoi, Sihanouk did hope to receive amounts sufficient to substantially offset the loss of U.S. support. Between 1963–1967, Cambodia concluded multiple aid agreements with both China and the USSR amounting to approximately $15 million (with each country providing roughly half that total), around $12 million of which was provided as grant aid and the remainder as credit.[14] Negligible amounts of economic or military aid were also provided by some other communist bloc states, including Czechoslovakia, East Germany, and Yugoslavia. However, the combined amount of communist bloc aid to Cambodia never came close to offsetting the assistance provided by the U.S., with one estimate of communist aid between 1963 and 1966 (adjusted for inflation and valued in U.S. dollars) placing it around 20–30% of the annual amounts previously provided by Washington.[15]

The significance of the downturn in foreign aid and the associated souring of relations with the U.S. should not be understated. At a critical juncture of its existence as a new nation, when it was threatened with growing sources of instability both externally (Vietnamese insurgents operating in its territory) and internally (a slow resurgence of Khmer communists), Cambodia's military and its economy contracted, as did confidence in the regime's judgement and abilities. Although the country had acute need to improve its military, the reversal in political course had the opposite effect. For example, the Cambodian defense budget approached $45 million annually between 1964 and 1966, amounting to over 25% of the total national budget in 1964, but declined to 22% of a smaller total budget by 1966.[16] Damaged relations with the U.S. also complicated efforts to obtain spare parts for American-made weapons and vehicles, making some of the inventory (mostly aging surplus WWII equipment at the time of donation) unusable and further limiting Cambodian military capabilities. Chinese military aid proved to be a partial stop-gap measure, supplying enough small arms and ammunition to equip approximately 37,000 men as well as small numbers of anti-aircraft weapons and obsolete aircraft between 1964 and 1965.[17] A U.S. intelligence assessment of the condition of the Cambodian military painted an enfeebled picture of its capabilities in 1964–65:

> The army, which accounts for 32,000 out of a total of 35,000 men in the regular armed forces, is capable of little more than carrying out an internal security role. The army suffers from a poorly developed logistical system, inadequate training, and a shortage of good officers. The army is not large enough nor sufficiently well organized and trained to resist an attack... The Cambodian navy received little aid from communist sources and remains a small force with only 1,400 men. It is capable of little more than coastal and river patrolling aimed at preventing smuggling and other violations of Cambodia's territorial waters... The (1,400-man) air force has relatively few aircraft and is handicapped by shortages of jet pilots, skilled technicians, spare parts

and communications... The Cambodian military could put up only a limited and brief resistance against full-scale invasion by its neighbors.[18]

Table 2: Estimated Communist Bloc Aid to North Vietnam 1955–1971 (in millions of U.S. $)

	1955-1964	1965	1966	1967	1968	1969	1970	1971	Total
Economic Aid (total)	630	135	290	475	615	685	610	600	4,040
USSR	235	95	160	235	305	385	345	315	2,075
China	285	35	70	120	120	90	60	100	880
E. Eur./other	110	5	60	120	190	210	205	185	1,085
Military Aid (total)	140	270	455	650	390	225	155	180	2,470
USSR	70	210	360	505	290	120	70	100	1,725
China	70	60	95	145	100	105	85	75	735
E. Eur./other	Negl.	Negl.	Negl.	Negl.	Negl.	Negl.	Negl.	5	10
Total Aid	770	405	745	1,125	1,005	910	765	780	6,510
USSR	305	305	520	740	595	505	415	415	3,800
China	355	95	165	265	220	195	145	175	1,615
E. Eur./other	110	5	60	120	190	210	205	190	1,095[19]

As shown, Sihanouk's rash break with U.S. aid had a negative impact on Cambodia's economy. Soon after relations soured, the Cambodian currency, the Riel, declined in value, many imported goods were hoarded, nervousness on the part of the business community led to a flight of capital abroad, and financing proved more difficult and more expensive to obtain.[20] The regime undertook reforms aimed at limiting the economic decline, including austerity measures to control the budget deficit and, perhaps more significantly, nationalizing much of Cambodia's import-export trade and the commercial banking sector.[21] Rice had previously accounted for around one-third of the country's exports, and, although Cambodia had a record rice harvest in 1963–64, the reforms caused farmers difficulty in obtaining credit to finance the harvest; they even had difficulty obtaining enough jute bags for collection and storage, bags that had previously been supplied via the USAID program—meaning a large portion of the harvest was lost to spoilage.[22] Such problems also extended to other export crops, and in addition to agricultural failures, the scheme to nationalize commercial banks eliminated almost all commercial credit for other business sectors, which, in turn, facilitated broad declines in construction and other economic activity.[23]

Sihanouk managed to nominally increase Cambodian trade with communist bloc nations during this period, but not enough to offset larger economic declines. The regime had also managed to elicit modest increases in French aid, but this too only offset a small fraction of the economic retrenchment. The overall effect of the reforms intended to ease the economic transition away from the U.S. worsened an already bad situation, facilitating widespread disruptions with the harvest and crop export, decreased credit availability, increased cost of living, accelerated unemployment, and expanded discontent among the population.[24] The traditional core elements of Cambodian leadership—the bureaucracy, business elite, military, and royal family—were increasingly concerned by both the economic downturn triggered by Sihanouk's policies and, perhaps even more so, his efforts to facilitate greater Chinese and other communist nations' influence within Cambodia.[25] At this juncture, no organized opposition to Sihanouk emerged from the country's power structure, with elites instead endeavoring to lobby Sihanouk to undertake more measured, cautious, and centrist policies. These developments could potentially be regarded as among the first major cracks in the Sihanouk regime and provided propaganda opportunities to Cambodian communists who would initiate an open insurrection against the government in 1967.

The Gulf of Tonkin incident was the trigger that dramatically escalated U.S. involvement and, in turn, intensified the Indochina conflict. On August 2, 1964, the USS Maddox, a destroyer primarily tasked with patrolling and electronic surveillance—but which also engaged in covert actions (e.g., shelling) against coastal targets—exchanged fire with three North Vietnamese torpedo boats attempting to discourage its presence several miles off the coast near Haiphong. Which vessels fired first and whether the salvos were intended by either party as warnings rather than a deliberate attempt to damage or sink the enemy remains in dispute.[26] The USS Maddox reported the incident as an attack, and a second U.S. destroyer was dispatched to reinforce its operations when, on the night of August 4, both vessels reported being attacked by a squadron of North Vietnamese vessels that were alleged to have fired as many as 20 torpedoes. However, years later, investigations ultimately revealed that the second "attack" on August 4 had not actually occurred and was instead the result of initially misinterpreted radar, sonar, and communications intercepts on the part of the U.S. ships that mistakenly thought enemy boats/torpedoes were in proximity.[27] Considerable questions existed—even on the part of the U.S. military—at the time of the report as to the veracity of the August 4 incident. United States President Lyndon Johnson's administration and the national media nevertheless portrayed the attack as factual and used what became known as the "Gulf of Tonkin incident" to elicit support for broader U.S. involvement in Vietnam; indeed, Johnson successfully lobbied Congress for what was essentially carte blanche approval (Gulf of Tonkin Resolution) to combat the spread of communism in Southeast Asia, including exponential increases in deploying U.S. troops.[28]

Throughout the early-mid 1960s, increasing numbers of troops were mobilized in North and South Vietnam; gradually, the number of U.S. military advisors in the South expanded and military engagements between the North and South increased in frequency and intensity. The latter trend, and the severity of fighting in Vietnam (Second Indochina War), escalated significantly in the second half of the decade, beginning in 1965. For example, North Vietnamese military forces expanded from an estimated 250,000 in mid-1965 to nearly 500,000 by 1967.[29] At the start of 1965, only 25,000 U.S. military personnel were in South Vietnam, ostensibly in advisory and training rather than combat roles, but 184,000 were present by the end of the year and 385,000 by 1966, peaking at over 500,000 by 1968.[30] Military fatalities among South Vietnamese forces were estimated by one source at 7,457 in 1964, increasing to 12,716 in 1967, and 27,915 in 1968.[31] The U.S. only had 216 fatalities in 1964, rising to 11,363 in 1967, and peaking at 16,899 the following year.[32] Casualty statistics for North Vietnamese and VC forces (as well as for Cambodia and Laos in this time period) are unreliable, but the Vietnamese communists are believed to have suffered greater casualties than their opponents and followed the same general pattern of increase throughout the decade.

Vietnamese Encroachment

As the war continued to intensify, Vietnamese communists repeatedly and flagrantly utilized the territory of neighboring Laos and Cambodia. Both the North Vietnamese military and Viet Cong insurgents in South Vietnam increasingly turned to territory across the borders for sanctuary, setting up bases of operation as well as transit and communication routes. Preparations for the Ho Chi Minh Trail, for example, were initiated in 1959 and intended to facilitate movement of communist forces and supplies between North and South Vietnam. The primary infiltration routes were built through South Vietnam's western mountains and through the demilitarized zone separating North and South Vietnam, but secondary routes were created through the territory of Cambodia and Laos to be used as needed for supplementary transit or if the main route was threatened.[33] As the war in Vietnam intensified and U.S. military pressure increased so also did Vietnamese communists' reliance upon Cambodia and Laos. In 1960, the first of many Vietcong bases was established inside Cambodia, facilities that served as transit points and supply depots for both North Vietnamese and VC forces transiting back and forth.[34]

Initially, Hanoi also decided to make practical use of the ethnic Cambodian communists it trained in North Vietnam as well as much of the existing communist network in Cambodia to support the war effort in the South, rather than using them to cultivate revolution in Cambodia. At the time, most communist supporters within Cambodia were members of the ethnic Vietnamese minority and were the focal point of Hanoi's efforts. Elements of Cambodia's Vietnamese community increasingly supported the Vietcong guerilla movement, and thousands of the youth joined the VC's ranks, in part because Hanoi controlled the Vietnamese-language media in Cambodia and used it for propaganda purposes.[35] Front organizations were established to garner support and obtain and funnel food and medical supplies. In the early 1960s, the North Vietnamese regime also sought to bolster and enhance the Cambodian communist cadres it was hosting in its own territory, expanding both their political and military training and increasing efforts to recruit in northeastern Cambodia. By 1967, an estimated 4,000 ethnic Khmer revolutionaries recruited from Cambodia were training in North Vietnam in addition to the substantial number that had already been deployed to assist communist efforts in the South.[36]

While the Vietnamese communist presence in Cambodia during the early to mid-1960s was in theory mostly surreptitious, the presence of North Vietnamese forces within Laos was more overt. By the early 1960s, military advisors from several nations, including the U.S. and Soviet Union, had a presence in Laos. Out of concern for possible escalation in the Laos Civil War between the Royalist government and communist guerrillas and the possibility of direct conflict between the forces of those external powers present, an agreement was signed in 1962 reaffirming Laos's neutrality and prohibiting foreign troops, with the exception of a small force of French trainers. While the U.S. and USSR withdrew their military presence in observance of the latter, North Vietnam ignored the agreement and kept most of its 6,000-man force in Laos.[37] The Vietnamese recognized Laos's critical value (and Cambodia's) in keeping supply/transit lines between North and South open and also recognized that the Pathet Lao communist insurrection in Laos would potentially falter without the support of Vietnamese forces, which provided the shock troops and backbone of the communist insurgency.[38] As the Second Indochina War intensified, rather than withdraw its forces—as called for in the 1962 Accords—North Vietnam and VC forces, in effect, invaded portions of Laos, increased their troop strength, and became more aggressive in engaging Royal Laos forces, actions which culminated in the defeat of the last large royalist forces in 1968 and the installation of a communist regime two years later.[39]

Sihanouk's Naïve Support of North Vietnam

Sihanouk's phase of cultivating closer ties to communist states was not limited to China or the Soviets. His government was, at least to some degree, aware of expanding North Vietnamese activity within Cambodia and of their recruitment and training of Cambodian revolutionaries. Such activities were tolerated due to improved relations with North Vietnam and the reality that the communists' vitriol was being directed against South Vietnam and the Diem regime rather than Cambodia. Sihanouk's police and military largely overlooked the machinations of VC/North Vietnamese propagandists, fundraisers, couriers, recruiters, and buyers.[40] South Vietnam became increasingly incensed over the latter arrangement and, by 1965, border incidents had become common, wherein Saigon's forces attempted to interdict such activity through incursions into Cambodian territory. South Vietnam (as well as Thailand) also began supporting Cambodia's Khmer Serei (Free Khmer) anti-communist movement, which had assumed a public stance of political opposition to Sihanouk due to his overtures to China, the Soviets, and North Vietnam.[41]

Throughout much of the decade, until the start of the Cambodian Civil War in 1967, cordial and often cooperative relations existed between the Sihanouk regime and North Vietnam, with Hanoi even sharing intelligence with Phenom Penh concerning the U.S. and South Vietnam, for example. Sihanouk remained convinced the North was poised to win the war and the U.S. could not prop up the South much longer. This perception guided his political actions for many years, and the U.S. bombing campaign and expanding military actions directed against North Vietnam in 1965 did nothing to assuage his thinking. In that year, Sihanouk hosted a conference between leaders of North Vietnam, the Viet Cong, and the Pathet Lao. The conference publicly condemned what was described as U.S. aggression within the region. It also helped facilitate an attack by leftist Cambodian students upon the U.S. Embassy in Phenom Penh, which preceded the official severing of diplomatic ties between Cambodia and the U.S. Sihanouk's relationship with Hanoi and the VC became further cemented when the Vietnamese made a formal request to purchase Cambodian rice. The food shipments, financed by China, began in 1966, and Cambodia supplied over 60,000 tons of the much-needed food staple to VC insurgents.[42] Further complicating Sihanouk's claims asserting Cambodian neutrality, shipments of Chinese arms and ammunition to the VC were also initiated in 1966 and reached an estimated 20,000 tons by 1969.[43]

Sihanouk's optimism in cultivating a burgeoning, stable relationship with Vietnamese communists was naïve. At the same time Hanoi and the VC were extracting accommodations from Sihanouk, Vietnamese-trained Khmer communists began to infiltrate Cambodia. Initially, they arrived covertly and in smaller numbers; by 1967, however, as many as 3,000 had reentered Cambodia behind the goal of recruiting and garnering support for a resurgent Cambodian communist movement and insurgency.[44] By 1968, the numbers of Vietnamese-trained Khmer communist revolutionaries infiltrating back into Cambodia accelerated and, by this time, were mostly soldiers rather than political operatives or civilians.[45] Rather than a rogue operation on the part of Khmer Viet Minh to facilitate revolution in their homeland, the developments reflected a conscious and deliberate strategy on Hanoi's part. A declassified intelligence report summarized North Vietnam's new policy shift concerning Cambodia and the Sihanouk regime:

> Hanoi decided to begin actively supporting a rebellion in Cambodia . . . (via) a large-scale increase in the number of Khmer infiltrators from North Vietnam and the start of guerrilla warfare in the Cambodian countryside. The policy was designed to be carried out covertly and in such a way that Hanoi could plausibly disavow it. The obvious reason for secrecy was that an overt communist insurrection in Cambodia was at odds with the Viet Cong need to keep their Cambodian bases open and the arms flowing. Three reasons have been advanced to explain their involvement:
> 1. The communists . . . may have felt the need to take out insurance in the case the Cambodians decided to renege. They were far from confident that Sihanouk, whom they viewed as the best of a bad lot was secure. They feared the rise of Cambodia's right-wing.
> 2. The communists may have decided to take advantage of long-standing grievances on the part of certain (regional/ethnic) segments of Cambodia's population to exert leverage . . . Furthermore, communist intelligence was aware of the restiveness and of the sorry state of the Cambodian army and police.
> 3. Bolstered by the 1968 Tet Offensive, Hanoi may have decided the time was ripe for a major step toward its long range goal of putting a communist government in Phnom Penh.[46]

Growth of the Ho Chi Minh Trail and Communist Supply Routes

The primary focus of the Second Indochina War was an attempt on the part of Vietnamese communists to subdue the non-communist, U.S.-backed South Vietnamese government and absorb that territory into a unified state under a communist regime. Accordingly, the communists' military operations largely entailed (1) North Vietnamese military forces and irregular communist forces under their control invading the South, as well as (2) sustained efforts to attack and undermine the South Vietnamese government and security structure from within via an internal insurgency that received weapons, training, and other support from the North. Throughout much of the conflict, the military operations of South Vietnam and its principle supporter, the U.S., were largely reactive in nature, one key element of which entailed efforts to halt or at least impede the movement of communist military personnel and supplies into the South. Interestingly, early in the conflict, U.S. intelligence was aware of large volumes of weapons, ammunition, and other supplies arriving in North Vietnam from China or the USSR. However, out of concern for potentially escalating the war and triggering direct conflict with Moscow or Beijing, the U.S. initially opted against direct strikes upon depots, railroads, or ports in the North and instead attempted to strike supplies once they had been broken down into smaller volumes en route to the South.[47]

The latter approach to interdiction proved to be largely ineffective. Many of the transit routes wound through remote and thickly forested territory, which proved difficult to identify and strike from the air. Also, as the war intensified, the nature of the Ho Chi Minh Trail became increasingly complex and decentralized and progressively shifted west into Laos and Cambodian territory, allowing the communists far more diversity and spatial distribution in infiltration routes. Despite the singularity of the term "Ho Chi Minh Trail," the transit network was never one single route, and the Ho Chi Minh Trail had, at its peak, expanded into a well-organized network of up to 12,000 miles of roads, trails, and paths.[48] An example of the expansion appears in a declassified 1971 U.S. intelligence assessment of how far the transit network had evolved in southern Laos. In 1965, the CIA assessed that 340 miles of routes existed in the southern Laos panhandle, which had expanded to 1,200 miles by 1968 and 2,000 miles by 1971, with 40,000–50,000 personnel and around 2,500 trucks tasked with moving supplies through Laos, organized into 16 regional logistical commands, each with multiple engineer, transport, and anti-aircraft battalions.[49]

Having originated merely as footpaths through the jungle, supplies transiting through the route were initially borne on the backs of porters. Insight into the volume of supplies that could be transported via footpaths can be gleaned from a 1952 Vietminh decree outlining suggested loads for porters as displayed in Table 3. When the Ho Chi Minh Trail initiated operations, a typical load for an individual on a footpath would be approximately four rifles or a 44-pound box of ammunition.[50] The modest volume of supplies that could be transited by foot as indicated by such statistics was offset to a great degree by thousands of porters tasked with moving supplies through the trail network. Many routes were also widened and otherwise improved over time, allowing a gradual increase in the volume of supplies as the transit medium shifted from porters and foot-traffic to bicycles, animal-drawn carts, and, ultimately, Soviet-made trucks. As the Ho Chi Minh Trail network expanded, it became increasingly effective in channeling large volumes of communist troops and supplies to the South. A U.S. intelligence report estimated that, between 1965 and 1970, the trail facilitated the movement of 630,000 North Vietnamese troops, 100,000 tons of food, 400,000 weapons, and 50,000 tons or 600 million rounds of ammunition into South Vietnam from Laos alone.[51]

Table 3: Vietminh Guidelines – Loads for Human Porters

Type of Load	Normal Load (pounds)		Normal Journey (miles per day)	
	Level Terrain	Mountains	Level Terrain	Mountains
Rice	55	30	15 (day)	9 (day)
Arms	33/44	22/33	12 (night)	7 (night)[52]

The war's evolving nature led to ongoing changes in communist transport logistics. Evidence exists of at least some previous troop and supply movement from North Vietnam through Cambodia, but Hanoi officially authorized the Ho Chi Minh Trail's extension through Cambodia in 1965; this segment of the route was dubbed the Sihanouk Trail. By the mid-1960s, U.S. and South Vietnamese forces had succeeded in placing increasing pressure on supply routes running directly between North and South Vietnam which, in turn, placed the communists in a position of greater dependency on Laos and, later, Cambodia to facilitate the movement of supplies and troops. Between 1965 and 1970, the Sihanouk regime permitted large volumes of arms and ammunition shipments from communist bloc nations through the Cambodian port of Sihanoukville and then via land routes to communist Vietnamese bases openly operating along the border with South Vietnam. By 1968, this arrangement provided up to one-half of the supplies needed by communist forces in southern South Vietnam.[53] As reflected in the snapshot of increasing Chinese shipment volumes provided in Table 4, by the late

1960s, bombing campaigns by the U.S. Air Force and other interdiction efforts in Laos and Vietnam made Cambodian supply routes increasingly important. Realizing this, and also out of justified concern that the Sihanouk regime could be toppled or might otherwise end the open-access policy for sea/land routes, Vietnamese communists continued to expand the trail network in eastern Cambodia and increasingly linked the latter network to existing trails/roads in Laos in the event transit needed to be shifted toward more covert routes in the trail network.

Table 4: Chinese Communist Supply Deliveries to the port of Sihanoukville, Cambodia for VC/NVA Forces, 1966–1969 (in tons)[54]

December 1966	1,060
February 1967	2,100
March 1967	2,960
October 1967	1,130
January 1968	2,490
March 1968	2,410
August 1968	2,650
January 1969	3,040
April 1969	3,760

*Intelligence estimates only available for select months during the period but reflect increasing volume over time.

Table 5: Chinese Communist Weapon and Ammunition Deliveries to Sihanoukville for VC/NVA Forces– 1966–1968 (in tons)[55]

Year	Weapons	Ammunition
1966 (December)	20	980
1967	770	5,010
1968	1,130	5,250

*Table 4 provides Chinese delivery estimates of all shipment types in support of VC/NVA forces, including food, clothing, arms, medicine, and other supplies. Table 5 is specific to estimates of weapons/ammunition deliveries.

U.S. Bombing Campaign and Cambodian Public Sentiment

The U.S. became aware of the ever-expanding supply network's transiting arms, personnel, and other resources needed to sustain expanding communist military efforts in Vietnam. In an effort to stem the flow of supplies and manpower, the U.S. initiated aerial bombing campaigns of the Ho Chi Minh Trail and the network of bases supporting its operation, including covert reconnaissance and bombing of Cambodian targets beginning in 1965. Initially, the undisclosed U.S. bombing operations in Cambodia were limited in intensity and geographical scope, but as the Vietnam conflict intensified so too did the air campaign. A significant escalation in the U.S. aerial campaign in Cambodia, known as Operation Menu, was launched in March 1969, in which six geographically distinct target zones (codenamed: Breakfast, Lunch, Snack, Dinner, Supper, and Dessert) in mostly eastern areas of the country selected for more intensive bombardment (carpet bombing) in an effort to halt or at least impede the Trail.

The magnitude of the aerial bombing campaign was immense, particularly for the relatively modest geographical scale involved. Cambodia has slightly less than 70,000 square miles, comparable in size to the U.S. states of Missouri or North Dakota or the nations of Uruguay or Syria, and most of the ordinance was dropped in roughly the eastern 40% of Cambodia, close to the borders with North and South Vietnam. (See Map 1: Cambodia and its Relative Size and Location in Chapter 1.) A U.S. Air Force database declassified and released by the Clinton administration in 2000 revealed a far more intense bombing campaign than previously disclosed or suspected. The data indicated that, between 1965 and 1975, a total of 113,716 sites had been targeted by 230,516 sorties that dropped 2,756,941 tons of ordinance in Cambodia alone.[56] The actual numbers are almost certainly higher, as the data contained reporting gaps for brief intervals during the period. For perspective, the Allies dropped a combined total of 2 million tons of ordinance during the entirety of WWII.[57] While many areas subjected to intense bombing were remote and sparsely populated, civilian casualties were nonetheless substantial. Estimates of civilian fatalities caused by the prolonged bombing operations vary greatly, ranging from under 100,000 to over 600,000, with the majority of academic studies placing estimates between 150,000 and 300,000.[58] In addition to the civilian and military casualties incurred, hundreds of thousands of Cambodians were displaced, having lost their farms, homes, and livelihoods.

The campaign failed to shut down the Ho Chi Minh Trail or significantly impede the communist war effort. However, it infuriated much of the

Cambodian population, particularly following the intensification of the bombing campaign in 1969. The bombing served as an important propaganda and recruitment tool for the Khmer Rouge, driving tens of thousands who might not have otherwise done so to support the communist insurrection and aid its rise; indeed, at the conclusion of the bombing campaign, communist forces actually controlled more Cambodian territory.[59] Kiernan and other scholars contend that the U.S. escalation of the Vietnam conflict and, in particular, the massive U.S. carpet bombing campaign in Cambodia destabilized the country economically and politically to such a degree that they were the most important factors in the rise of what was once a small and ineffectual Khmer communist movement.[60]

Evolving Political Dynamic

Sihanouk's flirtation with the left, which he further committed to in 1965 when he broke with the U.S. and aligned with China and North Vietnam, soon began to undermine his rule. For example, after a brief period of economic growth, large amounts of Cambodian rice—the country's leading export—by 1966 were being purchased "unofficially" and smuggled across the border to support communist efforts in Vietnam, substantially reducing a primary source of much-needed tax revenue and foreign exchange.[61] This and other deleterious economic impacts, such as the decline in western foreign aid caused by the geopolitical realignment of Cambodia, strained Sihanouk's support among the country's business class. This segment of society initially continued to support Sihanouk while lobbying the regime for a more moderate and neutral path; however, it increasingly turned away from him. Sihanouk's inability to manage the declining economy was not the sole consideration in growing dissatisfaction with his government. Many elements of Cambodia's political center and right were justifiably concerned about the drift away from neutrality—a foreign policy political stance called for in the 1954 Geneva Accords—the associated increased alignment with communist states, and the growth of the country's own far left. Even elements of the Cambodian far left became increasingly defiant of Sihanouk and his supporters, going so far as to openly call for the regime's removal as well as making public claims that leftist guerrillas were primarily responsible for achieving Cambodian independence rather than the political machinations of the embattled leader.[62]

The national elections of 1966 delivered a resounding referendum against Sihanouk and many of the policies he had pursued in recent years via a shift of the country's electorate to the right. Conservatives won 75% of National Assembly seats and elevated the pro-U.S. and staunchly anti-communist Defense Minister Lon Nol to the post of Prime Minister.[63] For reasons that are not entirely clear—perhaps out of growing weariness of attempting to micromanage every aspect of government—Sihanouk, who in the past appointed the Prime Minister and senior government officials, announced he would defer to the new conservative-dominated legislature in making the appointments. Concomitantly, the new government seated not just Lon Nol as Prime Minister but also an entire slate of right-wing appointees, many of whom were critical of Sihanouk. Yet again realigning his flexible politics with his perception of prevailing trends and in response to anti-government demonstrations by leftist groups, Sihanouk gave Lon Nol and the conservative-dominated government the latitude they desired to crack down on communist leaders and activism.

Fearing arrest or worse, many communist leaders consequently abandoned their professional double-lives, went into hiding, and fully devoted themselves to fomenting revolution.[64] At the same time the government cracked down on communists, Sihanouk appointed what was, in effect, a left-of-center advisory government in opposition, ostensibly to play an oversight role, and appointed a loyalist as Lon Nol's replacement as head of the military. Surprise over the degree of the cabinet's shift to the right and away from his control may have motivated these moves that aligned with his tendency to pit segments of Cambodia's polity against each other.[65] The ruler's evolving cycles of political gamesmanship, in which he attempted to at least cultivate the illusion of kinship to or tolerance of the left and its integration in some form within his government, would prove useful in a few years when Sihanouk again politically pivoted toward China and the Khmer Rouge.

Upon becoming General Secretary of the communist party in 1963, Pol Pot set about consolidating a disunited, ideologically factionalized organization into a more cohesive and hierarchical body mirroring the agenda of his own more militant faction that favored armed rebellion and usurpation of power rather than influencing gradual, peaceful change via the ballot box or integration within the existing government. The members of the more radical Pol Pot faction who integrated into traditional roles for a time mostly did so for utilitarian purposes, such as recruiting new members and supporting themselves financially. Those who served as teachers or professors, for example, were able to recruit increasing numbers of middle-class Cambodians to their cause; many of their former students became revolutionaries themselves, going on to become teachers or otherwise recruit future generations of supporters for the Khmer Rouge.[66] The latter recruitment efforts were important in sustaining the movement in the 1950s– early 60s as limited progress had been made in recruiting rural peasants.

Amid the intensifying government crackdown on the left, Pol Pot soon dropped any pretext of his party being a big-tent organization in which different leftist agendas were potentially integrated, including those of left-wing moderates and socialists who may have favored democratic norms/ approaches. To a great degree, the shift was the result of experiences Pol Pot and several Khmer Rouge colleagues had between 1965 and 1966 during a self-imposed exile, a period when they made prolonged political visits to North Vietnam, China, and North Korea. North Vietnamese leadership derided their Cambodian counterparts for the nationalist agenda embraced by the Khmer Rouge and insisted the Cambodian communists subordinate their interests to those of Vietnam and its war; specifically, Hanoi wanted the Khmer Rouge to delay the Cambodian revolution until the Vietnamese communists had prevailed in their struggle.[67] Always distrustful of the Vietnamese and resentful of their attempts at controlling Cambodia's communist movement and interference in Cambodian politics, Pol Pot and his faction became increasingly determined to transition away from Hanoi's influence. While avoiding open confrontation with his North Vietnamese patrons—as he still needed their support—Pol Pot left Hanoi feeling increasingly alienated and subordinated by his hosts. His delegation next travelled to China, which actively courted their Cambodian comrades with Beijing's more self-reliant and aggressive vision of communist revolution, a tactic which apparently won the Khmer Rouge over in ideological alignment and in terms of forging a new national alliance.[68] Addressing the formative impact of the trip and its aftermath upon the geopolitical alignment of the Khmer Rouge movement, Chandler states:

> Prudently, Pol Pot said nothing to the Vietnamese about his change of heart. Back home, he established his headquarters in a remote, heavily

wooded section of the country. For the next four years (1966–70), with a group of like-minded colleagues, he lost touch with everyday Cambodian life, polished his utopian ideas, nourished his hatreds, and thought about seizing power.[69]

At the conclusion of the grand tour of East Asia's communist bloc, the name of the organization was changed in 1966 from the somewhat more inclusive and integrative-sounding Worker's Party of Kampuchea (the successor organization of the Pracheachon since 1960) to the Communist Party of Kampuchea, hereafter regarded in this work as synonymous with the Khmer Rouge. At the same time the party leadership facilitated the name change, the decision was also made to reorganize and relocate the party's headquarters in exile, which had initially been situated just inside the South Vietnamese border in territory (Tay Ninh) controlled by the Viet Cong. They did so ostensibly to move to a safer location in the interior of northeast Cambodia away from U.S. bombing but in actuality to eliminate Vietnamese oversight and influence.[70] By 1967, the Khmer Rouge openly called for armed revolution, in defiance of Hanoi's wishes. The decision to undertake a national military uprising was made not by plebiscite within the movement's membership but by a core cadre of leaders in Pol Pot's faction: Pol Pot himself; Ieng Sary, who later served as Foreign Minister in the Khmer Rouge regime; Nuon Chea, Party Deputy Secretary and Head of the National Assembly under the Khmer Rouge; and So Phim, military head of the Party's Eastern Zone.[71] In coming years, the faction's core leadership also became gradually more open in terms of realigning the movement away from Vietnam and toward China. Such decisions convey the increasingly authoritative, oligarchical, and often secretive manner in which policy was determined within Cambodia's communist movement.

A key influence upon Pol Pot and the emerging agendas of his faction during this period was the Chinese Cultural Revolution, initiated at the beginning of 1966. The future Cambodian dictator and members of his inner circle had visited China at the onset of the Revolution and appear to have embraced and perhaps misinterpreted much of what they witnessed, including Mao's policies of class warfare, iconoclasty, purges, and forced mobilization of portions of the urban population for manual labor in the countryside.[72] In spite of early evidence of the failures of such dystopian programs in China, Pol Pot and Khmer Rouge leaders embraced earlier Maoist experiments first introduced in the Great Leap Forward that related to fully and rapidly committing to collectivization. These experiments included closing schools and universities and operating from the belief that all people regardless of background and station should engage in manual labor in egalitarian societies.[73] Pol Pot would not only adopt many such failed Maoist strategies but also radicalize many such programs further and adopt new societal experiments that transcended the boundaries of even China's Cultural Revolution, such as abolishing money.[74]

Sihanouk inadvertently aided in the emergence of the more radical and pro-Chinese Pol Pot faction within the ranks of the country's far left by integrating and to some degree pacifying more moderate socialists, leaving militant elements to assume leadership roles in the evolving Cambodian far left. For example, the regime tended to favor integrating/mainstreaming (granting appointments to) those with formal educations, which tended to be those educated abroad, either in Europe or Vietnan, and many such French and Vietnamese-educated socialists tended to favor more gradual and moderated paths to change and were often more inclined to political negotiation and compromise.[75] Many such leftists were successfully integrated into mainstream Cambodian society/politics, some even becoming political moderates through concluding that initial goals, such as decolonization and neutrality, had been achieved. Consequently, leadership opportunities were vacated within the country's far left for the more radical and pro-Chinese elements, that is, the Pol Pot faction.[76] Additionally, the regime's sporadic repression of communists tended to primarily target the more orthodox longtime party activists, often due to their sympathies with Vietnamese communists. This repression forced up to one-third of Cambodia's original communist party members to flee to Vietnam and concomitantly permitted the newer generation of communists, including Pol Pot's faction, to gain standing and assume leadership roles.[77] Paradoxically, under Sihanouk, Cambodian military officers accepted bribes and sold/delivered supplies, Cambodian farmers commonly sold large volumes of food to the NVA/VC, and the regime continued to honor its own arrangement with the Vietnamese and ignore their ever increasing presence on Cambodian soil; they did so at the same time Phnom Penh called upon the Cambodian military and population to fight the Khmer Rouge, portraying the insurrectionists as Vietnamese lackeys.[78]

Onset of Khmer Rouge Insurgency

According to records in the Soviet archives from Moscow's embassy in Phnom Penh, the Khmer Rouge began formulating specific plans for insurrection as early as 1966.[79] Traditional communist doctrine contended that revolution must originate from an oppressed and alienated working class—or at least that the latter class would constitute the rank and file, with leadership roles generally assumed by educated, urban revolutionaries. For some time, the communists had endeavored to build networks of potential militants primarily among the rural peasantry, as there were too few urban workers in Cambodia at the time to serve as a sizable nucleus for a revolution.[80] This ideologically conventional model of communist revolution was proving frustrating for the Khmer Rouge, as their efforts to organize and galvanize Cambodia's peasant population had at best experienced limited and geographically patchy success. Various considerations, often in combination, contributed to the communists' initially limited progress in winning over Cambodia's agrarian poor. Rural Khmers possessed a very traditional culture/mindset that was not easily reoriented toward new ideals; additionally, ethnic Khmers were distrustful of their historical rivals, the Vietnamese and Chinese, and were often aware that the latter and other foreign influences were intertwined with Cambodia's communist movement. The far left made some progress in expanding their propaganda capabilities, with leftist newspapers comprising more than half the daily circulation of Khmer-language papers by 1963—up from just 20% of total circulation in the late 1950s; nevertheless, this strategy had limited impact in reaching the largely illiterate rural peasantry, and such organs and their publishers were vulnerable to regime crackdowns.[81]

In addition to the U.S. bombing of Cambodian territory, other developments also began to play into the Khmer Rouge's hands in the latter 1960s that would aid in their propaganda and recruitment and serve as catalysts for their insurrection. The conduct of the newly conservative National Assembly and cabinet provided the Khmer Rouge with propaganda opportunities to recruit the politically disaffected via government crackdowns on leftists and democratic norms in general; the largely deserved reputation for government corruption; and, as of 1969, restoration of diplomatic ties with the U.S. amid an intensification of the fighting in Vietnam and escalation of U.S. bombing in Cambodia. Significantly, Sihanouk's efforts to keep Cambodia out of the expanding war in Indochina in part entailed giving Vietnamese communists and their Cambodian Khmer Rouge allies de facto control over as much as 20% of the country's territory. The latter policy greatly concerned conservative elements within Cambodian society, which, upon achieving an increased measure of control over the government in 1966—and largely with Sihanouk's acquiescence—began efforts to reduce communist influence/control with Cambodia, be it foreign (North Vietnam, Viet Cong, etc.) or domestic in nature. The Khmer Rouge were also able to cultivate alliances with, and recruit members from, the ranks of several indigenous tribal populations in remote areas of the country's north, which distrusted the national government.

Arguably, the single most important trigger in the Cambodian Civil War's eruption and the start of the shift in increasing rural support for the Khmer Rouge were developments related to the wholesale purchasing and taxation of rice. Traditionally, rice growers would sell their harvest at a set, pre-determined price, paid for and taxed in Cambodian currency. Given the dominance of rice as an export, such taxes were an important source of funding for the government. As the war in neighboring Vietnam escalated, so too did demand for food and other resources. Buyers acting on behalf of China and Vietnamese communists increasingly bought Cambodian rice surreptitiously, often paying higher rates in foreign currency and, in turn, smuggling the food staple into South Vietnam, thereby denying the Cambodian government tax revenues. A U.S. intelligence report from the era thus explained the smuggling problem's nature along the Cambodian-South Vietnamese border:

> There has always been a good deal of private trading and smuggling of rice across the Cambodian-South Vietnamese border, particularly in the delta region. In 1965, however, coincident with the buildup of North Vietnamese Army units in the rice-deficit South Vietnamese highlands, the communists began to make extensive private purchases of rice in Cambodia, smuggled through northeastern Cambodia to communist forces in Laos and South Vietnam . . . It is known that this smuggling was on a large enough scale to disturb Sihanouk because of the loss of tax revenue and foreign exchange earnings involved.[82]

Potentially of even greater concern than the rice itself was the increased encroachment upon Cambodian territory by Vietnamese communists, apparently transcending far beyond any arrangement made with Sihanouk.[83] The Cambodian government began increasing efforts to curtail smuggling operations in the mid-1960s through roadblocks and more frequent confiscation of unauthorized goods. However, the logistics of controlling the goods smuggling across the largely remote 700-mile border with South Vietnam was daunting, certainly given the meager size and capabilities of Cambodian military forces and the endemic corruption within the government and military.[84] Efforts were nonetheless undertaken. Upon becoming Prime Minister, anti-communist Lon Nol dispatched troops and tax collectors to oversee the state-sanctioned purchase of rice at lower government rates and restore the much-needed revenue stream. Unrest began to foment in many of the country's key rice-producing areas, including Battambang province in the northwest (see Map 3: Provinces of Cambodia) where irate farmers attacked government tax collectors. As such disorder began to spread, almost certainly exacerbated by Khmer Rouge agitation of the peasantry, Lon Nol and conservatives advocated a harsh response, which met with Sihanouk's approval as he was traveling abroad at the time. Martial law was declared, and additional military forces were dispatched that proceeded to kill hundreds of peasants and lay waste to scores of farms and even entire villages. Sihanouk deflected blame for the civil disorder and bungled response onto Lon Nol who, along with certain other conservatives, was forced to resign. Sihanouk, aware of the activities of the far-left in encouraging the peasantry during the chaos and publicly describing the uprising as a "pro-communist rebellion," abolished the leftist counter government he initially established and ordered the arrest of many known communists. However, he appointed other leftists not associated with the Pol Pot Maoist faction to cabinet posts vacated by the conservative officials in an apparent effort to counterbalance the right-wing elements that remained in the government.[85]

ONSET OF CAMBODIAN CIVIL WAR

Map 3: Provinces of Cambodia

Although the April 1967 outbreaks of disorder in the rice-producing areas were quelled, the violence marked a turning point in that, for the first time, significant numbers of the rural peasantry began to embrace the Khmer Rouge and its revolutionary message. Peasants' distrust in the Cambodian government and Sihanouk himself became increasingly common in subsequent years. For approximately the next year, the Khmer Rouge leadership was preoccupied with reorganizing, recruiting, and attempting to find paths forward with the Cambodian revolution, with only occasional public manifestations of their activities. In November, for example, the communists organized anti-U.S./imperialism demonstrations in the capital to gain public attention during a visit by Jacqueline Kennedy. The following February–March, the Khmer Rouge undertook small-scale military strikes in remote areas of the northeast, apparently with the goal of seizing arms and other supplies from government outposts and for the propaganda and recruitment benefits a few small victories could potentially offer.[86]

By the fall of 1968, Khmer Rouge activity had become more common, with the communists capturing territory (though still modest in total area) principally in northern areas of the country. As the Cambodian Army retook camps from the insurgents, they found better facilities for training and propaganda; evidence of more sophisticated administration—including programs for drafting peasants, intelligence gathering, and collecting "taxes" from local populations under their control—as well as large caches of food and other supplies, which suggested the rebellion was becoming more widespread and increasingly better organized.[87] The insurrection, though, was hardly on the verge of victory in the late 1960s. As of late 1968, fewer than 5,000 poorly armed Khmer Rouge were scattered across largely rural and isolated areas of northern and eastern Cambodia, and they lacked coherent strategy and leadership for moving forward.[88] However, their numbers were steadily increasing, and what was largely still a regional nuisance was potentially poised to evolve into a significant military threat. As awareness of the latter reality reached Phnom Penh, combined with ever more violations of Cambodian territory and the country's ostensible neutrality by Vietnamese communists, the political pendulum once more swung to the right. In 1968, anti-communist Lon Nol was reinstated as Defense Minister and as Prime Minister the following year.

Throughout 1969, the Khmer Rouge rebellion spread considerably beyond the remote localized patches of the country where it originated. By summer, the insurgency engulfed Cambodia's northeastern-most provinces of Ratanakiri and Strung Treng and, to a lesser degree, Mondulkiri and Preah Vihear. By fall, the government only controlled a minority of cities and towns in much of the northeast and maintained control only of major roads during daytime, amid reports of the Khmer Rouge fielding entire battalions of combatants against government forces.[89] Up to 50,000 Vietnamese communist forces had infiltrated into Cambodia's northern and eastern provinces by 1969, established in numerous bases of various size, function, and importance—an alarming reality that Sihanouk chose to ignore in public comments.[90] As the security climate in Cambodia continued to deteriorate, Sihanouk found it increasingly difficult to whitewash his prior collaborations with the Vietnamese communists and Cambodian far left and his ill-conceived policies that helped facilitate their exponentially expanding presence within the country. His efforts in the late 1960s to improve the situation, such as formally requesting the North Vietnamese government and Viet Cong respect Cambodian territory/neutrality and stop aiding the Khmer Rouge insurgents, yielded no substantive results. The latter political realities would ultimately lead to Prime Minister Lon Nol deposing Sihanouk the following year while also significantly intensifying the Civil War.

Map 4: Main Roads of Cambodia – Points of Khmer Rouge Attack, March-April 1970

Endnotes

1. Central Intelligence Agency, "Communism and Cambodia," (February 1972). Accessed March 17, 2022.
2. Ben Kiernan, *How Pol Pot Came to Power: Colonialism, Nationalism, and Communism in Cambodia, 1930–1975* (New Haven, CT: Yale University Press, 2004).
3. David Chandler, *Brother Number One: A Political Biography of Pol Pot* (Boulder, CO: Westview Press, 1999).
4. Central Intelligence Agency, "Intelligence Memorandum: Cambodia---Population and Manpower of Indochina," (September 1, 1954). Accessed February 2022.
5. U.S. Department of State – Office of the Historian, "Foreign Relations of the United States, 1955–1957, Vietnam, Volume I – Document 278: Dispatch From the Ambassador in Vietnam (Reinhardt) to the Department of State," (November 29, 1955). Accessed January 2022.
6. Ronald Frankum, *Operation Passage to Freedom: The United States Navy in Vietnam, 1954–55* (Lubbock, Texas: Texas Tech University Press, 2007); Central Intelligence Agency, "Vietnam: Where We Are and How We Got There," (May 1, 1964). Accessed February 2022.
7. Kiernan 2004.
8. Philip Short, *Pol Pot: Anatomy of a Nightmare* (New York: Henry Holt, 2004).
9. Kiernan 2004.
10. Central Intelligence Agency, "Intelligence Memorandum: Communist Military Aid to Cambodia, 1963–66," (May 1967). Accessed January 2022.
11. Central Intelligence Agency, "The Situation in Cambodia," (December 20, 1963). Accessed March 2021.
12. Ibid.
13. CIA, December 1963.
14. CIA, May 1967.
15. Ibid.
16. CIA, May 1967.
17. Central Intelligence Agency, "Intelligence Memorandum: Cambodia's Foreign Policy," (December 1, 1965). Accessed February 2021.
18. CIA, May 1967.

19. Central Intelligence Agency, "Intelligence Memorandum: Cambodia---Patterns and Trends in Soviet Military Assistance to North Vietnam," (April 17, 1972). Accessed March 2021.
20. CIA, December 1963.
21. Central Intelligence Agency, "Economic Intelligence Memorandum: Cambodia's Deteriorating Economy," (April 1964). Accessed March 2022.
22. Ibid.
23. CIA, April 1964.
24. Ibid.
25. CIA, December 1963.
26. Edwin Moise, *Tonkin Gulf and the Escalation of the Vietnam War, Revised Edition* (Annapolis, MD: Naval Institute Press, 2019); Lora Anne Viola, "The Gulf of Tonkin Incident and Deception in American Foreign Policy," in Laura Bieger and Christina Lammert eds. *Revisiting the Sixties: Interdisciplinary Perspectives on America's Longest Decade* (Berlin: Free University of Berlin/Campus Verlag, 2013).
27. Tal Tovy, *The Gulf of Tonkin: The United States and the Escalation in the Vietnam War* (New York: Taylor and Francis, 2021).
28. Brian VanDeMark, *Into the Quagmire: Lyndon Johnson and the Escalation of the Vietnam War* (New York: Oxford University Press, 1995); H.R. McMaster, *Dereliction of Duty: Johnson, McNamara, the Joint Chiefs of Staff, and the Lies That Led to Vietnam* (New York: HarperCollins, 1998).
29. Central Intelligence Agency, "DRV Manpower, Armed Forces and Reinforcement Capability," (1967). Accessed March 1, 2022.
30. Gordon Martel, *Twentieth-Century War and Conflict: A Concise Encyclopedia* (New York: Wiley-Blackwell, 2014).
31. Jeffrey Clarke, *United States Army in Vietnam: Advice and Support: The Final Years, 1965–1973*, (Washington, D.C: Center of Military History, United States Army, 1988).
32. National Archives: Vietnam War U.S. Military Fatal Casualty Statistics, https://www.archives.gov/research/military/vietnam-war/casualty-statistics. Accessed April 2022.
33. Central Intelligence Agency, "Communism and Cambodia," (February 1972). Accessed March 17, 2022.

34. CIA, February 1972.
35. CIA, February 1972.
36. Ibid.
37. Roland Paul, "Laos: Anatomy of an American Involvement," *Foreign Affairs* 49(3) 1971, pp. 533–547.
38. Ang Cheng Guan, "The Vietnam War, 1962–64: The Vietnamese Communist Perspective," *Journal of Contemporary History* 35(4) 2000, pp. 601–618.
39. Joshua Kurlantzick, *A Great Place to Have a War: America in Laos and the Birth of a Military CIA* (New York: Simon and Schuster, 2017).
40. CIA, February 1972.
41. A.J. Longman, *Political Terrorism: A New Guide to Actors, Authors, Concepts, Data Bases, Theories, and Literature* (New York: Taylor and Francis, 2017).
42. CIA, February 1972.
43. Ibid.
44. CIA, February 1972.
45. Ibid.
46. CIA, February 1972.
47. John Correll, "The Ho Chi Minh Trail," *Air Force Magazine*, November 1, 2005.
48. John Prados, *The Blood Road: The Ho Chi Minh Trail and the Vietnam War* (Ann Arbor, Michigan: University of Michigan Press, 1999).
49. Central Intelligence Agency, "Intelligence Memorandum: The Ho Chi Minh Trail," (March 1971). Accessed April 2022.
50. Correll 2005.
51. Central Intelligence Agency, "Intelligence Memorandum: Statistics on Enemy Manpower and Supplies," (February 8, 1971). Accessed January 2022.
52. Central Intelligence Agency, "Intelligence Memorandum: The Ho Chi Minh Trail," (August 1961). Accessed April 2022.
53. Central Intelligence Agency, "DCI Briefing Memo: The Communist Use of Sihanoukville," (May 18, 1970). Accessed April 2022.
54. Central Intelligence Agency, "Intelligence Memorandum: The Sihanouk Route," (February 23, 1971). Accessed April 2022.
55. Ibid.

56. Taylor Owen and Ben Kiernan, "Bombs Over Cambodia," Yale University: Genocide Studies Program, October 2006. https://gsp.yale.edu/sites/default/files/walrus_cambodiabombing_oct06.pdf. Date accessed: June 1, 2022.
57. Owen and Kiernan 2006.
58. James Tyner, *The Killing of Cambodia: Geography, Genocide and the Unmaking of Space* (New York: Routledge, 2008).
59. William Shawcross, *Nixon, Kissinger and the Destruction of Cambodia* (Lanham, MD: Cooper Square Press, 2002); Kenton Clymer, *The United States and Cambodia, 1969–2000: A Troubled Relationship* (New York: Routledge, 2013).
60. Ben Kiernan, *The Pol Pot Regime: Race, Power, and Genocide in Cambodia under the Khmer Rouge, 1975–79* (New Haven, CT: Yale University Press, 1996).
61. Kiernan, 2004.
62. Kiernan, 2004.
63. Kiernan, 2004.
64. Chandler, 1999.
65. David Chandler, *The Tragedy of Cambodian History: Politics, War and Revolution Since 1945* (New Haven, CT: Yale University Press, 1991).
66. Kiernan, 2004.
67. David Chandler, *A History of Cambodia: Fourth Edition* (Boulder, CO: Westview Press, 2008).
68. Chandler, 2008.
69. Ibid, 247.
70. Short, 2004.
71. Joel Brinkley, *Cambodia's Curse: The Modern History of a Troubled Land* (New York: Public Affairs, 2012).
72. Chandler, 1999.
73. Short, 2004.
74. Ibid.
75. Kiernan, 2004.
76. Ibid.
77. Kiernan 1996.
78. Chandler 1991.
79. Dmitry Mosyakov, "The Khmer Rouge and the Vietnamese

Communists: A History of Their Relations as Told in the Soviet Archives," in Susan Cook ed. *Genocide in Cambodia and Rwanda* (New York: Routledge, 2006).
80. Chandler, 1999.
81. Kiernan, 2004.
82. Central Intelligence Agency, "Cambodian Shipping, Sales and Assistance to North Vietnam and the National Front for the Liberation of South Vietnam," (March 1967). Accessed February 2022.
83. Central Intelligence Agency, "Cambodia and the Vietnamese Communists: A New Phase?" (June 1966). Accessed January 2022.
84. Ibid.
85. Central Intelligence Agency, "The President's Daily Brief," (April 6, 1967). Accessed May 2022.
86. CIA, February 1972.
87. CIA, February 1972.
88. Chandler, 1991.
89. CIA, February 1972.
90. Sak Sutsakhan, *The Khmer Republic at War and the Final Collapse* (Washington, DC: U.S. Army Center for Military History – Indochina Monographs, 2010).

Expanding Civil War and Vietnamese Involvement

As of 1970, the Khmer Rouge insurrection had gradually expanded over the preceding three years but remained largely contained by government forces throughout most of the country. Though poised to continue spreading slowly, the revolt was still constrained by various factors. Such elements included limited appeal among the population and continued restraint (e.g., providing only limited and surreptitious support to the Khmer Rouge) on the part of patron communist states, including North Vietnam, that were attempting to simultaneously maintain existing, if strained, relationships with the Cambodian government. In March, anti-communist elements of the government and rival political elements removed the ostensibly centrist Prince Norodom Sihanouk as chief of state. Sihanouk's regime, the Kingdom of Cambodia (1956–1970), was supplanted by the short-lived Khmer Republic (1970–1975) under Lon Nol. The deposed prince aligned himself with the communists in seeking to overthrow the new government amid a rapidly intensifying Cambodian Civil War. Sihanouk's removal was undertaken largely out of concern for the escalation of the Khmer Rouge rebellion and the associated presence of increasing numbers of communist Vietnamese troops within Cambodian territory, as well as disenchantment in some government circles with Sihanouk's often authoritarian and capricious management style. Conservative elements perceived Sihanouk as soft on Cambodian communists, allowing them to gradually grow in strength and numbers; additionally, his faux neutrality policies facilitated the establishment of Vietnamese bases and troops on Cambodian soil.

The Lon Nol government's attempt to implement a state of strict neutrality, including a demand for the departure of all Vietnamese communist forces in Cambodia, not only facilitated an escalation in the country's civil war but also added interstate conflict, as communist Vietnamese (NVA and VC) forces directly and effectively engaged Cambodian troops. U.S. bombing campaigns inflicted heavy casualties on Cambodian communists until their cessation in 1973, but, together with brief incursions from U.S. and South Vietnamese ground troops, they only served to buy the besieged government additional time. The Republican government engaged in multiple attempts to implement ceasefires between 1973 and 1975—replete with offers of power sharing and amnesty for Khmer Rouge forces—and proposed negotiations to end the war garnered support internationally, even from North Vietnam, but were ignored by Pol Pot and the resurgent Khmer Rouge. After consolidating political control over the Khmer Rouge and the opposition coalition, Pol Pot steered Cambodian communism toward China, using Beijing as a hedge against Vietnamese influence and control. By 1974, government forces were largely encircled in Cambodia's capital and main urban centers and reduced to a principally defensive posture that, after progressive decline, finally collapsed in April the following year. This collapse placed Cambodia in the hands of one of the most brutal and dystopian regimes in modern human history.

Sihanouk Deposed

Sihanouk had already lost much of his control over the government to the mostly conservative National Assembly and cabinet in the months leading up to his ousting, and a sequence of events in March 1970 facilitated his removal while he was abroad on state visits. On March 11, amid a broader uptick in anti-Vietnamese sentiment and violence among ethnic Khmers, Cambodian demonstrators attacked and damaged the diplomatic missions of North Vietnam and the Viet Cong. The following day, Lon Nol, after having taken no action to prevent or quell the still spreading violence against ethnic Vietnamese citizens, made a formal apology to the Vietnamese communists for the attacks on diplomatic compounds. However, he also proceeded to demand all Vietnamese troops withdraw from Cambodian soil within 72 hours and, apparently overestimating the Cambodian army's capabilities, threatened a military response if the Vietnamese failed to comply. The Prime Minister also closed the Port of Sihanoukville to Vietnamese communists and suspended their contracts for rice deliveries.

EXPANDING CIVIL WAR AND VIETNAMESE INVOLVEMENT

Map 5: Cambodian Cities

From Paris, Sihanouk criticized the move to the right and conveyed his desire to restore the country to his vision of neutrality.[1] However, rather than returning to Cambodia immediately, he proceeded with scheduled visits to Moscow and Beijing and appealed to both for support and for both to pressure Vietnamese communists to not exacerbate the political situation. Years later, in his memoirs, he claimed the Moscow meetings had been successful, although he declined the Soviet offer of a jet to return him to Phenom Penh during the political crisis and even extended his stay in Moscow by two additional days to schedule additional meetings. He also claimed the Soviets offered increased aid, though it may have been contingent upon both his canceling the visit to China in favor of immediately returning home to rally support for his position and Cambodian alignment with the USSR and away from Beijing.[2] On March 18, Lon Nol called upon the National Assembly to hold a plebiscite on whether Prince Sihanouk should be retained as Chief of State. The conservative-dominated body voted overwhelmingly 86–3 to remove him, effectively ending the Cambodian monarchy and establishing Lon Nol as Head of State.[3] Arriving in Beijing the following day, Sihanouk weighed whether to accept his fate and go into retirement in exile or, alternatively, to resist the political developments and form an opposition government in exile that would, out of necessity, require alignment with both the Khmer Rouge and Vietnamese communists.[4] With the encouragement of his Chinese hosts and their pledges of support, he chose the latter option in yet another of his many political realignments.

Despite his ouster, Sihanouk did not lack support in Cambodia. Many members of the upper and middle classes had benefited from his policies economically, whether through government contracts, appointments to government jobs, or otherwise. More importantly for the insurrection, large numbers of the country's rural poor continued to revere Sihanouk as much as they held Lon Nol and conservatives in contempt, due in large part to the Cambodian military's brutality toward peasants. Beginning on March 20, the deposed ruler issued a series of statements in which he denounced his removal as illegal, proclaimed the dissolution of the Lon Nol government and National Assembly, and announced he was forming a new government and resistance organization in exile.[5] Between March 26 and 30, violent demonstrations in support of Sihanouk—likely facilitated in part by communist agitation—erupted in several provinces and threatened to spread to the capital. The Cambodian military and police brutally quelled the protests by firing on the crowds and killing hundreds of demonstrators, after which Sihanouk publicly appealed to unarmed supporters to not take to the streets and risk their lives on his behalf.[6]

During his tenure, Sihanouk—like many Cambodian politicians, including elements among the communists—helped rouse national sentiment by often criticizing the Vietnamese and the loss of Cambodian territory to the latter, xenophobic and nationalistic messages that appealed to both ethnic Khmer peasants and the Khmer Rouge.[7] In the years prior to his removal, leftist propaganda, including that of the Pol Pot faction, had generally been more critical of Lon Nol and other right-wing leaders than the ostensibly centrist and neutral Sihanouk; indeed many within the country's left viewed Sihanouk as the lesser threat in Phnom Penh. In the years prior to his ouster, for example, the policy of the Viet Cong was to not criticize or otherwise mention Sihanouk by name in any of their propaganda. For many years, the left also continued to exploit Sihanouk's pseudo-neutrality and his often naive and accommodating policies toward communist elements. In recent years, Sihanouk subjected the Khmer Rouge to vacillating periods of harassment and persecution, juxtaposed against alternating periods of tolerance. They now made common cause with the deposed ruler and sought to recruit many of his supporters to their movement. His history of at least partial cooperation with the Vietnamese communists and other communist regimes/movements within the region also helped facilitate support among those states. Reflecting that reality and the increasing belligerence of the new government in Phnom Penh, North Vietnam and the Viet Cong withdrew their diplomats from Cambodia amid statements of support for Sihanouk's position from Vietnamese as well as Laotian communists.[8]

Sihanouk's removal by anti-communist elements of the Cambodian government facilitated a new political alliance and helped drive substantial numbers of ethnic Khmer peasants to the Khmer Rouge movement. From Beijing, the deposed leader described his removal as a coup and urged his supporters to "head for the jungle" and actively resist the new government in open rebellion.[9] Vietnamese communists took full advantage of Sihanouk's realignment and the temporary confusion the transition caused by attempting to recruit disaffected Cambodian soldiers, border guards, and citizens previously loyal to Sihanouk.[10] In addition to the ethnic Khmers who were joining the insurgency in increasing numbers, the communists in Cambodia drew significant strength from segments of the country's minorities. As of 1970, ethnic Vietnamese comprised approximately 7% of the population and ethnic Chinese around 5%, with substantial numbers of both groups either members of some party-run organization or otherwise pro-communist.[11]

Coalition/Opposition Government in Exile and Government Military Mobilization

From China, Sihanouk announced the formation of a coalition government while in exile, the Royal Government of the National Union of Kampuchea, which in French (*Gouvernement Royal d'Union Nationale du Kampuchéa*) formed the acronym GRUNK, by which the organization would become known. The political coalition between the pro-royalist forces loyal to Sihanouk and the more-numerous Khmer Rouge was termed the National United Front of Kampuchea (Front Uni National du Kampuchéa) or FUNK, which also came to refer to the newly formed opposition government's communist-dominated military forces. Although Sihanouk had often been their oppressor, the Khmer Rouge recognized the opportunity to recruit his supporters into their movement and gain some measure of additional political legitimacy (e.g., China recognized the GRUNK as the legitimate Cambodian government) by participation in the coalition government, and they accepted Sihanouk as the opposition forces' figurehead and publicly called for unity among opposition ranks. Several Khmer Rouge leaders were included in the new opposition government, including Hou Youn as Minister for Cooperatives (agricultural collectivization) and Hu Nim as Minister of Information (both of whom would later be killed in internal Khmer Rouge purges) as well as Khieu Samphan, who served as Deputy Prime Minister and officially as Defense Minister, though most military forces were under Pol Pot's de facto control.

At least initially, FUNK combat forces largely depended upon the communist Vietnamese troops' numbers and fighting capabilities in Cambodia. In organizing combat units, ethnic Khmer fighters were customarily integrated with more seasoned and better equipped Vietnamese forces, with ethic Khmers often the minority within such integrated combat battalions. At the time of Sihanouk's ouster in March 1970, the CIA estimated that 15,000–20,000 NVA/VC combat forces were in Cambodia in addition to between 5,000 to 10,000 Khmer communist troops—not including local militias.[12] By late 1971, the number of NVA/VC troops in Cambodia had risen to 50,000–60,000, around half of which were combat troops.[13] Due to a combination of factors, including low motivation (many fighters were conscripted into service), generally poor training, and fewer modern weapons, Cambodian communists' combat effectiveness was considerably lower than their Vietnamese counterparts.[14] Accordingly, the integrated (combined Khmer and Vietnamese) FUNK units that were most effective against the Cambodian military were those with higher percentages of Vietnamese troops.[15] Vietnamese training gradually improved the capacities of the FUNK units' ethnic Khmer communist elements, and the total size of FUNK forces also increased as the Civil War progressed, reaching 35,000–40,000 in 1972.[16] As the war continued and their numbers and capabilities improved, autonomous ethnic Khmer units became more common and larger in size, with battalion and regimental strength units deployed by the mid-point of the fighting and entire Khmer Rouge divisions organized and fielded in 1974–75.[17]

The coalition established behind the goal of toppling the Lon Nol regime was deeply fractured and became increasingly dysfunctional over the course of the Cambodian Civil War. Significant differences of opinion existed concerning political ideology, with centrists and royalists outnumbered by leftists. Communists were broadly polarized into radical as opposed to more moderate camps, with each of the latter camps also containing internal factions. Among radical communists, for example, the Khmer Viet Minh— the ethnic Khmer who had been in exile or trained in North Vietnam or VC-held areas of South Vietnam—were usually given better arms and supplies by the Vietnamese, often received better training, possessed an air of superiority, and felt entitled to leadership roles over the local Khmer Rouge; they, in turn, viewed the Khmer Viet Minh with suspicion, resentment, and as Hanoi's puppets. A detailed U.S. Department of Defense analysis noted that three basic factions existed among the FUNK's ethnic Khmer ranks:

1. Khmer communists and Khmer Viet Minh who had gone underground prior to Sihanouk's removal and who had already committed to a prolonged total war in pursuit of complete victory rather than a compromised outcome. The most radical political factions, which had initially opposed using Sihanouk as the revolution's figurehead and were also opposed to certain cultural traditions such as the practice of Buddhism. Pol Pot's Maoist faction was the prevalent group among the radicals who were ethnic Khmer.
2. The (comparatively) orthodox faction within the Khmer communist movement under the leadership of Khieu Samphan, Hu Nim, and Hou Yuon, all of whom had been integrated into leadership roles in the coalition opposition government due to their willingness to cooperate with Sihanouk.
3. The group known as the Khmer Romdas ("Liberation Khmer"), who were Sihanouk loyalists. Generally leftist and even communist, but opposed to the Khmer Viet Minh and the more radical Khmer Rouge and eventually engaged in open fighting with the latter during the Civil War.[18]

In Phnom Penh, the new government sought to better organize itself, including its military. The successor of Sihanouk's military, which had been known since independence as the Royal Khmer Armed Forces, was the renamed and reorganized Khmer National Armed Forces (*Forces Armées Nationales Khmères*) or FANK. The size and capabilities of the Royal Khmer Armed Forces had been modest, certainly in comparison to the military of North Vietnam and the Viet Cong. Sihanouk's government commonly allocated military personnel to such public works as road building rather than military training or other appropriate security roles that might yield practical experience. The Cambodian military had also long been enfeebled by corruption, with personnel commonly accepting bribes and selling supplies—including military hardware and ammunition—to the NVA/VC; they even used Cambodian military trucks to deliver such contraband. Graft had been widespread under Sihanouk and remained endemic throughout the new regime's brief tenure. Having served as the country's Defense Minister, such realities could not have been lost upon Lon Nol when his government assumed a more confrontational posture against the Vietnamese. The latter move may have reflected an optimistic assessment that the Vietnamese would not risk direct war with Cambodia and a consequent widening of the regional conflict. Additionally, a potential hope was that Hanoi would at least make concessions while the FANK was in the process of strengthening. Among the first changes to the Cambodian military were the departures, by resignation or removal, of officers loyal to Sihanouk. The new government's nationalistic and anti-Vietnamese rhetoric and its hardline stance against communism and foreign (Vietnamese) encroachment upon Cambodian soil also helped yield many new recruits from the ranks of ethnic Khmer nationalists when the Lon Nol regime publicly called for volunteers to bolster the military. However, when conscription was implemented, deferments were granted to university students and many other members of the middle and upper class, and the deferments remained in place throughout the Civil War even as manpower shortages in the military became acute.

Precise estimates of the Cambodian military forces' size are difficult due to widespread corruption. For example, officers commonly padded enlistment roles with non-existent soldiers and/or failed to report casualties or desertions in order to pocket the salaries of phantom troops. At the time of Sihanouk's removal, there were likely between 30,000 and 35,000 personnel in the Cambodian military, less than the maximum of 40,000 allowed by the country's constitution. The Cambodian Army comprised by far the largest force within the FANK, with some 32,000 troops initially, with the number of personnel in the Air Force and Navy comprising a small percentage of military forces, with 1,300 men and 15 aircraft and 1,600 men and 11 boats respectively.[19] At the onset of direct conflict with Vietnam, the Army's combat forces included some 30 infantry battalions, up to 15 separate infantry companies, one artillery battery, one anti-aircraft battery, one armored reconnaissance regiment, and various support battalions (e.g., engineer, transport) deployed throughout Cambodia but primarily concentrated in the northeast and around the capital in the south.[20] Reserve forces were even more modest, consisting of only two light infantry battalions and elements of the support battalions.[21]

In the first weeks of direct conflict with NVA/VC forces, the Cambodian government called for a general mobilization and established recruiting stations throughout the country for the large numbers of volunteers, mainly high school and post-secondary students.[22] The efforts to rapidly bolster the size of the Cambodian military included (1) reducing recruit training time by half, (2) calling up former active or reserve personnel who had not maintained an active schedule of military training, and (3) integrating many of the lightly armed, minimally (if at all) trained paramilitary local-level self-defense forces, along with their antiquated rifles that were so outdated as to make ammunition difficult to obtain.[23] New additions to the military were commonly blended with existing personnel, giving many FANK units a roughly even mixture of troops with at least some training and experience combined with equivalent numbers that had been provided with minimal-to-no training.[24] The intention behind such blended units was that more experienced personnel could aid in completing the new arrivals' training and guide them in operations, but in practice, the blended units were often decimated during their first engagement against far better trained, better armed, and more experienced NVA/VC forces.[25]

Expansion of Direct Vietnamese (and U.S.) Involvement

Although Hanoi had not supported Pol Pot's launching a Cambodian communist insurrection prior to the conclusion of the war in Vietnam, once the Khmer Rouge undertook the rebellion, Vietnamese communists felt they had little choice but to aid their comrades and help coordinate their operations to some degree. While Sihanouk had remained in power, Vietnamese support of the Khmer Rouge insurgency was surreptitious and somewhat limited in scope. However, following Sihanouk's removal in March 1970, Cambodia's new government assumed a more aggressive posture toward communist forces. The change in policy officially reflected pursuit of a more strict neutrality from Phnom Penh but empowered North Vietnam to lift what restraint it had shown toward the previous regime and, in turn, drove the Republic of Cambodia to align itself with South Vietnam and the U.S..[26]

North Vietnamese and Viet Cong forces quickly took the initiative and went on the offensive in Cambodia, consistently routing outmatched Cambodian forces. In April, just two weeks after Sihanouk's removal, Vietnamese communist forces at the request of the Khmer Rouge initiated successful campaigns to expand control far beyond their original base areas near the Laos and South Vietnam borders, seizing five Cambodian provinces in the first 10 days of operations.[27] Many Cambodian military or police posts were overrun with minimal or no resistance, with defenders commonly fleeing, surrendering, or even joining the ranks of the communist forces, facilitating the capture of substantial quantities of weapons and other supplies. Viet Cong forces claimed to have seized 10,000 weapons and 600 tons of ammunition in just the first two months.[28] By the end of July, communist forces had gained control of most of Cambodia's northeast, advanced into northwestern areas nearly to the Gulf of Thailand and the Thai border, and also established smaller zones of control south and southwest of Phnom Penh.[29] The speed of the developments and degree of military ineptitude on the part of government forces raised concerns both in Cambodia and internationally as to the new regime's prospects.

After rapidly driving Cambodian military forces from much of the country, the communists began efforts to recruit local Khmers into their military units; create governmental infrastructure in communist-held areas; and collect taxes, food, and supplies from local populations to support their ongoing military operations.[30] Such organization facilitated continued communist progress militarily and, by late 1971, Vietnamese and Khmer Rouge forces had full or partial control of at least 53 of Cambodia's 131 districts. These forces were also able to undertake limited operations and partly contest government control in roughly 40 other districts.³¹ The speed with which the communists captured territory since Sihanouk's removal may have left approximately one-half of Cambodia's seven million people under their control by mid-1971, as many had been unable to flee initially or stayed hoping the new rulers would be an improvement over the Lon Nol regime.³² However, in the last years of the Civil War as the brutal and authoritarian nature of the Khmer Rouge was made increasingly clear, many Cambodians trekked to areas still held by the government, leaving only a fraction of the country's population in the majority of Cambodian territory that had fallen under communist control.

The escalation in the Cambodian Civil War, facilitated largely by the direct intervention of North Vietnamese and Viet Cong military forces, led to deeper U.S. involvement in the conflict. Prior to the 1970 coup in Phnom Penh, the Nixon administration had focused on a two-prong approach to the security climate in Cambodia: (1) efforts to improve relations with the government, which were largely successful and resulted in restoration of diplomatic ties and U.S. aid, and (2) the escalation of the secret U.S. bombing campaign, which ultimately failed to significantly impede the movement of personnel or supplies across the porous border.³³ Washington purposefully undertook both of the latter approaches as alternatives to the direct intervention of U.S. ground troops in Cambodia, which was not initially viewed as an option.³⁴ U.S. assistance to Cambodia resumed in April 1970 and increased substantially during the Lon Nol administration, totaling $1.18 billion in military aid and $503 million in economic assistance between 1970 and 1975.³⁵ Phnom Penh also received training support or other aid from South Vietnam and, to a lesser degree, South Korea, Indonesia, Laos, the Philippines, Taiwan, and Thailand, which included, among other sources of assistance, outdated (e.g., U.S.-made M1 rifles dating to WWII) or captured weapons, ammunition, and other supplies.³⁶ Aside from the donation of existing (outdated) or captured supplies, the assistance rendered by other nations to Cambodia, such as the cost incurred to send trainers, was generally reimbursed to the donor nations via various U.S. aid programs.³⁷

Initially, the Nixon administration was uncertain as to how to interpret or respond to the change in government, and divergent opinions existed both within the State Department and the White House. For the first few days following the transition in Phnom Penh, the possibility appeared to exist that the Lon Nol regime might continue Cambodia's efforts to avoid direct conflict with Vietnam and, given Sihanouk's past political resiliency, U.S. observers may have even allowed for the possibility of the deposed leader's return to power in some capacity as a stabilizing agent.[38] Such uncertainty prevented the U.S. from endorsing the new regime initially.[39] However, Sihanouk's announcement of a coalition with the communists and call for rebellion, combined with Phnom Penh's confrontational posture toward Vietnamese communists which, in turn, elicited a belligerent Vietnamese counter-response, removed any doubt as to prospects for stability. The rout of Cambodian military forces by the Vietnamese in the opening days of direct fighting between the countries caused considerable alarm in both Phnom Penh and Washington. Lon Nol briefly attempted to affirm Cambodia's continued neutrality by announcing that neither the communist Vietnamese (North Vietnam and the Viet Cong) and South Vietnam nor U.S. should have troops on Cambodian soil. The sudden deterioration in Cambodia's security situation facilitated a rapid reversal in the latter position and led the Lon Nol government to formally request U.S. military intervention, a request that was accommodated mere days later, with U.S. ground forces entering Cambodia on May 1.[40] Between April and June, some 30,000 U.S. troops and approximately 40,000 South Vietnamese troops pushed communist forces away from their sanctuaries along the South Vietnamese border and into the interior, where the communists continued to effectively engage the ill-prepared Cambodian military.[41]

Prior to the direct intervention of U.S. ground forces, the military of South Vietnam (ARVN – Army of the Republic of Vietnam) interceded to engage NVA/VC troops on Cambodian soil. A "hot pursuit" arrangement had previously existed wherein ARVN units could pursue NVA/VC fighters for limited distances across the Cambodian border, but the direct attack upon FANK forces by Vietnamese communists facilitated larger scale ARVN military operations in the country. The U.S. helped in planning the ARVN's Cambodian operations and was interested in their actions both in terms of what they discovered/captured and also as a test of Vietnamization's progress in Indochina's broader conflict.[42] Concerns related to the latter stemmed from the ARVN's low pay, relative inexperience, and corruption, which undermined the effectiveness of many of their units. However, the ARVN hoped to take advantage of NVA forces being engaged against FANK forces to gain the upper hand and drive them away from many areas along the South Vietnam border.[43] Initiated first as border raids in March–April, by late April the ARVN executed its first of several major thrusts to capture or destroy major communist supply depots before they could be evacuated from former sanctuary areas, resulting in substantial NVA/VC casualties and captured supplies.[44] In addition to ground operations, South Vietnam's Air Force flew over 1,600 sorties in Cambodia—supported by over 300 USAF sorties—in the first phase of the Cambodian campaign and was effective in engaging fleeing NVA/VC forces and in identifying targets for ground troops.[45] By May, South Vietnam was aware of widespread ethnic violence in Cambodia targeting the country's Vietnamese minority. Part of the ARVN mission then shifted to opening escape corridors to facilitate the exodus of members of Cambodia's Vietnamese minority who wished to flee into South Vietnam.[46]

Several weeks after ARVN units began direct engagements with Vietnamese troops in Cambodia, the U.S. incursion (Task Force Shoemaker) involving some 12,000 troops in the first wave was initiated on May 1—with Washington providing the U.S. military only four days' notice. In an effort to mitigate intensifying public outcry among segments of the Cambodian (as well as U.S.) population concerning the U.S. military intervention, the White House announced that the U.S. operation would be limited in both duration and geographical scope—staying within 30 kilometers (18.64 mi) of the border to drive the Vietnamese out of their bases in former sanctuary areas.[47] Though the geographical constraints prevented U.S. forces from checking communist activity in the interior, the two-month campaign was largely successful in the short-term, inflicting substantial casualties on NVA/VC forces; dislodging them from many of their bases and transit corridors; disrupting networks of Vietnamese agents operating in Cambodia; capturing hundreds of tons of weapons, ammunition, and other supplies—up to 30% of the supplies the Vietnamese forces had in Cambodia; and diverting communist resources that would have at least in part been directed against FANK forces.[48] The operation caught the NVA by surprise, contributing to their decision to largely withdraw rather than offer stubborn resistance, perhaps reasoning it would be easier to replace supply caches than larger numbers of experienced officers and troops that would potentially be lost via offering more intense fighting.[49]

A more long-term international military intervention was considered in the Nixon Doctrine, which favored replacing U.S. troops in Southeast Asian conflict zones with a more long-term presence of allied Asian states' troops. Consideration was given to using troops from South Korea, Indonesia, and/or Taiwan to provide more long-term assistance in propping up the Cambodian government, but—aside from somewhat limited assistance rendered by a few neighboring states—the idea was not embraced in Washington due to fears of escalation.[50] The two-month U.S. military operation had achieved most of its objectives. Nevertheless, the Khmer Rouge effectively used the involvement of the U.S., as well as that of South Vietnam and Thailand, for propaganda and recruitment. The communists portrayed Lon Nol and his supporters as puppets of not only western imperialism but also of Cambodia's historical rivals within the region, allowing them at least partial success in countering the government narrative that the Khmer Rouge and FUNK were puppets of Vietnam and China. Arguably, the most significant long-term impact of the U.S. ground troop incursion into Cambodia was to inadvertently polarize the population even further, driving more Cambodians to the Khmer Rouge and further undermining popular support for the government and accelerating the Civil War.[51]

Strained Relations Between Khmer Rouge and Vietnamese Patrons

While the Vietnamese were one of the Khmer Rouge's and FUNK forces' main patrons during the Civil War, significant mutual animosity and mistrust existed, giving rise to numerous disputes. Sources of the discord included the NVA/VC treatment of Khmer forces as subordinate "younger brothers;" the distribution of taxes and supplies obtained from subject populations; travel restrictions—some imposed by the NVA/VC on the Khmer, others imposed by the Khmer upon the NVA/VC; and the initial unwillingness of the Vietnamese to adequately arm Khmer units with modern weapons that the Hanoi had at its disposal.[52] The shortage of modern arms among ethnic Khmer units in the early phases of the Civil War apparently reflected Vietnamese mistrust of their Cambodian comrades, with the customary practice being the short-term loan of newer arms to Khmer units only for specific Vietnamese-led/sanctioned missions, after which the weapons would be returned to the NVA/VC.[53] Such discordant relations not only contributed to demoralization and desertion among the ranks of ethnic Khmer fighters but also facilitated firefights between FUNK forces—including Khmer Rouge guerillas—and NVA/VC troops.[54] Beginning with an early period of the Sihanouk regime's persecution of Cambodian communists in 1954–55, many ethnic Khmer radicals fled across the border into North Vietnam or VC-held areas of South Vietnam. Several thousand Cambodian communists crossed the border, and many stayed until Sihanouk's outsing. The Vietnamese communists imparted significant, prolonged military, political, and administrative training to this cadre and had expectations that this group of Khmer Viet Minh would eventually return to Cambodia and form the nucleus of that country's communist movement and, reflecting Hanoi's patronage, would ally the Cambodian movement with that of Vietnam. Soon after Sihanouk's removal and the onset of direct conflict between Cambodia and the NVA/VC, the first waves of several thousand Cambodian communists who had been in Vietnam returned to participate in the resistance, though up to one-third died en route from bombings, disease, and accidents.[55] Upon arrival, rather than assuming leadership over the Cambodian communist movement, the returnees were treated with suspicion by the Khmer Rouge who regarded them as pro-Vietnamese collaborators and spies, and most were eventually purged or reduced to servile or insignificant roles in coming months/years during the Civil War.[56]

During the first years of the Civil War, the animosity the Khmer Rouge felt toward the Vietnamese communists was, to some degree, kept in check as Pol Pot and other leaders recognized the movement needed Vietnamese support. However, relations between the Khmer Rouge and their Vietnamese counterparts deteriorated in the final two years of the conflict. As soon as most NVA/VC forces withdrew from Cambodia in 1973, the Khmer Rouge engaged in public anti-Vietnamese demonstrations; dismantled pro-Sihanouk units under their authority—many of which, if not pro-Hanoi, had at least been willing to cooperate with Vietnam and/or were composed of more moderate leftists; and finished the purge of Khmer communists who had returned from exile in Vietnam or otherwise demonstrated sympathies to Hanoi.[57] Sporadic fighting even erupted between Khmer Rouge and NVA/VC units when, during the withdrawal of the Vietnamese forces from Cambodia, the latter tried to repatriate their military equipment rather than leave it for Cambodian comrades' use.[58]

As the Civil War continued, Pol Pot and his inner circle grew increasingly resentful of Vietnamese advice and their own dependence on Hanoi. In particular, they viewed Vietnam's acceptance of the 1973 ceasefire terms and the associated withdrawal as a betrayal, and the Cambodian communists strengthened their resolve to win the war themselves. The temporary halt in Vietnamese deliveries of military aid to the insurrectionists and the Khmer Rouge demand that all VC troops withdraw from Cambodian soil made such a stance even more necessary.[59] The movement's doctrine even began to reflect the widening political rift with Vietnam, as Pol Pot and Khmer Rouge leadership began to emphasize such concepts as self-reliance and increasingly added anti-minority, xenophobic rhetoric to their propaganda.[60] In 1974, Pol Pot and the Khmer Rouge leadership constructed a revisionist history of Cambodian communism, in which they downplayed Vietnam's contributions, dropped references to many foreign influences, such as Marxism/Leninism, and incorrectly described the country's communist movement as having originated not through foreign influences (e.g., Vietnam) but from within the native Khmer Issarak independence movement.[61]

Despite public political rhetoric to the contrary and his disdain for the Vietnamese, Pol Pot grasped that the Khmer Rouge likely did need military aid and other resources to achieve victory, and by 1974, the leader swallowed his pride and initiated renewed appeals to Vietnam for additional material support. By this time, Hanoi clearly understood Pol Pot and his faction's increasingly anti-Vietnamese stance, along with their unwillingness to defer to Vietnamese leadership. However, rather than attempting to remove Pol Pot or strengthen other Cambodian factions that might seek to counter his influence, Hanoi provided the aid the Khmer Rouge requested without any preconditions.[62] The Vietnamese may have seen the renewal of military aid as a means to restore positive relations with Khmer Rouge leadership, or they merely did not want accelerating political turmoil with Cambodia at the time they were organizing the final push in South Vietnam in their own conflict.[63] Whatever the motive may have been for restoring the flow of arms to the Khmer Rouge, it bolstered the latter's capabilities and, in so doing, further strengthened Pol Pot's leadership position.

Communists Gain Territory and Momentum

With increased U.S. aid and support, the Cambodian military had more firepower and near complete control of the air. FANK troop strength increased significantly since the entry of the Vietnamese in the Civil War. Beginning with no more than 35,000 personnel at its reorganization in 1970, troop strength had risen to as many as 200,000 by July 1972.[64] However, even as some improvements were realized within the Cambodian military, FANK forces remained poorly led and lacking in discipline, and, as the Civil War progressed, their morale deteriorated further. They became increasingly reluctant to engage in combat, resulting in a minority of Cambodian forces doing most of the fighting which, in turn, led to fatigue and burnout among the better units.[65] Government forces also suffered from command and control issues caused by inadequate communication capacity and lack of transport systems.[66] A declassified report prepared for the U.S. National Security Council during this period reveals examples of other significant shortcomings of FANK forces:

> FANK now considers that more than 130,000 personnel have been (sufficiently) trained. However, this figure includes the entire 35,000 original force whose training was of dubious quality as well as all those trained since 1970 who have become casualties or deserters. Some people have been trained twice–usually in different skills. I would conclude that no more than half of the FANK has thus far received effective training . . . The enemy/FANK kill ratio dropped to 0.7:1 last December (1971) but returned to about 2:1 in recent months (spring/summer 1972). However, the improved ratio appears to be due more to better FANK results against the less effective Khmer communists, who are carrying a sharply increasing part of the action, than any improvements in FANK.[67]

Several developments aided the growth of the Khmer Rouge and their appeal throughout the Civil War. From the onset of the Republic, using Sihanouk as the figurehead of the resistance gave it legitimacy in the eyes of much of the Cambodian population, particularly the peasantry, whose adherence to cultural traditions would have otherwise made communism unpalatable for most. Recruitment was also aided by the increasingly authoritarian tendencies of the Lon Nol regime, which eroded civil liberties as the Civil War progressed, and also by the brutality of Republican forces toward the peasant class. The Lon Nol regime eventually abandoned efforts to contest large swaths of the country, failing to protect many rural populations from the communists' forcibly conscripting them, "taxing" them, or stealing their food, and failing to resist encroachments of NVA/VC troops. Instead, the government concentrated what dwindling forces they could muster in defense of major urban areas and the transport corridors that linked them. By 1968, the Khmer Rouge had redoubled efforts to recruit fighters in rural areas and small villages, but they experienced limited success until Sihanouk's removal.[68] Such efforts were eventually aided by an influx of significant numbers of Vietnamese or Vietnamese-trained Khmer political cadres into Cambodia following the change in government in 1970. While the Khmer Rouge may not have embraced the arrivals, the scale of the latter development and the importance of the influx of trained political organizers—as well as fighters and military trainers—from across the border in bolstering the Khmer Rouge should not be understated. A declassified U.S. intelligence report from this era, which assessed the contributions of the Viet Cong in particular, noted the following.

> Viet Cong advisors began to report for duty across the border in late March 1970. By mid-April, there were reports of Vietnamese communists serving in Red Cambodian infantry units. As the communist invasion of Cambodia took over more territory and the Khmer structure grew in size and complexity, Viet Cong calls for cadres to serve in Cambodia became increasingly frequent. At first, the orders specified a preference for Khmer speakers, and Cambodian Proselytizing Sections throughout the delta in southern Vietnam were rapidly drawn down. But as weeks passed, standards relaxed, and calls for manpower widened to include most of South Vietnam. In May, for example, the northern Viet Cong province of Quang Da was ordered to muster several hundred cadres for service in Cambodia. By late 1970, so many cadres had left for Cambodia from the southern half of South Vietnam that Viet Cong operations there suffered severely . . . (Continuing through) the spring of 1971, large numbers of Vietnamese political cadres infiltrated into Cambodia over the Ho Chi Minh Trail. The large majority served

with Cambodian units in myriad roles including as specialists such as cryptographers, as advisors to Khmer communist military and political organizations or helping the communist training establishment.[69]

The brutal conduct of the Lon Nol regime did much to erode its popular support and turned many in the civilian population toward the insurrectionist cause. Government forces commonly engaged in human rights abuses toward peasants or others, often under the guise of wartime security measures. For example, ethnic minorities, particularly ethnic Vietnamese (many of whom had lived in Cambodia for generations), were targeted from the start in the nationalistic, xenophobic rhetoric of the new government in an apparent effort to curry favor among the ethnic Khmer majority by appealing to widely held ethnocentric, nationalistic attitudes. Government rhetoric condemning the NVA/VC invasions of Cambodian territory quickly evolved into a campaign of hatred and persecution of ethnic Vietnamese in general. In May 1970, government troops and police killed thousands of ethnic Vietnamese civilians, including women and children, in and around Phnom Penh, dumping many of their bodies into the Mekong River. Violence including smaller-scale massacres also targeted Vietnamese minorities in many other parts of the country either by government forces or by ethnic Khmer civilians spurred on by government rhetoric.[70] During the decade, over 400,000 members of Cambodia's ethnic Vietnamese minority were expelled or fled to (mostly South) Vietnam, with an estimated 200,000 fleeing to South Vietnam in 1970 alone.[71]

The new regime accused Cambodia's Vietnamese minority of supporting NVA/VC forces which, while true for some, belied the reality that large numbers of the ethnic Vietnamese as well as Chinese communities had never been sympathetic to the communists. Ironically, in response to the Cambodian government/population's directing violence and persecution against them, many members of Cambodia's Vietnamese minority fled to South Vietnam while South Vietnamese soldiers and Khmer Krom (ethnic Cambodians trained in and armed by South Vietnam) volunteer units were actively engaged against communist forces in Cambodia to shore up the security of the Cambodian government. Reflecting the persecution and violence directed against Cambodia's Vietnamese minority, census data reveals that their numbers decreased from around 364,000 in 1962 to just 165,000 by 1973.⁷² Making a feeble effort to explain and deflect the widespread violence directed against the minority to the newly allied government of South Vietnam, Phnom Penh claimed that it was difficult to distinguish between VC supporters and innocent Vietnamese. Official government comments concerning the violence directed against the ethnic Vietnamese minority fell short of an apology—though bowing to Saigon, Lon Nol agreed to permit the emigration of up to 500,000 of Cambodia's Vietnamese minority into South Vietnam—and no segment of the ethnic Khmer majority, including the country's Buddhist monks, publicly condemned the violence.⁷³

Pol Pot Cements Status as Leader

The Khmer Rouge were both militarily and politically unprepared for Sihanouk's overthrow and the escalation of the Civil War in 1970. Both developments apparently caught the communists by surprise. Militarily, the Khmer Rouge had previously focused on small-scale guerilla warfare in largely localized pockets, as they lacked the manpower, arms, and other resources to do otherwise. After 1970, their ranks began to expand to numbers they had not previously possessed, but training and equipping the Khmer fighters would take time. Consequently, they were placed in a position of dependency upon NVA/VC troops between 1970 and 1973. Without direct Vietnamese guidance, the Khmer Rouge, under the guise of either GRUNK or the communist party, also lacked the political and administrative experience to govern the sizable numbers of people or large swaths of territory that were being captured from the government largely due to Vietnamese military actions. A 1972 intelligence report encapsulated the latter situation in the first years following direct Vietnamese intervention:

> Sihanouk's overthrow and the VC invasion of the Cambodian interior in the spring of 1970 transformed the Khmer Party's problem and prospects overnight. As armed Vietnamese propaganda teams swept into hundreds of undefended Cambodian hamlets, the communists found themselves willy-nilly in the business of big government. The newly created "Liberation Committees" led by pro-Sihanouk Cambodians, were often no more than a collection of bewildered peasants and monks, entirely lacking the sinews of Party control.⁷⁴

Throughout much of the Civil War, the leadership of the Khmer Rouge and its role and position within the complex political dynamic remained secretive. Although largely in de facto control, Pol Pot remained in hiding and was not formally named as an official of the coalition for the first year. Khieu Samphan was publicly proclaimed as Defense Minister and Commander of FUNK military forces and as the head of the Khmer Rouge, which China officially portrayed as fighting on behalf of Sihanouk.[75] In March 1972, Pol Pot was acknowledged as the head of the armed forces of the coalition. From that point forward, he held responsibility for overall military strategy as well as most other major decisions, including the rejection of the cease fire proposed by North Vietnam and the Cambodian Republic in 1972 and several other overtures to end the fighting in 1973–75.[76] However, the formal anointing of Pol Pot as leader was known only to the inner circle of the movement's leadership. Outsiders, even those with whom the Khmer Rouge were ostensibly allied, did not have a complete picture in terms of the group's leadership or Pol Pot's position as the ultimate authority. For example, Soviet archives reveal that, in 1973–74, Moscow mistakenly perceived Khieu Samphan and Ieng Sary as the leaders of the Khmer Rouge.[77]

As the Civil War progressed, the number of Khmer communist forces grew exponentially compared to previous decades. Whereas French intelligence had estimated the combined total of communist combat troops and their local militia cells at around 7,000 in the early-mid 1950s, by 1972, they were estimated to have 15,000–30,000 combat regulars (the bulk of FUNK coalition forces) and likely possessed substantially larger numbers of supporting guerilla militia.[78] The quality of Khmer communist fighters gradually improved as well in terms of training, experience, and weapons. For roughly the first half of the insurrection against Republican forces (1970–72/73), NVA/VC soldiers did most of the serious fighting against Cambodian government troops or Phnom Penh's foreign allies, as had also been the case in neighboring Laos, with the indigenous rebel forces largely assuming secondary, supporting roles in both countries. However, as indigenous communist forces (ethnic Khmers in Cambodia, ethnic Laotians in Laos) grew in number and capability, they assumed greater roles in the fighting.

A period of "Khmerization" during the Civil War occurred in 1972–74 as NVA/VC troops increasingly withdrew from Cambodia, pursuing instead a push for final victory in their own conflict. The declining Vietnamese presence facilitated a transition in the nature of the Cambodian conflict from foreign forces engaging in an invasion—constituting an interstate conflict—to that of a true civil war, though a proxy conflict in which each side had outside backers. In turn, the political standing of the Khmer Rouge was in a sense enhanced both domestically and internationally, as they were perceived as not merely subordinate to an invading force of a neighboring state but the vanguard of an increasingly well organized and effective organization.[79] The latter, combined with increasing popular support for the insurrection, waning support for the government, and intensification of the fighting, shifted the momentum of the Civil War, bolstered the confidence of the Khmer Rouge/FUNK and further undermined the morale of government forces.

Khmer communists had always comprised the majority of FUNK forces and, among the various strands of Khmer communists, Pol Pot's radical Maoist faction emerged as dominant during the Civil War. Rivals for leadership roles in Cambodia's communist movement also existed. For example, Tou Samouth was the cofounder of the pro-Soviet/Vietnam Kampuchean People's Revolutionary Party (KPRP, later renamed the Worker's Party of Kampuchea) and leader of its more orthodox wing. His disappearance in July 1962, likely at the hands of Pol Pot who increasingly viewed him as an obstacle to his own ambitions, allowed for the latter to succeed him as leader of the Party, a status which he continued to consolidate in subsequent years. Sihanouk's actions in either drawing more moderate leftist/socialist elements out of the country's communist movement and into the political mainstream or, conversely, persecuting many of the original Khmer communist activists further served to clear the field for Pol Pot's faction, as did purges and political circumvention of those Khmer communists perceived to be aligned with Vietnam. The withdrawal of Vietnamese troops from Cambodia further weakened the political standing of any remaining Hanoi or Soviet-leaning Khmer communists.

In the early 1970s, the factions within Cambodian communism (and the FUNK more broadly) greatly mirrored a divergence of opinion among groups concerning Sihanouk's possible role in any future reorganization of Cambodian politics. They comprised (1) those Khmer communists who did not necessarily trust Sihanouk but were willing to cooperate with him in the coalition for their own ends; for example, he provided political legitimacy and, through his support in Beijing, potentially provided a counterbalance to Hanoi's influence; (2) those communists (the Pol Pot faction) whose opposition to Sihanouk predated his removal in 1970 and were at least initially less willing to tolerate him as the figurehead of the insurgency; and (3) those communists and others among the insurgent ranks who supported Sihanouk's return to power.[80] Differences of opinion concerning Sihanouk's appropriate role also existed among the communist patrons of the Khmer Rouge, with China supporting the deposed ruler having a role in the new state; Hanoi being wary and conflicted, based on a long history of antipathy with Sihanouk; and Moscow being apparently opposed to his return, based on his alliance with Beijing.[81] Some of these differences in opinion among Cambodian factions and between Beijing and Hanoi were smoothed over by Sihanouk's formal 1973 tour of the Cambodian territory—which had fallen under communist control—and his meetings with Khmer Rouge and FUNK leaders, including Pol Pot. A declassified U.S. intelligence document notes the political significance of the visit, which, although not a cure for existing distrust and a history of poor relations (e.g., Sihanouk and Pol Pot likely despised each other), may have helped facilitate enough understanding on the part of Sihanouk and the Khmer Rouge that they could continue to tolerate each other, recognize each other's potential usefulness in the symbiotic arrangement, and continue using each other for their respective political needs. The report observes:

> From all indications, the central purposes behind that undertaking seem to have been to enhance the legitimacy of Sihanouk and his "government" and to give him and the Khmer communist leaders a chance to reconcile their differences. With regard to his political relations with insurgent leaders, Sihanouk upon his return emphasized that as the result of his discussions with them, they fully support him as their "chief of state" . . . The public relations between Sihanouk and the Khmer communists remain cordial and cooperative. In a press interview, Sihanouk stated that the Khmer communists told him that he would be chief of state "until the end of his life". He also quoted Ieng Sary as saying that he, Sihanouk, was "the cement, the guarantee of the union of Cambodians." Despite the surface sweetness, the real

relationship between Sihanouk and the Khmer communist leadership is fragile.[82]

The genesis of many of the dystopian and iconoclastic policies the Khmer Rouge would eventually implement upon their seizing power remains unclear. Due to the secrecy surrounding Pol Pot's early leadership and the evolution of Khmer Rouge ideology and policy, it is difficult to establish a timeline as to when they formulated their future plans for Cambodia. However, Pol Pot's and the Khmer Rouge's radical, sociopathic vision and the atrocities they would ultimately commit were often foreshadowed by developments that unfolded in areas that fell under their control during the Civil War. For example, larger-scale experiments with agricultural collectivization were undertaken in areas under Khmer Rouge control by 1973 and, when collectivization and other totalitarian and iconoclastic edicts (e.g., "re-education" efforts, anti-Buddhist/religious attitudes) were not embraced by the local populations, the communists meted out brutal punishments, including torture and executions. Perhaps even more telling, in March 1974, after the southern city of Oudong fell to the Khmer Rouge, large swaths of the city were leveled, and virtually the entire population of 20,000 people was forcibly herded into the countryside where those identified as communist class/political enemies (teachers, officials/loyalists of the Republican government, etc.) were executed and the remainder forced into slave labor.[83] However, even with such occurrences during the war, few foresaw the bizarre, murderous, Orwellian policies that Pol Pot and his followers would undertake on a national scale at war's end.

Much of Pol Pot's dystopian vision for Cambodia's future appears to have been at least partially conceptualized previously but became formalized as policy at the June 1974 meeting of the Central Committee. This meeting was a turning point for Pol Pot and the Khmer Rouge in that plans were finalized for not just the final stages of military operations but also those related to certain critical actions that would be taken upon seizing power, including driving the populations of Phnom Penh and other government-held cities into the countryside, where ostensibly they could pose less threat (e.g., urban guerilla resistance to the Khmer Rouge regime) and could be forced into agrarian work through the justification of food shortages.[84] Also, several other radical policies were adopted at this conference, policies that came to be infamously associated with the Khmer Rouge, including the abolishment of money, private property, and the rejection of foreign (even humanitarian) aid behind the goal of utopian self-sufficiency—though such policies were not publicly disclosed until Pol Pot's regime came to power.[85]

Khmer Rouge Victory

As early as 1973, many observers began predicting the FANK's and Lon Nol regime's imminent collapse. To a great degree, the earliest such concerns stemmed from the cessation of U.S. bombing and offensive air campaigns that many perceived as one of the last obstacles to Khmer Rouge victory. While the Khmer Rouge publicly downplayed the impact of U.S. bombing, between 10,000 and 16,000 or up to one-half of Pol Pot's frontline combat forces had been killed in the final weeks of bombing through August 1973, a brief intensification designed to buy the Cambodian government time to shore up its capabilities.[86] In the short-term, the bombing shattered the Khmer Rouge's attempt to encircle Phnom Penh and ended their first major push to end the war militarily.[87] The Paris Accords in January 1973 that facilitated a U.S. ceasefire in South Vietnam also contained a provision in which Washington agreed to sunset the Cambodian theater of USAF operations. U.S. air strikes officially ceased on August 15, placing the full burden on the Khmer (government) Air Force, which, after suffering heavy losses years earlier, had been largely reconstituted with U.S. assistance in the preceding two years. To the surprise of many, the refurbished KAF performed well, initially running large numbers of daily combat sorties as well as effective reconnaissance and transport roles. However, the government's air power could not reverse the turning tide of the Civil War, certainly as its capabilities declined over the course of the next two years through attrition.

By 1973, approximately 60% of Cambodia's population lived in the 25% of the country's territory that remained under government control.[88] By the middle of the following year, the noose was tightening, but government forces still held most major urban areas, including most provincial capitals and shrinking portions of the countryside. However, Phnom Penh had been largely cut off from most other cities, including provincial capitals, and such fragmentation meant that the pockets of FANK forces could not support each other militarily and were increasingly left to defend their respective pockets in isolation, surrounded by the enemy.[89] This reality further undermined morale and recruitment efforts for government forces while it bolstered both for the insurrectionists. For example, in late 1974, a CIA assessment of the five FANK infantry divisions deployed to Phnom Penh judged only two to be capable of offensive action; the remaining divisions and some 20,000 various militia and other units were undermined chiefly by worsening manpower problems, with casualties and desertions outpacing conscription/recruitment efforts.[90]

In one of the last major campaigns of the Civil War, the Khmer Rouge prioritized the capture of Mekong Delta territories. The river system served as the primary supply route for the capital and had become especially important as a lifeline after sections of main roads leading to Phnom Penh had fallen. (See Map 4: Main Roads of Cambodia in Chapter 3.) While communist units had previously operated in the area—e.g., shelling river traffic at certain points along the route—the closing of the Mekong River to Phnom Penh before the end of the dry season (June) was established as a top communist military priority for 1975, a goal correctly seen as the key to capturing the capital and winning the war. Reflecting the importance of this objective, 10,000 Khmer Rouge troops were assigned to the Mekong interdiction effort, and 20,000–25,000 additional communist troops were tasked with tying down 40,000–45,000 FANK forces in proximity to Phnom Penh so they could not be redeployed to reinforce or intervene in the Mekong campaign.[91] Monsoon rains and associated flooding of areas in proximity to the Delta and its tributaries would impede military operations including efforts to halt shipping. (See Map 6: Cambodian Flood Plains.) The last supply ships to reach Phnom Penh via the river route arrived in January. By February, with the remnants of the Cambodian Navy unable to de-mine the route and other government forces unable to dislodge the communists from the banks or prevent heavy shelling of supply convoys, efforts to supply the besieged city via the Mekong concluded.

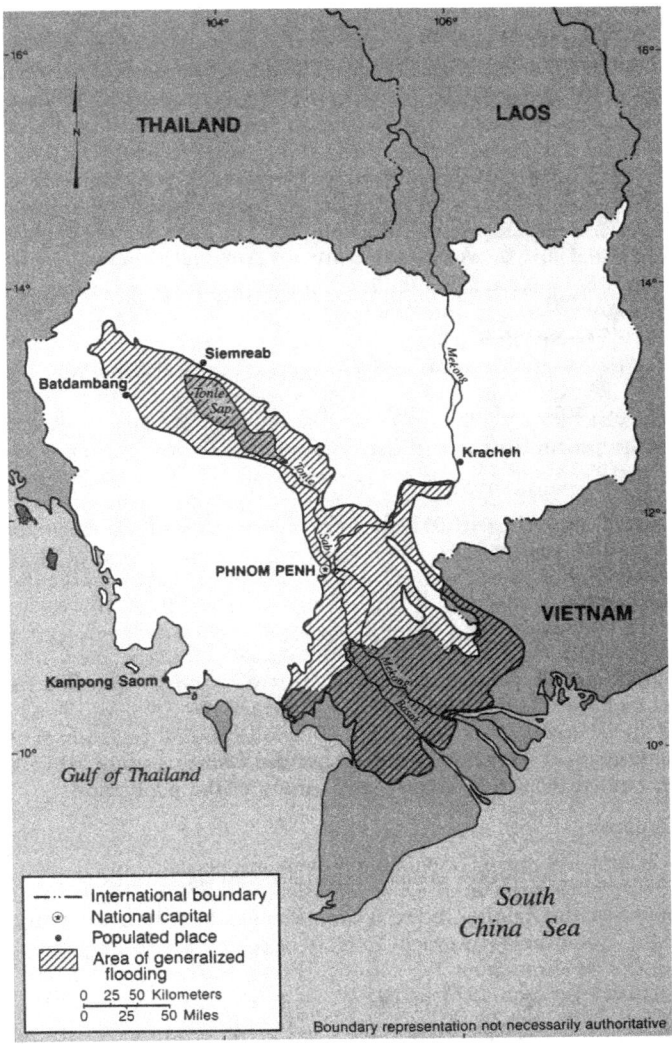

Map 6: Cambodian Flood Plains

As more territory and more transport corridors fell to the Khmer Rouge and government-held positions were reduced to encircled and isolated pockets, the logistics of supplying government strongholds became increasingly more difficult, adding supply shortages to the growing list of problems the imperiled government faced. Cambodia's population became increasingly dependent on food imports as fighting and Khmer Rouge control spread to the county's farming regions, causing many farmers to flee their fields as the communists advanced. As illustrated in Table 6, between January 1 and April 1, 1975, supply deliveries in three critical categories to Phnom Penh were a fraction of the deliveries during the same period of the previous year, despite increased need. By 1975, the Mekong River route, the lifeline for supplying the capital via cargo ships, had been largely cut off with airlifts able to only partly offset the imbalance, as the data illustrates. As conveyed in Table 6, worsening transport problems led to reduced stocks of critical supplies, with the capital holding only a 10-day reserve of rice by April 1975, for example.

An influx of large numbers of refugees into Phnom Penh and other remaining government-held areas exacerbated the supply shortage. The capital's population and many other cities under government control had grown exponentially since the Civil War's emergence in the late 1960s, largely driven by refugee arrivals. The urban population concentrations grew at an accelerated pace as the tide of war turned, fighting spread, and more Cambodian territory fell to Khmer Rouge control. For example, UN data puts Phnom Penh population estimates at 450,000 in 1966, doubling to 900,000 by 1970, and doubling again to over 1.8 million by 1974.[92] By April, with most of Cambodia's rural territory and smaller towns under communist control, streams of refugees inundated Phnom Penh and other cities still held by the government. In the final weeks of the war, as many as 6 million Cambodians were in government-held areas—with up to half that number in the capital—as opposed to as few as 1 million in areas under communist control.[93] Not all refugees had necessarily been supporters of the Lon Nol regime; however, having directly experienced or heard of the even more authoritarian and brutal tendencies of the Khmer Rouge, many viewed the Cambodian government as the better option. With nowhere to house such numbers, the refugees were overcrowded into nearly every public space, including schools, temples, and parks; they endured discomfort and inadequate food, medicine, and other supplies, with thousands ultimately succumbing to starvation or disease.

Table 6: Supply Deliveries to Phnom Penh via Mekong/Airlift (in metric tons)[94]

	January 1– April 9, 1974	January 1– April 9, 1975	
	Mekong	Mekong	Airlift
Total	181,000	18,050	52,800
Rice	84,300	6,750	21,900
Petroleum	48,700	5,300	9,500
Ammunition	48,100	6,000	21,400

Table 7: Critical Stock Inventories in Phnom Penh – April 9, 1975[95]

	Stocks (metric tons)	Days of Supply	Daily Consumption Rate (metric tons)
Rice	6,400	10	645
Petroleum	4,400	14	327
Ammunition	5,200	12	433

Throughout the first months of 1975, as the position of FANK forces became more untenable and many of its remaining experienced units suffered from combat fatigue, morale sank ever lower, and the manpower crisis accelerated. Personnel losses between January 1 and April 1 totaled around 22,300, including 6,600 desertions.[96] In desperation, the military attempted to reassign headquarters and support personnel to combat units to partly offset the losses, but similar efforts attempted previously were unsuccessful, as desertion rates among desk and rear echelon soldiers were high, with many of the transfers never reporting to their newly-assigned combat units.[97] Dwindling military equipment also had an impact on morale and combat effectiveness in the final stage of the war. As of mid-March 1975, for example, of the 70 remaining armored personnel carriers (APCs) in the capital district, only 44 were operational, a significant setback for FANK forces that had previously relied upon APCs as a means of rapidly responding to emerging hotspots along the front lines.[98] In the closing months of the war, U.S. military aid funds had been increasingly used to procure much-needed ammunition rather than finance the purchase or repair of military hardware.[99]

Since 1974, overly optimistic speculation suggested the Khmer Rouge could possibly be persuaded to accept a cease fire and negotiate terms if Lon

Nol stepped aside as head of state. Members of the international community, including Japan and the Association of Southeast Asian Nations (ASEAN) member-states, exerted pressure for the leader to step down and leave the country, accompanied by a chorus of international pleas to the Khmer Rouge and FUNK to accept a ceasefire. Perhaps seeing this environment as the best chance for a negotiated settlement, Lon Nol acceded to the appeals on April 1 then departed by plane, never to return.[100] Sutsakhan provides a poignant account of the brief hope that arose in the capital and other remaining government-held cities following Lon Nol's departure, a hope that would unfortunately prove to be short-lived.

> The departure . . . gave evidence of a real effort on the part of the Khmer government to reach a peaceful and honorable solution to the struggle. The government called for a purge of certain key people (many linked with Lon Nol and/or who were particularly objectionable to the Khmer Rouge) . . . Everyone rejoiced, especially the civilian population from the highest placed to the most humble. It was thought, not unreasonably, that real negotiations would take place and that peace was at hand. The troops were tired of fighting, the ammunition was running low, supplies were increasingly difficult to deliver to the troops at the front as the battle raged around the besieged capital. People waited for a miracle which only the U.S. could provide–military air support. Everyone hung on the radio listening for news from the U.S. Alas the decision (no renewal of U.S. military air support) was announced soon and caused an immediate and general panic.[101]

Pol Pot and the Khmer Rouge never intended to agree to a ceasefire or a negotiated, compromised settlement with a weakened government on the verge of collapse and likely fully committed to complete military victory as early as 1973. In the early years of the Civil War when the Khmer Rouge were little more than a subservient client of the Vietnamese communists and victory was far from assured, Pol Pot was willing to placate Hanoi on occasion by insincerely pledging to consider their wishes, such as their insistence that the possibility of an armistice and negotiated settlement with the Cambodian government be pursued.[102] The withdrawal of NVA/VC troops from Cambodia, combined with a series of Khmer Rouge military victories against FANK forces in early 1973, instilled sufficient confidence in the Cambodian communists that the pretext of deference to Hanoi was largely dropped along with any willingness to accept anything less than complete military victory and the removal of the Republican government. Soviet archives reveal that, as early as April 1973, Hanoi had advised Moscow that they no longer exerted any real control over the Khmer Rouge, including the manner in which Pol Pot would direct the Civil War.[103]

President of the Senate Saukham Koy became interim President of the Republic on April 1, 1975, following Lon Nol's ostensibly temporary departure. After less than two weeks in office, the new interim government realized the Khmer Rouge were not amenable to a ceasefire or a negotiated outcome and that direct U.S./international intervention was not forthcoming. On April 12, the Acting President accepted an invitation from Washington and fled the capital aboard a helicopter during the U.S. military evacuation of its remaining Embassy staff. The departure came as a surprise to the government and population. The U.S. Embassy had privately approached some senior Cambodian government and military leaders with offers of evacuation. Nearly all refused, however, opting to stay and share the fate of the Cambodian people; this choice would cost the lives of most officials who remained in Phnom Penh. An emergency government (Supreme Committee) was hastily convened with Lt. Gen. Sak Sutsakhan appointed as its chairman, and the new government again approached the Beijing-based GRUNK through the UN and Red Cross with an appeal for a ceasefire and negotiations, even offering to transfer power to the Sihanouk-headed GRUNK. These appeals were rejected.[104]

While supplies, including ammunition, continued to be air dropped into Phnom Penh by the U.S. and a significant number of defenders remained in the city, each day witnessed more setbacks and brought the capital closer to collapse, with Khmer Rouge forces closing from multiple directions. (See Map 7: Final Khmer Rouge Assault on Phnom Penh.) In the final days, hordes of refugees flooded into the city, and the Khmer Rouge utilized them as human shields for their advances and also infiltrated their ranks with spies and saboteurs. By the 17th, as Khmer Rouge fighters had breached most of the city's outer defense perimeter and were beginning to penetrate the suburbs, the interim government considered evacuating to a provincial capital and continuing to function and resist from that location in the country's north near the Thai border, but no aircraft were immediately available for a large-scale government evacuation. The leaders at that point decided to remain in Phnom Penh.

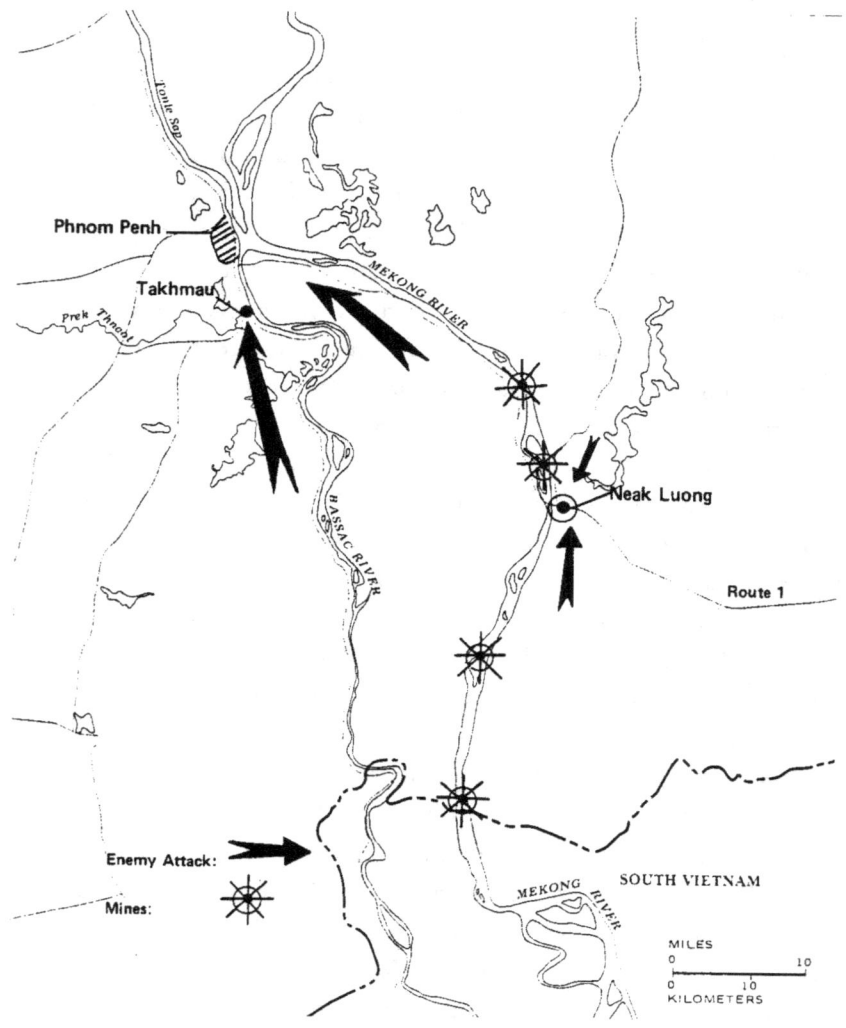

Map 7: Final Khmer Rouge Assault on Phnom Penh

Later the same day when a handful of Cambodian military helicopters arrived, the acting head of state and a small number of government officials and their families were persuaded to evacuate mere hours before the Headquarters of the General Staff fell to Khmer Rouge troops.[105] By the following day, only pockets of resistance remained in Phnom Penh, amid radio broadcasts proclaiming communist victory and in which captured government officials and military commanders called for an end to resistance in the capital. As the Khmer Rouge and its leadership had never publicly revealed their plans for the nation upon seizing power, no one was certain what to expect from the revolutionaries, apparently including the revolution's figurehead, Sihanouk, who provided the oblivious prediction to a group of U.S. Senators close to the end of the Civil War that his Khmer Rouge allies planned to establish a constitutional monarchy in the tradition of socialist-leaning Scandinavia.[106] During the 1970–75 Civil War, between 500,000 to 700,000 Cambodians were killed, mostly civilians who had been caught in the conflict's crossfire, but the casualties and suffering of the five-year Civil War would pale in comparison to the horrors that would be inflicted upon the Cambodian people under Khmer Rouge rule.[107]

Endnotes

1. R.B. Smith, "The International Setting of the Cambodia Crisis, 1969-1970," *The International History Review* 18(2) 1996, 303-335.
2. Smith 1996.
3. David Chandler, *A History of Cambodia* (Boulder, CO: Westview Press, 2000).
4. Smith 1996.
5. Smith 1996.
6. Smith 1996.
7. Jennifer Berman, "No Place Like Home: Anti-Vietnamese Discrimination and Nationality in Cambodia," *California Law Review*, 84(3) 1996, 817-874.
8. Smith 1996.
9. Central Intelligence Agency, "Communism and Cambodia," (February 1972). Accessed March 17, 2022.
10. CIA 1972.
11. CIA 1972.
12. Central Intelligence Agency, "Assessment of Cambodian Military Situation – Memorandum for President Nixon," (December 15, 1970). Accessed January 30, 2022; Central Intelligence Agency: Directorate of Intelligence, "Intelligence Memorandum: VC/NVA Combat Forces in Cambodia Since the Deposition of Sihanouk," (March 1972). Accessed April 15, 2021.
13. CIA December 15, 1970.
14. Central Intelligence Agency, "Intelligence Memorandum: Khmer Communist Combat Forces in Cambodia," (November 1971). Accessed March 30, 2022.
15. CIA November 1971.
16. Sak Sutsakhan, *The Khmer Republic at War and the Final Collapse* (Washington, DC: U.S. Army Center for Military History – Indochina Monographs, 2010).
17. Sutsakhan 2010.
18. Ibid.
19. GlobalSecurity.org, "Forces Armées Nationales Khmères (FANK)," Accessed January 10, 2022.
20. Sutsakhan 2010.

21. Ibid.
22. Martin 1994.
23. Sutsakhan 2010.
24. Sutsakhan 2010.
25. Ibid.
26. Christopher Paul, Colin Clarke, Beth Grill and Molly Dunigan, "Cambodia, 1967-1975," in Christopher Paul, et al. eds. *Paths to Victory: Detailed Insurgency Case Studies* (Washington DC: RAND Corporation – National Defense Research Institute, 2013).
27. Dmitry Mosyakov, "The Khmer Rouge and the Vietnamese Communists: A History of Their Relations as Told in the Soviet Archives," in Susan Cook ed. *Genocide in Cambodia and Rwanda* (New York: Routledge, 2006).
28. CIA 1972.
29. Central Intelligence Agency, "Intelligence Memorandum: Khmer Communist Combat Forces in Cambodia," (November 1971). Accessed March 30, 2022.
30. CIA, November 1971.
31. Ibid.
32. CIA, February 1972; Sutsakhan 2010.
33. Peter Drivas, "The Cambodian Incursion Revisited," *International Social Science Review*, 86(3/4) 2011, 134-159.
34. Drivas, 2011.
35. Yusof Ishak Institute, "Timeline: U.S.-Cambodian Relations," *Contemporary Southeast Asia* 32(3) 2010, 467-468.
36. Central Intelligence Agency, "Evaluation of OASD/SA Study: The War in Cambodia – Annex G: Abbreviated Military Assistance Plan, Cambodia," (May 21, 1971). Accessed February 15, 2022.
37. Kenton Clymer, *The United States and Cambodia, 1969-2000: A Troubled Relationship* (New York: Taylor and Francis, 2013).
38. Smith 1996.
39. Drivas 2011.
40. Smith 1996.
41. Chandler 1991.
42. John Shaw, *The Cambodian Campaign: The 1970 Offensive and America's Vietnam War* (Lawrence, KS: University Press of Kansas, 2008).

43. Shaw 2008.
44. Clymer 2013.
45. Shaw 2008.
46. Ibid.
47. David Schmitz, *Richard Nixon and the Vietnam War: The End of the American Century* (New York: Rowman and Littlefield, 2014); Clymer 2013.
48. White House, "Memorandum for the President: Report of Hanoi Reaction to U.S. Moves in Cambodia," (June 4, 1970). Accessed May 1, 2022.
49. Kenneth Conboy, *The Cambodian Wars: Clashing Armies and CIA Covert Operations* (Lawrence, KS: University Press of Kansas, 2013); Shaw 2008.
50. Central Intelligence Agency: Office of National Estimates - Memorandum, "Communist Reactions to the Entry into Cambodia of Troops from Non-Communist Asian States," (May 28, 1970). Accessed May 5, 2022.
51. Gregory Daddis, *Withdrawal: Reassessing America's Final Years in Vietnam* (Oxford, UK: Oxford University Press, 2017).
52. Mosyakov 2006, 56; CIA November 1971.
53. CIA November 1971.
54. Ibid.
55. Philip Short, *Pol Pot: Anatomy of a Nightmare* (New York: Henry Holt, 2004); Chandler 1991.
56. Short 2004; Chandler 1991.
57. Chandler 1991.
58. Ibid.
59. Marie Alexandrine Martin, *Cambodia: A Shattered Society* (Berkeley, CA: University of California Press, 1994).
60. David Chandler, *Brother Number One: A Political Biography of Pol Pot* (Boulder, CO: Westview Press, 1999).
61. Chandler 1999.
62. Mosyakov 2006.
63. Ibid.
64. Central Intelligence Agency, "The Situation in Cambodia – Memorandum for General Haig/National Security Council", (August

11, 1972). Accessed June 14, 2022.
65. CIA August 11, 1972.
66. Central Intelligence Agency, "Evaluation of OASD/SA Study: The War in Cambodia", (May 21, 1971). Accessed February 15, 2022.
67. CIA August 11, 1972, 2.
68. CIA February 1972.
69. CIA February 1972, 81-82.
70. Berman 1996.
71. Ramses Amer, "The Ethnic Vietnamese in Cambodia: A Minority at Risk?" *Contemporary Southeast Asia* 16(2) 1994, 210-238; Peter Poole, "The Vietnamese in Cambodia and Thailand: Their Role in Interstate Relations," *Asian Survey* 14(4) April 1974, 325-337.
72. Poole 1974.
73. Chandler 1999.
74. CIA February 1972.
75. David Chandler, *Brother Number One: A Political Biography of Pol Pot* (Boulder, CO: Westview Press, 1999).
76. Chandler 1999.
77. Mosyakov 2006.
78. CIA February 1972.
79. Sutsakhan 2010.
80. Central Intelligence Agency, "Intelligence Memorandum: The Khmer Insurgent Factions and the Influence of Peking, Hanoi, and Moscow Thereon," (July 20, 1973). Accessed December 15, 2021.
81. CIA July 20, 1973.
82. Ibid.
83. Donald Kirk, "Cambodia 1974: Governments on Trial," *Asian Survey* 15(1) 1975, p. 53-60; Sydney Schanberg, "Town is Devastated in Cambodian 'Victory.'" *New York Times* July 28, 1974.
84. Chandler 1999.
85. Ibid.
86. Chandler 1991.
87. Chandler 1999.
88. Chandler 1991.
89. Sutsakhan 2010.
90. Central Intelligence Agency, "Status of FANK's Infantry Divisions,"

(December 10, 1974). Accessed February 15, 2022.
91. National Security Council Memorandum, "Likelihood of Communist Closure of Mekong," (January 16, 1975). Accessed March 2, 2022.
92. United Nations Department of Economic and Social Affairs – Population Division: World Population Prospects. https://population.un.org/wpp/.
93. Sutsakhan 2010, 163.
94. Central Intelligence Agency, "Survey of Communist Military Developments in Indochina," (April 10, 1975). Accessed April 15, 2022.
95. CIA April 10, 1975.
96. CIA April 10, 1975.
97. CIA April 10, 1975.
98. CIA April 10, 1975.
99. CIA April 10, 1975.
100. Sutsakhan 2010.
101. Sutsakhan 2010.
102. William Shawcross, *Sideshow: Kissinger, Nixon and the Destruction of Cambodia* (New York: Cooper Square Press, 2002).
103. Mosyakov 2006.
104. Sutsakhan 2010.
105. Sutsakhan 2010.
106. Joel Brinkley, *Cambodia's Curse: The Modern History of a Troubled Land* (New York: Public Affairs, 2012).
107. Martin 1994.

The Dystopian Khmer Rouge Regime, 1975–1979

During the Civil War, the Khmer Rouge maintained secrecy concerning the movement's leadership structure, ideological precepts, and policies it planned to undertake. Using Sihanouk as a figurehead further aided the communists in their efforts to disguise their radical agenda and the violent dystopian actions they would ultimately unleash upon the Cambodian population. Rather than being terrified at the fate that awaited them, the population was lulled into a sense of complacency by Khmer Rouge propaganda and the pretense of normalcy and positive reforms. However, upon seizing power, the Khmer Rouge immediately undertook large scale executions of those associated with the previous regime in addition to using the forced exodus of all cities and establishment of a nationwide network of labor camps as a means of killing and punishing regime enemies and those the communists callously deemed as non-producers.

The militant, dystopian policies of Pol Pot's communist faction abruptly abolished private property, currency, schools, stores and other public businesses, and any societal vestige deemed to be foreign in origin or "reactionary" in nature, including all languages other than Khmer and all religions. In lieu of traditional wage payments, the captive nation enslaved in agrarian labor camps was compensated for their intense forced labor with starvation rations mainly composed of small servings of rice grossly inadequate for the manual labor with which they were tasked. Similar to previous Soviet machinations, even as the nation starved, the Khmer Rouge seized and exported "surplus" rice, though the original plan to use the rice to buy machinery and facilitate industrialization and related inept schemes aimed at modernization never really materialized. Instead, much of what little revenue was generated—almost entirely via agriculture—was directed toward weapons and ammunition to equip the Khmer Rouge military for possible conflict with Vietnam. Either directly through execution or torture or indirectly through starvation, overwork, or disease, nearly 2 million people perished in less than four years during the brief Khmer Rouge regime.

Much of the murderous violence perpetrated by the Khmer Rouge assumed the form of ethnic cleansing in which multiple non-Khmer minority groups were persecuted and killed at a far higher rate than the general population, including Cambodia's ethnic Vietnamese. The international community, both the west and communist bloc, was aware of the nature and magnitude of the Khmer Rouge genocide even in its earliest phases but remained largely silent due to Cold War politics and the unwillingness of other nations to alienate the Pol Pot regime, given its political and strategic significance within Indochina and its position in the non-aligned community of nations. The Khmer Rouge regime's international relations were largely characterized by isolationism and conflict, including boundary disputes and armed border incursions of varied intensity and frequency directed against all three neighboring states: Laos, Thailand, and Vietnam. Genocidal actions toward Cambodia's ethnic Vietnamese minority coupled with Pol Pot's reckless, increasingly aggressive provocations along the shared border eventually led Vietnam to invade Cambodia, toppling the regime in January 1979 and reducing the Khmer Rouge to the status of a rump state in control of a small percentage of the country's territory in the remote northwest.

"War Communism" and the Radical Efforts to Transform Society

The concept of "war communism" originated during the Russian Revolution and refers to the initial phase of the revolution in which various sweeping, systemic ideological/political and economic transformations perceived as necessary by authoritarian communist leadership are abruptly implemented in order to consolidate and secure the communist's hold. In their classic analysis of the Soviet economic system, Gregory and Stuart regarded war communism as an "abortive attempt on the part of inexperienced leadership to attain full communism without going through any preparatory intermediate stages" and as a system in which the economy "operated without direction, either from the market or from planners."[1] Rather than undertaking the moderated course of a more long-term transition, the radical Bolshevik leaders, emboldened by their initial military triumph, naively believed that just as armed struggle had toppled the previous regime, the fabric of traditional society could also be conquered and replaced essentially by going to war with the old order–via direct frontal assault rather than a war of gradual attrition and that in so doing, they could accomplish in mere years what previous governments had been unable to achieve in generations.[2] Nikolai Bukharin, a prominent Bolshevik leader and economist who favored more measured approaches, described the war communism approach as a "*leap* into socialism."[3] For decades, scholars have debated whether the focus of war communism is primarily economic or political and whether the pursuit of the more radical, accelerated transformation was a manifestation of communist doctrine or the non-ideological result of practical necessity. For example, did it use temporary, expedient measures to stave off complete economic and/or regime collapse immediately following or during the course of a national crisis, such as the Bolshevik (Counter) Revolution, Cambodian Civil War, etc.[4] While wading into all of the nuances of the latter debates is beyond its scope, this work considers that the phenomenon of war communism provides an applicable lens through which the dystopian Khmer Rouge regime can also be viewed.

This revolutionary experiment in abrupt socio-economic transformation was by almost any standard an abject failure that created and exacerbated rather than ameliorated problems. Scholars regard the Bolsheviks' pursuit of war communism (e.g., hunger and starvation caused by the forcible seizure of food from the rural peasants) as one of the key defining characteristics of the Red Terror era of early Soviet history.[5] Evidence exists that the belligerent and radical approaches typical of war communism did more damage to the economy than had been done by years of war.[6] In 1921, the Bolsheviks abandoned this approach due to the economic chaos and political/social strife it was generating in favor of more gradual, moderated policies, such as a slower pace of conversion to collectivization and state-owned monopolies. Members of the inner circle of Khmer Rouge leadership (e.g., the Paris Group) surely would have been aware of the failed history of "war communism" in early Soviet history through their political training in France or the readings they undertook as a part of the indoctrination process. By the time they had seized power, Pol Pot and some members of the Khmer Rouge hierarchy should also have attained an even clearer understanding of

China's adaptation of the model via the deplorable failures of the Great Leap Forward that concluded in 1962. Accordingly, it is difficult to rationalize why Pol Pot and the Khmer Rouge not only embraced the concepts and policies associated with war communism but also implemented an even more radical, iconoclastic, and malevolent manifestation of the model than attempted in the USSR or China.

A key characteristic of war communism's political dimension is counterrevolution and the elimination of internal enemies who may potentially serve as obstacles to the new order, actions that revolutionaries may deem especially necessary if the goal of the ascendant regime is totalitarian control. The literature acknowledges concerns and prescribed actions for preventing or quelling counterrevolution as fundamental to communist doctrine, lying at the heart of Marx's vision of class warfare and underpinning Lenin's arguments in favor of violent revolution and authoritarian control (e.g., the dictatorship of the proletariat).[7] Much of the conduct the Khmer Rouge undertook upon seizing power can be regarded as preemptory actions designed to prevent organized resistance to the new order. Pol Pot and other leaders appeared as, or more, concerned with eliminating those they perceived as enemies as they were with economic transformation or other initiatives, first killing officials and supporters of the former regime then quickly transitioning to the large-scale disempowerment and murder of those they deemed class or ideological enemies.[8] The Khmer Rouge intended many of the actions they took to radically restructure Cambodia's economy or society to serve counterrevolutionary functions. For example, Fein asserts that "by destroying any independent economy, eliminating the marketplace and money, and by virtually annulling kinship solidarity and preventing new groups from forming, the Khmer Rouge destroyed any basis for opposition."[9]

Upon seizing power, the Khmer Rouge maintained the intense secrecy with which it had conducted its affairs during the Civil War. The leadership structure of the Khmer Rouge was a closely held secret, not even divulged to the rank-and-file membership let alone to outsiders. Upon coming to power, it did not overtly convey even the ideological alignment of the controlling political order. Pol Pot's Communist Party of Kampuchea initially hid behind the vague name of "Angkar," meaning *The Organization*. They neither publicly extolled Marx, Lenin, Stalin, or Mao until the latter's death in 1976 nor officially proclaimed the ruling party/government as communist until the following year.[10] Scholars have suggested that the Khmer Rouge and the actions it undertook were not purely ideological in nature but instead resulted from a combination of both radical communist ideology/thought (e.g., war communism) along with political and cultural influences of the Khmer population and the predilections of the regime itself, including nationalism and xenophobia.[11] Such an observation has some merit but is not unique to the Khmer Rouge, as every manifestation of political ideology—including communism—to some degree melds with national/cultural perspectives and the interpretations of the regime implementing the ideology. Nor were the ideological perspectives of the Khmer Rouge or the contrivances they would unleash upon Cambodia adopted suddenly upon or just prior to their ascendancy. Rather, Pol Pot and the movement's leadership had merely succeeded in keeping their ideological alignment and their plans obscured from a population steeped in tradition and unlikely ever to knowingly consent to a brutal, dystopian agenda rooted in communist doctrine.

Additional Ideological Influences

Khmer communists had long been factionalized into myriad competing camps: veterans and newcomers, radicals and those with more orthodox interpretations, pro- or anti-Vietnam, pro- or anti-China and between those inclined more toward authoritarianism, nationalism, and ethnocentrism versus those who hoped for some degree of consensus and inclusion within the movement as well as the future Cambodian state. The emergence of the Pol Pot faction as dominant entailed a long-term process of eliminating or sidelining competing factions, beginning initially with purging Khmer Issarak veterans and progressing to other establishment leaders of party factions, Khmer Viet Minh returnees and others who identified with Hanoi, and, ultimately, any voice within the party that dissented with Pol Pot's edicts and radical Maoist vision. The Khmer Rouge regime resulted not from compromise and melded perspectives among ideological strands within Cambodia's communist insurgency but from the militant, ill-conceived utopian vision of Pol Pot's Maoist faction and the reality that the latter cabal succeeded in eliminating competing voices to become the last faction standing. This is not to say that the Pol Pot cabal was something other than communist, as aspects of the conduct and precepts of Pol Pot's Khmer Rouge were grounded in various aspects of communist doctrine, including the early Bolshevik perspectives related to war communism examined at the start of this chapter.

In a 1978 interview with journalists from communist Yugoslavia, Pol Pot, when asked about the ideological foundations of the Khmer Rouge regime, stated that "We are building socialism without a model. We do not wish to copy anyone; we shall use the experience gained in the course of the liberation struggle."[12] Such claims that Khmer Rouge actions were somehow innovative and without precedent are largely without merit, as nearly all aspects of the dystopian regime were indeed based in part upon the foundations of prior communist doctrine or societal experiments. Parallels appear in the communist dogma and policies of Soviet, North Vietnamese, and Thai (insurgent) communist models.[13] As many scholars have noted, Pol Pot and the Khmer Rouge considered their revolution to be Maoist in nature and adopted many policies from China, including many of the radical experiments undertaken in the Great Leap Forward and Cultural Revolution.[14] Similar to China, when the attempts at radical socio-economic retooling failed in disastrous fashion, blame was deflected to imaginary traitors and saboteurs rather than the gross stupidity, incompetence, and naiveté of communist policymakers. Pol Pot and Ieng Sary publicly credited China with being an ideological model, and the Khmer Rouge adopted and took to extreme levels such Maoist precepts as the persecution of Buddhism and romanticizing of rural, agrarian life.[15] At one point, Pol Pot even termed the radical societal experiments the Khmer Rouge undertook as the "Super Great Leap Forward" (essentially, a slogan for the regime's first and only four-year plan from 1976 to 1980). The Khmer Rouge victory in Cambodia and emulation of many of Mao's policies may have been symbolically important for China in illustrating to its own people and the world that the Chinese ideological model of communism was viable.[16] In examining the support China rendered to the Khmer Rouge regime, Mertha concludes that Beijing's incentive was to facilitate a counterbalance to the rival, Soviet-aligned Vietnamese and out of ideological kinship with the realization that the Khmer Rouge sought to adopt many Maoist policies.[17]

For example, orthodox Marxist-Leninist doctrine does not call for the abandonment or destruction of cities, but Pol Pot found partial precedent

THE DYSTOPIAN KHMER ROUGE REGIME, 1975–1979

for this radical course of action in Mao's Great Leap Forward. Several years into China's communist regime, Mao saw that—among many other problems—support for communist policies was potentially weaker among urban populations/workers and also that agricultural quotas were not being met, despite "progress" with the collectivization of farmland.[18] Mao envisioned a solution to both problems in ordering large numbers (though not entire cities) of urban workers into the countryside to undertake farm labor. In his estimation, this strategy would aid in indoctrinating the city workers through political instruction and the egalitarian experience of peasant labor. Perhaps more importantly, he saw the allocation of additional labor as a means to potentially offset shortages of both farm machinery and farm workers—much of China's rural population had shifted to cities in recent years—and, in turn, increase food production. The agricultural dimension of the Great Leap Forward was ill-conceived, poorly planned, chaotically executed and led to such a decline in agricultural output that as many as 45 million citizens died of starvation or related causes in the span of just three years, making it perhaps the largest human-induced famine in world history.[19] While they may not have known the exact magnitude of the catastrophe and its death toll, the Khmer Rouge leadership could hardly deem it as anything other than a failure on a massive scale. The Khmer Rouge regime also mirrored other features of China's Great Leap Forward or Cultural Revolution, including the banning of religion and other cultural traditions, forced collectivization, and abolishment of privately owned land.

Numerous other examples exist of Khmer Rouge policies that were perhaps modeled in part on earlier precedents in other communist states. Pol Pot also witnessed the deployment of urban workers to assist in agricultural production in Yugoslavia, though in this case, workers were given adequate training and tools and were not enslaved or toiling under exceedingly adverse conditions. The Tito regime also encouraged marriage among the country's various groups in an effort to promote ethnic cohesion. Pol Pot and other members of the Paris Group would likely have been aware of this practice, though it is unknown if it factored into the common Khmer Rouge practice of forced pairings between Khmer Rouge fighters and non-communist Khmer peasants, which the regime saw as a means of political control rather than multicultural unification. The standardization of political purges common to China, North Korea, and the Stalinist regime also characterized the Khmer Rouge. Forced relocation of populations and/or the insertion of ethnicities comprising the national majority into the territory of "others" was practiced in the USSR (e.g., Ukraine, the Baltic States) and China (e.g., Tibet) before the Khmer Rouge undertook similar, though potentially even more brutal, practices. Commitments to seizing previously lost lands and settling territorial disputes occurred in the USSR and North Korea (e.g., Pyongyang's desire to "re-unify" the Peninsula under its control) before becoming a defining characteristic of Khmer Rouge foreign policy decades later. An argument could be made that, at least in early periods of Chinese and North Korean communism, the agrarian life and the peasant was heralded as the societal ideal, though not to the near complete exclusion of urban/industrial concerns as was the case under the Khmer Rouge. Pol Pot had previously visited North Korea and witnessed a level of secrecy and utter isolation from the rest of the world that was largely unparalleled even among communist states—until the Khmer Rouge replicated the approach during their own brief tenure. Despite an acrimonious relationship, many Khmer Rouge policies appear to have been modeled after Vietnamese communism, including the concept of "smashing" vestiges of bourgeois/western ideals or other enemies that came to be featured in Pol Pot's rhetoric.[20] Virtually no initiative embraced by the Khmer Rouge regime, including its most callous and brutal actions, was without at least some precedent in other communist states. What may have been unprecedented (though arguably, the Soviet Red Terror and Mao's Great Leap Forward and Cultural Revolution served as precursors in these respects as well) was the lack of foresight and planning, level of incompetence, radical degree/speed of implementation, and sociopathic disregard for human life, even by the standards of most authoritarian states.

Phnom Penh and the Forced Urban Exodus

Most refugees (the majority of the population) in Phnom Penh and other government-held cities at the time of the Republic's capitulation were abjectly poor. While not necessarily committed to or against any political ideology, they had been ill-treated by the deposed Republic. Many therefore may have been potentially amenable to complying with or even supporting the new regime were the latter even moderately responsive to their needs. Many among the civilian population, including refugees, were pleased to be rid of the former regime and fled to government-held cities to escape the fighting rather than in support of the Republic or opposition to the communists. However, the Khmer Rouge regarded even the homeless, hungry refugee populations with suspicion and disdain for having fled areas that had been "liberated" by the communists. The Khmer Rouge regarded city residents even among the worker/peasant class with similar contempt for having remained in government-controlled areas. Like many extremist movements, the Khmer Rouge needed enemies in order to galvanize their base of supporters toward the goal of revolutionary struggle. With the collapse of the Cambodian government—the target of the communists' hatred for many years—the civilian population, including even impoverished peasants with no link to the Lon Nol regime or anti-communist activism, became the focus of Khmer Rouge revolutionary terror and the victims of the radicals' ill-conceived societal experimentation.

The decision to drive the populations out of Phenom Penh and other cities appears to have been finalized in early 1975, though other radical future policies, such as the eradication of the traditional economy, may have first been discussed among senior leaders at the mid-1974 party meeting—such intentions had only been known to a handful of senior leaders closest to Pol Pot.[21] Shortly before the fall of Phnom Penh, at a meeting of senior party leaders, many such plans were divulged to high-ranking Khmer Rouge leaders, though not yet made public. Hou Youn, a cofounder and senior leader of the Communist Party of Kampuchea and member of the FUNK Central Committee who had previously advocated a middle path between communism and capitalism, expressed misgivings about the proposed forced removal of urban populations, abolishment of the traditional economy, and other radical plans that Pol Pot revealed at the conference.[22] In an early example of the internal purges that later became characteristic of the regime, Hou Youn disappeared after voicing such objections and is thought to have been executed by the Khmer Rouge or, alternatively, to have died in a prison or "re-education" camp after they seized power.

On April 17, following the departure of the acting Head of State and amid radio broadcasts in which remaining officials of the deposed Republic and its military called upon what military units were left to surrender and for civilians to remain calm, a chaotic situation unfolded in Phnom Penh. While waning pockets of resistance remained, exhausted Khmer Rouge units began to penetrate the city from all directions. Some inhabitants welcomed their arrival with cheers, including an odd group hastily organized by General Lon Non, former Interior Minister and brother of former Prime Minister Lon Nol. The ostensibly nationalist group self-described as the "Monatio" (*National Movement*) and composed primarily of students, imitated the dress of the Khmer Rouge, drove through the city waiving Khmer Rouge banners, encouraged the surrender of remaining police and military forces, and occupied certain buildings, including the Ministry of Information, apparently out of a misguided notion that they could effect a power sharing arrangement with the communists. The Khmer Rouge tolerated the group for a few hours before taking them into custody and executing them along with their leader Lon Non, whose name—and those of most other senior government officials/supporters—had been placed on lists of those persons Sihanouk and the Khmer Rouge had ordered killed once the city fell.

Many of the city's former defenders, exhausted and demoralized, were at least relieved the fighting ended and did not appear to understand the horrific fate that awaited most of them. Many Cambodians in Phnom Penh and other capitulating cities, even including those from privileged classes, may have been lulled into a false sense of reassurance and optimism due to Sihanouk's having been portrayed as a leader of the rebellion as well as the FUNK's disingenuous promises of civil liberties, leniency, and reconciliation in victory, the respect of personal property, and permission to emigrate for those who wished to do so.[23] Such misplaced trust and optimism even permeated the ranks of leadership, the reason many government officials opted to remain. An account by the Republic's last Minister of Information who ultimately survived the war described initial attitudes of resigned relief that characterized some of the city's defenders at the time of capitulation:

> In front of the Prime Minister's house, soldiers and civilians, young and old, marched northward. They were cheering, jostling one another. Soldiers and sailors and airmen tore off their insignia and threw hats and scarves into the air. Jeeps loaded with civilians and students drove to and fro in a mad pace. Armored personnel cars paraded from Independence Monument to Wat Phnom. Soldiers tore the magazines from their tommy guns, shouting, "Peace! Peace!"[24]

THE DYSTOPIAN KHMER ROUGE REGIME, 1975–1979

Incessant, deceitful, and disarming Khmer Rouge propaganda had in part facilitated such attitudes by frequently referencing Sihanouk and such familiar Cambodian cultural traditions as tenets of Buddhism. Upon seizing control of the Information Ministry and radio airwaves, the new communist regime called upon all leaders of the former government to convene at the Ministry "to discuss ways of restoring order to the capital," and the 50 or so Republican officials and bureaucrats who complied—and many of their aids and family members—were promptly executed.[25] Cormack described the latter ruse and other initial efforts to illicit cooperation as "the first in a series of brilliantly orchestrated lies which the Khmer Rouge set in motion to secure their hold on a people psychologically ready to eat out of their hands."[26] While some bureaucrats and other functionaries of the deposed Republic likely surrendered hoping for leniency, senior figures, including former Prime Minister Long Boret and Sihanouk's cousin and political rival Prince Sirik Matak, would have known their names had been added to lists of those who were to be executed, as the FUNK had publicly announced such lists; and accordingly, many senior officials and other Cambodians fearful of the communists initially sought refuge in the French Embassy. Just after seizing the capitol, however, the Khmer Rouge demanded the Embassy expel all of the approximately 600 Cambodian nationals who attempted to take refuge at the site, all of whom were arrested and presumably executed.

While white flags continued to be raised over buildings across the city, scattered pockets of defenders fought to the death, even after having run out of ammunition in some cases, as they may have possessed a more lucid understanding of the militant, sadistic nature of the Khmer Rouge and what fates would be meted out to government forces/supporters who surrendered. Many also chose suicide as their final act, as did Admiral Vong Sarendy, Chief of Naval Forces, who shot himself as his headquarters—one of the last remaining government strongholds in the city—was overrun by communist insurgents. As more Khmer Rouge forces poured into the capitol, they disarmed troops and police, forced them to remove their uniforms, and, in a practice common to many communist revolutions around the world, forced them to write accounts of what roles they played in the former government—in effect, written confessions of their complicity in supporting the previous regime. Soldiers and police were then marched to the Olympic Stadium where they would be executed. Most higher ranking government officials, after writing their "biographies," were executed at the Phnom Penh Sporting Club, often by beheading on the tennis courts, though conflicting accounts exist of how certain former leaders were put to death.

Khmer Rouge fighters were often teenagers or even pre-teen adolescents and commonly recruited or conscripted from the ranks of abjectly poor, rural, uneducated youth, a demographic strata that Pol Pot viewed as malleable and useful instruments of his revolution. Many of the fighters had been raised in such deprived conditions and remote locations that, prior to the Civil War, they had never learned to read or write; never used money; and had never seen any form of technology, such as electronics, indoor plumbing, or automobiles; but had lived the same subsistence lifestyle experienced by their ancestors for centuries. Numerous accounts exist of the young Khmer Rouge soldiers being bewildered by the things they began to experience upon entering into the cities. Some drank from toilet bowls thinking they were what functioned as wells in the city or ingested cans of motor oil or toothpaste thinking the latter food items.[27] The mere appearance of the Khmer Rouge fighters as they continued to enter Phnom Penh was sobering to many of the city-dwellers who may have previously deluded themselves into thinking the communists would be innocuous. Witness accounts illustrate that the brief initial relief some of the city's population felt at the cessation of fighting quickly transitioned to dread as the dirty and disheveled Khmer Rouge soldiers were observed to be "ill at ease…they never smiled at all or even looked like Cambodians…their faces were worn and expressionless, speaking not a single word and surrounded by deathly silence as they marched along the boulevards."[28] Many of the guerillas would have already harbored distrust, animosity, and even anger toward Cambodia's middle/upper classes and, having been removed by the Khmer Rouge from any stabilizing family influences, were receptive to the radical political indoctrination of the communists related to class warfare—including the group's dogma that city-dwellers were corrupt and decadent and had long exploited and oppressed the peasants. Kenneth Quinn, former Ambassador to Cambodia, provides a concise observation of the nature of the revolutionaries and why they would unleash such dystopian misery upon the population:

> A small group of alienated intellectuals, enraged by their perception of a totally corrupt society imbued with a Maoist plan to create a pure

socialist order in the shortest possible time, recruited extremely young, poor and envious cadres, instructed them in harsh and brutal methods learned from Stalinist mentors and used them to destroy physically the cultural underpinnings of the Khmer civilization and to impose a new society through purges, executions, and violence.[29]

Phnom Penh was divided into five distinct sectors with each temporarily under the autonomous control of a different Khmer Rouge commander and occupation force. Initially, communication problems and the general chaos of the city's fall led to some degree of confusion, inconsistency of policy/actions, and even conflict among the various Khmer Rouge forces/sectors.[30] Depending on the sector, the degree of brutality and the capricious nature of treatment being meted out across the capital on the first day varied somewhat, as did orders to evacuate. By midday on April 17, the first day of Khmer Rouge occupation, much of the city's population was driven out forcibly, told the evacuation was only temporary and that they would be able to return after three days. Evacuation orders were issued in the northern sector the following morning, with residents only given 10 minutes' notice to gather provisions for what they were told would be a two-day period of exile from the city.[31] Justifications cited for the "temporary" evacuation depended on which Khmer Rouge units civilians encountered and varied between the need to purge the cities of the former government's counter-revolutionary forces who were allegedly threatening an urban insurgency, and/or that the Americans were planning immanent and massive air strikes against Phnom Penh and other Cambodian cities. Once the city's inhabitants were driven out, one of the radical regime's first actions was to destroy houses of worship (e.g., the main Catholic Cathedral) and other specific buildings including the Central Bank that the Khmer Rouge regarded as symbols of western traits, such as "reactionary religion" or "decadent capitalism."[32]

Scarce academic scholarship exists related to the conditions during the forced evacuations. However, much is known from the accounts of those who survived the ordeal. Callously, even hospitals were not spared evacuation orders, with many patients still in their wheeled hospital beds being pushed along roads by relatives and others limping or crawling the best they could manage despite fresh surgical incisions or other serious injuries/conditions.[33] As many as 20,000 hospital patients in various states of infirmity were forcibly ejected into the streets on the first day, with many lying helpless and ultimately being shot or otherwise dying in the same spot in which they had been dumped by the Khmer Rouge outside the hospital grounds.[34] During this forced evacuation, civilians faced confusion; in some cases, on the first day, chaos was sewn by newly arrived Khmer Rouge units unaware of the evacuation orders that, in turn, issued conflicting orders to civilians to stay in their homes. Those civilians who initially resisted orders to leave the city or otherwise failed to carry out orders of Khmer Rouge fighters were threatened, beaten, or summarily executed. Short notes that the "anger of the young men who had emerged from the jungle was directed at those who had been living in comfort…(and) directed against those who were better educated or better off."[35]

The treatment meted out to those jamming the roads out of the capital also varied widely depending on the sector and which Khmer Rouge units they encountered. For example, in some instances, very basic medical attention may have been allowed or orders even given to local populations along the routes to share food or other resources with those in need among the streams of evacuees. In other areas, however, the streams of urban refugees were met with indifference at best and were commonly brutally treated and subjected to summary execution for falling behind, refusing to relinquish their car or motorbike, or committing other often slight infractions. Looting by Khmer Rouge soldiers was also common, with fighters taking the contents of abandoned homes and buildings as well as items—such as motorbikes and watches—at gunpoint directly from displaced civilians along the crowded routes.[36] Consistent along all routes leading out of the city were the numerous checkpoints the Khmer Rouge established to filter evacuees. These checkpoints enabled the identification of those whose skills might be needed by the new regime; they also enabled the identification and subsequent execution of former soldiers, police, or functionaries (and family members) of the deposed government who had escaped capture when the previous government fell.

Reflecting the xenophobia of the Khmer Rouge, as well as their desire to isolate the new regime from international scrutiny as it undertook genocide and other crimes, all foreigners were rounded up throughout the city. Journalists, businessmen, missionaries, and others were ordered to gather at the French Embassy for eventual expulsion by arduous truck convoys to the Thai border some 250 miles away. The Khmer Rouge refused repeated requests by the French government to evacuate the 600 or so foreign nationals—many of whom were elderly or had medical conditions—by aircraft on standby in neighboring Laos. They refused despite the fact that Prince Sihanouk, as the new regime's chief diplomat, had apparently consented to the evacuation by air, a refusal that provided one of many telling indications of how little influence/control Sihanouk possessed in the new communist order. The roundup of all foreigners even applied to the diplomatic personnel in Phnom Penh's remaining embassies, including those of the Soviet Embassy, which had been fired upon by Khmer Rouge fighters at one point. Instead of maintaining conventional bilateral diplomatic ties with foreign governments, the Khmer Rouge pursued a path of near total diplomatic isolation. They isolated themselves even from communist states and some western governments such as France that were willing to formally recognize the new regime and exchange diplomats/embassies. Little more than a figurehead imparting some sense of legitimacy, Sihanouk essentially was used as a roving ambassador and the international face of the regime (see Chapter 4, pages 21 and 27).

Justifications the Khmer Rouge provided for the forced expulsions of urban populations were essentially three-fold; they were necessary (1) as a security measure aimed at preventing counter-revolution and organized resistance in the cities, (2) to allocate additional temporary labor to increase agricultural production and prevent mass hunger/starvation and as a prerequisite to the latter, and (3) to rebalance the country's population in the aftermath of the rural exodus to the cities during the Civil War. In April 1975 when the Khmer Rouge seized power, the population of Cambodia was estimated to have been 7.3 million.[37] The first justification needs to take into consideration that the Khmer Rouge likely had no more than 68,000 troops—many of whom were conscripted child soldiers rather than disciplined adult revolutionaries—and had only around 14,000 party members. The prospect of trying to maintain control over the capital and country with such an imbalance of numbers may have been initially intimidating to the revolutionaries who, in turn, coldly calculated that forcibly driving the population into the countryside and disrupting any existing social order might make Cambodia's population easier to control until the communists could bolster their numbers and formulate a path to governing.[38] Specifically, expelling the population from the cities would prevent the Khmer Rouge from becoming bogged down in urban guerilla counterinsurgency operations should organized resistance cells form in opposition to their rule.

However, given the depleted state of ammunition (see Table 2), seizing the surrendering government forces' arms, the reality that most government forces were interred or executed within days/weeks of the Khmer Rouge takeover, and the previous unwillingness of other citizens to take up arms in defense of the former government against the Khmer Rouge, it seems highly improbable that any anti-communist elements could organize anything resembling an effective, coordinated resistance campaign. The emergence of organized resistance would also have been deterred by the climate of fear and intimidation the communist regime cultivated in its first phase. Further, since the U.S. and other western nations had opted against continued support for the Republic in its waning days, it seems unlikely that external support would have been forthcoming had any anti-communist resistance cells miraculously organized following the fall of the capital. The argument that emptying Cambodia's cities was perceived by the Khmer Rouge as a necessary security strategy to prevent organized rebellion (urban guerilla warfare) is implausible; indeed, it mistakenly assumes the capacity for rational analysis and decision-making on the part of the Pol Pot regime and that it was not inclined to paranoia. Whether organized internal resistance to their continued rule would have materialized or not, the brutal actions of the Khmer Rouge, including the forced redistribution of population and associated destruction of the existing social order, did have the psychological effect of intimidating and cowing survivors of the forced exodus, as noted in a declassified intelligence report.

> Psychological as well as material factors, such as the feeling of rootlessness, separation from other family members, newly found poverty and the fear of cruel punishments have effectively prevented former city-dwellers from resisting the totalitarian rule of the new regime. Indications are that despite the relatively small number of guards assigned to the individual agricultural collectives–equivalent (in population) to the former villages–resistance to the Khmer Communist administration has manifested itself mainly in the form of attempted escape rather than in outbreaks of physical hostility against the regime.[39]

THE DYSTOPIAN KHMER ROUGE REGIME, 1975–1979

Regarding the second justification, it also strains credulity to argue that the mass expulsions from the cities were primarily undertaken (or justifiable) via any legitimate plan or concern to utilize the population as agricultural labor in order to combat food shortages. Aside from vague notions of using urban workers as supplemental agrarian labor that may have been implanted into Pol Pot's mind from his observations in Yugoslavia and China, no evidence exists of any detailed, logical plans having been formulated concerning how the urban populations would be trained, equipped, or organized to engage in productive agricultural work. The elderly, children, and the infirm, such as the patients driven from hospitals, would have been as ineffective at agricultural labor as they would have been as elements of an urban anti-communist insurgency, thus undermining the Khmer Rouge justifications for expelling entire urban populations en masse. The indiscriminate nature of the forced exodus of entire cities in death marches conveys not just a callous disregard for human life but also a likely deliberate, calculated effort to quickly cull many of those the Khmer Rouge deemed as non-producers, those who were physically the weakest and so unlikely to contribute much or anything by way of their labor, regardless of their politics. In addition to the physical inability of many of the captives to perform the difficult manual labor, the near complete absence of agricultural training or competent supervision for assigned tasks as well as the widespread lack of agricultural implements aside from captives' own hands or the crudest of improvised tools, such as sticks or rocks for digging, further challenges the portrayal of the cities' forced evacuations as a measure thoughtfully intended to address the decline in agricultural output.

Food reserves in Phnom Penh had indeed been largely exhausted by the time the city had fallen (see Table 2). However, the new regime was already receiving increased food aid from Vietnam, and other communist countries quickly increased shipments of food and other supplies—most notably China, which shipped nearly 19,000 metric tons of rice along with large volumes of fuel and other supplies in July alone and continued to support the Khmer Rouge regime with large-scale shipments of aid, including food, throughout Pol Pot's tenure.[40] Massive amounts of emergency food aid and other humanitarian assistance would have almost certainly been provided by international organizations and western nations had they been allowed by the regime, but such a scenario ran afoul of the militant Khmer Rouge commitment to autarky. For example, the International Committee of the Red Cross (ICRC) and the United Nations Children's Fund (UNICEF) were the last international relief organizations remaining in Cambodia at the time of the Khmer Rouge takeover in April 1975, and both initially hoped to continue their relief missions. UNICEF airlifted large volumes of supplies just prior to the fall of the capital and had stocked 130 tons of powdered milk and 15 tons of protein supplements as well as medical equipment and other supplies and vainly sought Khmer Rouge permission to fly in supplies after their victory.[41] Following Sihanouk's removal in 1970 and the subsequent escalation of the Civil War, the ICRC, in conjunction with the International Federation of Red Cross and Red Crescent Societies and the national Red Cross Societies of around 20 countries, undertook emergency operations in Cambodia to assist the hundreds of thousands of displaced people with food, medicine, and other relief.[42] Following the Khmer Rouge victory, representatives of the Red Cross indicated planes were standing by to airlift medical supplies and other aid, but permission to enter Cambodian airspace was not forthcoming.[43] Upon seizing power, the Khmer Rouge banned the presence of international relief organizations, ejected representatives of UNICEF and the Red Cross, and abolished the Cambodian Red Cross in addition to refusing offers of humanitarian aid from other nations. Such actions clearly convey that Pol Pot and the leadership of the Khmer Rouge revolution had no interest in saving the lives or ameliorating the suffering of the Cambodian people.

Concerning the third justification—inexorably linked with the second—prior to the Civil War, the majority of Cambodia's population had been rural/agrarian and years of fighting and the refugees' flight to cities had predictably disrupted agricultural production, with much former farmland remaining disused. The third justification, that is, restoring the rural-to-urban population balance, was publicly stated by the Khmer Rouge regime as the necessary first step in reversing declines in agricultural output. For example, Cambodia had reached a record production of 2,479,000 metric tons of milled rice in 1970, with output dropping to 648,000 tons by 1975.[44] However, rather than selectively relocating those refugees who had previously evacuated from agricultural areas and other urban residents who may have otherwise had prior agricultural experience, the radical new regime forcibly expelled the entire urban population without regard to background or ability. The actions were not a restoration of a demographic balance but a radical experiment in turning the entire country into a collection of poorly planned/organized agricultural collectives subjected to slave labor. The experiment in totalitarian control proved to be an abject failure, with national rice yields dropping further to an estimated 600,000 metric tons in both 1977 and 1978, the final two years in which the regime was in power.[45] Due to declines in domestic food production, exports (except black market activities) of many Cambodian agricultural products—including the primary staple, rice—had been halted by the Lon Nol government throughout much of the Civil War in the early 1970s. However, under the Khmer Rouge, despite further declines in domestic food production and the regime's use of the excuse that urban expulsions and population "redistribution" were undertaken to ward off starvation, Pol Pot resumed large-scale food exports while the Cambodian people starved; for example, 20,000 metric tons of rice was estimated to have been exported in 1976 and 19,000 tons the following year.[46] Potentially, more food had been available to the general population of Cambodia in the last year of the Republic—even amid the intense fighting of the Civil War disrupting agriculture—than was available during the first year of the inept and callous communist regime, which forcibly gathered much of what little rice had actually been produced to feed its military, place in storage, or export in order to finance Pol Pot's military or his naive vision of rapid, radical economic reform.[47]

Such actions undermine any claims by the regime or communist apologists that the forced expulsion from the cities and efforts to "rebalance" the rural-urban population were undertaken to prevent hunger or to support any other justifiable goal. The death marches from the cities and the establishment of myriad agricultural collectives and forced labor camps (e.g., to dig irrigation canals) throughout the country, combined with ongoing filtering and forced relocations among the camps, were meant to in part accomplish the same objective behind the mass executions of former soldiers, police, and officials/supporters of the Republican government: the elimination or at least punishment of potential enemies of the new Khmer Rouge order. For example, in 1975 and again in 1978, hundreds of thousands of people, mostly among categories targeted for persecution rather than experienced farmers, were relocated to sparsely settled and barely habitable areas of the country, where many perished.[48] The communists could not (at least quickly/initially) murder all those who did not embrace their radical agenda, but the unfathomable cruelty with which their radical experiment was carried out conveyed a desire to *punish* urban populations, reviled by the Khmer Rouge as traitors and enemies in terms of class and ideology.[49] Khmer Rouge hatred toward their enemies within Cambodian society was likely intensified by years of hardship and struggle throughout the Civil War. In turn, the communists likely sought to inflict extreme hardships in living and working conditions, such as imposing 12–18 hour workdays while providing starvation rations, on the Cambodians who failed to support the insurgency—in addition to attempting to inculcate the population into Pol Pot's naive, unattainable vision of an agrarian utopia.[50] If other purposes were also intended by the forced relocations into agricultural collectives, such objectives were coupled with the goals of punishing or eliminating large swaths of Cambodian society and terrorizing the population into acquiescing to the new regime's radical order.

Iconoclasty and Societal Destruction

Upon seizing power, the Khmer Rouge embarked on what was likely the most radical, dystopian attempt to completely remake every facet of society ever undertaken in modern human history. Their goal was not merely to eradicate potential enemies among the country's people but to destroy nearly all vestiges of former Cambodian life. Reflecting the abrupt transition to the new Khmer Rouge vision of society and Cambodia's rebirth as well as a repudiation of the country's past, the regime abolished the traditional calendar and proclaimed April 17, 1975 as the first day of "Year Zero." As stated earlier, Pol Pot and many other Khmer Rouge leaders studied in France and read French history; they adapted the idea of discarding the past with this new calendar from similar actions French Revolutionaries undertook following the overthrow of their country's monarchy. Much hypocrisy was present in Khmer Rouge leadership: they were ethnocentric and xenophobic, yet most were among the privileged few in Cambodia who had lived/studied abroad—where they absorbed many foreign ideas related to revolution and otherwise; they were anti-religion, despite many, including Pol Pot, having received religious teachings from an early age and even having attended religious schools (e.g., as a young man, Pol Pot spent a year at a Buddhist monastery and later attended a French

Catholic elementary school); they were anti-establishment when most were from elite backgrounds and benefited from having been members of the traditional establishment in some capacity—as had their families; and they espoused hatred of intellectuals and education, yet most were well-read, multilingual, and had formal, post-secondary educations. Such ironies aside, the Khmer Rouge regime would take a radical course of iconoclastic reforms in their pursuit of a new utopian society, and as stated earlier, they modeled most of these reforms in part upon precepts or policies (many failed) of other communist states.

The economy was to be an agrarian autarky, with nearly the entire civilian population tasked with farming or engineering projects, such as building dams and digging irrigation ditches/canals by hand, in support of that objective. The regime sought to gradually industrialize and brought in advisors and technicians from China and North Korea to assist in that goal, but any drive toward industrialization would need to be financed almost entirely by agricultural surplus, which was established as a top priority, even as the population starved.[51] Import substitution measures were also implemented to not only facilitate Pol Pot's vision of self-reliance but also redirect scarce revenue toward acquiring industrial equipment and other manufactured items that could not be produced in Cambodia.[52] Currency was abolished, and the country's enslaved population would be "paid" for their forced labor in modest (often starvation-level) food rations based upon the type and intensity of labor performed. Capitalism was eliminated in favor of a centrally planned economy controlled by the regime, though little evidence exists of logical, detailed planning or anything resembling competent economic management on the part of the Khmer Rouge. No markets or private businesses remained, and private property/homes and virtually all other personal possessions were banned. Those who resisted discarding personal items, even possessions as innocuous as books, clocks, photographs, housewares, or clothing of any higher quality than work-clothes, were subject to being deemed as enemies by the Khmer Rouge, accused of clinging to outmoded, decadent capitalist ways.[53]

The traditional economy and its manifestations, such as material possessions, were not the only targets of the revolutionaries; the social structure of Cambodia was slated for destruction as well. The bizarre, forced exodus of urban populations into agrarian labor camps and the near abandonment of the cities remains largely without precedent in human history. Though Phnom Penh and other cities were not completely depopulated, only a select few were permitted to remain in cities: high ranking government or party officials/functionaries, security forces, and those with certain technical skills needed by the regime. The Khmer Rouge regarded capitalism, modernity, foreign influences, and urban lifestyles as moral contaminants to be cleansed by forcing nearly the entire population into agrarian servitude.[54] However, the communist regime did not restrict its societal experimentation to "urbicide;" it also attempted to wipe out the traditional ways of rural peasant life by eliminating kinship networks and economic and cultural traditions.

All aspects of Khmer culture and society were subject to assault, including such fundamental cornerstones as religion. Over 90% of the Cambodian population was Buddhist, and the religion had served as a defining cultural tradition among ethnic Khmer and as the official state religion since the 13th century. The Pol Pot regime nevertheless regarded Buddhism as the "cause of our country's weakness" and closed all temples and destroyed or defaced most Buddhist statuary and temples, with those temples left standing re-tasked to some other purpose intended to defile them, for example, as livestock sheds, torture sites, etc.[55] Despite a guarantee of religious freedom within the Khmer Rouge "constitution," the observance of any religious faith was prohibited, and even engaging in private prayer could lead to severe punishment. By the end of the Khmer Rouge regime in early 1979, as few as 100 Buddhist monks remained alive in the country, with as many as 25,000 out of a total of some 65,000 monks and initiates—around 1% of the pre-genocide national population—having been executed outright and thousands of others killed by starvation, overwork, or disease, with most survivors having fled abroad.[56] Of the 2,680 monks and novices from the country's eight largest monasteries, only 70 are known to have survived.[57]

Cambodian educational institutions were targeted for destruction as well. As of 1969, before the intensification of the Civil War, the country had 5,275 elementary schools, 146 secondary schools and nine post-secondary institutions.[58] The Khmer Rouge not only closed all schools but also destroyed 90% of the school buildings; emptied their libraries—burning books and other contents—destroyed nearly all other educational resources, including laboratory equipment; and repurposed the few surviving buildings for political training, prisons, or other regime-related functions.[59] Small numbers of elementary schools were operated in the latter part of Khmer Rouge rule, focused primarily upon agricultural training.[60] Reflecting the intense degree to which education was targeted by the revolutionaries, between 75 and 90% of those who had been teachers or professors, 96% of college/university students, and up to 67% of secondary students are estimated to have died during the brief tenure of the Khmer Rouge.[61]

The totalitarian regime sought to eradicate virtually every vestige of traditional life, including such customs as holidays, material culture, and even the family unit, the most basic thread in the fabric of human society, also came under assault. In addition to the widespread loss of family members to execution or imprisonment, the revolutionaries invested deliberate effort into altering family structure by separating family members, often through frequent forced relocations among work camps or forced marriage, for example, of non-communists to Khmer Rouge fighters. Forced removal and political brainwashing of children and other state-sanctioned efforts aimed at altering family structure became the state-mandated norm, and children were not allowed to cry or display emotion when separated from family members under threat of beatings or worse. As an example of the regime's experimentation with familial/social fabric, by around 1976–77 and in Orwellian fashion, children older than six were removed from their families to live in group settings designed to facilitate indoctrination by the Khmer Rouge.[62] This indoctrination of the young intended not just to train children ideologically and in regime loyalty but to eliminate all their empathy for other human beings, to train them to spy on parents and other family members and report any transgression, even if that led to the family member's execution; ultimately, the children were being inculcated to function as obedient soldiers, executioners, and torturers for the Khmer Rouge.[63]

Endnotes

1. Paul Gregory and Robert Stuart, *Soviet Economic Structure and Performance* (New York: Harper and Row, 1974) pp. 43-49.
2. Bertrand Patenaude, "Peasants Into Russians: The Utopian Essence of War Communism," *The Russian Review* 54(4) 1995, pp. 552-570.
3. Lars Lih, "Bukharin's 'Illusion': War Communism and the Meaning of N.E.P.," *Russian History* 27(4) 2000, pp. 417-459.
4. For example, Roberts asserts that war communism and its radical approaches were a product of communist doctrine, Dobb contends that rather than ideology/doctrine, the phenomenon reflected desperate, temporary measures to address crises, and Carr argues war communism reflects a combination of both ideology and temporary expediency: Edward Carr, *A History of Soviet Russia: The Bolshevik Revolution, 1917–1923* (New York: W.W. Norton, 1985); Maurice Dobb, *Soviet Economic Development Since 1917* (London: Routledge, 2012); Paul Roberts, "War Communism: A Re-Examination," *Slavic Review* (29)2 1970, pp. 238-261.
5. Stephane Courtois, Nicolas Werth, Jean-Louis Panne, Andrej Paczkowski, Karel Bartosek, and Jean-Louis Margolin, *The Black Book of Communism: Crimes, Terror and Repression* (Cambridge, MA: Harvard University Press, 2001).
6. Andrei Markevich and Mark Harrison, "Great War, Civil War and Recovery: Russia's National Income, 1913 to 1928," *The Journal of Economic History* 71(3) 2011, pp. 672-703.
7. Lewis Brownstein, "The Concept of Counterrevolution in Marxian Theory," *Studies in Soviet Thought* 22(3) 1981, pp. 175-192.
8. Elizabeth Becker, *When the War was Over: Cambodia and the Khmer Rouge Revolution* (New York: Public Affairs, 1998).
9. Helen Fein, "Revolutionary and Antirevolutionary Genocides: A Comparison of State Murders in Democratic Kampuchea, 1975 to 1979, and in Indonesia, 1965 to 1966," *Comparative Studies in Society and History* 35(4) 1993, pp. 796-823.
10. Ben Kiernan, in "External and Indigenous Sources of Khmer Rouge Ideology" in *The Third Indochina War: Conflict between China, Vietnam and Cambodia, 1972–1979*, O. Westad and S. Quinn-Judge eds. (New York: Routledge, 2006), 187–206

11. Kiernan, 2006.
12. Eva Mysliwiec, *Punishing the Poor: The International Isolation of Kampuchea* (Oxford, UK: Oxfam, 1988), p. 48.
13. Alexander Hinton, *Why Did They Kill: Cambodia in the Shadow of Genocide* (Berkeley, CA: University of California Press, 2005).
14. Kiernan, 2006; Yinghong Cheng, *Creating the New Man: From Enlightenment Ideals to Socialist Realities* (University of Hawai'i Press, 2009).
15. Ian Harris, *Buddhism in a Dark Age: Cambodian Monks Under Pol Pot* (Honolulu, HI: University of Hawaii Press, 2013).
16. Chenyi Wang, "The Chinese Communist Party's Relationship with the Khmer Rouge in the 1970s: An Ideological Victory and a Strategic Failure," Working Paper 88, Cold War International History Project. Washington, DC: Wilson Center, December 2018.
17. Andrew Mertha, *Brothers In Arms: Chinese Aid to the Khmer Rouge* (Ithaca, NY: Cornell University Press, 2019).
18. Jean-luc Domenach and Mark Selden, *The Origins of The Great Leap Forward: The Case Of One Chinese Province* (New York: Taylor and Francis, 2019).
19. Xin Meng, Nancy Qian, and Pierre Yared, "The Institutional Causes of China's Great Famine, 1959-61," *Review of Economic Studies* 82(4) 2015, pp. 1568-1611.
20. Stephen Heder, *Cambodian Communism and the Vietnamese Model: Volume I – Imitation and Independence, 1930-1975* (Bangkok, Thailand: White Lotus, 2004); Mai Elliot, *RAND in Southeast Asia: A History of the Vietnam War Era* (Santa Monica, CA: RAND Corporation 2010); David Chandler and Ben Kiernan, "Decisions of the Central Committee on a Variety of Questions," in David Chandler, Ben Kiernan and Chanthou Boua eds. *Pol Pot Plans the Future: Confidential Leadership Documents from Democratic Kampuchea, 1976-1977* (New Haven, CT: Yale Center for International and Area Studies, 1988).
21. David Chandler, *The Tragedy of Cambodian History: Politics, War and Revolution Since 1945* (New Haven, CT: Yale University Press, 1991); Ben Keirnan, *How Pol Pot Came to Power: Colonialism, Nationalism, and Communism in Cambodia, 1930-1975* (New Haven, CT: Yale

University Press 2004).
22. Kenton Clymer, *The United States and Cambodia, 1969-2000: A Troubled Relationship* (New York: Routledge, 2013).
23. Phillip Short, *Pol Pot: Anatomy of a Nightmare* (New York: Henry Holt, 2005).
24. Chhang Song, "The Final Hours of the Khmer Republic", *The Khmer Times*. April 16, 2015.
25. Don Cormack, *Killing Fields, Living Fields: An Unfinished Portrait of the Cambodian Church – The Church That Would Not Die* (Grand Rapids, Michigan: Monarch Books, 2001), p. 165-166.
26. Cormack, 2001 p. 165.
27. Short, 2005.
28. Short, 2005 p. 268.
29. Kenneth Quinn, "Pattern and Scope of Violence," In *Cambodia, 1975-1978: Rendezvous with Death*, Karl Jackson ed. (Princeton, NJ: Princeton University Press, 1989).
30. Michael Vickery, *Cambodia, 1975-1982 – 2nd Edition* (Chaing Mai, Thailand: Silkworm, 1999).
31. Vickery 1999.
32. Benny Widyono, *Dancing in the Shadows: Sihanouk, the Khmer Rouge, and the United Nations in Cambodia* (New York: Rowman and Littlefield, 2008), p. 9.
33. Ben Kiernan, *The Pol Pot Regime: Race, Power, and Genocide in Cambodia under the Khmer Rouge, 1975-79* (New Haven, CT: Yale University Press, 1996).
34. Cormack, 2001.
35. Short, 2005 p. 270.
36. Cormack, 2001.
37. Russell Ross, *Cambodia: A Country Study* (Washington DC: Federal Research Division – Library of Congress, 1990).
38. Becker 1998.
39. Central Intelligence Agency, "Research Study – Democratic Cambodia: An Experiment in Radicalism," (December 1976). Accessed April 10, 2022.
40. Margaret Slocomb, *An Economic History of Cambodia in the Twentieth Century* (Honolulu, HI: University of Hawaii Press, 2010); Mertha 2019.

41. David Andelman, "French Express Concern on Embassy in Cambodia," *New York Times*. April 27, 1975, p. 28.
42. International Committee of the Red Cross, https://www.icrc.org/en/doc/resources/documents/misc/cambodia-history-091209.htm; https://www.icrc.org/en/doc/resources/documents/interview/cambodia-interview-011209.htm. Accessed May 30, 2022.
43. Andelman, 1975.
44. U.S. Department of Agriculture (a) data as cited in: https://www.indexmundi.com/agriculture/?country=kh&commodity=milled-rice&graph=production. Accessed June 5, 2022.
45. USDA (a)
46. U.S. Department of Agriculture (b) data as cited in: https://www.indexmundi.com/agriculture/?country=kh&commodity=milled-rice&graph=exports. Accessed June 6, 2022.
47. David Chandler, *A History of Cambodia* (Boulder, CO: Westview Press, 2008); Zachary Abuza, "The Khmer Rouge Quest for Economic Independence." *Asian Survey* 33(10) 1993, pp. 1010-1021.
48. Hinton, 2005.
49. Marie Alexandrine Martin, *Cambodia: A Shattered Society* (Berkeley, CA: University of California Press, 1994).
50. Martin, 1994; CIA, December 1976.
51. Karl Jackson, Cambodia, *1975-1978: Rendezvous with Death* (Princeton, NJ: Princeton University Press, 2014).
52. James Tyner, *From Rice Fields to Killing Fields: Nature, Life, and Labor Under the Khmer Rouge* (Syracuse, NY: Syracuse University Press, 2017).
53. Haing Ngor, *Survival in the Killing Fields* (New York: Little, Brown Book Group, 2012).
54. Ryan Bishop and Gregory Clancey, "The City as Target or Perpetuation and Death," in Stephen Graham ed. *Cities, War and Terrorism: Towards an Urban Geopolitics* (New York: Wiley, 2008), pp. 54-76.
55. Francois Ponchaud, *Cambodia: Year Zero* (Ann Arbor, MI: University of Michigan Press, 2008), pp. 126.
56. Charles Keyes, "Buddhism and Revolution in Cambodia," *Cultural Survival Quarterly*. September 1990; Charles Wallace, "Buddhism

Rising Again from the Ashes of Cambodia," *Los Angeles Times*. June 19, 1990.
57. Ben Kiernan, "By Any Measure, Pol Pot Engaged in Genocide," *New York Times*, September 4, 1990.
58. Thomas Clayton, "Building the New Cambodia: Educational Destruction and Construction under the Khmer Rouge, 1975-1979," *History of Education Quarterly* 38(1) 1998, pp. 1-16.
59. David Ayres, "The Khmer Rouge and Education: Beyond the Discourse of Destruction," *History of Education* 28(2) 1999, pp. 205-218; Clayton, 1998.
60. Damien de Walque, *The Long-Term Legacy of the Khmer Rouge Period in Cambodia* (United States: World Bank, Development Research Group, Public Services Team, 2004).
61. Clayton 1998, p. 7.
62. Ben Kiernan, *Genocide and Resistance in Southeast Asia: Documentation, Denial, and Justice in Cambodia and East Timor* (United States: Transaction Publishers, 2011), p. 23.
63. Dith Pran and Kim DePaul eds., *Children of Cambodia's Killing Fields: Memoirs by Survivors* (New Haven, CT: Yale University Press, 1997).

The Khmer Rouge Genocide

One purpose of forcing the entire population into a national network of agricultural collectives was so that those the communists deemed as enemies could be executed on a mass scale in more rural, isolated settings, wherein presumably fewer people would bear witness to the atrocities. The majority of executions were perpetrated upon whole groups at a time and in close proximity to the sites at which victims would be dumped into mass graves. The Documentation Center of Cambodia, an NGO that documents and researches the Khmer Rouge regime and its crimes, has estimated that over 22,000 mass grave sites exist, each containing up to several hundred bodies, though all such sites may never be discovered and the exact number never known.[1] The execution and burial sites are widely scattered across most of Cambodia's territory and correlate closely with the locations of the thousands of agricultural collectives and labor camps from which the victims were drawn. Many killing fields were concentrated around the main population centers from which people had been driven, particularly Phnom Penh and the southeastern areas of the country.

The Khmer Rouge also perpetrated a large number of killings, torture, and other crimes at sites created solely for such purposes. The most infamous political prison of the Khmer Rouge era was Tuol Sleng, known by the Khmer Rouge as S-21, one of the 189 known political prisons officially designated as "interrogation centers" operated by the communist regime. Based in a former high school in Phnom Penh, this site was used primarily to torture, extract "confessions" from, and execute Khmer Rouge soldiers and those in leadership positions of the movement who had been targeted for purging by Pol Pot and his inner circle. The latter reflected the growing distrust on the part of Khmer Rouge leaders of their own followers throughout the tenure of the regime, often due to failure to meet unrealistic goals of agricultural production or other objectives established by senior leadership.[2] Initially, those killed at the site were dumped in mass graves on or adjacent to it, but as the internal purges and the numbers of those executed at Tuol Sleng began to increase, a larger site for mass graves was selected outside the city. By around 1977, the bodies of those who were executed or died from torture on the Tuol Sleng site were transported a few miles south of the city to the notorious Choeung Ek site, which ultimately contained at least 129 mass graves. Prisoners at Tuol Sleng who relented under torture and provided a "confession" were trucked in large numbers to Choeung Ek—having been told that they were being sent to a political re-education camp—and promptly executed there, frequently in an improvised and brutal manner.[3]

The sadistic cruelty the Khmer Rouge displayed at such sites is nearly beyond comprehension. A forensic analysis of a random sample of over 500 remains previously exhumed at the site revealed the majority had been killed by either blunt- or sharp-force trauma to the skull, with only 1 gunshot wound identified in the sample.[4] A similar forensic study of 6,426 skulls exhumed from Choeung Ek identified a total of 28,083 individual traumatic wounds, some of which were inflicted through torture or abuse prior to execution and many of which also indicated that multiple blows were commonly needed in the crude execution process, with the most common skull traumas identified as caused by wooden clubs (12,237), steel bars/axles (5,806) and knives (3,563).[5] Such forensic studies closely correlate to witness testimony that most victims executed on site at Choeung Ek were killed by blows to the back of the head or neck with any hard object that was conveniently available, including rifle butts, agricultural tools (e.g., hoes or spades), or the steel axles removed from oxcarts. Given that out of as many as 20,000 people the Khmer Rouge sent to Tuol Sleng less than a dozen are known to have survived, it is reasonable to characterize the site and many other such sites as death camps.[6] Concerned that the children of executed parents might one day seek revenge, the communist regime established a policy wherein if both parents were to be executed, their children would also be killed. This policy was even carried out against infants and the very young, and the remains of countless babies and other children murdered by the Khmer Rouge have been found in mass grave sites throughout the country. Today, the Tuol Sleng and Choeung Ek sites are the two primary memorials to those murdered during the Khmer Rouge genocide.

Distinct phases occurred in which segments of Cambodia's population were targeted by the Khmer Rouge for punishment or execution or, in the lexicon of the regime, "smashing." The manner of treatment meted out, including even the methods used to execute those the regime perceived as its enemies, also reflected to a degree which phase the Khmer Rouge genocide was in at a given point in time. The initial phase of the communists' mass killings entailed the elimination of military forces, government officials, and others associated with the previous regime. The majority of those targeted in this phase were killed within days or weeks. In this opening phase, most elements of the former regime and others directly executed (as opposed to dying via exhaustion, hunger, etc.) were likely shot. The initial phase also corresponded with the elimination of many, perhaps most, of those the Khmer Rouge regarded as expendable—such "non-producers" as the elderly, very young, and infirm—via the death marches and lack of food and medicine and the otherwise harsh conditions in the agricultural collectives and labor camps. The latter situation and the sociopathic callousness of the communist regime is reflected in a common Khmer Rouge warning that "to keep you is no gain, to lose you is no loss."[7] This first of the three phases of the Khmer Rouge terror appears to have the lowest death toll, in large part because (1) it was the shortest time period of the phases, in part due to (2) the Khmer Rouge regime's becoming increasingly murderous in ensuing weeks/months, and also (3) because insufficient time had passed for deaths from certain causes, such as malnutrition or starvation, to have peaked. Attempting to calculate the death toll of the first few weeks specifically in Phnom Penh, Kiernan estimated that less than 1% or nearly 11,000 of the capital's total population of some 2 million died en route during the initial weeks of the forced exodus and around 10,000 had been summarily executed in the capital within days of its fall.[8] Some estimates place both of the latter death tolls higher, and the numbers would certainly increase if an accurate count existed for the entire country—rather than just the capital—during the first weeks/months of Khmer Rouge rule.[9]

Once most of the officials, soldiers, police, civil servants, and other human vestiges of the former government had been eliminated, the violent revolutionary zeal of the communists quickly turned to those they deemed broadly as class enemies or who were otherwise perceived to potentially run afoul of the new order. Several categories within the population were targeted in this respect, including not just the former economic and political elite but also educated/professionals in general: teachers, lawyers, doctors, those who spoke a foreign language, and even those who wore glasses—the logic apparently being that eyeglasses could identify those who were well-read.[10] The Khmer Rouge reviled foreign influences, and those with family or other ties abroad or who had even travelled internationally were subject to being targeted for killing or intense persecution. As stated earlier, religion was also deemed an anti-Khmer and politically reactionary influence, including Buddhism which had diffused into Southeast Asia from ancient India. Previous identities and loyalties were targeted for elimination in favor of new revolutionary ideals; for example, acceptance of a hierarchical social order and concepts of karma were Buddhist tenets that ran afoul of radical communist doctrine.[11] Khmer Rouge propaganda frequently referred to Buddhist monks as "worms" or "leeches" who consumed rather than produced resources.[12] Non-Khmer ethnic minorities were also targeted by the xenophobic and ultra-nationalist Khmer Rouge; because both identities overlap, it can be difficult to draw a clear distinction between the hatred the regime harbored toward ethnic minorities as opposed to the animosity they felt toward religious communities. Noting the latter and the degree to which minority ethnicities would either be killed or forced to flee, Mowell observed the following.

> Prior to the Pol Pot regime, the largest non-Khmer ethnic minorities in Cambodia were the Chinese and Vietnamese populations, which were predominantly Buddhist, and the Cham population which was largely Muslim. The latter three communities comprised approximately 15% of Cambodia's population prior to the Khmer Rouge. However, after only two years of large-scale efforts to kill or drive out its professed enemies, the Pol Pot regime claimed that the three groups collectively constituted only 1% of the national population.[13]

This second phase began mere days or weeks after the communists seized power and potentially peaked in terms of casualties by around 1977–78, though the ill-treatment and murders of those perceived to be members of such categories continued through the end of the regime. The overwhelming majority of those who died during the Khmer Rouge terror belonged to one or more of the categories that began to be targeted in this phase, roughly the first two to two-and-a half years of the regime. The second phase (as well as the third) was additionally characterized by the improvised, garish, and cruel methods of execution mandated in lieu of shooting in order to save ammunition. Despite Cambodia's secretive and almost totally isolated nature under the Khmer Rouge, awareness of the magnitude of the regime's crimes was possible early in the regime due to journalists, diplomats, and other foreigners present for the first few weeks as well as a small but steady trickle of survivors escaping across the borders with eyewitness accounts. Additionally, governmental understanding of unfolding events was likely aided by communication intercepts and other intelligence operations. A declassified CIA report from December 1976 conveys that, fairly early in the era of Khmer Rouge control, even if not fully acknowledged or condemned in public at the time, the U.S. and likely many other members of the international community possessed a clear understanding of the radical and violent nature of the regime and the scale of suffering and death it caused, noting that "the unprecedented cruelty with which the experiment was carried out resulted in the death of hundreds of thousands of people including almost the entire educated stratum."[14] Reflecting the shocking mortality rates during this second phase of the genocide, the report estimated that by late 1976—scarcely one and a half years into Khmer Rouge rule—over 10% of Cambodia's population had likely already perished due to a combination of executions, hunger, disease (e.g., malaria), and other factors.

The nature of Khmer Rouge crimes early in the regime was also addressed in the press and made known to the general public, both almost from the start and increasingly over time. Even before Phnom Penh's fall to the Khmer Rouge, many policymakers publicly warned of bloodbaths in Cambodia if the communists seized power. Such fears stemmed from Khmer Rouge conduct during the Civil War, including the torture and execution of captured government troops or functionaries as well as the rhetoric Khmer Rouge leadership espoused (e.g., the need to "smash" enemies was not merely allegory). In the first weeks of the communist regime, some 7,000 Cambodian refugees had escaped into Thailand, some of whom had been in the cities and subsequent death marches and witnessed or were informed en route by other survivors of widespread atrocities. Outside Cambodia, enough information was emerging from survivor accounts and other sources to cultivate an understanding of the horrors being inflicted upon its population. In July 1975, just weeks after the Khmer Rouge seized power, in among the first examples of alarm bells sounded by major international media outlets concerning the genocide, a *New York Times* editorial noted that "the picture begins to emerge of a country that resembles a giant prison camp with the urban supporters of the former regime being worked to death on thin gruel and hard labor and with medical care virtually non-existent."[15] The piece succinctly explained how the unique political circumstances (e.g., self-proclaimed neutrality) of Cambodia served to quell international outcry: the communist bloc remained silent as the Khmer Rouge were ostensibly communist; western nations remained silent out of fear of facilitating an end to Pol Pot's feigned neutrality or alienating other officially non-aligned nations at the height of the Cold War; and non-aligned states avoided public condemnation perhaps because of the prominence Cambodia held within that bloc. The article noted that

> Were Cambodia a non-communist and non-Third-World country, the outraged protests from the developing and communist countries would be deafening... Members of (the U.S.) Congress who rightly criticized the undemocratic Lon Nol regime have a special obligation to speak up. Few if any have been heard from. The UN is (also) silent. That silence must be broken.[16]

A range of factors contributed to the minimal outcry in the U.S. It partly reflected lack of widespread public awareness as developments in Cambodia were to some degree lost amid other headlines of the time, such as the fall of South Vietnam or the multitude of domestic problems facing the country. Similar to obliviousness during the Holocaust, it is likely many people also could not conceive of the magnitude of the atrocities being committed and may have discounted such information as exaggeration at best and completely fabricated propaganda intended to discredit the Khmer Rouge regime at worst. At least initially, disbelief of the reports was widespread, and academics and others—particularly on the left—were quick to publicly downplay the mounting evidence of atrocities. For example, British Sociologist Aiden Foster-Carter asserted that the Khmer Rouge were merely mobilizing the workforce to enhance agricultural productivity and combat hunger, an oft repeated claim even today. American academic and far-left political activist Noam Chomsky downplayed the eyewitness accounts of those who escaped the Khmer Rouge as the exaggerated and politically motivated propaganda of the deposed former Cambodian Republic's supporters. Even as the months and years passed and incontrovertible evidence of Khmer Rouge atrocities mounted, apologists—again, mainly on the left—continued to deny or downplay the crimes of the Pol Pot regime. In the early 70s, the political climate in the U.S. was partisan and highly polarized, with conservatives warning of the carnage that would ensue in Indochina if communist regimes were established as partial justification for continuing U.S. military intervention/aid. Even before the ascendency of the Khmer Rouge, unpopular U.S. President Gerald Ford and others from generally conservative perspectives warned of the "bloodbath" that would result in Cambodia if the communists seized power, at the same time elements of the American left asserted the new Pol Pot regime would bring "peaceful rule" to Cambodia—thereby apparently accepting Sihanouk's public rhetoric spinning the Khmer Rouge agenda as democratic.[17] Coming in the wake of the Vietnam War and the reality that hawks had used similar justifications for U.S. involvement in that conflict, by the mid-1970s, many on the left were disinclined to heed warnings or evidence concerning the Khmer Rouge. Attempts to raise concern as to Khmer Rouge actions on the part of the by-then scandal-tainted and politically weakened Ford regime and its conservative supporters in Congress were largely ignored as the atrocities in Cambodia continued.

The third and final phase of the Khmer Rouge genocide (1977–1979) roughly the last two years the group remained in power, with each of the phases overlapping to some degree—was characterized by paranoia that fellow Khmer communists were betraying the revolution and its leadership. Thus, the Pol Pot regime turned on many of its own soldiers and functionaries. For example, by this point, the regime was still in the process of eliminating class enemies and other perceived obstacles in the general population, actions that characterized the previous phase. Accordingly, most executions and other deaths during the third phase were continuations of targeting the same groups from the previous genocide period. However, now for the first time in significant numbers, Khmer Rouge fighters, leaders, and their families were also being detained, tortured, and executed for alleged disloyalty (e.g., many were accused of being spies for Vietnam or other foreign powers) or counterrevolutionary thought or action. Those in the Eastern Zone were targeted to a greater degree, as they were perceived as being more ideologically mainstream communists and, due to proximity to Vietnam, were also commonly suspected of being under Hanoi's influence. At least some of the regime's paranoia regarding the influence of Vietnamese communists may have had basis in reality, though the charges levied against many victims were often likely exaggerated or even completely fabricated, such as the case of Hu Nim who served as the Minister of Information during the first two years of the Khmer Rouge regime before being arrested and forced under torture to confess to being a U.S. agent. Purging the ranks of imagined traitors reflects growing regime paranoia and is perhaps how many of the senior leaders rationalized the near complete failure of their radical societal experiments. The cannibalization of fellow militants, however, was at least to some degree likely a conscious exercise in deflecting blame from the inept senior leadership and the failure of its ill-conceived, dystopian policies.

Torture/execution centers existed at regional, district, and commune levels, with many such sites converted from former Buddhist temples.[18] Methods of execution and torture varied depending upon location as well as time period. As an example of the latter, the Khmer Rouge upon seizing power initially had most former supporters and functionaries of the Republican government shot in the first days/weeks. However, shortly after they came to power and out of concern for preserving finite supplies of ammunition—all of which had to be imported—the regime, as stated above, employed a diverse range of garish, improvised, and merciless methods of execution in lieu of wasting bullets. In addition to the methods noted in Chapter 6, page 2, many victims were executed by asphyxiation, drowning, being dropped from heights or bashed against hard surfaces, disembowelment, and various other methods.[19] Some methods of execution were so sadistic—such as the apparently standardized Khmer Rouge practices for executing infants and toddlers—that they will not be recounted in this work.

The use of torture by the Pol Pot regime to extract "confessions" was widespread, systematic, and similar to that of the Nazis. Torture and executions were often well-documented in interrogators' logs and manuals and often even accompanied by photographs of the victims.[20] Torture methods varied widely and included beatings, sexual assault, use of pliers and other tools to inflict bodily trauma, cutting/stabbing, suffocating, acid application, hanging victims from hooks, electric shock, and such psychological approaches as forcing victims to watch the torture of others. Sexual assaults were not confined to regime-sanctioned torture, and many survivor accounts convey that rape at the hands of Khmer Rouge guards was a common occurrence in work camps and prisons. Many victims also died via medical experimentation, such as live dissection, organ removal (certain organs such as gall bladders would be removed, dried, and sold for use in folk medicine in China), and experiments to determine how long it would take victims to die from blood loss via various types of traumas, with nearly all such murders having been perpetrated without any form of anesthesia.[21]

Estimates vary concerning the total number of people killed in the Khmer Rouge genocide. Initial estimates offered by the Vietnamese government suggested well over 3 million dead; Vietnam apparently used this inflated number, one with little basis in evidence, to help justify their invasion of Cambodia on humanitarian grounds. Heuveline provides an example on the lower end of credible attempts at estimating the death toll; through statistical simulations of demographic data, estimating that around 1.2 million died, though this number is significantly below most other reputable figures.[22] While the exact number will never be known, most credible estimates derived from formal research place the death toll just below the 2 million mark, with Kiernan, for example, proposing a range of between 1.67 million and 1.87 million or between 21 and 24% of the national population.[23] Yale University, which has undertaken exhaustive U.S. State Department-funded research into the Khmer Rouge genocide, places the death toll at approximately 1.7 million or 21% of the population.[24] Such statistics are even more startling when considering the fact that the regime was in power for less than four years: April 1975 to January 1979. Attempts to estimate the death toll of the Khmer Rouge terror are usually specific to the brief period in which they functioned as the government of all Cambodia. For nearly two decades after being deposed, however, Pol Pot and his followers maintained a rump state and continued a low-intensity guerilla war in rural parts of the country and were directly or indirectly responsible for the deaths of perhaps several hundred thousand additional people during this time period.

To illustrate the complexities involved in calculating the death toll, an exact estimate of the fatalities based upon pre- and post-Khmer Rouge demographic data is hampered by imprecise and sometimes conflicting population estimates both before and after the Khmer Rouge came to power. At approximately the time of the Khmer Rouge takeover, early 1975, Cambodia had a population of between 7.3 and 7.5 million with an annual growth rate of 2.8% which, in turn, should have yielded a population of approximately 8.4–8.6 million by 1981.[25] The official figure released by the Cambodian government estimated the national population to be 6.7 million in 1981, although 6.3–6.4 million is likely more accurate.[26] If the lowest of the latter 1981 population estimates (6.3 million) is subtracted from the highest projection for what the population should have been in 1981 (8.6 million), 2.3 million people are missing. If the higher estimate of the actual 1981 population (6.7 million) is subtracted from the lowest projection (8.4 million), then 1.7 million are missing. Both of the latter figures of 1.7 and 2.3 million would need to take emigration and return-migration into account. Further complicating estimations of the death toll is the lack of clarity as to how many people fled (rather than died) and/or returned to the country after having fled the Khmer Rouge. While the Khmer Rouge were in power, unauthorized travel on roadways was nearly impossible, and the borders were sealed. Consequently, only small numbers are thought to have escaped the country during the Khmer Rouge era—and most of those likely at the very beginning—thus, the impact of in/out-migration may not be significant in attempting to calculate the death toll using national population data. Using standard demographic data, such as estimating what future population levels should have attained based on the growth rate of prior years, is also problematic because fertility rates under the Khmer Rouge would have declined due to hunger, maltreatment, and other adverse conditions.

The exact number/ratio of victims who were directly executed or died during torture versus those who died of various other causes, such as exhaustion/overwork, hunger, disease, suicide, injury/abuse, or medical experimentation will also never be known. Heuveline, using statistical modelling, proposed that out of an overall estimated death toll of around

1.2 million, over 700,000 (58.3%) were violent deaths (e.g., via execution or torture).[27] Chandler estimated at least 1.7 million died, of which around 200,000, or less than 12%, died via direct execution, and 1.5 million of less direct causes, such as starvation, overwork, and disease.[28] However, the Khmer Rouge were responsible for such deaths, as it was through the communists' brutal policies that conditions were created to cause such losses, often by deliberately overworking or withholding food or medicine from targeted groups.

As an example of the latter, the Khmer Rouge understood most of the population was hungry and malnourished, yet many of the regime's policies ignored that reality. Average daily caloric intake in Cambodia had declined from an estimated 2,190 in 1972 to 1,884 in 1974 as the Civil War progressed, and dropped substantially further under the communist regime at the same time they imposed grueling, unrelenting manual labor upon most of the population.[29] Prior to the Khmer Rouge, peasants in Cambodia consumed an average of around 700 grams of rice daily.[30] Rations under the communists—the method of "payment" utilized by the regime after currency had been abolished—varied over time. Depending on one's classification and the type of work assigned, the initial ration for most city evacuees was around 250 grams of rice daily and as conditions worsened, even those tasked with the most intense labor were often given as little as 50–125 grams of rice daily, combined with very little, if any, other supplemental rations (e.g., a small amount of fish paste would occasionally be distributed)—a grossly insufficient diet for sustained hard labor.[31] Even in the face of widespread malnutrition and hunger, the Khmer Rouge prohibited foraging for wild plants and other supplemental food sources for personal consumption beyond the meager rations officially distributed, as such foraging would, in effect, acknowledge the inadequacy of the regime's efforts to supply food. Starving, desperate people nonetheless risked punishment—even including summary execution—to eat grass and other wild plants, insects, and such small animals as lizards or frogs; some resorted to cannibalism of the corpses of those who had already succumbed to the deplorable conditions.[32] Consumption of such substances out of desperation to quell hunger contributed to dysentery and other diseases, and many were also sickened or died due to the unwitting consumption of poisonous wild plants.

Isolationist and Discordant Foreign Relations

Throughout 1975, the Khmer Rouge regime pursued a policy of near complete international isolation. The few countries with which it maintained official diplomatic ties were mostly other communist states that the regime deemed not to be puppet states of Moscow, including Albania, China, Cuba, North Korea, Romania, and Yugoslavia. They also maintained relations with communist Laos, despite its orbit with the USSR and also with non-communist Thailand. Though they, in theory, exchanged formal diplomatic recognition with each of the latter states, the Khmer Rouge stopped short of permitting all to have embassies in the country and allowed very few foreign diplomats to be physically present, even from among the few states with which it established official ties. Short provides insight into the severe paranoia-inspired restrictions the Khmer Rouge imposed upon the small number of diplomats allowed into the country:

> Apart from the Chinese, who were allowed to retain their old Embassy, the other countries were assigned living and working quarters. The side roads were barricaded off and the diplomats were not permitted to walk more than 300 yards up and down the street without an escort and official permission . . . Embassies were not allowed to employ Cambodian staff. They were not allowed cars. They were not allowed to visit the Foreign Ministry . . . and the one-way telephone system which operated meant that the (Foreign) Ministry could call them but they were not allowed to call out.[33]

In Pol Pot's Cambodia, there were initially not only few foreign diplomats but also no foreign journalists; no representatives of NGOs or other international organizations; no access across land and maritime borders that remained closed; no scheduled international flights; nor were there even international telephone, telegraph, or postal linkages to the outside world.[34] By 1976, the Khmer Rouge began to display at least some willingness to expand diplomatic ties within the international community. They exchanged formal recognition with a growing list of non-communist states, primarily in what was then called the third world—a segment of the international community in which the Pol Pot regime hoped to establish a leadership role—including Egypt and Burma (Myanmar), for example.

The regime participated in some international conferences among non-aligned and developing nations. The Khmer Rouge also negotiated formal recognition, though not a bilateral exchange of embassies, with several industrialized nations, including Denmark, Italy, Japan, Norway, and Sweden. The main criterion for the Khmer Rouge in establishing formal relations appears to have been the willingness of the other state to abide by the restrictive terms the Pol Pot regime set, including not insisting upon opening an embassy.[35]

Attitudes toward the Khmer Rouge regime on the part of many nations were driven by larger geopolitical considerations. The U.S., Thailand, and China were all concerned at the prospect of a Vietnamese-dominated Indochina; some movement along that path had already happened with Vietnamese alignment with Laos—cemented in a 1977 friendship pact—as well as Hanoi's attempts to influence the communist movement in Cambodia. Global Cold War-era politics also served as a consideration, as the U.S. and China regarded communist Cambodia as a potential counterweight to neighboring Vietnam and Laos, both of which were aligned with the Soviet bloc. While it did not overtly aid the Khmer Rouge during its tenure in Cambodia, the U.S.—like other western nations and most of the world—tacitly tolerated the Khmer Rouge by remaining largely silent in the face of mounting, incontrovertible evidence of their atrocities. However, throughout its time in power, an intense anti-American outlook was a defining characteristic of the Khmer Rouge regime. Its anti-U.S. rhetoric was more intense than that of most other communist regimes in the era and was used as partial justification for the continued repression of the population and also as a scapegoat (e.g., imperialist sabotage) for the regime's many failures.

"Nonalignment" and Communist Party Portrayals/Interactions

A defining characteristic of Khmer Rouge foreign policy was its ostensible (feigned) commitment to non-alignment, as stated earlier, driven chiefly by the goal of preserving autonomy and preventing foreign encroachment upon Cambodian territory. Pol Pot most likely reasoned that, via membership and standing in the nonaligned community of nations, Cold War powers and their proxies would not be incentivized to interfere in Cambodian affairs and, ideally, some states might grant unconditional aid to his government in an (unrequited) effort to woo the regime—which proved to be correct in China's case. For example, western nations would be reluctant to interfere or even offer criticism out of concern for driving the ostensibly neutral regime closer toward communist alliances/ideology, and the Soviet bloc would not seek to offer provocation for fear of driving the Khmer Rouge closer to Beijing. Reflecting this presumptive commitment to neutrality, as well as the country's prior history with foreign intervention, the regime's constitution expressly prohibited the establishment of foreign bases on Cambodian soil. Pol Pot's pursuit of a nonaligned stance not only facilitated pledges of nonparticipation in military blocs and regional alliances but also led the Khmer Rouge government to initially mask its ideological nature and refuse to publicly acknowledge that it was communist in orientation.

Initially, rather than publicly proclaiming the new regime as communist or even officially acknowledging the existence of the Khmer Communist Party (KCP), Khmer communists contrived a façade they termed the "revolutionary organization," also commonly referred to as "the organization" or *Angkor*. The KCP remained a secretive organization, as did its leadership structure (e.g., the CIA and other external observers did not initially realize Prime Minister Pol Pot and KCP Secretary General Saloth Sar were the same person until around 1975), yet the KCP and Pol Pot faction retained full control over the government and political agenda of the regime.[36] To camouflage its communist nature, the regime also adopted the politically ambiguous term "Democratic Cambodia" as the official name of Cambodia. A detailed intelligence assessment of the situation in the early period of Khmer Rouge rule suggested that the communist ideological orientation of the regime and the reality that it was controlled by the KCP (and the mere fact of the KCP's existence) initially remained hidden for a combination of reasons.

1. Claiming no direct ties to the communist bloc better positioned the Khmer communists to claim membership in the nonaligned community of nations, which Pol Pot saw as a strategy to help preserve Cambodian autonomy;
2. Many years of existence as a guerilla insurgency instilled a strong sense of secrecy and elitism, and the transition to an overt political existence proved difficult;

3. Were the KCP to transition from its long-standing status as an underground organization, the transition would necessitate the expansion of membership which, in turn, might dilute the Party's revolutionary discipline and change it into a looser, less cohesive organization;
4. The communists wanted to avoid identifying the Party and its leadership as being responsible for regime actions that resulted in the displacement, death, and misery of millions; and
5. Hiding the KCP and its influence over the new regime better enabled the Khmer Rouge to disavow their earlier ideological and organizational connection to Vietnamese communism, ties that Hanoi might potentially seek to utilize to exert control over or interfere in Cambodian political developments.[37]

Largely Discordant Regional Interactions

The Pol Pot regime had better relations with Thailand than any other non-communist state, at least initially. Following decades of military rule that had been aligned with the U.S. Cold War anti-communist agenda, Thailand transitioned in 1973 to a brief period of democracy and a policy of geopolitical coexistence. Thailand's democratic government was among the first to recognize the Khmer Rouge regime, though several points of contention existed between the countries. Up to 50,000 or more refugees ultimately fled across the Thai border due to the Khmer Rouge takeover. Some of these refugees were former Lon Nol soldiers and functionaries who had taken Cambodian military vehicles with them. Phnom Penh wanted the return of both the refugees and military equipment and also initially (unsuccessfully) sought Bangkok's permission to pursue fleeing Cambodian soldiers across the Thai border. Boundary disputes also existed, with the Khmer Rouge alleging Thailand had taken advantage of the Cambodian Civil War to occupy portions of territory along the border. Numerous incursions occurred along the land borders, with the Khmer Rouge planting mines in Thai territory, abducting villagers, and looting food; incidents also occurred in disputed areas of the maritime boundaries in the form of Khmer Rouge attacks on Thai fishing vessels and engagements between the maritime security forces of both countries.[38] Leftist elements in Thailand attributed at least some of the border conflicts to the presence of ex-Lon Nol military forces that the Thai military had allowed to use certain areas along the border as sanctuaries.[39]

An additional potential source of friction was the continued presence of U.S. troops in Thailand, a holdover from the previous military regime in Bangkok. For years, U.S. troops had been deployed to seven military bases operated by the Pentagon primarily behind the goal of combating communism within the region. From these bases, supplies were airlifted in an effort to prop up the Lon Nol regime. During the period of Thai democracy, 1973–76, much domestic public sentiment in that country supported ending the U.S. presence there. Interestingly, however, the Khmer Rouge declined to join Vietnam and Laos in their 1975 demand that Thailand order a full withdrawal of all remaining U.S. forces from its territory. In 1976, apparently reflecting Pol Pot's initial desire for better relations with Cambodia's western neighbor amid strained relations with Hanoi, Phnom Penh likewise did not join in Vietnam's propaganda campaign condemning the Thai military coup that toppled the democracy and restored conservative, anti-communist policies in Thailand.[40] Despite the rapidly deteriorating relations with Vietnam, however, the Khmer Rouge in 1977–78 resumed and escalated attacks on Thai border areas. They were also accused by the Thai military of aiding Thailand's communist insurgents and even of assisting them in attacks on targets and in the forced conscription of villagers in Thailand—apparently behind the goal of helping the Thai communist insurgency establish a "liberated zone" in their country.[41] Tensions between the two governments related to the border disputes, and the skirmishes only started to subside in late 1978.

As was also the case with Thailand and Vietnam, a contentious element in relations between the Khmer Rouge regime and neighboring Laos was the disputed border and irredentist forces stemming from the spatial distribution of ethnic Khmer and other populations in proximity to national boundaries. In the colonial era, the exact border had never been precisely delimited, and ethnic Laotians living in areas claimed by Cambodia and ethnic Khmers living in areas claimed by Laos further bolstered each nation's overlapping claims (by virtue of habitation) and exacerbated tensions related to the disputed boundaries. At its historical zenith, the ancient Khmer Empire occupied much of Indochina. On that basis, some Khmer Rouge leaders claimed rightful Cambodian ownership of much of Laos far beyond the contemporary border (see Chapter 1). Khmer Rouge fighters occasionally crossed the border and fired on Laotian civilians in an effort to assert Cambodian claims to the disputed territory.[42]

Like all other segments of the Cambodian population, members of the ethnic Lao minority—including some remote communities that were semi-nomadic—were rounded up into forced labor camps. The Khmer Rouge treated the Lao minority harshly; they banned the Lao language, and many died due to poor conditions or were directly executed, including some who had initially been communists. Several thousand ethnic Lao and others managed to flee across the border from the Khmer Rouge, adding an additional source of tension between the countries as the Pol Pot regime expected the return of refugees.[43] The strained relations between Laos and Pol Pot's Cambodia were ironic in that both countries at the time had communist governments, though the Khmer Rouge regarded Laos as being under the control of Vietnam and the Soviet Union. As the only country in Indochina militarily weaker than Cambodia, Laos was in no position to resolve the border dispute, the periodic Khmer Rouge incursions, or the mistreatment of ethnic Lao minorities in Cambodia via armed conflict, nor were the thinly spread Khmer Rouge forces capable of doing anything more to Laos and its sovereignty than be an occasional nuisance.

Despite having been directly aided by Vietnamese communists throughout most of the Civil War and the reality that most Chinese aid to communist Cambodia initially moved through Vietnam, the Pol Pot faction never wavered in their distrust and hatred of their historical rival Vietnam. While relations between the Cambodian communists and Hanoi were often strained at best during the Cambodian Civil War, Pol Pot and the Khmer Rouge once in power quickly assumed an increasingly confrontational stance against the country that had previously been a benefactor and was ostensibly still an ally. Much of this posturing stemmed from territorial disputes, including some that were initially driven by Hanoi. Pol Pot was already dissatisfied over the transfer of historically Khmer lands to Vietnam under French colonial rule decades earlier when, almost immediately following communist victory in their war with the South, Hanoi essentially invalidated previous boundary agreements made with the Sihanouk regime, conveyed that fresh negotiations should be convened concerning how the colonial boundaries were drawn, and asserted Vietnamese ownership of lands and territorial waters that were claimed by Cambodia.[44] Perhaps one of the main points of contention with boundaries was the "Brevie Line" which established the colonial maritime boundary during the period of French control, but Hanoi disputed the boundary and, in turn, the ownership of Puolo Wai and potentially other islands came into question.[45] Mere weeks after Phnom Penh fell, Khmer Rouge forces initiated attacks on multiple islands claimed by Vietnam off the coast of the Mekong Delta. They inflicted damage and casualties, landed troops, and took over 500 local inhabitants captive—all of whom were eventually executed—before ultimately being driven out by local Vietnamese defense forces and apologizing for what Phnom Penh characterized as a misunderstanding, offering the excuse that the encroachments were the result of the Khmer Rouge troops' incorrect understanding of geography in the area.[46]

In the first weeks of May, the dispute over maritime boundaries facilitated aggression by Pol Pot's forces toward international shipping in what they regarded as their territorial waters. The Khmer Rouge seized multiple Vietnamese fishing boats and other vessels and executed their crews and either captured or fired upon ships from multiple other nations, seizing the commercial freighter USS Mayaguez on May 12.[47] The latter triggered a U.S. military response, including the insertion of Marines on a nearby island in an effort to rescue the crew members. The ensuing engagement on May 15, regarded as the last battle of U.S. involvement in Indochina and the only direct engagement between U.S. and Khmer Rouge forces, resulted in 18 U.S. fatalities (including three MIAs who were presumed dead), 50 wounded and three downed helicopters. The Khmer Rouge lost at least 15 troops (likely more) in the ground fighting and an unknown number in sea engagements that resulted in the sinking of four of their patrol boats.[48] Unknown to the U.S. when the operation began, the ship's crew had been initially taken to the mainland and released just prior to the start of the engagement. The engagement with U.S. forces substantially weakened the already precarious Khmer Rouge military position in the area, in effect aiding Vietnamese forces in their temporary rout of the Cambodian communists from several disputed islands before Hanoi ordered the withdrawal of their military.[49]

Conflict had also erupted early over the Khmer Rouge desire for Vietnamese forces to withdraw from Cambodian soil along the land borders, an issue that was often linked to the territorial disputes. With the fall of

Saigon and the final communist victory in the South, the Khmer Rouge expected Vietnamese communist forces to withdraw from former sanctuary areas they utilized in Cambodia during the war. After the Vietnamese failed to withdraw from many such areas along the border, Phnom Penh made a formal request for Hanoi to order their withdrawal and received an obtuse response indicating some of the territory in question was Vietnamese, so their troops would remain.[50] The latter situation facilitated sporadic, isolated conflicts between Khmer Rouge and Vietnamese forces along almost the entirety of the shared border nearly from the start of the Pol Pot regime, and the condition continued to deteriorate over time. As border disputes continued and skirmishes and incursions into Vietnamese territory by Khmer Rouge units became more common, the Vietnamese government may have been complicit in several unsuccessful assassination attempts against Pol Pot as well as at least one coup attempt that may never have evolved much beyond the preparation stage.[51]

Not all Khmer Rouge relations with regional neighbors were marred by conflict, with China being the best example of a positive bilateral relationship—though one forged out of Pol Pot's dependency on unconditional aid from Beijing. Within months of the Khmer Rouge victory, China extended approximately $1 billion in interest-free loans to the Pol Pot regime, the largest aid package Beijing had ever provided to a single country.[52] China also provided other forms of assistance, including humanitarian aid and technical and military advisors. As noted earlier (see Chapter 5, pages 4 and 7–10), the disastrous failures of China's Great Leap Forward (1958–62) and Cultural Revolution (1966–1976), as well as China's ideological and policy conflicts with the Soviet Union, appear to have served as a strong incentive for Mao's support of the Khmer Rouge regime in Cambodia. Beijing saw the Khmer Rouge as a chance to demonstrate that the Maoist model of communism could potentially succeed internationally. China's increasingly alienated relations with Vietnam (and Hanoi's primary backer, the USSR) also incentivized efforts to support the Maoist Khmer Rouge as a regional geopolitical hedge and as a means of bolstering China's influence within Southeast Asia.

Beijing also initially viewed its support for the Khmer Rouge as a relative bargain. During the Cambodian Civil War, the amount of aid China provided to the Khmer Rouge was modest in comparison to the support Beijing offered to Vietnamese communists during the same period: 316 million yuan versus over 5 billion respectively between 1971 and 1975.[53] Early examples of Chinese aid to Pol Pot's government included such material aid as food, fuel, medicine, and other emergency aid; as well as personnel, such as advisors, trainers, and specialists, including Chinese Navy staff dispatched to help clear mines in the Mekong River.[54] In his analysis of Chinese Aid to the Pol Pot regime, Mertha concludes that the relationship was essentially one-sided, with Beijing providing largely unconditional support and the Khmer Rouge providing virtually nothing tangible (e.g., no military bases or useful natural resources) in return.[55] However, as noted in the discussion of ideological patterning, China perceived its relationship with the Khmer Rouge regime to offer political and symbolic benefits. Given the continuing deterioration in relations with both the Soviets and Vietnamese, Beijing's recognition of the potential political value of its favorable relations with Cambodia meant that aid continued even after Mao's death in 1976.

Most communist regimes, including China, followed a transnational, parallel approach to relations with political counterparts in other states. Communist countries maintained official bilateral diplomatic ties through the reciprocal exchange of embassies/diplomats. The latter would customarily be simultaneously combined with formal party-to-party linkages between the communist party leadership of both nations, through which the communist parties could exchange ideas concerning ideology, policy, etc. Cold War political discord was not limited to the east-west dynamic, and doctrinal disputes commonly erupted over what communist policy should be and, in some instances, resulted in the severing of direct ties between the communist parties of states. For example, Cambodia under the Khmer Rouge and China in the same era did not have direct party-to-party relations with most Soviet bloc regimes, as both Beijing and Phnom Penh regarded the Soviets and their satellite states as having betrayed the tenets of true communism. The initial unwillingness of the Khmer Rouge regime to publicly identify itself as communist or even officially acknowledge the existence of the KCP enabled Pol Pot to avoid forming formal party-to-party relations with other communist regimes.[56] In official, public discussions of Cambodian relationships with other communist states, the Pol Pot regime usually omitted any reference even to parties, using other verbiage such as "governments" or "peoples" instead.[57] As discussed in Chapter 6, such a strategy was designed to serve several purposes, including maintaining the illusion of neutrality to serve the regime's goal of inclusion in the nonaligned community of nations, cultivating the appearance of neutrality in the political conflict between Beijing and Moscow, and potentially preventing political interference and ideological contamination from other communist movements.

The communist parties of China and the Khmer Rouge regime recognized each other as orthodox, non-revisionist ideological movements, and the regimes drew nearer to each other over time despite any effort on the part of Pol Pot to present a public image of neutrality. From the establishment of Khmer Rouge rule, Beijing was by far the regime's biggest benefactor, despite Chinese realization early on that the Khmer Rouge were brutal and directly or indirectly killing a large portion of Cambodia's population. The Chinese government almost surely understood the nature and magnitude of the Khmer Rouge genocide as it unfolded; nevertheless, their support of Pol Pot was unwavering. China's support of the Khmer Rouge regime even continued to increase while ethnic Chinese minorities residing in Cambodia were being targeted alongside other ethnic minorities for more intense persecution and maltreatment, including bans on foreign languages and forcible reforging of socio-cultural identities. The Chinese government remained publicly silent concerning Khmer Rouge crimes so as to not discredit one of their few allies abroad.[58] Kiernan notes that, out of a total population of as many as 425,000 ethnic Chinese in Cambodia, up to one-half perished in the Khmer Rouge genocide—over twice the death rate of urban ethnic Khmer.[59] Becker notes, however, that Beijing's continued public and financial support may well have spared the ethnic Chinese minority in Cambodia from being subjected to even worse treatment, including a policy of total eradication similar to that directed by the Khmer Rouge toward Buddhist monks or Muslim Chams.[60] So steadfast was Beijing's support of the Khmer Rouge that, when Vietnam toppled the regime, Chinese diplomats and thousands of military and technical trainers/advisors fled with Pol Pot's deposed government into exile to remote enclaves along the border of Thailand.

Escalating Conflict with Vietnam

Throughout the first years of Khmer Rouge rule, the Vietnamese government remained optimistic that improved relations with Phnom Penh could be obtained, and Hanoi undertook bilateral summits and other efforts toward that goal. However, the Vietnamese did not appear to grasp the degree of animosity the Khmer Rouge harbored toward them and possessed a poor understanding of the political dynamic of the secretive regime. Indeed, they incorrectly concluded in late 1976 that the "bad people" Pol Pot and Ieng Sary had been deposed, thus further cultivating false hope in Hanoi for an improved political dynamic.[61] By the fall of 1977, relations between the Khmer Rouge regime and Vietnam had deteriorated substantially, and Hanoi had largely accepted the futility of reconciliation efforts. In September, Khmer Rouge troops crossed into Vietnam's Tay Ninh Province, a territory once claimed by the Khmer, and massacred nearly 300 Vietnamese civilians in five villages.[62] Justification for the incursion and massacres seem to be twofold: (1) during a time of heightened paranoia concerning alleged Vietnamese sympathizers within Pol Pot's regime/military, the aggressive foray into Vietnam allowed the Khmer Rouge commanders responsible to demonstrate their loyalty and (2) gave Pol Pot evidence to display to China concerning the alignment of his regime with Beijing.[63] Thousands, possibly tens of thousands, of civilians, both ethnic Vietnamese and ethnic Khmer, are thought to have been murdered in the Khmer Rouge raids of Vietnamese territory, a primary factor in the Vietnamese decision to invade.

In the same year, the Pol Pot regime also resumed military conflict with Vietnam over the disputed Kampuchea Krom territory, historically Khmer lands that the French colonial administration in 1949 had reassigned to Vietnam, much to the anger of Cambodians (see Chapter 1). Vietnam, and the French colonial government prior to independence, colonized the region with over 1 million ethnic Vietnamese, often resettling them on lands taken from ethnic Khmer. Throughout 1977, the Khmer Rouge undertook numerous cross-border incursions into the disputed region of Vietnam, with each of the attacks often resulting in the massacres of dozens or even hundreds of Vietnamese civilians. Perhaps the single worst such incident was the massacre at Ba Chuc when, on April 18, 1978, 3,157 civilians—both Vietnamese and ethnic Khmer—were killed by Khmer Rouge forces that crossed the border before retreating from the approaching Vietnamese Army.[64] The escalating conflict with Vietnam worsened the already dire living conditions for the Cambodian people as the Khmer Rouge seized large quantities of the rice harvests, as stated earlier, to feed the military or to export to China in exchange for arms while simultaneously imposing stricter food rations, longer working hours, and higher agricultural quotas on the captive national population.[65]

In December-January 1977–78, Vietnamese forces altered what had up to that point been their largely defensive, reactionary posture and successfully attacked numerous Khmer Rouge positions along the border, destroying several units/bases and pursuing Pol Pot's forces to within 35 miles of Phnom Penh before withdrawing—apparently concluding at the time that attempting to occupy the entire country was impractical.[66] Vietnamese forces easily routed Khmer Rouge opponents in most of the engagements. They reported that many Cambodians warmly received them as liberators. Further, when they withdrew back to Vietnam, thousands of Cambodians, many of whom were ethnically Khmer, went with them to escape Pol Pot's rule.[67] The latter realizations may have factored into Hanoi's reevaluation of whether it should undertake an invasion to remove the Khmer Rouge regime. Despite the 1977–78 incursion by Vietnamese forces and their own poor performance militarily, the Cambodian communists resumed bellicose posturing and rhetoric almost as soon as Hanoi's forces had withdrawn across the border.

The increasingly aggressive actions the Pol Pot regime took toward neighboring Vietnam are puzzling, given the massive gap in military strength between the countries. Khmer Rouge military capabilities as of late 1978 were modest at best, with useful modern weaponry and certain types of ammunition in short supply. For example, the Khmer Rouge possessed a handful of operational light tanks, around 200 armored personnel carriers in various states of (dis)repair, and virtually no air force as opposed to a Vietnamese inventory of around 900 tanks and a 12,000-man air force with over 300 combat aircraft.[68] Total Khmer Rouge troop strength was approximately 70,000 (compared to around 615,000 in the Vietnamese military[69]) which was only nominally larger than it had been at the time the Cambodian Republic was deposed. Additionally, due to purges of many of the seasoned Khmer Rouge veterans, a large percentage of the Khmer Rouge forces were poorly armed/trained child soldiers whose only experience was in brutalizing captive civilians in labor camps. Such glaring disparities would have been known to Pol Pot, who may have miscalculated that Vietnam could be cowed into acquiescence in order to avoid further open conflict or that, in order to preserve harmony among the communist states of Indochina, such external powers as China or the USSR would persuade the Vietnamese to compromise. In addition, xenophobic anti-Vietnamese rhetoric, the confrontational posture the regime took against Vietnam, and the publicly-espoused goal of recreating a modern Angkor Empire by regaining historically lost territories were all also used for propaganda purposes in an effort by the Khmer Rouge to cultivate support for their regime among the ethnic Khmer majority.

Attempted negotiations between the Khmer Rouge and Vietnam failed to end the disputes or diffuse tensions. In the wake of the failed talks and amid continuing border skirmishes/incursions undertaken by Pol Pot's forces and belligerent, confrontational public rhetoric, Vietnamese troops invaded a portion of southeastern Cambodia in late 1978. They succeeded in creating what they termed a "liberated zone" and founded the Kampuchean United Front for National Salvation (KUFNS), comprised in part of ethnic Vietnamese as well as ethnic Khmer—including Khmer communists—who fled Cambodia due to the Khmer Rouge.[70] Vietnam used the territory they captured in this initial phase as the staging area for a full-scale Cambodian invasion, intended to remove the Khmer Rouge from power and install a communist regime friendly to Hanoi; this plan was initiated on Christmas Day 1978. Given the disparity in the size, training, weaponry, and overall readiness between the military forces of Vietnam and Cambodia, Pol Pot's persisting in confrontational actions toward his vastly more powerful neighbor is unfathomable, especially in the face of mounting Vietnamese anger and clear signs that Hanoi was potentially poised to undertake full-scale conflict. However, assuming that the conduct of the Khmer Rouge regime was that of a rational actor, driven by logical norms and paradigms explaining state behavior, is perhaps an inherently flawed presupposition.

Endnotes

1. Documentation Center of Cambodia. http://dccam.org/homepage Accessed August 1, 2022.
2. United States Holocaust Memorial Museum, "S-21, Tuol Sleng," https://www.ushmm.org/genocide-prevention/countries/cambodia/case-study/violence/s-21. Accessed August 1, 2022.
3. David Chandler, *Voices from S-21: Terror and History in Pol Pot's Secret Prison* (Oakland, CA: University of California Press, 2000).
4. Julie Fleischman, "Analysis of skeletal demographics and traumatic injuries from the Khmer Rouge–period mass gravesite of Choeung Ek, Cambodia," *Forensic Anthropology* 2(4) 2019, pp. 347–365.
5. Katherine Gruspier and Michael Pollanen, "Forensic Legacy of the Khmer Rouge: The Cambodian Genocide," *Academic Forensic Pathology* 7(3) 2017, 415–433.
6. David Chandler, *The Tragedy of Cambodian History: Politics, War and Revolution Since 1945* (New Haven, CT: Yale University Press, 1991).
7. United States Holocaust Memorial Museum, 2022.
8. Kiernan, 1996.
9. For example, based on the accounts of survivors, Barron and Paul, Martin, and Ponchaud regard the initial phase as being characterized by more killings and other atrocities perpetrated by the Khmer Rouge than did Kiernan: John Barron and Anthony Paul, *Murder of a Gentle Land: The Untold Story of Communist Genocide in Cambodia* (New York: Reader's Digest Press, 1977); Martin 1994; Francois Ponchaud, *Cambodia Year Zero* (New York: Penguin Books, 1977).
10. USC Shoah Foundation, "Cambodian Genocide," https://sfi.usc.edu/collections/cambodian-genocide. Accessed August 15, 2022.
11. Hinton, 2005.
12. George Wright, "Monk Tells of Persecution of Buddhists Under Khmer Rouge," *The Cambodia Daily*, February 17, 2015.
13. B.D. Mowell, "Religious Communities as Targets of the Khmer Rouge Genocide," in *The Routledge Handbook of Religion, Mass Atrocity, and Genocide* eds. Sara Brown and Stephen Smith (New York: Routledge, 2022), p. 196. The 1% figure quoted by Pol Pot is likely an exaggerated undercount, but nonetheless reflects the Khmer Rouge agenda in eliminating non-Khmer populations as observed by: Ben

Kiernan, "By Any Measure, Pol Pot Engaged in Genocide." *New York Times*, September 4, 1990.
14. CIA, December 1976, p. iv.
15. *New York Times* Editorial, "Cambodia's Crime," *New York Times*. July 9, 1975, p. 30.
16. Ibid.
17. Donald Kirk, "The Cambodian Bloodbath Debate," *New York Times*. April 5, 1975, p. 29.
18. Rosemary O'Kane, "Cambodia in the Zero Years: Rudimentary Totalitarianism," *Third World Quarterly* 14(4) 1993, pp. 735–748.
19. Kenneth Robinson, Howard DeNike and John Quigley eds., *Genocide in Cambodia: Documents from the Trial of Pol Pot and Ieng Sary* (Philadelphia, PA: University of Pennsylvania Press, 2012); Ian MacKinnon, "Khmer Rouge's Chief Torturer Tells Court of 'Heartfelt Sorrow' Over Killings," *The Guardian*. March 31, 2009; Harris, 2013.
20. Hurst Hannum, "International Law and Cambodian Genocide: The Sounds of Silence," *Human Rights Quarterly* 11(1) 1989, pp. 82–138; United States Holocaust Museum, 2022.
21. Ben Kiernan and Eve Zucker, *Political Violence in Southeast Asia Since 1945: Case Studies from Six Countries* (New York: Taylor and Francis 2021); Patrick Falby, "Court Hears of Khmer Rouge Torture Methods," *The Sydney Morning Herald*. April 1, 2009; Robinson, De Nike and Quigley, 2012.
22. Patrick Heuveline, "The Boundaries of Genocide: Quantifying the Uncertainty of the Death Toll During the Pol Pot Regime (1975–1979)," *Population Studies* 69(2) 2015, pp. 201–218.
23. Ben Kiernan, "The Demography of Genocide in Southeast Asia: The Death Tolls in Cambodia, 1975–79, and East Timor, 1975–80," *Critical Asian Studies* 35(4) 2003, pp. 585–597.
24. Yale University – Genocide Studies Program, "Introduction to Cambodian Genocide Program," https://gsp.yale.edu/introduction-cambodian-genocide-program. Accessed August 5, 2022.
25. Slocomb, 2010; Ross 1990.
26. Ross, 1990.
27. Heuveline, 2015.
28. David Chandler, *Voices From S-21: Terror and History in Pol Pot's Secret*

Prison (Berkely, CA: University of California Press, 1999).
29. Slocomb, 2010; Martin, 1994.
30. Martin, 1994.
31. Vickery, 1999; Martin 1994.
32. Martin, 1994.
33. Short, 2005, pp. 332–333.
34. Short, 2005.
35. CIA, 1976.
36. Ibid.
37. CIA, 1976, pp. 2–3.
38. Puangthong Rungswasdisab, "Thailand's Response to the Cambodian Genocide," Yale University Genocide Studies Program: https://gsp.yale.edu/thailands-response-cambodian-genocide. Accessed August 25, 2022.
39. Ibid.
40. CIA, 1976.
41. Stephen Morris, *Why Vietnam Invaded Cambodia: Political Culture and the Cause of War* (Stanford, CA: Stanford University Press, 1999) pp. 78–81.
42. Kiernan, 1996.
43. Ibid.
44. Becker, 1998.
45. Kiernan, 1996, p. 112.
46. Kiernan, 2004.
47. Central Intelligence Agency, "The Rescue of the S.S. Mayaguez and Its Crew," (May 23, 1975). Accessed August 30, 2022.
48. Christopher Lamb, *The Mayaguez Crisis, Mission Command, and Civil-Military Relations* (United States: Joint History Office, Office of the Chairman of the Joint Chiefs of Staff, 2018).
49. Ralph Wetterhahn, *The Last Battle: The Mayaguez Incident and the End of the Vietnam War* (Boston, MA: Da Capo Press, 2001.
50. Becker, 1998.
51. Nayan Chanda, *Brother Enemy - The War After the War: A History of Indochina Since the Fall of Saigon* (New York: Collier Books, 1988).
52. Kiernan, 2004.
53. Wang, 2018.

54. Ibid.
55. Mertha, 2014.
56. CIA, 1976.
57. Ibid.
58. Wang, 2018.
59. Ben Kiernan, "Kampuchea's Ethnic Chinese Under Pol Pot: A Case of Systematic Social Discrimination," *Journal of Contemporary Asia*, 16(1) 1986, pp. 18–29.
60. Becker, 1998.
61. Dmitry Mosyakov, "The Khmer Rouge and the Vietnamese Communists: A History of Their Relations as Told in the Soviet Archives," in Susan Cook ed. *Genocide in Cambodia and Rwanda* (New York: Routledge, 2006), p. 66.
62. Yale University – Genocide Studies Program, https://gsp.yale.edu/cgp/cbio/y03100. Accessed July 25, 2022.
63. Chanda, 1988.
64. James Pringle, "When the Khmer Rouge Came to Kill," *New York Times*. January 7, 2004.
65. Kiernan, 2004.
66. Mosyakov, 2006.
67. Chanda, 1988; Mosyakov, 2006.
68. Morris, 1999, p. 103.
69. Ibid.
70. Wilfred Deac, *Road to the Killing Fields: The Cambodian War of 1970–1975* (College Station, TX: Texas A&M University Press, 1997).

The Rump State and Vietnamese Occupation, 1979–1991

Significant information gaps exist in the conduct and motivations of the Khmer Rouge regime during its brief stint in power as Cambodia's government. Arguably even less is known concerning aspects of the Khmer Rouge leadership during its prolonged status in exile as a rump state following the Vietnamese invasion. Large scale killings stopped not out of any moral awakening or ideological transformation but due to the recognition by the remnant Pol Pot regime that the human capital remaining under its control was sorely needed as sources of labor in the remote, undeveloped areas of western Cambodia in which the Khmer Rouge still operated. The Vietnamese were largely successful in geographically confining the Khmer Rouge remnants away from the food producing areas, population centers, and other key areas of Cambodia, increasing the dependency of Pol Pot's rump state on both what laborers they were able to conscript and foreign aid.[1]

The conflict would continue for many years as a low-intensity proxy war with China, the U.S., ASEAN, and many western nations supporting the Khmer Rouge and/or other opposition groups and the Soviet bloc supporting Vietnam and the client regime Hanoi installed in Cambodia. The civil war was stalemated as Vietnamese forces and their Cambodian allies failed in repeated annual attempts to drive guerillas out of the remaining small pockets of Cambodia the rebels controlled, and the insurgents were unable to drive out the Vietnamese or recapture any significant Cambodian territory. In 1982, the three main opposition forces—the Khmer Rouge; Prince Sihanouk's royalist faction known as FUNCINPAC; and the pro-western, right wing Khmer People's National Liberation Front (KPNLF)—collaborated to a limited extent in forming a coalition government in exile. As Soviet-bloc aid began to decline in the late 1980s, making its occupation more financially burdensome, Vietnam committed to reducing and eventually withdrawing its forces while working to shore up its client state's capabilities in Phnom Penh, including the Cambodian government's military. Amid the protracted fighting and the slow, incremental progress at economic/societal recovery and nation-building, the international community eventually helped facilitate the 1991 Paris Peace Accords, intended to bring peace, reconciliation, and democratization to Cambodia.

Vietnamese Invasion

Following South Vietnam's collapse in 1975, most of the communist Vietnamese military was demobilized. However, following ongoing border incursions by the Khmer Rouge, many of which were characterized by the massacre or abuse of Vietnamese civilians and the looting and destruction of farms and villages, Hanoi began to remobilize its army to reinforce and secure the border, recapture lost territory, and undertake retaliatory raids against Pol Pot's forces.[2] With relations continuing to deteriorate, the Khmer Rouge regime severed diplomatic ties with Hanoi at the end of 1977, publicly proclaiming that Cambodia's greatest threat was Vietnam rather than the U.S. or imperialism.[3] What started as sporadic and usually low-intensity border incidents in previous years became a near constant state of military incursions, counter-incursions, and skirmishing along the full frontier by 1978. During this time, Vietnam seized progressively more Cambodian borderlands, though as yet only a small percentage of the country's overall territory. By 1978, Hanoi had also begun a propaganda campaign aimed at delegitimizing the Khmer Rouge regime (e.g., frequent public references were made to the genocidal violence the Khmer Rouge committed) and to give credence to Hanoi's efforts to remove it from power.[4] The decision to invade Cambodia may have also been made early in that year, as Vietnam spent much of 1978 recruiting and training troops, calling up reservists, reorganizing units, and formulating meticulous battle plans; by the summer, Hanoi informed Moscow of the planned invasion and asked for Soviet acquiescence.[5]

While they recognized the conflict was worsening, the U.S. and many other observers had not anticipated the full-scale Vietnamese invasion and occupation of Cambodia. The U.S. intelligence community was aware

THE RUMP STATE AND VIETNAMESE OCCUPATION, 1979–1991

of Vietnamese sponsorship of a small but growing anti-Pol Pot resistance movement in exile, and many analysts assumed the Vietnamese capture of swaths of Cambodian border territory meant such areas were to be used as sanctuary territory for a prolonged campaign waged by the Khmer insurrectionists, armed and trained by Hanoi.[6] The mistaken conclusion that Hanoi preferred such a long-term resistance campaign was misread by most analysts in the U.S. as constituting Vietnam's conscious alternative to full-scale invasion and occupation. They maintained this view even as Vietnamese forces continued building up in strength along the border in numbers far beyond what would be needed to support pro-Hanoi Cambodian guerrillas or quell Khmer Rouge border incursions. However, China possessed a clearer sense of the escalating conflict and was concerned about the prospect of a Vietnamese invasion of Cambodia. In 1978, Beijing began attempting to moderate the Khmer Rouge's anti-Vietnamese actions and rhetoric—particularly their aggressive provocations along the border—they also called upon Pol Pot to halt the purges that had weakened the Cambodian military. The Chinese, however, met with little success, and their efforts were likely too late given that Hanoi had already committed to invasion.[7]

The Vietnamese invasion plan utilized a massive force of 18 infantry divisions supported by naval, armor, artillery, and other ancillary units in coordinated, simultaneous large-scale assaults along five fronts spanning the entire border, a plan designed to quickly overwhelm with superior numbers.[8] Ultimately, some 200,000 Vietnamese troops supported by around 20,000 disaffected Cambodians armed and trained by Hanoi would be unleashed to overwhelm Khmer Rouge defenders.[9] As Vietnamese forces continued to mass in staging areas along the border, the Khmer Rouge understood what the buildup signaled and launched pre-emptive attacks into Vietnam on December 20–21, resulting in Hanoi's moving up the original invasion timetable to Christmas Day.[10] The key objective was Phnom Penh as the seat of government, upon which multiple Vietnamese columns would converge after quickly shattering Khmer Rouge forces in proximity to the frontier. Defending against the onslaught, the Khmer Rouge fielded approximately 15 understrength divisions, each of which was less than one-half the size of a Vietnamese division—fewer than 4,000 in a Cambodian division compared to 8,000 in Vietnamese divisions.[11] Reflecting such disparities in manpower, training, and equipment favored Vietnamese forces, and the course of the fighting was largely one-sided. While it encountered pockets of stubborn Khmer Rouge resistance, the Vietnamese offensive threw Pol Pot's military into disarray, and within mere days of the start of the campaign, Pol Pot's military was in shambles and only capable of delaying tactics and insurgency operations. A key goal of Vietnam's military operation was to overrun Cambodia quickly enough that China would not be able to effectively intervene on the Pol Pot regime's behalf. The latter objective was achieved, to the point that outcomes and timetables exceeded Hanoi's initial expectations.

The speed with which Vietnamese forces overwhelmed defending units and penetrated Cambodian territory surprised the Khmer Rouge. By January 6, 1979, less than two weeks after the invasion began, Vietnamese forces had crossed the Mekong River in two different locations and were quickly converging on Phnom Penh. Correctly assessing that the remaining forces at his disposal were insufficient to halt the advancing columns or otherwise hold the capital, Pol Pot ordered the city's immediate evacuation before all escape routes were cut off. Phnom Penh's population, which had grown to approximately 50,000 Khmer Rouge officials, bureaucrats, and other regime-approved workers and their families, was ordered to evacuate westward by any available means; leaders and their families escaped by air, rail, or vehicle convoy; others, by foot.[12] Pol Pot and remaining senior officials fled the following morning mere hours before Vietnamese troops began entering the city's outskirts amid a chaotic, disorganized, and confused backdrop reminiscent of the fall of the Cambodian Republic a few years earlier. The capital's fall materialized so quickly and the Khmer Rouge government was so inept in its evacuation that most wounded were left behind along with significant resources, including intact aircraft and large quantities of military equipment and other supplies.

While many of the city's workers were either indoctrinated supporters of the regime who fled willingly or were coerced into evacuating with government forces, not all the rank-and-file workers in Phnom Penh chose to flee; instead, many apparently went into hiding within the city to avoid evacuation. Many workers in Phnom Penh had been forced to toil long hours under conditions described as "Dickensian" by some of the scant foreign observers who had been allowed a glimpse behind the regime's operational curtain.[13] Though they may not have harbored any inherent affection for the Vietnamese, significant numbers of Cambodians in the

THE RUMP STATE AND VIETNAMESE OCCUPATION, 1979–1991

capital—as in many other parts of the country—regarded Hanoi's invasion as a means to end their suffering under Pol Pot's rule and welcomed the Vietnamese as liberators. Reflecting this perspective as well as the hatred most Cambodians felt toward the Pol Pot regime, many Khmer Rouge functionaries, supporters, or soldiers who in parts of the country either chose not to evacuate from the advancing Vietnamese forces or fell behind along their routes of retreat were attacked and even beaten or hacked to death by infuriated fellow Cambodians.[14] However, such episodes were not the norm and, as Chanda notes, after several years of brutal Khmer Rouge rule, most of the Cambodian population sought to reject violence and revenge.

> The widespread killings, especially under the Khmer Rouge regime from April 1975 to January 1979 have taught Cambodians the need to avoid revenge if only to stop the cycle of violence. With few exceptions, the transition after the Vietnamese invaded was relatively peaceful. Khmer Rouge leaders Pol Pot and Ieng Sary were sentenced to death in absentia but the (Vietnamese-installed – People's Republic of Kampuchea) PRK government did not attempt to bring anyone else to justice. The Cambodian people themselves have been more forgiving than one could imagine in a similar situation anywhere else.[15]

The Khmer Rouge initially predicted the Vietnamese advance would stall after Phnom Penh's capture due to not only Hanoi's forces becoming spread increasingly thin but also the planned intensification of guerrilla resistance in territories under Vietnam's control, a resistance campaign that largely failed to materialize in occupied Cambodia. However, in the weeks following the capital's fall, Khmer Rouge forces were progressively driven back and repeatedly forced to relinquish more territory and relocate further west. By March, central Cambodia and virtually all remaining cities and towns had also been overrun, and the shattered remnants of the Khmer Rouge—including approximately 20,000–40,000 remaining troops and militia—had fled into remote, inaccessible jungles along Cambodia's border with Thailand.[16] Conditions along the Thai border were primitive, with few useful resources initially, meaning jungle land had to be cleared for the planting of subsistence crops, and endemic malaria afflicted many and ultimately claimed thousands of lives.

International Reactions

Thailand functioned as a close ally of the U.S. throughout much of the Cold War, hosting some 48,000 U.S. troops and receiving nearly $1 billion in U.S. military assistance between 1951 and 1971, but most U.S. troops were withdrawn by 1976, meaning Thailand became solely responsible for its own defense, a reality that tested the Thai military/government when Vietnam invaded neighboring Cambodia at the same time Thailand was fighting its own communist insurgency.[17] The number of Vietnamese troops deployed in Cambodia (approximately 160,000) in 1979 exceeded the total troop strength of the Thai military; Vietnamese forces were also well equipped, and most possessed considerable combat experience.[18] Vietnamese military incursions into Thai territory—usually in pursuit of Khmer Rouge forces that often attempted to use Thai territory as sanctuary—were common throughout much of the 1980s. This reality, combined with fighting between the Khmer Rouge remnants and Hanoi's forces along the frontier, displaced large numbers of both Thai and Cambodian civilians near the border. By early 1980, as many as 1 million Cambodians were displaced internally or externally, with some 100,000 Cambodian civilians having fled into Thailand to avoid the conflict.[19]

Although Vietnamese forces were within 300 km (186 mi) of Bangkok and made temporary incursions into and shelled Thai territory along the border—usually in engaging Khmer Rouge forces that, again, used Thai territory and the porous borders as sanctuary—Thailand largely tolerated these realities. Instead, they opted against significant military buildup or retaliation in much the same non-escalatory manner that Bangkok had reacted to Khmer Rouge border provocations during the Pol Pot regime.[20] Thailand chose to deal with the Vietnamese crisis politically/diplomatically through alliance building, including renewing close ties with the U.S., drawing closer to China and ASEAN, and inviting UN observers to monitor Vietnamese activities along the border.[21] Raymond (2020) suggests that Thailand used these moderated strategies in lieu of military escalation because (1) the Thai government thought the Vietnamese occupation of Cambodia would be more short-term in nature; (2) it possessed intelligence indicating no Vietnamese plans to invade Thailand; or (3) Bangkok's alliances with international partners, including the U.S. and China, would be sufficient to deter a Vietnamese invasion.[22] While bilateral relations with

THE RUMP STATE AND VIETNAMESE OCCUPATION, 1979–1991

Thailand were often strained when Pol Pot was in power (due to border disputes/incursions among other sources of friction), the Thai government provided continuing tacit support to the post-invasion Khmer Rouge remnants, regarding them as a buffer against the Vietnamese. The latter perception of Pol Pot's forces as a hedge against Hanoi had been formed in Bangkok even before the Vietnamese invasion; thus, practical geopolitical considerations incentivized the Thai government to largely ignore the atrocities of the Khmer Rouge regime.[23]

Thailand and the other four ASEAN member states—Indonesia, Malaysia, the Philippines, and Singapore—were all non-communist, and most were dealing with their own leftist insurgencies at the time of the Vietnamese offensive against the Khmer Rouge. An initial primary goal of ASEAN, in addition to economic and broader political cooperation, was communism's containment within Southeast Asia. ASEAN in the latter respect was, to a degree, an effort on the part of participating states within the region to replace the defunct Southeast Asian Treaty Organization (SEATO – 1954–1977) that had originally been intended as a collective security regime to deter communism's spread. Thailand and other ASEAN members were deeply concerned that the Vietnamese invasion of neighboring Cambodia not only established a precedent for Hanoi to interfere in other states within the region but also that the Soviet backing of Vietnam signaled Moscow's willingness to exert its own influence within Southeast Asia and escalate the Cambodian-Vietnamese dynamic into a broader regional conflict.[24]

The world's preeminent intergovernmental organization proved to be as ineffective as ASEAN in resolving the Vietnamese invasion, at least initially. The UN paid little attention to Cambodia while the Khmer Rouge were in power, failing to condemn or formally investigate the genocidal actions of the Pol Pot regime, yet it did begin to involve itself in Cambodian affairs in the wake of the Vietnamese invasion and occupation.[25] A November 1979 UN resolution called in vain for the immediate withdrawal of all foreign military forces from Cambodia. ASEAN, as well as Sihanouk's machinations, succeeded in getting the UN increasingly involved in the Cambodian conflict, including the 1981 International Conference on Kampuchea convened by the UN General Assembly.[26] Although it accomplished little and was boycotted by Vietnam and the Soviet bloc, the latter conference helped establish an international commitment to a peaceful resolution and set an organizational precedent for future UN efforts that would ultimately help facilitate peace.

Initially, the Hanoi-installed Cambodian government opposed any direct UN intervention—including deploying international peacekeeping forces—interpreting such proposals as an affront to national sovereignty; indeed, Vietnam and Laos for several years supported the Phnom Penh government's objections. It also undertook other efforts to convey its autonomous status. In an effort to counter perceptions that it was merely Vietnam's puppet, the government changed the country's official name in 1989 from the People's Republic of Kampuchea (PRK) to the State of Cambodia.[27] Attempting to also establish at least partial control over Cambodia's security and diminish reliance upon occupying Vietnamese forces, the Hanoi-installed government implemented an unpopular conscription program when they were unable to attract significant numbers of volunteers. Conscription raised some 80,000 Cambodian government troops, compared to no more than 40,000 Khmer Rouge forces and 14,000 KPNLF and 10,000 FUNCINPEC troops.[28] Hoping to placate them, the financially strapped regime permitted poorly paid government conscripts to exploit the natural resources (timber, minerals, etc.) and levy "taxes" on local populations in their military districts. While they did not endear local populations to either the new government or its military, these practices did generally provide enough economic incentive for government troops to endeavor to hold their territory from opposition forces.[29] Dobbins, et al. in a RAND Corporation study provide a concise overview of the formation and significance of the opposition coalition, which included the Khmer Rouge and eventually coalesced into a coalition government in exile.

> (In addition to the Khmer Rouge) . . . Forces loyal to Prince Sihanouk, under the banner of the United Front for an Independent, Neutral, Peaceful, and Cooperative Cambodia (in French: *Front Uni National pour un Cambodge Independant, Neutre, Pacifique, et Cooperatif,* or FUNCINPEC), and forces loyal to Republican leader Son Sann, the Khmer People's National Liberation Front (KPNLF) were also entrenched along the border. Consequently, many of the camps effectively became paramilitary training centers. With support from China, ASEAN countries and the West, the groups opposed to the

THE RUMP STATE AND VIETNAMESE OCCUPATION, 1979–1991

Vietnamese backed regime organized into a government in exile named the Coalition Government of Democratic Kampuchea (CGDK).[30]

ASEAN member states unanimously condemned the Vietnamese invasion of Cambodia, refused to recognize the puppet government installed by the Vietnamese in Phnom Penh, and called for both the immediate withdrawal of Hanoi's forces and Cambodian self-determination by scheduling free and fair elections. ASEAN's efforts and those of other actors were initially insufficient to secure Vietnam's withdrawal from Cambodia or facilitate other steps (elections) called for to resolve the crisis. However, ASEAN's support as the primary regional cooperation regime combined with that of an eclectic mix of various other international actors—the U.S. and most western nations, China, North Korea—gave the deposed, murderous Khmer Rouge a level of international recognition and legitimacy they could not have attained otherwise. For example, the rump state was not only widely recognized bilaterally as Cambodia's legitimate government but also the remnant of what should have been the wholly discredited Pol Pot regime retained sole control of Cambodia's seat and vote within the United Nations until 1982—over three years after its ouster. In fact, they shared joint control of that seat/vote as a part of the coalition opposition government in exile until 1991 with the final Vietnamese withdrawal and Peace Accords.[31]

As in many other geopolitical issues during the Cold War, the communist bloc was divided as to Vietnam's Cambodian invasion. Laos was the only nation in Southeast Asia allied with Vietnam and publicly supportive of its actions in Cambodia. In July 1975, communist Laos laid the foundation of its political alliance with, and subservience to, Vietnam by signing a preliminary Treaty of Friendship and Cooperation, followed in 1977 by a 25-year Treaty of Friendship and formal acknowledgement that it was within Hanoi's sphere of influence.[32] At the request of the Vientiane, Vietnam deployed up to 60,000 troops to prop up the communist regime in Laos. The latter, combined with Laotian dependency on Hanoi (as well as Moscow) for material and economic aid, established Laos as Vietnam's sole military ally within the region. It also facilitated both the swift recognition of the Vietnamese-installed government in Cambodia and the Laos government's severed diplomatic ties with China.[33]

Vietnam likely would not have proceeded with its Cambodian invasion without at least tacit Soviet support, and the USSR remained the most significant source of international support for the ongoing occupation and for the Vietnamese-installed regime in Phnom Penh. In late 1979, the Soviet Union, the Congo, and Panama failed in an attempt to have the UN recognize the Vietnamese-installed regime as the legitimate government in Cambodia. Though by the following year, 29 countries (many of which were Soviet allies or client states) recognized the People's Republic, with nearly 80 states still acknowledging the Khmer Rouge as Cambodia's legitimate government.[34] Shifting Soviet policy during the 1980s would eventually factor into the ongoing Vietnamese occupation. In the early 1980s, Vietnam received as much as $1 billion in annual aid from Moscow, which subsidized much of Vietnam's expenses in maintaining its military presence in Cambodia. By the late 1980s, however, a reform-minded Gorbachev, seeking to moderate Soviet foreign policy and forge better relations with China and the west (and also motivated by the USSR's worsening economic difficulties that impeded its ability to maintain previous levels of foreign assistance), substantially reduced Vietnam's aid levels, a primary factor in Vietnam's 1989 announcement that it would withdraw its forces and end the occupation.[35]

China had been the primary source of aid to the Khmer Rouge both in the latter period of Pol Pot's insurrection against the Cambodian Republic and during Pol Pot's regime. This support continued despite several failures of China's foreign policy machinations related to Cambodia: Beijing had not succeeded in its efforts to moderate or control Khmer Rouge policies, including its maltreatment of its ethnic Vietnamese minority and aggression toward Vietnam. Chinese maneuvering had not prevented the Soviet-Vietnamese alliance that Beijing feared was an early phase of Moscow's plans to encircle China and extend Soviet influence within China's geographical domain; and China failed to prevent Vietnam from invading Cambodia.

An agreement between China and Thailand forged shortly after the Vietnamese invasion afforded Khmer Rouge forces sanctuary in Thailand and shipments of Chinese arms and other supplies through Thai territory in exchange for Beijing ceasing all support for the Thai Communist Party and its insurgency.[36] With full U.S. support of the Sino-Thai cooperation to prop up Pol Pot, China shipped military supplies to Thailand by sea; the Thai

Army, in turn, delivered these supplies to Khmer Rouge camps. Food and other supplies were also provided to the Khmer Rouge by China, the ethnic Chinese minority in Thailand, and the Thai military.[37] At its height, U.S. funding (covert and otherwise) to the Khmer Rouge and other opposition forces never exceeded a few million dollars annually. In contrast, Chinese aid—which, with U.S./western encouragement, was eventually extended to multiple opposition factions in addition to the Khmer Rouge—totaled up to around $100 million annually.[38] Such support enabled Khmer Rouge forces to substantially increase in both size (50–100%) and capability within less than a year after the invasion, becoming the most formidable military force among major opposition groups.[39] Despite the partial rebuilding of their forces and the level of support they received from China and other nations, the Khmer Rouge were never able to conduct military actions beyond insurgency operations, nor did they ever pose a serious threat in terms of expelling Vietnamese forces or overthrowing the Hanoi-installed government in Phnom Penh. In the first weeks of the Vietnamese invasion, the very survival of the Khmer Rouge was in question, leading China into direct military conflict with Vietnam in what was perhaps the most glaring example of discord within the communist bloc.

Sino-Vietnamese Border War

While China and Vietnam had been close allies in previous decades, with Beijing providing up to $20 billion in military and other aid to Vietnamese communists since 1951, their relations increasingly deteriorated beginning in the mid-1970s.[40] In November 1978, Vietnam and the Soviet Union signed a Treaty of Friendship and Cooperation that precipitated large shipments of Soviet military aid and further deterioration in relations with China. In turn, Beijing pursued improved relations, including security cooperation with other nations in Southeast Asia (e.g., ending support for Thailand's communist guerillas) as a strategy to contain the Vietnamese and their Soviet backers.[41] China publicly condemned Vietnam's invasion of Cambodia and, in a January 1979 statement to the UN, accused Vietnam of attempting to establish a regional federation under the control of Hanoi/Moscow with Soviet support.[42] Seeing that Vietnam was not content with a limited incursion into Cambodia and that widespread international condemnation of the invasion would not dissuade Hanoi, China opted for a large-scale military response in what was among the best examples of overt conflict among rival communist states during the Cold War.

In February, up to 600,000 Chinese troops attacked along the entirety of the disputed border with Vietnam at a time when three of Vietnam's four army groups were deployed in Cambodia—some elements of which were quickly recalled to help fend off the Chinese offensive.[43] China never offered an official public justification for its border war with Vietnam, but various combined factors drove its actions, as Zhang (2010) succinctly notes: (1) intent to counter Vietnam's aspirations to become the regional hegemon in Southeast Asia; (2) border disputes/incursions between China and Vietnam, which had been escalating with some 752 such incidents occurring in 1977 alone; (3) alleged maltreatment of ethnic Chinese minorities in Vietnam, mostly in the border region; (4) Vietnam's alliance with the Soviet Union, which sought to expand its influence within the region; and (5) the border war that would divert Vietnamese military forces away from the Khmer Rouge, China's ally, and perhaps halt or at least slow Hanoi's military advances in Cambodia.[44]

The Vietnamese had progressively reinforced the border through prolonged and escalating skirmishes in recent years. For weeks leading up to the attack, China consequently announced its plans for a punitive attack and even evacuated several hundred thousand of its citizens along the border. However, despite Hanoi's preparations, the scale of the attack along the entire frontier combined with superior Chinese numbers supported by armor, artillery, and air power initially overtaxed Vietnamese defenders, comprising approximately 100,000 regular military forces supported by some 150,000 militia.[45] A substantial force of around 300,000 Vietnamese troops was held in reserve for Hanoi's defense in the event of a breakthrough by Chinese forces in the north. Beijing also held back several hundred thousand troops, the bulk of its military, along the border with the Soviet Union and placed them on heightened alert, fearing Moscow might escalate the conflict by attacking China in support of Vietnam and, in doing so, potentially trigger WWIII.

While neither of the latter worst-case scenarios materialized, intense fighting raged across the more than 800-mile border for nearly a month. Within days of the initial offensive, Chinese forces penetrated up to 12 miles into Vietnam and ultimately captured a substantial amount of territory along the border, including several towns, before the initial offensive's momentum stalled amid mounting Vietnamese resistance both along the front and behind the lines through guerilla action. In early March, Beijing publicly proclaimed its objectives had been achieved and that it was accordingly withdrawing its forces from Vietnamese territory. As the Chinese forces withdrew, they either looted or purposefully destroyed much in Vietnam's northern provinces that had been initially captured, an action that had a lasting impact on the affected areas' economies and livelihoods. Both sides proclaimed victory in what was largely a stalemated and pointless conflict without a decisive outcome.

Just as it is difficult to estimate the exact numbers of troops involved in the conflict, the number of casualties incurred by each side is also subject to debate. To make their own forces appear more successful, both sides exaggerated the opposing force's size; similarly, they inflated estimates of enemy casualties and downplayed the numbers of their own killed and wounded. Credible estimates of Chinese casualties generally range from between 6,500 and 25,000 killed and between 31,000 and 37,000 wounded, with Vietnamese sources claiming to have inflicted significantly higher Chinese losses.[46] Most third-party estimates of Vietnamese losses suggest approximately 30,000 dead and a comparable or slightly larger number of wounded, with almost certainly inflated Chinese estimates of Vietnamese casualties substantially higher.[47]

China may have, in effect, punished Vietnam by inflicting damage and casualties, but it suffered substantial losses itself, and, given the speed with which Vietnamese forces had overrun the Khmer Rouge, nearly all populated areas of Cambodia had been taken over by Vietnamese forces by March when the Sino-Vietnamese War concluded. Likewise, the Vietnamese had managed to fend off the Chinese attack but only barely and at great cost. Military resources that Hanoi could have otherwise devoted to the Cambodia operation were diverted in line with China's objectives, but the Khmer Rouge had already been effectively routed and reduced to little more than a disorganized rabble by the time the Sino-Vietnamese War erupted. Had the war with China never materialized, it is highly unlikely that Vietnamese forces could have halted or impeded the Khmer Rouge retreat into Cambodia's remote western jungles or that Vietnamese forces could have effectively pursued Pol Pot's remaining forces into such remote areas to dislodge them in early 1979. In short, the Sino-Vietnamese War in and of itself did little to prop up or ameliorate the decline of the Khmer Rouge regime or alter the course of what would evolve into a prolonged, low-intensity guerilla war waged by Pol Pot's rump state along the Thai border of westernmost Cambodia.

Pol Pot's Rump State and Prolonged Low-Intensity Guerilla Campaign

Following its disastrous defeats stemming from the Vietnamese invasion, the Khmer Rouge partially rebuilt its military in subsequent years in the remote, forested portions of the country to which it had fled. Its reconstituted forces were estimated to have achieved a peak strength of between 25,000 and 45,000. However, they were never again able to establish permanent control over any strategic or otherwise important region or major city of Cambodia or garner significant support from the country's population that they had subjugated and terrorized years earlier—though propaganda and indoctrination efforts directed principally to the peasant class would continue.[48] At its territorial height, the Khmer Rouge rump regime controlled only approximately 200,000 people, or around 5% of Cambodia's population at the time, via some 2,000 of Cambodia's 8,000 rural villages—mostly small and isolated—which, together with foreign aid, kept Khmer Rouge fighters and functionaries fed.[49]

In the wake of the invasion and the reduction in status to a rump state, the Khmer Rouge largely stopped mass killings but continued to engage in other egregious human rights violations. Thousands of people were trapped in camps behind the goals of forced labor and indoctrination, and thousands more who had initially escaped the Khmer Rouge were abducted from refugee camps across the border in Thailand and brought as laborers to Cambodian territory controlled by the Khmer Rouge.[50] Up to 60,000 Cambodian refugees had been taken from Thai-based camps into Khmer Rouge-controlled territory as sources of agricultural labor by late 1990, reflecting that the movement was maintaining its ideological position of reliance upon an agrarian base as political and economic cornerstones.[51]

The Khmer Rouge abandoned many of its more radical former economic policies, reversing course at least temporarily in allowing free markets, private property ownership, and other vestiges of capitalism. Banks and possession of foreign currency were legalized, and the rump state eventually printed its own currency that was pegged to the Thai baht and

U.S. dollar, though barter, especially rice, remained a common medium of exchange.[52] Mining and logging concessions were negotiated with private companies, primarily based in Thailand, which paid various fees to the Khmer Rouge and also built much-needed roads and other infrastructure in the areas under the group's control. This arrangement generated significant revenue for the Khmer Rouge: up to $100–150 million in 1990—more than the national budget of the Vietnamese-installed regime in Phnom Penh that year.[53] The degree to which such reforms (and occasional public pronouncements that the movement was no longer communist) were undertaken out of any genuine revision in Khmer Rouge ideology as opposed to being implemented out of temporary economic expediency and the regime's desperation to curry favor internationally or ensure its survival remains unclear. Other sources of income for the Khmer Rouge included taxing cross-border trade between Thailand and Cambodia and, eventually, exporting a limited range of agricultural products, including rice (93% of exports), rubber (5%), and various other crops (2%).[54] Such sources of self-reliant income would prove increasingly vital to the Khmer Rouge and its ongoing guerilla campaign as sources of foreign aid were eventually reduced or eliminated entirely beginning in the late 1980s.

Vietnamese-Occupied Cambodia

A defining characteristic of Cambodian communism was its divisive, fractious nature and its tendency to split into competing factions that harbored as much or more animus toward each other as they did toward rival non-communist polities within the country. Such discord was present prior to and during the Khmer Rouge regime as well as its period as a rump state. Ideological differences, internal power struggles, and brutal dystopian policies during the Pol Pot regime led to the defection of many disaffected Khmer Rouge, including the Cambodian communist faction led by Heng Samrin (Cambodian National Assembly President and de facto head of state, 1979–1992). Samrin and many others opposed to Pol Pot fled to Vietnam and were ultimately installed by Hanoi as part of its client regime, officially known as the People's Republic of Kampuchea (1979–1989) and, after 1989, as the State of Cambodia.

The Khmer communists who opposed Pol Pot and fled to Vietnam and aided in the Vietnamese overthrow of the Khmer Rouge regime had been justifiably harsh in their condemnation of the latter and its dystopian, genocidal policies. Reflecting opposition attitudes toward the Pol Pot cabal, these Khmer communists, together with Vietnamese forces that participated in the invasion and Pol Pot's overthrow, described their umbrella coalition as the Salvation Front.[55] Given the circumstances, one might expect that the Heng Samrin regime in Phnom Penh and the Vietnamese occupation forces would have engaged in retaliatory conduct and meted out harsh punitive justice to former Pol Pot soldiers or functionaries over whom they gained custody, but that was generally not the case. Particularly in the first years of the Vietnamese occupation, Cambodians identified and exposed many former Pol Pot supporters who had gone underground to escape responsibility. However, apart from a few cases in which mob justice was meted out by crowds, most former Khmer Rouge faced little-to-no punishment, with some being arrested by Cambodian or Vietnamese forces but normally released shortly thereafter and others interred in re-education camps in which they did not usually experience harsh treatment and were not detained for prolonged periods.[56]

Former Khmer Rouge were also integrated in large numbers into government positions, perhaps reflecting a belief on the part of the Heng Samrin faction and the Vietnamese that Khmer Rouge could be converted to their interpretation of communism more easily than the general Cambodian population or out of recognition that reconciliation, including forgiveness and reintegration of former Khmer Rouge, would be necessary to rebuild a stable Cambodian society.[57] Additionally, some Heng Samrin-aligned communists remained distrustful of the Vietnamese and potentially saw rehabilitated Khmer Rouge as the lesser of two evils—and perhaps hoped their reintegration into Cambodian society might help diminish Hanoi's influence and strengthen what had originally been established as little more than a puppet state.

Following the withdrawal of Vietnamese forces, concern nonetheless was raised over possible future attempts by the Khmer Rouge to return to power, even as one element of a broader governing coalition. Such concerns were exacerbated by Beijing's (perhaps the only possible moderating influence over the militants) assertion that it wielded limited control over Pol Pot's faction. One option initially considered was to seek the exile of Pol Pot and other senior leaders to China or some other state, but no

THE RUMP STATE AND VIETNAMESE OCCUPATION, 1979–1991

countries seriously contemplated extending an offer of asylum due to the Khmer Rouge genocide's stigma.[58] The Vietnamese-installed government in Phnom Penh and its sponsors in Hanoi actively took precautions against any effort on the part of the Khmer Rouge to regain power, such as organizing and training national military and local militia forces armed with Soviet-supplied weapons—including over 200,000 modern rifles as well as such higher-end weaponry as MIG-21 fighters.[59]

Prior to the Pol Pot regime, non-ethnic Khmer minorities had been proportionally overrepresented in leadership roles as heads of government agencies, bureaucrats, business leaders, etc. Given the numbers of ethnic minorities and those formerly in positions of power who had been killed or fled abroad during the Pol Pot dictatorship, a leadership vacuum opened after the Khmer Rouge were removed from power. In attempting to rebuild Cambodian society, even low/mid-level positions such as teachers, civil servants, and shopkeepers—essential for the functioning of any society—could not be adequately staffed due to the scope of the killings and the degree to which the genocide had targeted any visible vestige of the previous socioeconomic and political order. In part to address such personnel shortages as well as the consequences of the Khmer Rouge's targeting and decimating the ethnic Vietnamese minority that had been present in significant numbers just years earlier, Hanoi facilitated the resettlement of several hundred thousand ethnic Vietnamese in Cambodia in the years following the Vietnamese invasion.[60]

Even after ousting the Khmer Rouge from most of Cambodia, the Vietnamese and their client state found it difficult to initiate rebuilding the country. The timing of the invasion disrupted planting the annual rice crop, which, combined with Khmer Rouge efforts to steal or destroy rice and other food stocks as they retreated, ultimately resulted in a famine that claimed tens of thousands of lives. This food insecurity pattern would intermittently repeat for years, caused by either active fighting or landmines preventing normal agricultural processes.[61] The scale of national destruction the Khmer Rouge wrought, the shortage of engineers and other key labor segments and the effects of the ongoing guerilla war meant that Cambodia's infrastructure and even the most basic services, such as public utilities and medical care, would not attain even minimal standards for many years. The Cold War political dynamic meant that, initially, foreign aid and nation-building support for the Hanoi-installed Cambodian government came almost entirely from the Soviet bloc. Vietnam, the USSR, and Eastern European nations sent food, fuel, and machinery as well as engineers and other workers. Within a few years, western nations followed suit with significant aid to induce the Phnom Penh regime to participate in the peace process.[62]

1991 Paris Peace Agreement and Vietnamese Withdrawal

In the late 1980s, international efforts aimed at resolving the Cambodian Civil War intensified which, coupled with changing geopolitical circumstances on the part of many external powers involved in Cambodia, opened the door for progress to be made in peace efforts. China's initial position was that leaving the Hanoi-installed regime in place legitimized Vietnam's invasion and undermined Cambodian sovereignty. Beijing also stipulated that improved Chinese relations with the USSR and Vietnam depended on both countries backing away from their involvement in Cambodia.[63] China's position concerning the Vietnamese-installed regime in Phnom Penh eventually softened, and external developments also facilitated political pullback from Moscow and Hanoi. China had also initially supported restoring the Khmer Rouge to power but by 1988 had abandoned such demands in favor of a power-sharing arrangement among the main opposition groups under Sihanouk's leadership. Beijing also indicated that it would honor the results of a fair Cambodian election, though it continued its support for the Khmer Rouge and other opposition groups to maintain leverage over Vietnam.[64]

Reform-minded Gorbachev prioritized improved relations with China over wielding Soviet influence in Southeast Asia, even including Moscow's alliance with Vietnam.[65] In 1988, Moscow's shifting position was indicated when the USSR remained silent in the Sino-Vietnamese conflict over control of the Spratly Islands, essentially signaling Soviet deference to China in Southeast Asian affairs as well as the reality that the USSR had reduced its naval patrols and other vestiges of a military presence within the region.[66] The improved Sino-Soviet political dynamic, combined with deteriorating economic conditions in the USSR and Soviet bloc and a broader thaw in the Cold War dynamic, meant the Soviets and their Eastern European satellite states had, by the late 1980s, substantially reduced their aid to Vietnam and

THE RUMP STATE AND VIETNAMESE OCCUPATION, 1979–1991

its client state in Phnom Penh. Declining foreign aid, which at its height was approximately $1.8 billion annually, shifted the unsustainable financial burden of propping up the existing Cambodian government to Hanoi, which consequently became increasingly receptive to a negotiated settlement.[67] The financial strain on Vietnam was further exacerbated by Beijing's decision to maintain up to 300,000 troops along the Sino-Vietnamese border, requiring Hanoi in turn to deploy substantial numbers of troops near the border as a precautionary measure.[68]

China, the U.S., USSR, and ASEAN, as well as the Cambodian government and three main opposition factions, eventually supported a political settlement, including elections and international oversight. This support, combined with rising anti-Vietnamese sentiment in Cambodia and years of economic and political isolation, incentivized Vietnam to acquiesce.[69] However, the Khmer Rouge were initially obstructionists, refusing to negotiate until all Vietnamese troops were withdrawn and Hanoi's client regime in Phnom Penh was out of power.[70] The first of the two goals would soon be realized. Vietnam began drawing down its remaining 100,000-man force in the spring of 1989. The last of its soldiers (apart from technical advisors) withdrew by September of that year, ending a nearly 11-year occupation that, together with the initial invasion, had resulted in approximately 55,000 Vietnamese military fatalities, according to Hanoi.[71]

Following Vietnam's military withdrawal, international efforts focused on a negotiated settlement among the various Cambodian political factions to end the civil war, promote fair elections and other democratic norms, and prevent the resurgence of the Khmer Rouge—with the U.S. and many other former sources of international support shifting away from Pol Pot in favor of other opposition elements and the idea of a coalition democracy.[72] Negotiations culminated in the Paris Peace Accords adopted in October 1991. The agreement was signed by the four principle Cambodian political groups: the Kampuchean People's Revolutionary Armed Forces (the Hanoi-installed government), the Khmer Rouge (known officially as the Party of Democratic Kampuchea), the Khmer People's National Liberation Front (pro-west, anti-communist opposition group—essentially, reformulated Republican forces), the Funcinpec Party (National United Front for an Independent, Neutral, Peaceful and Cooperative Cambodia—Prince Sihanouk's royalist opposition group), and 19 foreign countries with interests in Cambodia and the conflict.[73] The Accords' primary objectives were to end the fighting and help facilitate political stability in Cambodia. Charlesworth succinctly explains the significance of the Accords and the creation of the UN Transitional Authority:

> The agreements established the UN Transitional Authority in Cambodia (UNTAC) and gave it responsibility to monitor the ceasefire, oversee the demobilization of the various armies and create a new political system. The creation of UNTAC, an initiative led by Australia, was the first time that the UN had taken over the functions of government across a country. It was designed in large part to allow China a face-saving method of withdrawing its support for the Khmer Rouge.[74]

The UN proposal that was ultimately adopted integrated ASEAN's original vision of a transitional Supreme National Council with six seats allocated to the Heng Samrin regime and six assigned to the opposition coalition. Additionally, until elections—overseen by international observers—could be implemented to form a new democratic government, Cambodia would temporarily be administered under what would be a two-year UN trusteeship, with the existing government in Phnom Penh retaining partial control.[75] As part of the 1991 Agreement, the Khmer Rouge and other members of the opposition coalition were not to attempt to create separate states, though certain actions of the Khmer Rouge—such as printing currency—ran afoul of such terms.[76] Pol Pot's faction also refused to draw down its forces and posed other obstacles to international intervention which, in turn, led the other opposition factions and Cambodian government to often limit cooperation with UNTAC mandates.[77] The inability of UNTAC to fully demobilize or disarm the warring factions permitted sporadic fighting between the groups to continue, even following a tenuous May 1991 cease-fire agreement brokered by the UN.[78] Despite such continued setbacks, the conditions were set for an end to the Cambodian Civil War and for democratization and reconciliation in the post-Cold War era.

Endnotes

1. Kelvin Rowley, "Second Life, Second Death: The Khmer Rouge After 1978," in Susan Cook ed. *Genocide in Cambodia and Rwanda* (New York: Routledge 2006), pp. 201–225.
2. Merle Pribbenow, "A Tale of Five Generals: Vietnam's Invasion of Cambodia," *The Journal of Military History* 70(2) 2006, pp. 459–486.
3. Joseph Pouvatchy, "Cambodian-Vietnamese Relations," *Asian Survey* 26(4) 1986, pp. 440–451.
4. Stephen Morris, *Why Vietnam Invaded Cambodia: Political Culture and the Cause of War* (Stanford, CA: Stanford University Press, 1999).
5. Pribbenow, 2006.
6. Rep. Les Aspin Press Release, "Intelligence Performance on the China-Vietnam Border," March 26, 1979 (Accessed July 21, 2022).
7. Chenyi Wang, "The Chinese Communist Party's Relationship with the Khmer Rouge in the 1970s: An Ideological Victory and a Strategic Failure," Working Paper 88, Cold War International History Project. Washington, DC: Wilson Center, December 2018.
8. Pribbenow, 2006.
9. Laura Southgate, *ASEAN Resistance to Sovereignty Violation: Interests, Balancing and the Role of the Vanguard State* (Bristol, UK: Bristol University Press, 2019).
10. Pribbenow, 2006.
11. Pribbenow, 2006.
12. Wilfred Deac, *Road to the Killing Fields: The Cambodian War of 1970–1975* (College Station, TX: Texas A&M University Press, 1997).
13. Ben Kiernan, *The Pol Pot Regime: Race, Power, and Genocide in Cambodia under the Khmer Rouge, 1975-79* (New Haven, CT: Yale University Press, 1996), pp. 444–445.
14. David Chandler, *Brother Number One: A Political Biography of Pol Pot* (Boulder, CO: Westview Press, 1999); Phillip Short, *Pol Pot: Anatomy of a Nightmare* (New York: Henry Holt, 2005).
15. Nayan Chanda, "Civil War in Cambodia," *Foreign Policy* (No. 76) 1989, pp. 29–30.
16. Southgate, 2019.
17. Gregory Raymond, "Strategic Culture and Thailand's Response to Vietnam's Occupation of Cambodia, 1979–1989," *Journal of Cold War*

Studies 22(1) 2020, pp. 4–45.
18. Raymond, 2020.
19. Southgate, 2019.
20. Christian Oesterheld, "Cambodian-Thai Relations During the Khmer Rouge Regime: Evidence from the East German Diplomatic Archives," *Silpakorn University Journal of Social Sciences* (14) 2014, pp. 107–128; Raymond, 2020.
21. Raymond, 2020.
22. Ibid.
23. Puangthong Rungswasdisab, "Thailand's Response to the Cambodian Genocide," in Susan Cook ed. *Genocide in Cambodia and Rwanda* (New York: Routledge 2006) pp. 79–126.
24. Raymond, 2020.
25. Hillary Charlesworth, "Swimming to Cambodia: Justice and Ritual in Human Rights After Conflict," *Australian Yearbook of International Law* Vol. 29 2010, pp. 1–16.
26. Esref Aksu, *The United Nations, Intra-state Peacekeeping and Normative Change* (Manchester, UK: Manchester University Press, 2003).
27. James Dobbins, Laurel Miller, Stephanie Pezars, Christopher Chivvis, Julie Taylor, Keith Crane, Calin Trenkov-Wermuth and Tewodaj Mengistu, *Overcoming Obstacles to Peace.* (Arlington, VA: RAND Corporation, 2013).
28. Dobbins, et al., 2013.
29. Joel Brinkley, *Cambodia's Curse: The Modern History of a Troubled Land* (New York: Public Affairs, 2011); Dobbins, et al., 2013.
30. Dobbins, et al., 2013
31. Paul Bellamy, "After the Killing Fields." *New Zealand International Review* 33(1) 2008, pp. 18–22
32. Southgate, 2019.
33. Khang Vu, "Vietnam's Sole Military Ally: The country's longstanding ties with its neighbor Laos constitute an alliance in everything but name," *The Diplomat* December 21, 2020.
34. Bellamy, 2008.
35. Raymond, 2020.
36. Zachary Abuza, "The Khmer Rouge Quest for Economic Independence," *Asian Survey* 33(10) Oct. 1993, pp. 1010–1021.

37. Abuza, 1993; Elizabeth Becker, *When the War was Over: Cambodia and the Khmer Rouge Revolution* (New York: Public Affairs, 1998).
38. Don Oberdorfer, "Schultz Opposes Military Aid for Guerillas in Cambodia," *Washington Post*. July 11, 1985, p. A–23.
39. Abuza, 1993.
40. Xiaoming Zhang, "Deng Xiaping and China's decision to go to War," *Journal of Cold War Studies* 12(3) 2010, pp. 3–29.
41. Southgate, 2019.
42. Southgate, 2019.
43. Pribbenow, 2006; Estimates of troop deployments vary between Chinese, Vietnamese, and western sources– China claimed to have only deployed around 200,000 troops; Vietnam claimed over 600,000 Chinese troops were deployed; third-party estimates generally place Chinese troop deployments somewhere between the two extremes– such as Southgate (2019) who estimated approximately 400,000.
44. Zhang, 20010.
45. King Chen, *China's War with Vietnam, 1979: Issues, Decisions, and Implications* (Stanford, CA: Hoover Institution Press, Stanford University, 1987).
46. Zhang Xiaoming, "China's 1979 War with Vietnam: A Reassessment," *China Quarterly* (No. 184) December 2005, pp. 851–874.
47. Raymond, 2020; Southgate, 2019.
48. Chanda, 1989; Abuza, 1993.
49. Abuza, 1993.
50. Chanda, 1989.
51. Abuza, 1993.
52. Bill Bainbridge and Lon Nara, "Last Days for Guerilla Currency," *Phnom Penh Post* August 3, 2001; Abuza, 1993.
53. Dobbins, et al., 2013; Abuza, 1993.
54. Abuzza, 1993.
55. David Hutt, "Cambodia Needs to Move Past the Narrative of 'National Salvation'" *The Diplomat*. Sept. 28, 2022.
56. Marie Alexandrine Martin, *Cambodia: A Shattered Society* (Berkeley, CA: University of California Press, 1994).
57. Martin, 1994.
58. Chanda, 1989.

59. Chanda, 1989.
60. Abdulgaffar Peang-Meth, "Understanding the Khmer: Sociological-Cultural Observations," *Asian Survey* (31)5 May 1991, pp. 442–455.
61. M. Leepson, "Cambodia: A Nation in Turmoil," Congressional Quarterly Editorial Research Reports (Vol. I) 1985. Washington DC: CQ Press. Retrieved from: https://library.cqpress.com/cqresearcher/document.php?id=cqresrre1985040508.
62. Evan Gottesman, *Cambodia After the Khmer Rouge: Inside the Politics of Nation Building* (New Haven, CT: Yale University Press, 2003).
63. Robert Ross, "China and the Cambodian Peace Process: The Value of Coercive Diplomacy," *Asian Survey* 31(12) December 1991, pp. 1170–1185.
64. Ross, 1991.
65. Ross, 1991.
66. Ross, 1991.
67. V. Largo. *Vietnam: Current Issues and Historical Background* (Hauppauge: NY: Nova Science Publishers, 2002).
68. Ross, 1991.
69. Central Intelligence Agency, "Cambodia: How Viable (is) the Heng Samrin Regime – An Intelligence Assessment," (June 1986). Accessed March 1, 2022; Aksu, 2003.
70. CIA, 1986; Ross, 1991.
71. Nick Williams, "Hanoi Puts Its Cambodia Toll at 55,000 Dead," *Los Angeles Times*. July 1, 1988.
72. Ross, 1991.
73. Charlesworth, 2010.
74. Charlesworth, 2010.
75. Peang-Meth, 1991.
76. Abuza, 1993.
77. Dobbins, et al., 2013.
78. United Nations, "Cambodia: UNTAC Background," https://peacekeeping.un.org/en/mission/past/untacbackgr1.html. Accessed September 18, 2022; Dobbins, et al., 2013.

Post-Cold War Cambodia

The UN Transitional Authority and associated national elections afforded Cambodians and international observers hope that the country was poised to enter a new era of stability and democratization. The FUNCINPEC electoral victory was not recognized by the post-Khmer Rouge communist regime, which leveraged its complaints and position of authority—and fears of a renewed civil war—to forge a coalition government and power-sharing arrangement with Sihanouk's faction within the framework of a reformulated constitutional monarchy. The Khmer Rouge rump state, understandably, failed to garner any popular support beyond the small populations it continued to control in remote western enclaves. Knowing their portion of the vote would be meager, the Khmer Rouge refused to participate in the election and, decrying its results and the continued control of the Vietnamese-installed regime in Phnom Penh, sustained their guerilla campaign.

Defections, internecine conflict, and the loss of aid from formerly supportive foreign backers all contributed to the progressive decline of the Khmer Rouge throughout the 1990s. Pol Pot was removed from power, tried, convicted, and placed under house arrest by a rival Khmer Rouge faction in 1997. He died while still in Khmer Rouge custody the following year, mere months before the last remaining pockets of Khmer Rouge guerillas surrendered. Following prolonged negotiations, legal proceedings jointly undertaken by the international community and Cambodian authorities were eventually initiated to bring those responsible for Khmer Rouge crimes to justice. Largely due to the Hun Sen government's interference, the Khmer Rouge Tribunals only facilitated eight indictments and three convictions, despite the misery wrought by the Khmer Rouge upon the Cambodian population. In addition to hopes for justice having been largely dashed, a regime comprised of many former Khmer Rouge functionaries—though with such varying political incarnations as name changes for the government and ruling party—has remained in power for decades and increasingly turned away from democratic norms in favor of corruption, de facto one-party rule, authoritarianism, and widespread human rights violations.

Transitional Period

The settlement afforded a significant degree of temporary administrative control of Cambodia to the UN under the direct auspices of the Secretary General (rather than the General Assembly—as Vietnam and its client regime in Phnom Penh resented and distrusted the UN legislative body for awarding Cambodia's seat/vote to the Khmer Rouge and later to the opposition coalition). The arrangement ostensibly allowed the UN Secretary General to temporarily control many aspects of Cambodia's government, a plan which, in addition to permitting a thaw in relations between China and Vietnam, in theory would also deprive the Vietnamese-installed regime of many incumbency benefits (e.g., attempting to leverage political patronage) leading up to national elections, in effect helping to level the political playing field for opposition groups.[1] However, while the Heng Samrin regime in Phnom Penh did make concessions in terms of ceding some governmental authority, it retained significant bureaucratic control and would go into the elections with potentially more influence over most of the Cambodian population than any of the opposition factions.[2]

UNTAC's mission officially began in March 1992 and, at its peak, UNTAC was staffed with over 21,000 military and civilian personnel from more than 100 countries.[3] UNTAC assumed at least partial control of many key sectors of Cambodia's government, including communications, finance, foreign affairs, and security, to help facilitate stability conducive to national elections.[4] Casualties subsided in factional fighting following the Vietnamese withdrawal and arrival of UNTAC peacekeepers and observers. In 1989, prior to peace negotiations, fighting resulted in approximately 1,000 fatalities; following the implementation of the Peace Accords, however, military deaths dropped to 200 in 1991.[5] The latter downward trend continued in subsequent years due to the stabilizing effects of the

UN mission and the subsequent elections and political reconciliation/reintegration, with combat fatalities dropping to 25–50 deaths per year between 1995 and 1998.[6]

One of the most difficult issues to address initially was the relocation of several hundred thousand Cambodian refugees close to the Thai-Cambodia border, many of whom did not want to relocate for fear fighting might resume leading up to or following the elections.[7] One of the greatest achievements of the UN mission in Cambodia was the successful repatriation and resettlement of approximately 370,000 refugees and displaced persons in time for the national election, a success facilitated by the UN's establishing legitimacy/credibility and cultivating trust with the local population and providing humanitarian aid throughout the process.[8] The UN offered a range of incentives to encourage resettlement, including providing essential housewares and other household supplies, food for 400 days, and promise of five acres of land in certain parts of the country—which, due to such logistical problems as clearing landmines and other unexploded ordinance, transitioned to providing cash grants to assist returnees in purchasing land in areas of their choosing.[9] The closure of refugee camps and resettlement of Cambodian refugees, many of whom had been exploited as laborers, to parts of the country beyond the control of the Khmer Rouge was, in effect, a significant blow to the Khmer Rouge. Combined with reduced or eliminated aid from foreign backers, this blow would undermine the economic viability and operational abilities of Pol Pot's forces.

Shortcomings occurred within the UNTAC mission, the largest of which was arguably the limited success experienced in the disarmament and demobilization of the warring factions' military forces and the consequent inability of the peacekeeping forces to entirely halt the fighting or the factions' intimidation and exploitation of the population—though as noted, the intensity of violence was reduced. However, UNTAC was accused of concealing and downplaying levels of violence between political factions as well as episodes of ethnic violence directed toward the Vietnamese minority and other human rights violations in order to promote more of a perception of normalcy than had perhaps been achieved in reality.[10] The scale and complexity of the mission, the speed with which it was assembled, and the Secretary General's inexperience in undertaking such operations meant instances of bureaucratic oversight and some resource mismanagement had indeed occurred.¹¹ Examples of such waste include over 300 largely unused UN vehicles and vast quantities of other goods lost or stolen and nearly $200 million spent on unnecessary prefabricated housing, unused equipment, and the elaborate remodeling of the UNTAC chief's official (though short-term) residence.¹² Far worse were allegations of smuggling, theft, substance abuse, child molestation and other sex offenses, and dereliction of duties on the part of some members of the UN peacekeeping and police forces, allegations that would again be levied against UN peacekeepers in Bosnia a few years later.¹³

The Khmer Rouge were likely the most belligerent faction concerning UNTAC operations and were among the most significant obstacles to the peace process. These obstacles included committing cease-fire violations; refusing UNTAC forces entry into territory under their control; delaying or outright refusing demobilization; and failing to disclose information concerning its forces, armaments, and mine fields on the grounds that (1) Vietnamese troops/advisors and their allies were still present in Cambodia and (2) no firm agreement had been reached with Vietnam prohibiting the re-entry of its troops.¹⁴ Khmer Rouge forces violated the ceasefire with increasing frequency, attacking other factions, directing violence against the ethnic Vietnamese minority, and even on occasion detaining UNTAC peacekeepers in the months leading up to the elections. Such conduct to some degree led other political factions to deviate from the peace plan's terms. For example, Sihanouk's royalist faction, FUNCINPEC, temporarily halted cooperation with UNTAC, citing violence directed against them—often at the hands of the Khmer Rouge. In February 1993, amid demands that UN forces do more to curtail the aggressive actions of Pol Pot's forces, the Cambodian government also launched a military offensive against the Khmer Rouge in an effort to recapture territory.¹⁵

1993 Elections, Coalition Government, and Constitutional Monarchy

The Khmer Rouge boycotted the 1993 elections in large part because UN promises to limit the political power and influence of the Phnom Penh regime had fallen short of expectations and consequently the Cambodian government's ruling party was poised to use its incumbency advantage (e.g., some measure of control over most of the country's territory and population) to prevail in the vote.¹⁶ At the time, Pol Pot's forces only controlled around 1% of the country's voting-age population and failed in their efforts to establish political networks or win over significant numbers from the rural populations in other parts of Cambodia.[17] Though such ongoing socio-economic problems as taxation, forced conscription, and a slow recovery from the effects of the war did not endear many rural Cambodians to the government in Hanoi, the Khmer Rouge never came close to their original goal of gaining one-third of the rural population's support. This target, if achieved, could have been politically leveraged for inclusion in any new government, or at least place the group in a better position to negotiate concessions.[18] The Khmer Rouge had not been overtly impeded from participating but knew they lacked enough support within the country to win a democratic vote or even a significant number of seats in the legislature; instead, they opted to attempt to retain control over the regions they occupied by decrying the fairness of the election and refusing to recognize its results. Though isolated, discredited by the horrors of their legacy, and increasingly weakened by factionalization as well as high rates of desertion, defection, and declining military capabilities, the Khmer Rouge would remain a substantial enough force that it continued as a consideration in Cambodian politics for most of the decade.

The process of national elections was not devoid of problems; overall, however, the elections were a success, certainly given the magnitude of violence and socio-economic upheaval the nation had endured in recent years. From the time campaigning officially began in April, most political factions engaged in propaganda and attempted voter manipulation and intimidation. Political factions both perpetrated and suffered increased (though not all pervasive) political violence. The killing or disappearance of political opponents/organizers was not rare in the weeks leading up to the election.[19] Much of the violence had been directed by the CPP against FUNCINPEC, the largest opposition party, which had its campaigns disrupted, party offices destroyed, and over 100 of its supporters killed.[20] Reflecting an uptick in nationalism and xenophobia—characteristic of, and partly driven by, the campaign rhetoric of most political factions—much of the chaos at the time disproportionately affected the ethnic Vietnamese minority, over 21,000 of whom had been displaced by political violence in the weeks leading up to the election.[21] However, despite such problems and the presence of some voting irregularities, an estimated 89.5% of the eligible population voted in what was by most accounts the first largely free and fair national election in Cambodian history.²² Dobbins, et al. provide a concise overview of the election results and the power sharing agreement and coalition government forged between the Hanoi installed communist regime—the leadership of which transitioned from Heng Samrin to Hun Sen—and the largest opposition group.

> Prince Sihanouk's FUNCINPEC came out on top with 45% of the vote (58 seats), followed by the CPP (government) with 38% (51 seats), the Buddhist Liberal Democratic Party with 4% (10 seats) and the Molinaka Party with 1% (1 seat). The CPP alleged misconduct and refused to recognize the election unless the CPP was brought in as an equal coalition partner . . . Fearing that the CPP would break with the accords and ignite a civil war, and given that the entire army and [much of the] government remained under CPP control, UNTAC and FUNCINPEC caved in to CPP demands and created a power-sharing government . . . [and] Norodom Ranariddh, head of FUNCINPEC and the CPP's Hun Sen became co-Prime Ministers.²³

The power sharing arrangement avoided a renewed civil war and partly unified Cambodia's major political factions against the remaining vestiges of Khmer Rouge but was not without flaws. Following the election, government troops were integrated with the non-Khmer Rouge political factions' forces to form the unified Royal Cambodian Armed Forces (RCAF) under a dual command structure.²⁴ However, ongoing internal factional rivalries and leadership divisions undermined the effectiveness of the RCAF for many years, limiting its ability to decisively engage the withering remnants of the Khmer Rouge and retake the territory still under the militants' control.²⁵ Throughout the arrangement's duration, tensions existed between the governing coalitions' two elements over a range of issues, including policy formulation and government position and contract allocations, with both coalition partners often alleging they were not being allocated their proportional share. Co-Premiers Hun Sen and Prince Ranariddh competed for support, often by promoting patronage and selling government appointments or contracts.²⁶

Sihanouk led the opposition coalition in the peace process culminating in the Paris Accords, but his health was declining, leading him to transfer leadership of FUNCINPEC to his son, Norodom Ranariddh, in 1992. The following year, in the aftermath of national elections and the formulation of the National Assembly, Sihanouk was instrumental in the Cambodian government's adopting a constitutional monarchy model, with himself reinstated as King and Ranariddh as Prince (in addition to serving as co-Prime Minister). The restored King advocated for the full re-integration of the Khmer Rouge in the government and called for new elections in which the Pol Pot faction could participate. These suggestions were rejected by both elements of the coalition government, which nonetheless regarded Sihanouk and the restoration of a monarchy as a means to reassure the Cambodian population. The King also, in effect, functioned as an agent of political stability and mediation in the often tumultuous relationship between the CPP and FUNCINPEC and the tenuous coalition government they formed.

Complicity of Post-Cold War Leaders in Khmer Rouge Actions

Interestingly, a large number of Cambodian government officials and political leaders, including those in senior leadership positions, had been former Khmer Rouge functionaries or sympathizers. Many of the highest ranking leaders of the Hanoi installed CPP regime formerly held leadership positions in Pol Pot's movement for years prior to defecting. For example, Heng Samrin was installed by Vietnam as the de facto head of the Cambodian government for some 13 years following the overthrow of Pol Pot and has served as a member of parliament since 1993, also operating as President of the National Assembly since 2006. He joined the Khmer Rouge early, served as a high ranking political organizer, and rose to the rank of divisional military commander before Pol Pot's purges of those perceived to be potential leadership rivals motivated his fleeing to Vietnam late in the Khmer Rouge regime.[27] Also, after initially joining the Khmer Rouge as a soldier and rising to the rank of battalion commander before defecting in 1977 and later aiding the Vietnamese in their invasion, Hun Sen assumed many leadership roles over the next decades, including Foreign Minister, Prime Minister, President of the CPP, and a long-time member of the National Assembly.[28]

Particularly in Cambodia's eastern districts—some of which were almost semi-autonomous for a time—examples exist of Khmer Rouge military commanders and other functionaries, including Heng Samrin, attempting to moderate and resist many of Pol Pot's edicts; these attempts ultimately resulted in internecine warfare as the regime dispatched troops to quell such dissent.[29] Nonetheless, even those Khmer Rouge leaders who later came to oppose Pol Pot had aided his rise to power, and many were accused of being complicit in atrocities. For instance, witnesses alleged Hun Sen's troops engaged in various war crimes under the Khmer Rouge banner, including massacres of Cham Muslims and ethnic Vietnamese civilians and slitting the throats of patients upon gaining control of hospitals in areas formerly held by rival forces.[30] Like most former functionaries and acolytes of the regime, both Samrin and Sen publicly downplayed their involvement with the Khmer Rouge and denied any complicity in war crimes or human rights violations.

Sihanouk had also actively supported the Khmer Rouge during their insurgency against the Republic and served in a figurehead role as the official Head of State for roughly the first year of Pol Pot's regime (see Chapter 5). During this time, he worked to cultivate international support and recognition for the Khmer Rouge. He also contributed an air of legitimacy to their rule, a role he fulfilled while usually living and travelling abroad. Sihanouk resigned his ceremonial role upon claiming to have first learned the full extent of Pol Pot's atrocities in 1976, at which point the regime kept him under house arrest until the Vietnamese invasion. Those who held such leadership positions for prolonged periods of Pol Pot's rule are highly unlikely to have been completely unaware of the regime's genocidal conduct and dystopian policies. Even in Sihanouk's case regarding his absence from the country throughout most of his period of service to the Pol Pot regime, it is implausible that he would not have had some idea as to the egregious crimes committed during the first year. While internal dissention clearly existed among the ranks of the Khmer Rouge, many in leadership roles apparently opted to defect and actively condemn the regime's actions and advocate its overthrow only after becoming fearful for their own safety. The number of people who went on to hold positions in the Cambodian government, military, or who otherwise became fully reintegrated into Cambodia and led successful lives after having been active participants in, and supporters of, the Khmer Rouge regime is disconcerting. However, many Cambodians and others in the international community held out hope that justice might eventually be achieved, at least for the worst offenders and the chief architects of the Khmer Rouge's nightmarish actions.

Justice Unrealized

Establishing a formal framework to adjudicate Khmer Rouge crimes was a lengthy process, gradually formulated through prolonged and often contentious negotiations between Cambodian authorities and the international community. In 1979, the Hanoi-installed government in Phnom Penh conducted a brief, five-day trial of two of the senior most Khmer Rouge leaders–Pol Pot and Ieng Sary, in which both were convicted in absentia of genocide and sentenced to death. However, this trial was widely regarded as a political action intended to legitimize Vietnam's invasion rather than as a legitimate legal process. In 1998, nearly two decades after the Pol Pot regime had been overthrown, co-Prime Ministers Norodom Ranariddh and Hun Sen both requested assistance from the UN in formulating legal mechanisms to bring those Khmer Rouge who were complicit in the genocide and other crimes to trial. The legal apparatus that eventually emerged was the Extraordinary Chambers in the Courts of Cambodia (ECCC), more commonly referred to as the Khmer Rouge Tribunal(s). The ECCC was, in effect, a dual or hybrid legal system: it served (1) technically as a Cambodian national court with the participation and support of Cambodian civil society, and (2) ostensibly as an international court with the participation of the Cambodian government so that cases were tried within the country rather than at the International Criminal Court or a UN venue, but still included the participation and oversight of the international community and was modeled after procedures found in international law.

However, Hun Sen and most of those in leadership roles in his government/party had been former Khmer Rouge, and many were likely participants in, or at least privy to, crimes perpetrated by the Khmer Rouge during either its insurgency against the Cambodian Republic or the Pol Pot regime. The latter reality was politically awkward and poised to not only embarrass and discredit the Hun Sen government and the CPP but also confronted many such individuals with the prospect of being formally charged and publicly tried in the proceedings. Additionally, while the UN was proposing a move forward with trying Pol Pot's former supporters for their crimes, a steady stream of Khmer Rouge defectors continued to abandon their former loyalties and reintegrate back into Cambodian society, often welcomed into the CPP as well. The Cambodian government even wooed such disaffected Khmer Rouge cadres despite the fact that these recruitment efforts would potentially be thwarted by an aggressive, functional campaign to prosecute former Khmer Rouge for crimes in which they had been involved. It remains unclear why Hun Sen would have initially agreed to move forward with public trials involving international oversight and participation. Perhaps he did so out of wishful thinking that UN proposals and discussions would never actually materialize into substantive action or, as Chivas suggested, to enhance his regime's credibility and chances of funding with the international community, but once the legal process began to take shape, Hun Sen and his government sought to undermine rather than help facilitate the ECCC's functioning.[31]

Obstructionism on the part of Hun Sen's communist regime was arguably the most significant obstacle the ECCC faced and the most significant factor in its limited success in bringing Khmer Rouge cadres to justice. Almost immediately Hun Sen seemed to regret his initial expression of support for an autonomous legal process involving the UN, and the regime began throwing up obstacles to delay or halt the proceedings; for example, they protested that such a body ran afoul of national sovereignty.[32] A primary source of contention was whether the composition of the court would be predominantly Cambodian (in which case the regime might presumably exercise control) or international. A complex bifurcated structure was ultimately created in which appointees of the Cambodian government and international representatives would together serve as co-judges, co-investigators, co-prosecutors, etc., with a supermajority required for certain decisions, such as the dismissal of charges.[33] Longstanding practices of patronage and endemic corruption had been reinstituted throughout the Cambodian government; these were present in Cambodia's staffing positions in the ECCC with unqualified and/or politically biased Cambodian judges, attorneys, and other staffers who often paid for their appointments or otherwise had connections to some source of corruption or undue influence, thereby undermining the process from the start.[34]

In 2006 the co-government arrangement with FUNCINPEC was dissolved, leaving Hun Sen and the CPP in sole control of the Cambodian government and in an even better position to manipulate the ECCC process. Because the dual structure of the ECCC required a supermajority for certain decisions, Hun Sen was able to use his regime's court appointments to manipulate the proceedings, including the number of indictments and which former Khmer Rouge were selected. While it acquiesced to some indictments, the regime attempted to limit the number of former Khmer Rouge targeted by the court and often intervened with attempts to shield specific individuals from prosecution. Perhaps the best example of such intervention was the initial attempt by the CPP government to obtain a pardon for Ieng Sary's 1979 sentence and absolve him from indictment by the ECCC. These actions angered what had, up to that point, been a largely complacent Cambodian population that now forced the regime to reverse course on the issue. Frustrated with such ongoing machinations and the inability of the ECCC to function effectively, many judges and other court staffers resigned in disgust. Additionally, many witnesses eventually withdrew their participation upon viewing the process as corrupted and futile.[35] Many international donors also halted contributions, adding financial difficulties to the already lengthy list of problems. Even the UN halted cooperation at intervals, citing the ECCC's inability to function without the Cambodian government's cooperation.[36]

In September 2022, the ECCC concluded its operations and, in its final act, denied the appeal of Khieu Samphan's guilty verdict. Following 16 years of ostensibly collaborative effort on the part of both Cambodian authorities and the international community and the expenditure of some $337 million, a surprisingly small number of former Khmer Rouge were indicted on multiple counts of crimes against humanity, genocide, or war crimes in addition to being charged with various (often multiple) crimes under Cambodian national law.[37] Of the nine persons formally indicted, only three (Kaing Guek Eav, Khieu Samphan, Nuon Chea) were found guilty, with each receiving a life sentence; two of the accused (Ieng Sary, Ieng Thirith) died during the legal proceedings; and four (Ao An, Im Chaem, Meas Muth, Yim Tith) succeeded in having their charges dismissed.[38]

Pol Pot, the chief architect of the Cambodian Genocide and the radical, catastrophically dystopian policies of the Khmer Rouge regime, ultimately escaped justice—though his end at least marked an ignominious fall from grace within the movement he founded. From its inception, the Khmer Rouge had always been a fractious polity, prone to internal discord, fragmentation, defection, and purges of real or perceived political rivals. Such internal dissention also characterized the militants during their period as a rump state in exile, though the Pol Pot faction retained control throughout most of this period. In 1979, perhaps as part of concerted efforts to make the Khmer Rouge rump state in exile more politically palatable to the UN as well as to potential backers in the international community, Pol Pot ostensibly stepped down as Prime Minister. Officially, one of Pol Pot's chief lieutenants, Khieu Samphan, became the head of the Khmer Rouge rump regime; Pol Pot, however, retained direct control of military forces and remained the de facto leader. Pol Pot's "retirement" was announced in 1985, at which point the Khmer Rouge's military leadership was officially transferred to Son Sen, Defense Minister and longtime Pol Pot loyalist and Central Committee member. Several years later, he would ultimately be executed on Pol Pot's orders for alleged disloyalty (negotiating with other Cambodian political factions). Although he was in declining health and relinquished much of his official political control, Pol Pot remained a dominant influence within the movement, gradually reasserting his leadership via obstructionist stances throughout the 1990s. These obstructions included influencing Khmer Rouge refusal to disarm, participate in the elections, and negotiate with the CPP government, and to resume fighting.

A key turning point in the declining Khmer Rouge internal dynamic transpired in 1996 when, amid intensifying internal dissention and mutinies, a mass defection of large numbers of remaining Khmer Rouge occurred under Ieng Sary and several other senior leaders. As had the FUNCINPEC opposition, the government of Hun Sen had actively courted Khmer Rouge defectors to strengthen its political base within Cambodia. At Hun Sen's urging, King Sihanouk initially granted Ieng Sary a pardon for his 1979 conviction and death sentence; he also promised amnesty against future prosecution in Cambodian courts. Consequently, Ieng Sary and around 4,000 of his soldiers—as many as half of all remaining Khmer Rouge fighters—defected to join with the Hun Sen government.[39] In addition to this significant blow in terms of manpower, the Khmer Rouge lost a large amount of territory and bases in the south that had been under the defecting faction's control. The weakened remaining Khmer Rouge degenerated into factional infighting and in 1997, outraged by the murder of Son Sen and his entire family on Pol Pot's instructions days earlier, Ta Mok—another long-time Khmer Rouge leader and Central Committee member—ordered Pol Pot's arrest. The former dictator was tried and sentenced by a Khmer Rouge court to life imprisonment, which, as stated, manifested as house arrest. These actions were supported by most remaining Khmer Rouge leaders. Before the area in which he was being detained fell to government troops, Pol Pot, frail and partially paralyzed by a stroke, died in his sleep on April 15, 1998. He was widely believed to have committed suicide by poison for fear of being captured by anti-Khmer Rouge government troops, but allegations that he was murdered by political rivals within the Khmer Rouge have also been levied. His body was cremated in accordance with Buddhist tradition, a cultural observance not afforded to many of the countless thousands who died as a result of Pol Pot's murderous, dystopian movement.

Few would deny that the ECCC tribunals fell far short of imparting justice to those who perpetrated crimes against the Cambodian people. The near-universal dismay at the judicial system's failure has manifested in varied degrees of criticism, such as the veiled, diplomatic U.S. Institute for Peace description of the proceedings' outcomes as "disappointing" and as constituting "a complex legacy."[40] Other appraisals of the effectiveness of the ECCC offer a more direct, forthright perspective, including that of the *New York Times* Foreign Affairs Editor who described the tribunals as a "farce heaped upon an insult" and as a "global embarrassment."[41] Though faulty, manipulated, and overwhelmingly incomplete, the efforts at prosecution could at least be potentially regarded as some official acknowledgement of the Pol Pot regime's crimes and as a means of moving beyond the Khmer Rouge's traumatic specter within Cambodian society, a turning point needed by many. The tribunals might also be regarded as an additional (if flawed) precedent for attempting to hold government officials accountable for such crimes, no matter how lengthy and bureaucratically difficult the process.

In addition to failing to prosecute the thousands of Khmer Rouge soldiers and leaders who were directly complicit in crimes, the courts had difficulty distinguishing what acts constituted genocide versus other classifications of crimes. For example, they considered whether genocide was the attempted extermination of a specific race or ethnicity, or might the term also be applied to efforts aimed at wiping out members of a particular political group (e.g., capitalists, non-communists, supporters of the previous political regime) or economic class.[42] If a clear distinction is made, the latter examples would constitute politicide or classicide respectively, but potentially not genocide. Chandler argues that the Khmer Rouge targeted political/class enemies for extermination rather than specific ethnicities, nationalities, or religious groups and thus, by definition, their actions were atrocities, war crimes, or crimes against humanity, as well as potentially crimes under national law (e.g., murder), but not genocide.[43] The UN Convention on Genocide defines the practice as "acts committed with intent to destroy, in whole or in part, a national, ethnical, racial or religious group."[44] The ECCC experienced difficulty applying some of the latter classifications, such as nationality, in that the Khmer Rouge were Cambodians committing crimes against other Cambodians. Such overlapping categories often made it difficult to determine if a group was targeted by the regime due to their political/economic status (not genocide?) or due to their ethnicity or religion (genocide). Ultimately, of the former Khmer Rouge indicted, seven were charged with genocide, of which only two were convicted—specifically for acts committed against ethnic Vietnamese and Cham Muslim minorities. The ECCC did not pursue legal standing in the form of a genocide charge on behalf of other ethnic minorities that appear to have suffered disproportionately or of other religious groups, including Buddhists and Christians.[45] Legal and academic debate continues as to what should be regarded as genocide and how international law should be applied.

Revisionism

Touring the S-21 Museum or other sites related to the Cambodian Genocide could be interpreted as remembrance of the victims and the horrors they suffered and as a somber form of educational tourism undertaken to grasp man's inhumanity as well as the need for international standards/laws related to human rights and the sanctity of life. However, with the support of the Ministry of Tourism, many local communities in former Khmer Rouge strongholds in often remote areas of northern and western Cambodia have attempted to promote a bizarre form of tourism in which visitors can tour historical Khmer Rouge sites, such as the internment site of Pol Pot's ashes or his former home. Many former Khmer Rouge and their descendants remain in these areas of Cambodia, some of whom still express respect and admiration for Pol Pot and other Khmer Rouge leaders and engage in revisionist whitewashing of the militant movement's crimes. Accounts exist of such Khmer Rouge apologists—particularly in the regions that were once group strongholds—engaging in revisionism by downplaying the scope of the killings; attributing most of the deaths to natural causes, such as famine caused by the war; redirecting blame to external actors, such as Vietnam or the west; and/or justifying the killings on the grounds that those who died were either criminals, immoral, or in some other respect deserving of their brutal fate.[46]

Attempts to deny or downplay the crimes of the Khmer Rouge have long been present outside Cambodia as well. While covering up or minimizing the atrocities of the Khmer Rouge could perhaps be expected from other communist bloc states during the Cold War, many such distorted realities emerged from within western nations as well. Many academics, journalists, and others, particularly those with far-left political leanings, initially refused to acknowledge the magnitude and horrific nature of the Khmer Rouge Genocide (see Chapter 6). In the 1970s, despite mounting evidence from survivors who witnessed Khmer Rouge atrocities prior to escaping the country or from other valid forms of intelligence concerning the regime's crimes, many leftists in the west perceived the Khmer Rouge as a positive and democratic trend for Cambodia and many dismissed reports of widespread killings and other human rights abuses as western (anti-communist) propaganda intended to discredit the new regime. For example, *Cambodia: Starvation and Revolution*, a book released in the U.S. during the first year of the Pol Pot regime, largely ignored survivor accounts and utilized limited information—apparently including publicly released Khmer Rouge propaganda—to paint the image of a necessary and largely successful agrarian "revolution," dismissing numerous dire reports of a chaotic, failed forced collectivization scheme and its devastating impacts as a myth.[47] Noam Chomsky, widely perceived initially as a Khmer Rouge apologist (see Chapter 6), famously heralded the regime as poised to usher in "a new era of economic development and social justice" and as an improvement over the western-aligned Cambodian Republic.[48] After 1979, however, in the wake of the Vietnamese invasion, incontrovertible evidence of Khmer Rouge atrocities was provided by Hanoi and new waves of Cambodian refugees who offered firsthand accounts of the dystopian nightmare they survived. Most western apologists who initially sought to downplay the regime's atrocities and portray Pol Pot's movement in a positive light ultimately embraced reality, moderated or reversed their original positions, and acknowledged Khmer Rouge crimes. However, pro-Khmer Rouge rhetoric from the era, such as naive justifications of the forced urban exodus as necessary in order to increase food production—a misconception which has been widely dispelled (see discussion in Chapters 4 and 5)—remain in the literature and may continue to distort perceptions of the Pol Pot regime and its policies.

A different type of Khmer Rouge revisionism has emerged since the 1970s. Voluminous amounts of irrefutable evidence from a diverse range of sources exists—and has been officially acknowledged as fact—establishing the guilt of the Khmer Rouge in the Cambodian genocide and other crimes. Accordingly, as it would be impossible to successfully deny that the Khmer Rouge perpetrated atrocities against the population of Cambodia, elements of the far left have sought to deny that Pol Pot's movement was communist in order to disassociate Khmer Rouge crimes from communist/socialist ideologies. For example, an article in the far-left publication *The Workers' Advocate* makes the strange claim that "the Pol Pot regime and the Khmer Rouge were not a communist movement, despite their (the Khmer Rouge's) claims."[49] Following Hanoi's invasion of Cambodia, the communist governments of Vietnam and its client state in Phnom Penh perhaps understandably endeavored to distance themselves from the Khmer Rouge also, in part, by denying that Pol Pot's movement was communist.[50] Far-left revisionists, however, ask the world to ignore (1) the ideological training and indoctrination of the Khmer Rouge and their leadership; (2) the body of communist political rhetoric extolled by the militants throughout most of the movement's existence; (3) the reality that nearly all other communist bloc states, including China, Vietnam, and the USSR, formally recognized the Pol Pot regime as Marxist-Leninist; and (4) the entirety of communist style policies, such as collectivization, pursued by the regime. Ignoring all such realities and embracing a distorted, revisionist view of Khmer Rouge ideology prevents potentially discrediting communism by virtue of association with Pol Pot's movement; thus, elements of the far left continue to undertake a campaign of obfuscation and denial.

Khmer Rouge Repudiation of Their Legacy?

Following the demise of the Khmer Rouge movement, many of its former leaders and acolytes undertook some form of conversion in their outlook and made public pronouncements that contrasted with their past identities as Khmer Rouge, doing so potentially for self-preservation. A curious example exists in the form of a large-scale religious conversion. Some 4,000 former Khmer Rouge have converted to Christianity since the movement's collapse in the late 1990s, though much skepticism exists concerning the motivation for the conversions which may reflect either efforts to escape earthly or spiritual justice—e.g., many such "awakenings" may have been strategically contrived to curry favor with western prosecutors—or out of a late-life desire to escape the karmic justice prescribed in Buddhist spiritualism as opposed to the redemption and forgiveness promised by Christian dogma to those who repent and seek forgiveness.[51] Perhaps the best known instance of such a transformative spiritual awakening was that of Kaing Guek Eav, also known as Comrade Duch, the former Director of the infamous S-21 prison at which some 18,000–20,000 victims were tortured and killed (see Chapter 6). He claimed to have become a born-again Christian late in his life and asked forgiveness for his sins.

Many former Khmer Rouge also claimed to have undergone political conversions, including the chief architect of the radical movement. Beginning in 1979 with the Vietnamese invasion, Pol Pot had altered his public political rhetoric, including expressions of anti-western sentiment, knowing that he needed the support of the U.S. and other western states to continue his guerilla campaign. After he had been removed from power in the unravelling rump state and placed under house arrest, Pol Pot was famously interviewed by American journalist Nate Thayer in 1997. In the interview, the deposed dictator continued to fling vitriol at the Vietnamese, either deflecting blame for the killings and Cambodia's other ills onto Hanoi or asserting that reports of Khmer Rouge atrocities were Vietnamese propaganda.[52] He insisted that his actions had saved Cambodia from Vietnamese domination, though he acknowledged the Khmer Rouge had "made mistakes," conveyed his wish that "Cambodia remain Cambodia and belong to the West," and his belief that "it is over for communism."[53] Similar comments had also been publicly made by other remaining Khmer Rouge leaders. At the time of the interview, a renewed offensive was being waged by Cambodian government troops against the last enfeebled pockets of Khmer Rouge. Although the west had already withdrawn support, the remnant Khmer Rouge had been making overtures, either out of naive hope of renewed aid or perhaps out of concern they might ultimately be handed over to western courts for judgement (by this time calls for such international tribunals were mounting).[54] Had such efforts aimed at reproachment with the west not been pursued in the last days of the Khmer Rouge, it seems unlikely Pol Pot or his Khmer Rouge captors would have acceded to an interview—the first the leader had given to a western journalist in some 20 years—or espoused pro-western or anti-communist rhetoric. Accordingly, as in the case of the alleged religious conversions, such dramatic reversals are difficult to accept at face value.

Most higher-ranking officials in the communist regime installed by Vietnam were former Khmer Rouge and, in many cases, held leadership roles in Pol Pot's movement. While many such persons were attached to the eastern zone cadres that ultimately rebelled against Pol Pot before fleeing into Vietnam, even these individuals would likely have either been complicit in various atrocities or had knowledge of them. Many of those cadres that rebelled against or fled the Khmer Rouge regime did so not out of moral conviction or ideological opposition but from self-interest after having been targeted—or fearing they soon would be—in Pol Pot's purges. Following the Vietnamese invasion and throughout the existence of Pol Pot's rump state, a steady stream of Khmer Rouge defectors, many of whom had undoubtedly been active participants in the movement's crimes, were welcomed by the successor regime in Phnom Penh and fully re-integrated into Cambodian society; indeed, some were even given leadership positions in the government and military. Leaders of the new communist regime and CPP may have publicly repudiated Pol Pot and the Khmer Rouge, but they did so while simultaneously hiding or downplaying their own roles in the crimes of the radical movement. As stated, the Hun Sen regime may have interfered in the functioning of the ECCC, restricting the number of former Khmer Rouge investigated and placed on trial, out of concern that the involvement of current government officials in Khmer Rouge atrocities would be publicly exposed.[55] Of the small number of those noted above as ultimately charged with crimes by the ECCC, only one ever admitted responsibility: Kaing Guek Eav (Comrade Duch) of the S-21 prison.[56] Other former Khmer Rouge leaders who remain in leadership roles in the Cambodian government, including Hun Sen and Heng Samrin, while publicly condemning the atrocities perpetrated under Pol Pot have denied involvement in, or knowledge of, such crimes. Many former Khmer Rouge have gone so far as to hide their identities and deny any past affiliation with the movement.

Contemporary Cambodia

Many perceive the Khmer Rouge's influence upon Cambodia as having ended with the Vietnamese invasion in 1978–79 or with the surrender of the last of the movement's guerilla factions and dissolution of its government in exile in 1998. However, the degree to which Khmer Rouge influence has ended—even into the third decade of the 21st century—is subject to interpretation. Cambodian communism has, from its emergence, been characterized by rivalrous factions and competing political agendas. Amid the civil war waged against the Republic, the most radical faction, led by Pol Pot, emerged as dominant and, upon seizing power, was able to impose its murderous and dystopian policies upon Cambodia (see Chapters 5 and 6). Under the Pol Pot regime, most other Cambodian communist factions at least initially either acquiesced willingly or were cowed into compliance with the regime's policies. While defections and even internal revolts against Pol Pot's rule became increasingly common by the second year of the regime, many (perhaps most) of the defecting Khmer Rouge cadres had to some degree been initially complicit in the regime's actions, and nearly all such defectors remained ideologically communist. As noted, not all such defectors from Pol Pot's regime did so out of moral qualms or ideological opposition to his policies; instead, they sought to save their own lives once the internal purges characteristic of Khmer Rouge leadership expanded.

These are the individuals who were installed by Vietnam after the Pol Pot regime was toppled. Rather than regarding the post-Pol Pot Cambodian government and political apparatus as something fundamentally new or diametrically opposed to what it replaced, a more accurate perception of it would be a less overtly malign, Orwellian, and incompetent variant of the Khmer Rouge. Certainly, distinctions existed in terms of ideology and policy. Among the most obvious examples of such was the absence of Pol Pot's fanatical, xenophobic, and naïve vision of Cambodia as an isolated autarky, as the Hanoi-installed regime was subject to external (e.g., Vietnamese) oversight and, due to its need for foreign aid and recognition, at least somewhat conscious of, and responsive to, international opinion. The Vietnamese-installed Cambodian government was nonetheless communist, authoritarian, inclined to use violence and intimidation—including extralegal killings—and rooted politically in such behaviors to the Khmer Rouge regime that it replaced.

Upon being brought to power by the Vietnamese invasion, as stated above and in Chapter 7, Cambodia's subsequent communist regime proclaimed the country the People's Republic of Kampuchea and then, in 1989–91, the State of Cambodia, which was followed by the brief period of UN transitional presence and subsequently with the restoration in 1993 of the Kingdom of Cambodia, a largely figurehead monarchy, in order to lend legitimacy and credibility to the Cambodian government. In order to broaden its popular appeal leading up to elections, also as stated above the governing party, originally called the Kampuchean People's Revolutionary Party—the revived name of an early faction within Cambodian communism—dropped the reference to "Revolutionary" and downplayed socialist rhetoric in being renamed the Cambodian People's Party (CPP) in 1991. The multiple changes in the name of the Cambodian state and the governing party arguably reflect more of an effort to rebrand, establish credibility within Cambodia and abroad, and distance the new communist order from the Pol Pot regime than a substantive change in policy or ideology. Examples exist of incremental political/governmental reform during the period, including the initial abandonment of one-party rule as of the 1993 elections, the official abolishment of capital punishment, and the governing party's efforts to distance itself from many conventional Marxist positions and rhetoric in the aftermath of the Cold War. As noted, however, a surprisingly high degree of continuity has existed in terms of Cambodia's leadership, with many former Khmer Rouge who once held leadership roles in the Pol Pot regime prior to their political evolutions wielding power many decades later. These include Hun Sen as Prime Minister (after stepping down as PM in 2023 and installing his son as his successor, Hun Sen retained his seat in the National Assembly and likely continues to exert considerable influence behind the scenes); Heng Samrin as President of the National Assembly; Chea Sim (longtime Khmer Rouge military commander) as Senate President and Head of the CCP until his death in 2015; and numerous former Khmer Rouge in the legislature, serving as heads of government ministries, or in other leadership capacities for many decades.

Cambodia is still governed by the CPP (via the restoration of de facto one-party rule) and, again, by many of the same officials who have run the country for decades and first rose to prominence under Pol Pot. It is now difficult to definitively ascertain the degree to which those who were former Khmer Rouge were complicit in atrocities decades ago or whether former communists have truly evolved from that ideological worldview as opposed to merely downplaying such views for political purposes. However, the present condition of Cambodia following decades of Heng Samrin, Hun Sen, and CPP control reveals a country that never fully achieved democracy and in which authoritarianism, human rights violations, and one-party rule have returned as norms. As of 2025 and for many years previously, Freedom House has assessed Cambodia as "not free," noting that recent national elections were conducted in a "severely repressive environment" with political opposition and human rights activists subjected to "harassment, intimidation and arrest."[57] Human Rights Watch has for many years linked the Hun Sen regime to various ongoing abuses, including "torture, arbitrary arrests, summary trials, censorship, bans on assembly and association, and a national network of spies and informers intended to frighten and intimidate the public into submission."[58] Although not approaching the scale of Pol Pot's genocidal policies, examples of political terror, including murders at the hands of the government, are not rare and usually go unpunished. A recent Human Rights Watch report stated the following.

> Hun Sen's main tactic has been the threat and use of force. During his time in power, hundreds of opposition figures, journalists, trade union leaders, and others have been killed in politically motivated attacks. Although in many cases the killers are known, in not one case has there been a credible investigation and prosecution, let alone conviction. Worse, many have been promoted: the Ministry of Defense and Ministry of Interior websites listing senior military and police officials are a veritable Who's Who of human rights abusers.[59]

In addition to the increasingly authoritarian government and its human rights abuses, Cambodia faces a multitude of other often interrelated challenges, many of which can be traced back to the era of military conflicts and the Khmer Rouge. Cambodia has experienced economic success in some respects, with an average annual growth rate of 7.6% between 1994 and 2015; this growth has, in turn, contributed to a significant reduction in rates of extreme poverty.[60] Though a range of socio-economic obstacles remain, including limited physical as well as institutional infrastructure, such as inadequate educational/healthcare systems—much of which has yet to fully recover from the Khmer Rouge—poor government planning; unrealized potential for agricultural/rural development due to the ongoing presence of unexploded mines or other ordinance stemming from prior wars (with only around half such areas thought to have been cleared); and difficulty in attracting sufficient foreign investment.[61] A contributing factor in many other lingering problems facing Cambodia is its consistent ranking as among the world's most corrupt countries, with Transparency International awarding it a score of only 24/100 on its corruption index in 2022.[62] While the overt persecution and maltreatment of minorities is less pervasive than in previous generations, instances of discrimination, including disenfranchisement perpetrated against ethnic Chinese, Vietnamese, and other minority groups, are not uncommon.[63] Contemporary Cambodia has made significant strides in overcoming the nightmare of Khmer Rouge rule and decades of war. However, a full, transformative recovery seems unlikely until the ascendance of new leaders who are not ideologically bound to the past and who repudiate communist and authoritarian ideals in favor of human rights and other democratic norms.

Endnotes

1. Robert Ross, "China and the Cambodian Peace Process: The Value of Coercive Diplomacy," *Asian Survey* 31(12) December 1991, pp. 1170–1185.
2. Esref Aksu, *The United Nations, Intra-State Peacekeeping and Normative Change* (Manchester, UK: Manchester University Press, 2003).
3. United Nations, "Cambodia: UNTAC Background," https://peacekeeping.un.org/en/mission/past/untacbackgr1.html Accessed September 18, 2022.
4. United Nations, 2022.
5. James Dobbins, Laurel Miller, Stephanie Pezars, Christopher Chivvis, Julie Taylor, Keith Crane, Calin Trenkov-Wermuth and Tewodaj Mengistu, *Overcoming Obstacles to Peace* (Arlington, VA: RAND Corporation, 2013).
6. Dobbins et al., 2013.
7. Aksu, 2003.
8. Jeni Whalan. "UNTAC's Successes – Elections, Refugee Repatriation, and Military Unification", *How Peace Operations Work: Power, Legitimacy and Effectiveness* (Oxford, UK: Oxford University Press, 2013); Trevor Findlay, *Cambodia: The Legacy and Lessons of UNTAC* (Oxford, UK: Oxford University Press, 1995).
9. Dobbins et al., 2013.
10. Wilfred Deac, *Road to the Killing Fields: The Cambodian War of 1970–1975* (College Station, TX: Texas A&M University Press, 1997).
11. Findlay, 1995.
12. Deac, 1997.
13. Deac, 1997.
14. Aksu, 2003.
15. Aksu, 2003.
16. Elizabeth Becker, *When the War was Over: Cambodia and the Khmer Rouge Revolution* (New York: Public Affairs, 1998).
17. Phillip Short, *Pol Pot: Anatomy of a Nightmare* (New York: Henry Holt, 2005).
18. Short, 2005.
19. Marie Alexandrine Martin, *Cambodia: A Shattered Society* (Berkeley, CA: University of California Press, 1994).

20. Becker, 1998.
21. Judith Banister and Paige Johnson, "After the Nightmare: The Population of Cambodia," in Ben Kiernan ed. *Genocide and Democracy in Cambodia: The Khmer Rouge, the United Nations and the International Community* (New Haven, CT: Yale University Southeast Asia Studies, 1993); Aksu, 2003.
22. Findlay, 1995.
23. Dobbins et al., 2013.
24. Dobbins et al., 2013.
25. Ibid.
26. Dobbins et al., 2013.
27. Carl Jackson, *Cambodia, 1975–1978: Rendezvous with Death* (Princeton, NJ: Princeton University Press, 2014).
28. Sebastian Strangio, *Cambodia: From Pol Pot to Hun Sen and Beyond* (New Haven, CT: Yale University Press, 2020).
29. Ben Kiernan, *Genocide and Resistance in Southeast Asia: Documentation, Denial & Justice in Cambodia & East Timor* (New York: Routledge, 2017).
30. Strangio, 2020.
31. George Chigas, "The Politics of Defining Justice after the Cambodian Genocide," *Journal of Genocide Research* 2(2) 2000, pp. 245–265.
32. Joel Brinkley, "Justice Squandered: Cambodia's Khmer Rouge Tribunal", *World Affairs* 176(3) 2013, pp. 41–48
33. Duncan McCargo, "Politics by Other Means? The Virtual Trials of the Khmer Rouge Tribunal," *International Affairs* 87(3) 2011, pp. 613–627.
34. Brinkley, 2013.
35. Brinkley, 2013.
36. Brinkley, 2013.
37. Associated Press, "After 16 years and 3 convictions, an international tribunal closes down in Cambodia," September 22, 2022. https://www.npr.org/2022/09/22/1124432798/cambodia-khmer-rouge-tribunal Accessed: November 14, 2022.
38. Extraordinary Chambers in the Courts of Cambodia. https://www.eccc.gov.kh/en Accessed: December 2, 2022.
39. Short, 2005; Extraordinary Chambers in the Courts of Cambodia.

https://www.eccc.gov.kh/en/indicted-person/ieng-sary-fomer-accused Accessed: December 12, 2022.

40. Nicole Cochran and Andrew Wells-Dang, "Never Again? The Legacy of Cambodia's Khmer Rouge Trials The Extraordinary Chambers in the Courts of Cambodia has issued its final decision, but still has an important role to play in peace and reconciliation," U.S. Institute for Peace. October 3, 2022. https://www.usip.org/publications/2022/10/never-again-legacy-cambodias-khmer-rouge-trials

41. Roger Cohen, "For Cambodia's Dead, Farce Heaped on Insult," *New York Times*, April 2, 2005.

42. B.D. Mowell, "Religious Communities as Targets of the Khmer Rouge Genocide," in *The Routledge Handbook of Religion, Mass Atrocity, and Genocide* eds. Sara Brown and Stephen Smith (New York: Routledge, 2022), pp. 195–204.

43. David Chandler, *A History of Cambodia* (New York: Routledge, 2007).

44. United Nations Office on Genocide Prevention and the Responsibility to Protect, "Genocide: Definition." https://www.un.org/en/genocideprevention/genocide.shtml Accessed: January 25, 2023.

45. Mowell, 2022.

46. Anne Yvonne Guilou, "The 'Master of the Land': Cult Activities Around Pol Pot's Tomb," *Journal of Genocide Research* (20)2 2018, pp. 275–289.

47. Gareth Porter and George C. Hildebrand, *Cambodia: Starvation and Revolution* (New York: Monthly Review Press, 1976).

48. Christopher Hitchens, "The Chorus and Cassandra: What Everyone Knows About Noam Chomsky," *Grand Street* 5(1) Autumn 1985, pp. 106–131; Michael Haas, *Genocide by Proxy: Cambodian Pawn on a Superpower Chessboard* (New York: Praeger, 1991).

49. *The Workers' Advocate*, "The lesson of the Kampuchean tragedy: The peasant revolutionary movement needs the leadership of the proletariat," *The Workers' Advocate* 15(3) March 1, 1985 in: Encyclopedia of Anti-Revisionism On-Line, Paul Saba (transcription/editing), https://www.marxists.org/history/erol/ncm-7/mlp-kamp.htm#:~:text=The%20Pol%20Pot%20regime%20and,concern%20with%20the%20working%20class.

50. Kate Freison, "The Political Nature of Democratic Kampuchea,"

Pacific Affairs 61(3) Autumn 1988, pp. 405–427.
51. Dene-Hern Chen, "The Former Khmer Rouge Cadres Who Turned to God for Salvation," *Post Magazine* February 16, 2017.
52. Nate Thayer, "Second Thoughts for Pol Pot," *Washington Post*. October 28, 1997.
53. Thayer, 1997.
54. *The Economist*, "Try Pol Pot," *The Economist* 303(8023) June 28, 1997, p. 17; Thayer, 1997.
55. Human Rights Watch, "30 Years of Hun Sen: Violence, Repression and Corruption in Cambodia," Human Rights Watch. January 12, 2015. https://www.hrw.org/report/2015/01/12/30-years-hun-sen/violence-repression-and-corruption-cambodia.
56. Extraordinary Chambers in the Courts of Cambodia, "Kaing Guek Eav," https://www.eccc.gov.kh/en/indicted-person/kaing-guek-eav Accessed: December 30, 2022.
57. Freedom House, "Freedom in the World: 2022 – Cambodia," https://freedomhouse.org/country/cambodia/freedom-world/2022 Accessed: January 2, 2023.
58. Human Rights Watch, 2015.
59. Human Rights Watch, 2015.
60. World Bank, *Cambodia - Sustaining Strong Growth for the Benefit of All* (Washington, D.C.: World Bank Group, 2017).
61. World Bank, 2017.
62. Transparency International, "Corruption Perceptions Index: 2022," https://www.transparency.org/en/cpi/2022 Accessed: January 8, 2023.
63. U.S. Department of State, "2021 Country Reports on Human Rights Practices: Cambodia," https://www.state.gov/reports/2021-country-reports-on-human-rights-practices/cambodia Accessed: January 20, 2023.

Appendix: Photo Gallery

Image A.1: French Union military forces engaging communist insurgents in an Indochina rice paddy c. 1950. (Source: U.S. Information Agency.)

Following WWII France attempted to reassert control over its colonial holdings in Indochina (Cambodia, Laos and Vietnam) which led to the First Indochina War, a Cold War-era proxy war in which insurgencies were undertaken in each of the French territories by coalitions of pro-independence elements including far-left factions. Fighting escalated progressively culminating in the end of French colonial rule in 1954, the partition of Vietnam and the independence of the communist-led state of North Vietnam and non-communist states of Cambodia, Laos, and South Vietnam. Post-independence communist insurgencies subsequently ensued behind the goal of establishing communist control of Cambodia, Laos, and South Vietnam in what became known collectively as the Second Indochina War, known in the U.S. as the Vietnam War.

Image A.2: Cambodian Prime Minister (and former King) Prince Norodom Sihanouk with U.S. President Dwight D. Eisenhower in 1959. (Source: U.S. Embassy, Phnom Penh.)

Crowned King in 1941, Sihanouk abdicated the throne in 1955, installing his father to the largely ceremonial throne and Sihanouk assuming the title Prince. The transition was made to legally permit Sihanouk to found a political party (the Sangkum) and actively campaign in Cambodian national elections in which his party prevailed, resulting in his appointment as Prime Minister. Sihanouk's rule of Cambodia was characterized by authoritarianism and by political vacillation between the political center, left, and right with numerous political coalitions and alliances (both in terms of domestic politics and international/Cold War politics) being forged, modified, and broken out of political expediency.

Many of his actions as Cambodian head of state directly or inadvertently aided in the rise of communism. For example, in forging a new national government in the years immediately following independence, Sihanouk integrated many leaders among Cambodia's socialists and less radical communists into his political party and government, inadvertently allowing the emergence of a leadership vacuum among socialists/communists which in turn permitted more militant elements including Pol Pot's faction to eventually assume leadership of the country's far left. Though his regime was officially neutral within the Cold War dynamic, Sihanouk eventually shifted away from the U.S./west and made overtures to the communist bloc. For many years he tolerated the use of Cambodian territory by North Vietnamese and Viet Cong forces in their war with South Vietnam. His complacency allowed Vietnamese communists to gain extensive footholds in Cambodia and also to nurture the rise of the Khmer Rouge and facilitate the Cambodian Civil War. Sihanouk's attitudes toward communists and his inability to stem the tide of their growing presence in Cambodia once it was entrenched, led to his removal from office and the establishment of the Cambodian Republic under Lon Nol in 1970.

Image A.3: The 3rd Congress of the Communist Party of Kampuchea (Khmer Rouge) in 1971. Pol Pot sits cross-legged in the front row visible between the rows of benches. (Source: CPA Media Pte Ltd.)

Most Cambodians were a very traditional and culturally conservative people who held Buddhism and other societal norms in high regard. Realizing this, and grasping that few Cambodians would knowingly embrace the radical iconoclastic precepts of communism, the Khmer Rouge and their Vietnamese communist patrons sought to hide the true nature of Pol Pot's nascent political movement from the population. Prior to and during the Cambodian Civil War (and even in the initial stage after seizing power) the Khmer Rouge did not publicly describe their movement as communist, with only the highest echelons of Khmer Rouge leadership understanding the true fanatical nature and nefarious agenda of the movement.

However, Khmer Rouge ideologies were heavily grounded in communist ideologies and almost entirely based upon the writings of various communist thinkers and the dystopian and brutal actions the Pol Pot regime undertook were largely based upon policies of previous communist regimes. The above image from a 1971 meeting of senior Khmer Rouge leadership conveys the commitment of the movement to communist ideals—note the hammer and sickle banner and the images of Marx, Engels, Lenin and Stalin prominently displayed. Elements of the international far left including western academics initially denied that the Pol Pot regime had committed atrocities or tried to downplay the magnitude and severity of Khmer Rouge crimes despite survivor accounts and other mounting evidence. Given, the overwhelming evidence of crimes which surfaced after the Khmer Rouge were toppled by Vietnamese forces, and realizing that the atrocities of the Pol Pot regime can no longer be denied or minimized, many communist apologists have now shifted to arguing that the Khmer Rouge were not communists, also an indefensible claim.

Image A.4: Khmer Rouge leaders Pol Pot (center) and Ieng Sary (right)—Deputy Prime Minister and Minister of Foreign Affairs of the regime—meet with Chairman Mao Zedong in Beijing, 1976. (Source: CPA Media Pte Ltd.)

A defining characteristic of Cold War-era geopolitics was not just the east-west dynamic of capitalist/western states pitted against communism, but also the eventual emergence of a polarized communist bloc comprised of the Soviet faction of communist nations and those communist states aligned with China. The Sino-Soviet rift emerged in the 1950s principally from differences over communist ideology/policy as well as border disputes and continued until the collapse of the USSR. While an insurgency movement, the Khmer Rouge generally avoided the emerging factionalization within the communist bloc. However, upon coming to power, the Pol Pot regime aligned itself with China, largely as a reflection of a rapid souring of relations between the Khmer Rouge government and Soviet-aligned Vietnam and Pol Pot's (ultimately unsuccessful) efforts to hedge his regime's security against Vietnam via cultivating a powerful external ally.

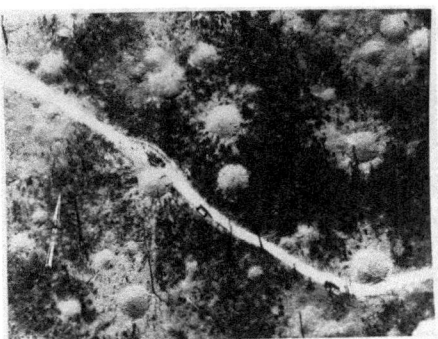 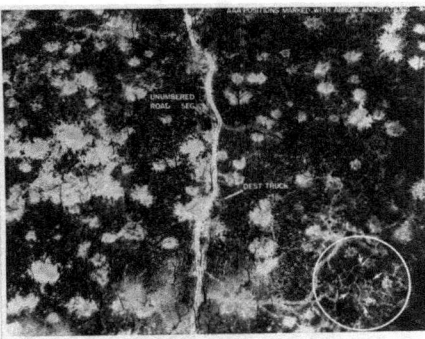

Images A.5 and A.6: Bombing of the Ho Chi Minh Trail. (Source: National Archives.)

In an effort to supply the ongoing campaign to topple the South Vietnamese government, in the 1960s through 1975, the North Vietnamese military and the Viet Cong guerrillas transited large volumes of supplies and troops through Cambodia and Laos along a network of routes collectively known as the Ho Chi Minh Trail. The reconnaissance photos above illustrate U.S. efforts to disrupt shipments along the route primarily via aerial bombing campaigns. Large bomb craters and destroyed vehicles are visible in the images. The circle highlights the position of Vietnamese anti-aircraft guns nearby. However the bombing campaigns had limited impact upon the overall flow of supplies and fighters as damage would quickly be repaired (e.g., bomb craters filled in) or the paths would simply curve around the damage as can be seen in the images. Narrower elements of the Trail such as footpaths or bicycle trails were nearly impossible to spot from the air and could still facilitate the movement of substantial amounts of troops and supplies.

Images A.7 and A.8: Varied Scale/Capacity of Ho Chi Minh Trail Segments. (Sources: A.7 – Stewart, Richd W. "Deepening Involvement, 1945–1965," Center of Military History, United States Army. A.8 – U.S. Air Force.)

APPENDIX: PHOTO GALLERY

References to the Ho Chi Minh Trail may conjure images of narrow, well-hidden footpaths and bike trails reflective of the image at top but the width, composition, and capacity of the Trail varied widely and included segments wide enough for large trucks and other vehicles. The second image depicts a North Vietnamese armored car transiting through Cambodia. Vietnamese communists became utterly dependant upon the Ho Chi Minh Trail through Cambodia and Laos to sustain their military operations and were thus highly committed to establishing and maintaining a significant military presence in both nations and also in helping to facilitate and strengthen indigenous communist movements in both.

Image A.9: U.S. President Richard Nixon's famous televised speech in 1970 sought to justify a larger-scale direct U.S. military intervention in eastern Cambodia, citing the progressive seizure of the country's territory by communist forces. (Source: National Archives.)

Cambodia and Laos were significant Cold War conflict zones. They were not merely transit routes for Vietnamese communist troops and supplies. A significant and progressively larger amount of territory in both countries was seized and utilized by the North Vietnamese military and the Viet Cong as staging and sanctuary areas, some of which are illustrated in the map above. Vietnamese communists established networks of camps to (re)organize and train fighters, serve as supply depots and also as fallback points that were less accessible to South Vietnamese or U.S./coalition troops and aircraft—that may have otherwise pursued communist cadres more successfully within South Vietnam. Such sanctuary zones also enabled Vietnamese communists to recruit, train, and supply slowly growing numbers of Cambodian and

Laotian communist fighters to advance civil war in their countries. U.S. and allied efforts to bomb communist sanctuary zones and communist transit routes led to Cambodian civilian casualties and damage to farms/property. Consequently, this may have played into the anti-western propaganda efforts of communists, inadvertently aiding in the rise of the Khmer Rouge movement, turning many in the population against the pro-U.S. Cambodian Republic and aiding in recruitment efforts.

Images A.10 and A.11: Large volumes of communist weapons and other supplies were captured or destroyed via the 1970 Cambodian incursion by U.S. and South Vietnamese forces. (Sources: A.10 – U.S. Air Force. A.11 – U.S. Army.)

APPENDIX: PHOTO GALLERY

In a significant escalation of the conflict, between April and July 1970, over 50,000 U.S. troops and nearly 60,000 South Vietnamese troops deployed into eastern Cambodia in an attempt to eliminate at least some communist sanctuary sites and disrupt portions of the Ho Chi Minh Trail. Vietnamese communist forces were caught off guard and often abandoned camps abruptly. Large volumes of weapons, ammunition, and other supplies were captured or destroyed, substantial casualties were inflicted, and supply lines were temporarily disrupted. Despite the initial successes of the temporary incursion, communist forces had established control over most of Cambodia, particularly the eastern and northern districts, within a year of the campaign.

Image A.12: Operation Eagle Pull – U.S. evacuation of Embassy staff and small numbers of Cambodian and other foreign nationals prior to fall of Phnom Penh in April 1975. (Source: U.S. Marine Corps.)

In Cambodia, the military fortunes of the pro-western Republic led by Lon Nol continued to deteriorate throughout the early 1970s in spite of the valiant, sustained efforts of the beleaguered Cambodian military aided by the U.S. and other allies. By around 1973, the majority of communist fighters in Cambodia were ethnic Khmer rather than North Vietnamese or Viet Cong troops and most Cambodian territory with the exception of most major cities was under their control. The deposed Prince Sihanouk was used as a political figurehead by the insurrectionists which lent credibility and cultivated the illusion of a more moderate opposition coalition, aiding in the appeal of the revolutionaries for some disaffected Cambodians. As Khmer Rouge strength grew and the situation became increasingly untenable, plans for the evacuation of the U.S. Embassy were formulated in early 1975. The evacuation was initiated in April, first via fixed-wing aircraft and later, due to Khmer Rouge shelling of the airport, concluded with the arrival of military helicopters dispatched from U.S. aircraft carriers, mere days before the fall of Phnom Penh to the Khmer Rouge on April 17. 1975 was a significant turning point in the Cold War with not only the fall of South Vietnam but also the collapse of non-communist governments and subsequent establishment of communist regimes in both Cambodia and Laos.

Image A.13: The U.S. cargo container ship Mayaguez c. 1975. (Source: U.S. Air Force.)

In one of the first manifestations of a discordant Khmer Rouge foreign policy toward most of the outside world, shortly after seizing power the regime assumed a belligerent and aggressive posture toward international shipping based upon a disputed maritime territorial limit. Within weeks of the fall of Phnom Penh, Khmer Rouge patrol boats had seized multiple Thai fishing boats, Panamanian and South Korean cargo ships, and had fired upon a Swedish vessel, claiming all had violated their maritime boundary.

On May 12, a U.S. freighter, the Mayaguez, was stopped and boarded while in international waters off the Cambodian coast and the 39 crew members were taken into custody. Regarded as an act of piracy by the U.S. government, U.S. military forces were dispatched to retake the ship and rescue the crew. Only after military operations had been initiated and casualties had been incurred did it become known that the Khmer Rouge had transferred all crew members of the Mayaguez to a fishing vessel already en route to release them unharmed. With 41 U.S. fatalities, most as the result of a helicopter crash, the Mayaguez incident marked the last U.S. casualties in the Vietnam (Second Indochina) War. Khmer Rouge belligerence toward other nations including all three countries sharing a border with Cambodia would continue to escalate.

Image A.14: Across Cambodia, Buddhist Temples and other places of worship were intentionally destroyed or defiled by the Khmer Rouge. (Source: Photo courtesy of the Documentation Center of Cambodia.)

Even by the standards of communism, the Khmer Rouge regime was one of the most iconoclastic, radical and brutal governments in human history. Pol Pot and his followers sought to eradicate a lengthy list of internal enemies including the educated or other class enemies, anyone associated with the previous government, anyone with connections to another country or political ideal, ethnic minorities, and also all communities of faith. This fanatical commitment to destroying all vestiges of traditional society also applied to Buddhism, the traditional faith of most Cambodians.

In addition to murdering those perceived as enemies within the Cambodian population, the Khmer Rouge sought a clean break from history and nearly all vestiges of traditional culture. Upon seizing power, the regime abolished the traditional calendar, proclaimed "Year Zero" to mark the genesis of their dystopian transformation of society, and proceeded to abolish most aspects of traditional culture: money, banks, private property/possessions, schools, books, foreign languages, all forms of religion, family/kinship ties, etc. Toward that end, it was not sufficient to merely prohibit Buddhist and other religious traditions/thought or to eliminate most of the Cambodia's monks and other religious clerics---even the religious sites themselves had to either be destroyed as can be seen in the image above or defiled by converting the building into a livestock pen, or some other degraded function.

Image A.15: Forced labor camp at a Khmer Rouge mandated dam/irrigation project c. 1976. (Source: Photo courtesy of the Documentation Center of Cambodia)

The bizarre and radical ideas of the Khmer Rouge related to self-sufficiency, collectivization and forced labor turned the entirety of Cambodia into a vast network of slave labor camps. The enslaved national population including women, children and the elderly and infirm was subjected to backbreaking work on starvation diets. The slightest infractions such as failing to follow an order or answer a question quickly enough could result in beatings, torture or execution. The Pol Pot regime and communist apologists claimed the forced expulsion of the entire Cambodian population from cities and their mobilization into agrarian slave labor camps was necessary to prevent starvation, a baseless claim that has been debunked.

In reality the forced labor camps provided means for the fanatical communist regime to subjugate the population, cow them into submission with brutality and propaganda, to identify and eliminate ("smash") anyone they deemed as a potential enemy of the militant new order, and destroy any vestige of traditional Cambodian civilization. It also presented an opportunity for the callous, murderous regime to eliminate all those deemed as "non-producers" such as the elderly via brutal conditions. The labor camps tended to be compartmentalized and isolated from each other, limiting the number of witnesses and any ability to disseminate word or to grasp the nationwide scale of egregious human rights abuses and mass killings. Hundreds of mass graves from the Khmer Rouge era have been unearthed with countless more yet to be discovered. The locations of most mass graves correspond to the locations of the forced labor camps with victims having died of overwork, starvation, disease, torture or execution.

Image A.16: Survivor art depiction of mass grave perpetrated during Khmer Rouge genocide. (Source: Peter Horree.)

During their brief tenure (1975-1979) as the government of Cambodia, the fanatical and sadistic communist regime killed approximately 2 million people or nearly 25% of the national population. Many were killed directly via execution or succumbing to beatings or torture and others indirectly due to the dystopian regime's policies via starvation, disease, or overwork. While the ethnic Khmer majority also suffered greatly under the communist regime, ethnic minorities such as Chams, Chinese and Vietnamese were disproportionately targeted, as were certain socio-political classifications of people such as communities of religious faith or those with any form of linkage to the previous government. Given the volume of deaths, mass graves were utilized by the Khmer Rouge throughout Cambodia to dispose of their victims. Such mass burial sites continue to be discovered in Cambodia today.

Image A.17: Memorial to Khmer Rouge victims near mass grave site. (Source: Mike Goldwater.)

Hundreds of the mass graves of Khmer Rouge victims have been unearthed across Cambodia with many more yet to be discovered. Mass grave sites were usually adjacent in proximity to larger forced labor sites and others near the many centers of torture and execution. As such sites are discovered, remains are exhumed and often placed in ossuaries which serve as memorials to the victims and as a testament to the crimes of the Khmer Rouge regime. Forensic analysis of remains is often undertaken which commonly reveals severe blunt force trauma wounds, reflecting the brutal, improvised execution methods used by the Khmer Rouge. Ammunition had to be imported and as the Pol Pot regime was obsessed with self sufficiency and also concerned with preserving stocks of ammunition and other military supplies for any future potential conflicts (i.e., with Vietnam) it did not want to waste ammunition on the large number of executions being undertaken.

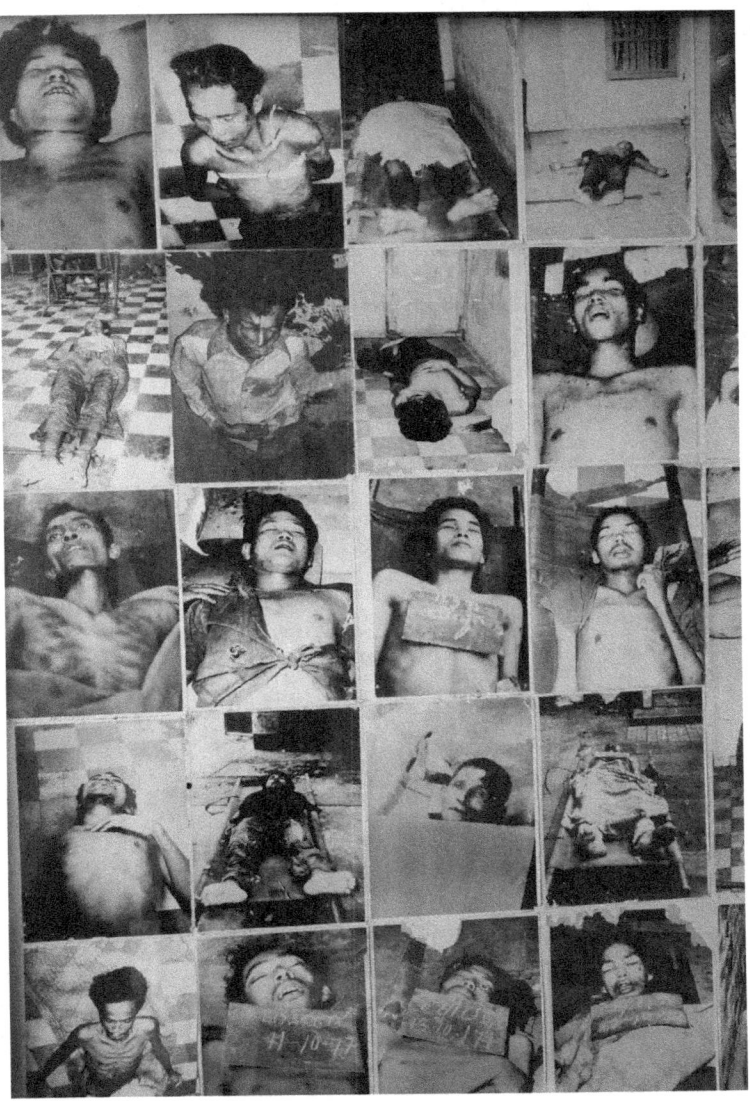

Image A.18: Postmortem photos of Khmer Rouge victims at Tuol Sleng (S-21) Prison taken by captors. (Source: Tom McShane.)

DYSTOPIAN DISCORD

The majority of those who perished at the hands of the Khmer Rouge, died at one of the countless slave labor camps or on forced death marches across the country and the deaths of such victims were usually undocumented. However, the dystopian totalitarian regime sought to identify and obtain "confessions" from certain regime enemies including members of Khmer Rouge leadership accused of disloyalty. Higher ranking Khmer Rouge political functionaries or military officers who fell under suspicion were sent to the Tuol Sleng (S-21) Prison in Phnom Penh, which is the most infamous of nearly 200 such sites across the country. Given its status as an interrogation/execution center for the elite, the Khmer Rouge made copious records of Tuol Sleng prisoners including photographing them upon arrival, keeping records of their "interrogations" and "confessions" (conducted/obtained via torture) and photographing their bodies if they died during torture or after their executions. Such records were used by the captors to prove to the regime that due diligence was being carried out at the prison and that those accused (almost always falsely) of being spies, traitors, saboteurs and regime enemies were being executed for their alleged crimes.

Image A.19: Photos of child victims of the Khmer Rouge taken upon their arrival at the Tuol Sleng (S-21) Prison, a center for interrogation (torture) and in almost all cases, execution, for higher ranking prisoners and their families. (Source: Tom McShane.)

The eventual collapse of the Khmer Rouge regime at the hands of Vietnamese troops came so rapidly that Pol Pot's forces had little time to destroy evidence of their crimes. For example, large volumes of photos and other records of victims at Tuol Sleng were left behind when the Khmer Rouge hastily evacuated the capital due to advancing Vietnamese troops in 1979. Many of these photos, records and other sources of evidence were placed on display when the Tuol Sleng prison was converted to a museum, the Tuol Sleng Genocide Museum.

Typically, if a Khmer Rouge leader was accused of disloyalty or other serious offenses, the accused and their entire family including children were sent to S-21 for "interrogation". If a confession could not be elicited from the accused under extreme torture, the Khmer Rouge anticipated that family members under torture would condemn their loved one and attest to their guilt to stop the pain. In addition to obtaining "confessions", the regime also sought to execute not just the accused but their family as well. Customarily, once "confessions" were obtained, the accused would subsequently be loaded into a truck and told they were being sent to a re-education camp, at which point they would be transited to a nearby mass grave site for execution. The Museum contains hundreds of photos of Tuol Sleng victims including women and (as seen above) children. Only a handful of prisoners are known to have survived Tuol Sleng, thus virtually every photo displayed is that of a S-21 fatality.

Image A.20: Survivor art depicting Khmer Rouge prison guards seizing children from parents accused of crimes against the regime. (Source: Universal Images Group North America LLC.)

The appalling, sociopathic cruelty of the Khmer Rouge extended to children as well. The radical new communist order wanted to break with every tradition of the past even going so far as to destroy the most basic thread of every society, the family unit. In the slave labor camps, children were removed from their parents and raised collectively by regime representatives so they could be brainwashed with propaganda and instilled with the worldview and values of the Khmer Rouge rather than that of their families. For example, children were trained to hate all classifications of people the Khmer Rouge deemed as enemies (e.g., the Vietnamese) and to serve the Khmer Rouge agenda with blind obedience whether that be as child soldiers, torturers, executions or any other task demanded of them.

Image A.21: Survivor art depicting executions and mass grave of infants and children at the Choeung Ek site which served as the killing and burial grounds for the S-21 Prison. (Source: Peter Horree)

If the Khmer Rouge targeted an individual for execution, the fate would normally also be meted out to their entire immediate family. This applied to

APPENDIX: PHOTO GALLERY

children as well, even infants and toddlers, as the regime was concerned the child may grow up to learn of the parent's fate and take revenge upon the Khmer Rouge and the new order. One of the excuses made by Khmer Rouge leadership and communist apologists/revisionists is that the unspeakably cruel widespread torture, mass executions and other examples of brutal conduct occurred not at the direction of the Pol Pot regime but rather as the result of the regime losing control of many of its soldiers/supporters who perpetrated such atrocities on their own initiative. The latter ludicrous argument blatantly ignores the reality that in the history of human civilization, no greater degree of centralized totalitarian control has ever been wielded over a population than the degree of control held and abused by the Khmer Rouge regime. Large amounts of evidence also confirms the degree of centralized control the Khmer Rouge leadership wielded over their barbarous regime. This includes the largely standardized methods of torture and execution implemented at thousands of different sites (conveying centralized training/instruction in what were often very specific methods) across the country including the unspeakably cruel, improvised methods used to murder infants and young children. Commonly, executioners and those using torture to interrogate victims were teenagers---indoctrinated by the Khmer Rouge to obey regime orders blindly and to not possess empathy or a moral compass---but in almost all cases, they were following orders that had been issued through the chain of command, as to do otherwise would invite a death sentence upon themselves and their superiors.

Image A.22: Khmer Rouge execution sites tasked with murdering infants and small children often utilized a "killing tree", a tree with a broad enough trunk that severe blunt force trauma served as the execution method. Many such trees now serve as memorial sites throughout the country. (Source: Danita Delimont)

APPENDIX: PHOTO GALLERY

Image A.23: Cambodian refugees, having fled across the border into Vietnam, being recruited by the Vietnamese military to organize an anti-Khmer Rouge, Hanoi-led communist fighting force, 1978. (Source: CPA Media Pte Ltd.)

Between 1976 and late 1978, the Khmer Rouge regime undertook widespread internal purges. Virtually every initiative undertaken by the radical and incompetent Pol Pot government had failed and Pol Pot had fallen far short of progress toward the utopian autarchy he and other Khmer Rouge leaders had envisioned. Examples of such policy failures include efforts to increase agricultural production via enslaving the entire nation as a labor force (agricultural output actually dropped from the already low levels during the Cambodian Republic/Civil War); the abysmal failure to achieve Pol Pot's vision of an emerging Cambodian industrial base; and the inability of the regime to settle territorial disputes (in some cases revived needlessly by Pol Pot) via threats, aggressive posturing and border skirmishes, even directed toward fellow communist states Laos and Vietnam.

To deflect responsibility, Khmer Rouge leadership increasingly blamed such failures on imagined internal enemies. Rather than conceding to its own incompetence or the reality that many policies were far too radical to be attainable, the regime blamed setbacks on internal traitors, spies, and saboteurs. Few in the regime were above suspicion or immune from being arrested and executed, from the lowliest foot soldier to the highest ranking political and military officials. As purges accelerated, many Khmer Rouge fled across international borders, particularly in eastern Cambodia which bordered Vietnam. By the latter period of Khmer Rouge rule, entire military units in the east defected and fled across the

Vietnamese border fearing they might be the next to be targeted by the purges. When defecting across the border, many Khmer Rouge units also took their families and other civilians (e.g., laborers in camps under their control) with them. By 1978, Vietnam was becoming committed to removing the Pol Pot regime and many of the refugees were recruited by Hanoi behind that goal as conveyed in the image above.

Image A.24: The bodies of Vietnamese civilians massacred by Khmer Rouge soldiers on Vietnamese soil during a border raid near the southern coastal city of Ha Tien in early 1978, one of many cross-border attacks by the Khmer Rouge collectively resulting in thousands of Vietnamese casualties. (Source: CPA Media Pte Ltd.)

As discussed in the book, territory in Indochina has changed hands among the region's populations for centuries. Lands that at one point may have been those of the ancestors of modern Cambodia over time shifted to the control of present-day Laos, Thailand or Vietnam. For example, during the French colonial era, significant territory was reallocated from Khmer control to Vietnam, particularly in the southern, Mekong Delta area. French colonial authorities also resettled large numbers of various other groups including ethnic Vietnamese into historically Khmer lands. The latter developments combined with imprecisely demarcated international borders have contributed to significant territorial disputes. The Khmer Rouge sought to reclaim at least much of the disputed territory via aggressive conduct rather than diplomacy, repeatedly perpetrating unprovoked incidents (e.g., shelling, cross-border incursions) along the borders with Laos and Thailand, and in particular with Vietnam. The Vietnamese minority in Cambodia was also one of several groups targeted in the Khmer Rouge genocide, provocations that ultimately culminated in Hanoi's invasion of Cambodia in December 1978.

Image A.25: Anti-Vietnamese Propaganda of the Khmer Rouge depicting Cambodians defending against the personification of Vietnam which is portrayed as a giant seeking to attack/devour Cambodia. (Source: Khmer People's National Liberation Front—Coalition Government of Democratic Kampuchea.)

Despite receiving military aid/training and other forms of support from Vietnamese communists for many years, the Khmer Rouge always resented the influence the Vietnamese exerted over their own movement and also harbored ill-will toward them as a historical rival of the Khmer people and usurper of Khmer territory. Once in power, the Khmer Rouge targeted Cambodia's Vietnamese minority (among other groups) for persecution and elimination. The Pol Pot regime also quickly assumed an increasingly antagonistic posture toward neighboring Vietnam, launching border raids and perpetrating massacres of Vietnamese civilians on Vietnamese territory that progressed in frequency and severity. Such incidents often occurred in areas of long-standing territorial disputes between the Khmer and Vietnamese, such as the Khmer Rouge attack upon the disputed island of Phu Quoc mere weeks after Pol Pot's victory in the Cambodian Civil War.

Image A.26: A destroyed Khmer Rouge tank in a flooded Cambodian field circa 1979. (Source: Mike Goldwater.)

A large disparity existed between the military capabilities of the Khmer Rouge military and that of Vietnam. Vietnamese forces not only outnumbered the Khmer Rouge 2–3:1, but most Vietnamese troops were well-equipped, disciplined, seasoned veteran fighters whereas a large percentage of the Khmer Rouge were child soldiers whose only experience was in brutalizing starving civilians. Those Khmer Rouge soldiers that did possess combat experience were generally more poorly trained/equipped/fed/led and less motivated than their Vietnamese counterparts. The Vietnamese also had vastly more armor and air capability, factors which collectively enabled them to inflict greater casualties upon and quickly rout most Khmer Rouge units.

The discord between the Khmer Rouge regime and Vietnam (as well as the associated Sino-Vietnamese Border War of 1979) well illustrates the reality that significant friction existed among many communist states in the Cold War era and beyond, which in many cases culminated in armed conflict. Near the top of a lengthy list of the most naive and foolish tenets of communism is the assertion that workers of the world will abandon their allegiances to nations, cultures, and all other societal identities and related historical grievances to embrace each other as fellow workers/socialists in a world unified by radical-left ideology. In reality, nearly all communist regimes have to varying degrees embraced ethnocentrism, racism, xenophobia, nationalism, scapegoating, and egregious human rights violations often disproportionately targeting specific groups. Most communist regimes have also undertaken some form of ethnic cleansing and/or other egregious crimes against humanity. Rather than realizing the harmonious, "utopian" visions of naive radical left thinkers, communist regimes have all facilitated the crimes, societal ills, and inclination toward conflict associated with authoritarianism.

Image A.27: This rare combat photo depicts Vietnamese troops storming Phnom Penh, January 1979. (Source: CPA Media Pte Ltd.)

The full-scale Vietnamese offensive was initiated on Christmas Day 1978 with over 150,000 troops along the entire national frontier. While some pockets of stubborn Khmer Rouge resistance persisted, most of Pol Pot's forces were destroyed within two weeks of the invasion. Following the fall of the capital on January 7, a new Hanoi-aligned communist regime (The People's Republic of Kampuchea) was proclaimed as remnants of the Khmer Rouge retreated further west where the regime would establish a rump state and continue to conduct low-intensity guerrilla operations against the Vietnamese occupation forces and new Cambodian regime for many years.

The Khmer Rouge would never again control significant amounts of Cambodian territory or any major city. For example, by 1980, only a few small pockets of thick, mountainous jungle in the northeast and a strip of remote, mountainous, forested territory along the border with Thailand remained under their control. However, the remoteness and inaccessibility of their jungle bases allowed them to hold out and continue waging what was essentially a harassment campaign for two decades. Pol Pot died in 1998 after being removed from leadership and placed under house arrest by a rival Khmer Rouge faction. The last Khmer Rouge guerrillas did not surrender until 1999 with almost none of their surviving leaders ever held legally accountable for their crimes despite an international tribunal.

Image A.28: Unexploded ordinance uncovered from Cambodian fields and rendered inert. (Source: Gary Todd.)

APPENDIX: PHOTO GALLERY

Image A.29: Contemporary efforts continue to de-mine the Cambodia-Thailand border. (Source: U.S. Department of Defense.)

A large amount of unexploded ordinance including artillery and mortar shells, grenades, mines, and aerial bombs remain in the ground throughout Cambodia as the remnants of many years of war. Due to the injuries and fatalities that still result from such military ordinance throughout the country, the U.S. and many other nations have assisted Cambodia in removing mines and other unexploded ordinance via providing training and equipment.

Select Chronology

c. 0-500 CE	Predecessors of the Khmer civilization characterized by numerous advancements including writing, partly due to the influence of neighboring cultures including that of India
c. 9th century CE	Ancestors of the Khmer people had established some degree of unity and had emerged as a regional power
802 CE	King Jayavarman II founded a unified Khmer Empire (Angkor Kingdom)
c. 13th century	Approximate period of zenith for the early Khmer civilization, after which it begins an extended period of slow decline including deteriorating military and economic circumstances relative to neighboring cultures including ancestors of the Thai and Vietnamese
c. 14th century	Angkor may have been the largest city in the world with a population approaching 1 million
15th–17th century	Period of significant Khmer decline due to competition with Thai and Vietnamese as well as other (e.g., environmental) factors
17th century	First phase of France's involvement in Indochina marked by the arrival of French Jesuit missionaries
19th century	Period of increasing Vietnamese influence and resettlement of significant numbers of ethnic Vietnamese into historically Khmer areas
Latter 19th century	Britain and France compete over territory in Indochina with France ultimately emerging in control of the territories that will become Cambodia, Laos and Vietnam

1863	French protectorate established in Cambodia
1887	Network of protectorates and other territories constituting present-day Cambodia, Laos and Vietnam are brought under unified colonial administrative structure, becoming collectively known as French Indochina
19th–20th centuries	Little economic or other benefit derived by Khmer people from French rule; a sense of Khmer nationalism begins to slowly evolve
1906–1907	The French seize territory in western Cambodia from Thailand via a brief war
1920s	The first communist movements begin to manifest in Indochina, often via elements among the ethnic Chinese minorities via the nascent Chinese Communist Party
1920s–1930s	Small communist cells established in Cambodia among elements of ethnic Vietnamese minorities
1930	Indochinese Communist Party founded by o Chi Minh to advance communist revolution regionally under Vietnamese leadership
1930s	Largely unsuccessful efforts undertaken by France to quell growth of communist cells in Indochina
1940s/50s	Select Cambodian students are sent by the colonial French government to study in Paris where many are recruited and radicalized by the French Communist Party, including Pol Pot and many other eventual leaders of the Khmer Rouge
1940s/50s	The radical left strengthens to become an increasingly important source of anti-colonial, pro-independence agitation in French Indochina
1940	Japan invades French Indochina, beginning with Vietnam and followed by Cambodia and Las the following year
1940–41	Franco-Thai War: Vichy French colonial regime cedes disputed western one-third of Cambodia's territory to Thailand
1940–45	Japan promotes anti-European/western and anti-colonial sentiment which helped further cultivate nationalism in Cambodia and elsewhere in Indochina

SELECT CHRONOLOGY

1941	Vichy French colonial government appoints a young Norodom Sihanouk the new King who contrary to the expectations of the French ultimately proved to be a proponent of Cambodian nationalism/autonomy
1945	At the urging of Japan in the closing days of WWII, Cambodia, Laos and Vietnam declared independence, though French colonial control was quickly re-established and in the case of Cambodia, the short-lived Khmer Issarak government fled and established a government in exile in Thailand until dissolving itself in 1947
1946	In an effort to placate the growing nationalist movement, Cambodia was given limited control over certain domestic affairs by France
1949	After generations of encouraging the resettlement of ethic Vietnamese into Cambodian territory (e.g., the ethnic Khmer had become a minority in the Mekong Delta region due to this colonial practice), the French government reassigned much of what had historically been Khmer territory to Vietnam, a source of significant resentment among Cambodians and eventually a source of strife between the Khmer Rouge regime and Vietnam
Late 40s–early 50s	Viet Minh guerrillas became increasingly potent fighters in Vietnam and in turn provided increased training and support to other communist movements in the region including Cambodia
1950	First national congress of Khmer Issarak - around one-third of the delegates were aligned with various communist factions
1950	France expands Cambodia's semi-autonomous status by granting it authority to establish diplomatic missions
1951	The regional but Vietnamese-led Indochinese Communist Party transforms into several national parties including the Kampuchean People's Revolutionary Party and the Vietnamese Workers' Party in an effort to minimize perceptions of Vietnamese dominance and in turn potentially stimulate more indigenous (e.g., Khmer) support for communist movements in neighboring nations

1950s	The numbers and influence of communists gradually grew, eventually becoming the majority element among Khmer Issarak pro-independence fighters; composition of communists in Cambodia gradually began to shift from mostly ethnic Vietnamese and Chinese minorities to ethnic Khmer
1953	Following a prolonged lobbying effort for international support, King Sihanouk proclaims full independence of Cambodia and initiates efforts to remove Viet Minh guerrilla forces, ordering them to withdraw from Cambodian territory back to Vietnam
1954	Geneva Conference officially concludes First Indochina War; Sihanouk refuses Soviet demands to partition Cambodia into two states with one designated as a communist-led zone as was done in Vietnam—a significant setback for Cambodian communism
1955	Pracheachon founded, the public political wing/party (front organization) of the early Khmer communists which failed to gain widespread support in national elections
1957	Cambodia declares neutrality in Vietnam conflict
1958–1962	China's "Great Leap Foreward," a disastrous experiment in collectivization and societal restructuring resulting in the deaths of tens of millions, primarily from regime-induced famine; Pol Pot appears to have nonetheless modeled many of his radical policies on the failed Chinese experiment
1959	North Vietnam officially declares a state of war with the South
1959	Failed plot to overthrow Sihanouk by right-wing Cambodians and backed by South Vietnam and Thailand led Sihanouk to question alliances with the west and to initiate overtures to communist bloc in an effort to better consolidate his political position
1959	Preparations initiated for Ho Chi Minh Trail through Cambodia and Laos
1960	Cambodian communists reorganized into a more focused and ostensibly more unified organization with a hierarchical and secretive leadership structure
1960	First Viet Cong bases established inside Cambodia

SELECT CHRONOLOGY

Early 1960s	Viet Cong expand the recruitment and training of Cambodian communist cadres
1963	Sihanouk government initiates crackdown targeting growing communist movement, forcing many of its leaders into hiding or exile
February 1963	Pol Pot elected General Secretary of the Workers' Party of Kampuchea
November 1963	U.S.-backed assassination of South Vietnam leader Ngo Dinh Diem worries Sihanouk concerning prospects for South Vietnamese victory and U.S. interference, leading Sihanouk to renounce all U.S. aid and forge alliances with the communist bloc while remaining officially nonaligned
August 1964	Gulf of Tonkin incident leads to large expansion of U.S. military involvement in Second Indochina War
November 1964	Sihanouk renounces all U.S. aid to Cambodia
1965	Sihanouk severs diplomatic ties with U.S. and begins to obtain smaller amounts of financial support from communist bloc while ostensibly maintaining Cambodia's neutrality
1965–1970	Loss of U.S. military/developmental aid results in economic problems including smaller Cambodian government budget including defense spending, leading to declining military capabilities at crucial point of expanding communist strength
1966	Cambodian elections aid conservative anti-communists and erode Sihanouk's power; pro-U.S. Defense Minister Lon Nol appointed Prime Minister; many Cambodian communist go into hiding or exile
1966–1976	China's Cultural Revolution, an Orwellian socio-political purge perpetrated by Mao Zedong resulting in the imprisonment, torture and death of millions which used as a model by Pol Pot and the Khmer Rouge
1967	Open revolt initiated by Cambodian communists against Sihanouk government, marking the formal start of the Cambodian Civil War
1968	NVA and VC forces defeat last large royalist military units in neighboring Laos, setting stage for communist regime two years later

Late 1960s	By this time, the VC were heavily dependant upon Cambodia as a supplier of food and a transit point through which weapons and other supplies flowed; NVA/VC attempted to balance favorable relations with Sihanouk regime while simultaneously accelerating efforts to infiltrate Cambodia with increasing numbers of communist fighters
March 1969	Operation Menu: significant escalation in U.S. bombing campaign in Cambodia primarily targeting the Ho Chi Minh Trail which had little impact upon VC supply routes but ultimately turned public opinion against the U.S./west and aided communist propaganda
May 1969	Sihanouk regime restores diplomatic ties with the U.S.
1969	Security climate continues to deteriorate with Khmer Rouge expanding their operations throughout much of Cambodia and large numbers of NVA and VC troops infiltrating northern and eastern provinces; Sihanouk appears weak and is increasingly criticized for his association with communists—he vainly requests the withdrawal of all Vietnamese forces from Cambodia
1970	As of early 1970, 15–20,000 Vietnamese troops were estimated to have been in Cambodia; Khmer Rouge troop strength was estimated to be 5–10,000
March 1970	Sihanouk and his regime (Kingdom of Cambodia (1956–1970) deposed by Lon Nol/conservatives who established the short-lived Khmer Republic (1970–1975)
1970	Following his ouster, Sihanouk established government in exile in China and aligns himself with communists behind goal of overthrowing Lon Nol government; many of Sihanouk's supporters in Cambodia turn to far left
April 1970	U.S. military and other aid restored; increased throughout period of Lon Nol government
1970	Khmer Rouge rebellion partially contained by Cambodian government forces, but continued to strengthen largely due to Vietnamese forces which had seized much of Cambodia's northeast

SELECT CHRONOLOGY

May 1970	At the request of Cambodia's Republican government around 30,000 U.S. troops and 40,000 South Vietnamese troops temporarily deploy in Cambodia to push back communist forces in parts of the country
1971	By late 1971, some 50–60,000 Vietnamese communist troops were deployed in Cambodia, a significant escalation which gave them full or partial control of 53 of Cambodia's 131 districts
1972–	"Khmerization" of communist forces in Cambodian Civil War gradually accelerated as ethnic Khmer fighters began to assume increasing responsibility for fighting government forces rather than NVA/VC troops
1973	By 1973 around 60% of Cambodia's population lived in the 25% of the country's territory remaining under the control of the Cambodian Republic—millions had fled communist-controlled areas
	U.S. bombing campaign ceases; most NVA/VC troops withdraw from Cambodia
1973–1974	Early radical Khmer Rouge experiments in collectivization, "re-education" and the brutalization and execution of large numbers of subjugated people were undertaken in areas captured by their forces
1974	Government forces largely encircled in the capital and major cities—reduced to primarily defensive posture
	Amid growing anti-Vietnamese rhetoric, Pol Pot and the Khmer Rouge present revisionist history of Cambodian communism in which Vietnam's contributions and foreign influence in general are downplayed
	At the meeting of the Khmer Rouge Central Committee several of the radical, bizarre plans of Pol Pot were first revealed to senior leadership including the forced depopulation of cities and the dystopian, iconoclastic restructuring of Cambodian society

1975	Early in the year the capital was cut off from river supply routes by Khmer Rouge offensives in the Mekong region; airdrops of food, ammunition and other supplies continued, but were insufficient in volume
	Personnel losses in the Cambodian military accelerated and became increasingly untenable
April 1, 1975	Lon Nol resigns and departs the country by plane hoping his removal will permit ceasefire negotiations
April 12, 1975	Upon realizing the Khmer Rouge were not agreeable to negotiations or a ceasefire, Cambodia's acting president fled the capital with remaining U.S. Embassy staff; an emergency government was established
April 17, 1975	Phnom Penh falls to Khmer Rouge; Pol Pot proclaims "Year Zero" marking the start of his sociopathic regime
April 18, 1975	Amid the forced population expulsions from the capital and all other cities, the Khmer Rouge initiates the first phase of large-scale executions begins, first targeting officials, military/police forces, bureaucrats, and supporters of the deposed Republic
1976	Pol Pot regime publicly extols communist doctrine and changed the official name of Cambodia from the Kingdom of Kampuchea (1975–1976), a name reflective of Sihanouk being used as a public figurehead initially, to Democratic Kampuchea (1976–1979)
	Khmer Rouge regime releases its first and only four-year plan, dubbed the "Super Great Leap Forward"—an attempt to emulate China's disastrous prior effort at societal transformation
1977	Khmer Rouge relations with Vietnam deteriorate further largely driven by territorial disputes and Khmer Rouge border attacks and killings of ethnic Vietnamese
	Pol Pot regime severs diplomatic ties with Vietnam citing Hanoi as the greatest threat to Cambodia

SELECT CHRONOLOGY

1977–1978	Rice/food production drops under influence of Khmer Rouge forced collectivization; much of what is produced is seized by the regime rather than distributed to starving population
	Approximate peak period of deaths during the Khmer Rouge regime
	Khmer Rouge resumed and escalated attacks in Thailand border areas in support of Thai communist insurgents
1977–1979	The Khmer Rouge regime begins to turn on itself via factionalization, scapegoating, and internal purges
1978	Vietnam initiates propaganda campaign to delegitimize Khmer Rouge; Hanoi begins organizing and training troops for Cambodian invasion
	China unsuccessfully attempts to de-escalate tensions between the Pol Pot regime and Vietnam
April 1978	Khmer Rouge forces cross border and murder over 3,000 Vietnamese civilians
	Following an initial 1977 incursion ending in withdrawal of its forces in January of 1978, later in the year Vietnamese forces again seize portions of southeast Cambodia to use as staging areas for planned invasion by Vietnamese and anti-Khmer Rouge Cambodian communists
November 1978	Vietnam and Soviet Union sign Treaty of Friendship facilitating increased Soviet aid
December 20, 1978	Anticipating an attack by Hanoi, Khmer Rouge launch preemptive strikes and shelling into Vietnam, escalating to fighting along much of the border by December 23
December 25, 1978	Vietnam initiates full-scale invasion of Cambodia with goal of toppling Pol Pot regime
January 1979	Vietnamese forces capture Phnom Penh; pro-Hanoi People's Republic of Kampuchea proclaimed; Pol Pot's remaining forces flee west and continue resistance via prolonged low-intensity campaign
February–March 1979	Sino-Vietnamese War

March 1979	Most Cambodian territory including all major cities overrun by Vietnamese forces and their Cambodian communist allies
	India, USSR, and most of Soviet bloc officially recognize the Vietnamese installed regime in Cambodia; Pol Pot's rump state remains recognized as the legitimate government of Cambodia by China, the U.S., the UN and around 80 other states
November 1979	United Nations vainly calls for ceasefire and withdrawal of all foreign military forces from Cambodia
1980s–present	Many former Khmer rouge (chiefly those that had defected to Vietnamese and Hanoi-installed regime in Phnom Penh) including Hun Sen assumed leadership roles in new government
1982	Due to the support of China and most western nations, Cambodia's seat/vote at the UN reverts to a Khmer Rouge dominated anti-Vietnamese Cambodian coalition, essentially leaving the seat under Khmer Rouge control until 1993
Late 1980s	Reduction in Soviet aid progressively strains Vietnam's ability to maintain presence in Cambodia; sources of foreign aid to Khmer Rouge rump state also declined
1989	As part of its efforts to counter perceptions that the communist regime in Cambodia was merely a puppet of Hanoi, the Cambodian government changed the country's official name from the People's Republic of Kampuchea to The State of Cambodia
1990s	Progressive decline of Khmer Rouge in territories still under their control
1991	Final withdrawal of Vietnamese forces from Cambodia; Paris Peace Accords establishes UN Transitional Authority in Cambodia (UNTAC)
March 1992	UNTAC mission officially begins—ultimately comprised of some 21,000 military and civilian personnel from over 100 countries
1993	Khmer Rouge remnant boycotts national elections, knowing they could not prevail

SELECT CHRONOLOGY

1994	Constitutional Monarchy reestablished (as figurehead) with Sihanouk reinstated as king; in declining health, he abdicates in 2004 with his son Norodom Sihamoni assuming the throne
1996	Mass defections of many remaining Khmer Rouge under Ieng Sary
1997	Rival Khmer Rouge leader/faction arrests and convicts Pol Pot
	Extraordinary Chambers in the Courts of Cambodia (ECCC – commonly known as the Khmer Rouge Tribunal) to prosecute Khmer Rouge leaders proposed and tentative agreement signed between Cambodian government and the UN
1998	Pol Pot dies while under house arrest imposed by rival Khmer Rouge faction
	Last significant pockets of Khmer Rouge guerillas surrender
1999	Ta Mok, the last Khmer Rouge leader who refused to surrender or defect to the new Cambodian government, was captured
2001	Cambodian government agrees to create national legal institutions/processes for prosecution of Khmer Rouge war criminals
2003	Cambodian government ostensibly reaches agreement with the UN concerning how the international community will participate jointly in the ECCC
2006	Political power sharing arrangement between the Cambodian People's Party (communists) and FUNCINPEC dissolved, leaving the CPP and Hun Sen as the sole governing authority
2012	Sihanouk dies
2022	ECCC formally concludes, having indicted a mere nine former Khmer Rouge, only three of which were found guilty

2023   Former Khmer Rouge battalion commander Hun Sen steps down as Prime Minister after nearly 25 years of authoritarian rule, appointing his son Hun Manet as his successor; such a dynastic pattern can be commonly seen in contemporary Cambodia as aging former Khmer Rouge seek to have their sons or other hand-picked designees installed in their former leadership roles upon retirement

List of Abbreviations

APC: armored personnel carrier
ARVN: Army of the Republic of (South) Vietnam
ASEAN: Association of Southeast Asian Nations
CGDK: Coalition Government of Democratic Kampuchea (coalition of various groups opposed to the Vietnam-installed, post-Khmer Rouge regime)
CIA: Central Intelligence Agency
Comintern: Communist International (1919–1943; political body led by the USSR which advocated the advancement of global communism)
CPK: Communist Party of Kampuchea (1966–1981; Pol Pot's communist faction—synomymous with the term "Khmer Rouge"; successor to earlier Cambodian communist political parties)
CPP: Cambodian People's Party (1991–present; renamed/rebranded successor party to the KPRP)
ECCC: Extraordinary Chambers in the Courts of Cambodia
FANK: French: *Forces Armées Royales Khmères* English: Khmer National Armed Forces (the military forces of the anti-communist Lon Nol government—successor to the Royal Khmer Armed Forces)
FUNCINPEC: French: *Front Uni National pour un Cambodge Indépendant, Neutre, Pacifique, et Coopératif* English: National United Front for an Independent, Neutral, Peaceful, and Cooperative Cambodia (pro-Sihanouk forces/faction)
FUNK: French: *Front Uni National du Kampuchéa* English: National United Front of Kampuchea (the coalition formed between King Sihanouk upon his ouster with the Khmer Rouge)

GRUNK: French: *Gouvernement Royal d'Union Nationale du Kampuchéa*
English: Royal Government of the National Union of Kampuchea (the government in exile established by King Sihanouk following his removal from power by the Lon Nol government)
ICP: Indochinese Communist Party
ICRC: International Committee of the Red Cross
IGO: intergovernmental organization
IR: international relations
KAF: Kampuchean (Cambodian) Air Force (the air forces of the Lon Nol government)
KCP: Kampuchean Communist Party (a synonymous variation of CPK)
KPNLF: Khmer People's Liberation Front (forces/faction that advocated a Cambodian Republic in opposition to the Vietnam-installed government following Hanoi's invasion of Cambodia)
KPRP: Kampuchean (Cambodian) People's Revolutionary Party (1951–1960; offshoot of the ICP which evolved into other communist organs to eventually become the CPK/Khmer Rouge)
KSA: Khmer Students Association (organization of radical Cambodian students studying in France, recruited by the French Communist Party)
KSU: Khmer Students Union (the successor organization to the KSA after the latter was banned)
KUFNS: Kampuchean United Front for Salvation (Vietnam-backed anti-Khmer Rouge communist organization founded in 1978)
NGO: non-governmental organization
NVA: North Vietnamese Army
PRK: People's Republic of Kampuchea (official name for the Vietnam-installed communist regime following Hanoi's invasion of Cambodia)
RCAF: Royal Cambodian Armed Forces
UN: United Nations
UNICEF: United Nations International Children's Emergency Fund
UNTAC: United Nations Transitional Authority Cambodia
USAF: United States Air Force
U.S.: United States
USS: United States Ship (designation for U.S. Navy vessels)
USSR: Union of Soviet Socialist Republics (Soviet Union)
VC: Viet Cong

Index

A

Afghanistan (Afghan-Soviet War), xix
agrarianism, xvii, xix, 17, 46, 48, 80, 114, 129, 134, 136, 145-146, 148-150, 198, 223, 247
agriculture, 4, 130, 147
"Angkar", 132
Angkor Wat, vii, 4-5
Ankor Kingdom, 16
anti-colonialism, xvi, 8, 14, 17, 31-34, 37, 264
anti-communist efforts (in colonial Cambodia), 31, 43
apologists (of communism/Khmer Rouge), ii, 147, 163, 223-224, 238, 247, 253
ARVN, 102, 103, 275
ASEAN, xxviii, 120, 185, 190-193, 203-204, 275
asylum, 241
atrocities, ii, vii, xiv, xxxi, xxxv-xxxvi, 114, 157, 162-163, 169, 191, 216, 222-229, 238, 253
attrition, 116, 131
autarky, 146, 149, 227, 289

B

Ba Chuc massacre, 179
Bao Dai, 59
Bolsheviks, 131

bombing, 60, 69, 72-75, 78, 80, 92, 101, 105, 115, 239, 268-269
border/boundary disputes, xxvii, xxx, 67, 175, 191, 239, 257
border fighting/incursions, xv, xxix, xxvi, 35-36, 39, 68, 75, 81, 100-103, 108, 130, 172-173, 178, 180, 186-187, 191, 195-198, 245, 255-259, 270-271
Britain, 6, 32-33, 35, 38, 59, 263
Buddhism/Buddhist, 3, 97, 110, 114, 134, 139, 148, 150, 160, 164, 177, 214, 221-222, 225, 237, 245-246
Bull, Hedley, xxxii-xxxiii
Burma/Myanmar, 6, 168

C

caloric intake, 167
Cambodia (see topical entries)
Cambodian (government) Army, 36, 63, 70, 84, 92, 99
Cambodian independence, xvii, xxxiv, 14-15, 19-20, 22, 24, 29-52
Cambodian National Assembly, 22, 43, 61, 76, 78, 80, 92-94, 191, 199, 210, 215, 228-229
Cambodian (government) Navy, 63, 99, 116
Cambodian People's Party, 228, 273, 275
casualties, 34, 37, 66, 74, 92, 98, 103, 107, 116, 123, 160, 174, 197, 210, 242-243, 245, 256, 259
Central Intelligence Agency, 16, 40, 71, 96, 116, 161, 170
Cham Muslims, 160, 177, 216, 222, 248
Chea Sim, 228
Chiang Kai-Shek, 31-32
Chinese (ethnic minority in Cambodia), xvii, 3, 8-9, 20, 29, 44-45, 47, 52, 95, 109, 160, 168, 177, 230, 248, 264, 266
Chinese Communist Party, 9, 45, 264
Choeung Ek mass grave site, 158-159, 252
Christians, 6, 31, 222, 225
class warfare, 11, 78, 132, 140
classical realism, xx-xxii, xxv, xxxi, xxxiii
coalition(s), xxxv, 14, 19, 21, 35, 42-43, 45, 92, 95-97, 102, 111, 113, 185, 192-193, 200, 203-204, 209-210, 212, 214-215, 235-236, 241, 243, 257, 272, 275

collectivization, xvii, 6, 79, 96, 114, 131, 135, 144, 147-148, 157, 159, 223-224, 246, 266, 269, 271
Comintern, 10-11, 16, 19, 275
communism (see topical entries)
communist bloc, xiv, xviii-xix, 38-40, 61-62, 64-65, 72, 78, 130, 162, 170, 193, 195, 223-224, 237, 239, 266-267
Communist Party of Kampuchea, 46, 48, 78, 132, 137, 237, 275
Comrade Duch (Kaing Guek Eav), 219, 225-226
conscription, 98, 116, 173, 192, 213
conservatives, xxxiv, 43, 58, 76, 80-82, 91-94, 163, 172, 237, 267-268
constitutional monarchy, 123, 209, 212, 273
constructivism (IR theory of), xx-xxi, xxvii
corruption/graft, 8, 60, 80, 82, 98, 102, 140, 210, 218, 230
Cultural Revolution, xvii, 78-79, 134-136, 175, 267

D

death marches, 145, 147, 159, 162, 250
death toll, 37, 66, 74, 135, 159, 165-166, 174, 203, 210-211, 245
decolonization, 6, 8, 30-31, 79
defections (Khmer Rouge), xxxvi, 199, 209, 213, 215-216, 218, 220, 226-227, 255-266, 272-273
DeGaulle, Charles, 31
Democratic Kampuchea, 193, 203, 270, 275
de-Stalinization, xix
disease, 105, 118, 130, 150, 161, 166-167, 247-248
Dulles, John Foster, 22, 38
Dutch Communist Party, 11

E

East Germany, 48, 62
Eastern Zone, xvii, 78, 164, 180, 215, 226, 255
economy, 8, 31, 63-64, 75, 130-132, 137, 149
educational institutions, 8, 79, 129, 150-151, 157, 246
elections, xxxvi, 39, 43-44, 46-47, 58-59, 76, 193, 202-204, 209-215, 220, 228-229, 236, 266-267, 272
English School (of international relations), xxi, xxxi-xxxiii

ethnic cleansing, xxxi, 130, 259

ethnic minorities, xv-xvii, xxix, xxxi, xxxv, 1, 9-10, 14, 17, 20, 30, 44-45, 50, 52, 67, 84, 95-96, 103, 106, 109-110, 130, 160, 173, 177, 194-195, 201, 211-213, 222, 230, 245, 248, 257-258, 264-266

ethnocentrism, xiii, xvi-xvii, xxix, xxix, 6, 109, 133, 148, 259

executions, 112, 129-130, 141-142, 147, 151, 157-159, 161, 163-165, 167, 247-254, 269-270

exiles, 23, 50, 77-78, 94-95, 105, 185, 187, 192-193, 220, 227, 265, 267, 276

Extraordinary Chambers in the Courts of Cambodia (ECCC), 217-219, 221-219, 226, 273, 275

F

factions, xvii-xix, xxxv, 18-19, 21-22, 35, 40-41, 44, 46, 97, 106, 112-113, 133, 195, 199, 203-204, 210-214, 220, 227, 235, 265

FANK, 98-99, 102-103, 107, 115-116, 119, 121, 275

famine/food insecurity, 5, 108, 114, 117-118, 131, 135, 142, 145-147, 149, 159, 167, 179, 201-202, 211, 223-224, 266, 270-271

filtering/checkpoints, 142, 147

flooding, 5, 116-117, 258

food shortages (see famine/food insecurity)

forced evacuation of cities, xxxv, 78, 114, 129, 136-149, 159, 224, 246-247, 250, 269-270

forced labor, xxxv, 78-79, 129, 135, 143, 145, 147, 149, 157, 159, 162, 167, 173, 179, 185, 198, 246-248, 250, 252, 255

foreign aid, xxxv, 15, 33, 50, 60-64, 75, 101, 106-107, 115, 119, 145-146, 170, 173, 175-176, 186, 194-195, 199, 202, 209, 211, 226-227, 267-268, 271-272

foreign relations of Khmer Rouge, 168-180, 186, 194-195, 199, 226-227, 267-268, 271-272

France, xxxiv, 6-8, 10-15, 19-24, 30-32, 35-38, 44, 46-47, 50, 57, 131, 143, 148, 235, 263-265, 276

Franco-Thai War, 12, 264

Free French government, 32

French Communist Party, 19, 44, 46, 48, 264, 276

French Foreign Legion, 37

French Indochina, 6, 11-12, 14, 29-30, 33-34, 36-37, 40, 43, 264
FUNCINPAC, 185
FUNK, 96-97, 104-105, 111-113, 120, 137-139, 275

G

Geneva Conference, 24, 36-45, 49, 51, 58-59, 75, 266
genocide, xxvii, xxxv, 130, 142, 150, 157-180, 186, 191, 200-201, 216-217, 219, 221-224, 229, 247, 251, 257
geopolitics, xiii-xiv, xviii-xix, xxii, xxxiv, 1, 12, 15, 29-32, 39-40, 44, 62, 75, 77, 169, 171, 175, 191, 193, 202, 238
Great Leap Forward, 79, 132, 134-136, 175, 266, 270
GRUNK, 95-96, 110, 121, 276
guerrillas, 39, 68, 75, 187, 239, 260, 265
Gulf of Tonkin Incident/Resolution, 65-66, 267

H

hegemony, xviii-xix, xxi, xxiii-xxvi, 4, 196
Heng Samrin, 199-200, 204, 210, 214-216, 226, 228-229
Ho Chi Minh, 9, 11-12, 16-18, 33, 59
Ho Chi Minh Trail, 67, 70-74, 108, 239-241, 243, 266, 268
Hou Youn, 47, 96, 137
human rights violations, xiv, xxvii, xxx, 109, 198, 210-211, 216, 222-223, 229-230, 247, 259
Human Rights Watch, 229
Hu Nim, 58, 96-97, 164
Hun Sen, 209, 214-220, 226, 228-229, 272-274
Hungary, xix

I

iconoclasty, xiv-xxxv, 3, 78, 114, 132, 148-149, 159, 237, 245, 269
ideology, vii-xv, xviii-xix, xxviii, xxxi-xxxii, xxxv, 1, 11, 17, 18, 29-30, 45, 48, 61, 76-77, 80, 97, 114, 129-136, 148, 151, 164, 170-171, 175-177, 185, 198-199, 224, 226-230, 238-239, 259
Ieng Sary, 19, 48, 78, 111, 113, 134, 178, 189, 217, 219-220-238, 273
imperialism, xvi, xxix, 3, 10-11, 84, 104, 169, 186
incursions

    into Cambodia, 36, 38-40, 69, 92, 103-104, 179, 186, 195, 242-243, 257, 271
    into Thailand, 7, 171, 190-191
    into Vietnam, 42, 130, 175, 178, 180, 186-187, 196
India, xix, 3, 8-9, 15, 33, 160, 263, 272
Indian National Congress, 8
indigenous communities, 49, 81
Indochinese Communist Party, 9-10, 18, 45, 264-265, 276
Indonesia, 101, 104, 191
Indonesian Communist Party, 11
infanticide, 158, 164, 252-254
insurgents, 15, 17, 22, 43, 45, 51-52, 57, 60-63, 67, 69, 84-85, 113, 134, 139, 172, 185, 235, 271
international relations, theory xx-xxxiii
international tribunal (see Extraordinary Chambers in the Courts of Cambodia)
isolationism, xxxv, 116, 130, 136, 143, 168-171, 203

J

Japan (WWII), 12-14, 22, 31-33, 120, 169, 264-265
Jayavarman II, 4, 263
Jesuits, 6, 263

K

Kampuchean People's Revolutionary Party, 46, 112, 203, 228, 265
Khieu Samphan, 19, 48, 96-97, 111, 219-220
Khmer
    Ancient, 2, 3, 7, 16, 160, 172, 263
    ethnicity, xv-xviii, xxii, xxix-xxx, 5, 8-9, 14, 16, 20-21, 35, 45-46, 48-50, 67, 80, 92, 94- 98, 104-105, 109-111, 150, 172, 177-178, 180, 201, 243, 248, 265-266, 269
    language, 3, 80, 129, 160, 177, 246
Khmer Communist Party, 170
Khmer Empire, 7, 172, 263
Khmer Issarak (Free Khmer), 2, 14-15, 17, 19-22, 34-36, 45, 61, 106, 133, 265-266

Khmerland, 41-42
Khmer People's National Liberation Front, 185, 192, 203
Khmer Republic, xxxiv, 91-123, 268
Khmer Rouge (see topical entries)
Khmer Serei, 69
Khmer Students Association, 19, 46, 276
Khmer Viet Minh, 18, 35-36, 45, 70, 97, 105, 133
Khrushchev, Nikita, xix
killing fields, 157-180
kinship networks, 132, 140, 144, 150-151, 160, 246, 251-252
King Norodom Sihamoni, 273
King Norodom Sihanouk (see topical entries)
King Sisowath Monivong, 13
Korea
    division of (Geneva Accords), 37, 40
    North, 77, 135-136, 149, 168, 193
    South, 101, 104, 244,
KUFNS, 180, 276

L

labor camps, xxv, 129, 147, 149, 151, 157-159, 165, 173, 179, 198, 246-247, 250, 252, 256
landmines, 171, 201, 211-212, 230, 261
Laos
    alignment with Vietnam, 15, 17-18, 42-43, 45, 50, 168-169, 193
    Civil War, 14, 23, 33-42, 57, 66-68, 71-72, 100, 111, 241
    territory/border dispute, xvii, 130, 172-173
level(s) of analysis (within international relations), xvi-xx
liberal theory/idealism (within international relations), xxvi-xxviii
Lon Nol, viii, xxxv, 76, 82, 84-85, 91-94, 97-98, 101-102, 104, 108-110, 115, 118, 120-121, 137-138, 147, 162, 171-172, 237, 243, 267-268, 270, 275-276
Long Boret, 139

M

Mao Zedong, xix, 132, 135, 238, 267

Maoism/Maoist, viii, 18, 79, 82, 97, 111, 133-134, 140, 175

Marx(ism), xx-xxi, xxix-xxxi, 10-11, 19, 46, 48, 106, 132, 134, 224, 228, 238

mass graves, 157-159, 247-248, 251-253, 273

Mearshimer, John, xxiv

Mekong Delta, 3, 14, 16, 29-30, 109, 116, 118-119, 174, 176, 188, 257, 265, 270

military assistance/training, xxxv, 16, 21, 50-51, 60, 62-64, 68, 101, 106, 108, 119, 178, 195, 243, 258

minorities (see ethnic minorities or religious minorities)

Missionaries (also see Jesuits), 6, 142, 263

Modus Vivendi Agreement, 35

Monatio, 138

N

National Assembly (of Cambodia), 22, 43, 61, 76, 78, 80, 92-94, 199, 215, 228

nationalism, xiii, xvi-xvii, xxxv, 1, 13-14, 22, 30, 34, 133, 213, 259, 264-265

Nationalist China, 31, 32

neorealism/structural realism (IR theory of), xx-xxviii, xxxiii

neutrality, xxxiv-xxxvi, 12, 39, 50-51, 58, 60-62, 68-69, 75, 79, 84-85, 91, 93-95, 100, 102, 162,   170, 177, 192, 203, 237, 266-267, 275

Ngo Dinh Diem, 58, 61, 267

Nixon, Richard, 101, 104, 241

non-governmental organizations (NGOs), xxvi-xxvii, 157, 168, 276

"non-producers", 129, 145, 159, 247

North Korea (see Korea, North)

North Vietnam, 34, 38-39, 41-44, 49-50, 52, 59-60, 62, 64, 68-70, 75, 77, 81, 91-92, 95, 97, 100, 105, 111, 134, 235, 237, 266

Nuon Chea, 78, 219

NVA, viii, xxxiv, 43, 51, 65-68, 70-73, 81, 92, 98, 100-103, 239, 241, 243, 267-268, 276

O

Operation Menu, 74, 268

INDEX

Ottoman Empire, 9

P
Paris Group, 44, 46-49, 131-135
Paris Peace Accords (1991), 186, 203, 272
Pathet Lao, 42, 68-69
patronage, 44, 61, 77, 91, 104-106, 113, 210, 214, 218, 237
peasant(s), xxxi, 11, 17, 19, 22, 46, 48, 58, 77, 80, 82-84, 94-95, 107-110, 131, 135-137, 140, 150, 167, 198
People's Republic of Cambodia/Kampuchea, xxxvi, 189, 192, 199, 228, 260, 271-272, 276
phases of Khmer Rouge Genocide, xxxv, 130, 159-164
Pol Pot (see topical entries)
Popular Socialist Community, 43
population "rebalancing", 143-144, 147
post-war resettlement, 201, 211, 257
post-WWII transitions, 12-19
Potsdam Conference, 32
power transition theory, xxi, xxiii
Pracheachon, 44, 46-47, 49, 78, 266
Prince Norodom Ranariddh, 214-215, 217
propaganda, 13, 61, 65, 67, 75, 80, 84, 94, 104, 106, 110, 129, 139, 160, 162-163, 172, 180, 186, 198, 213, 223, 225, 242, 247, 252, 257, 268, 271
proxy war, xix-xx, xxxiii, xxxvi, 34, 51, 112, 185, 235
pseudo neutrality, xxxiv, xxxvi, 95, 162
psychological control/intimidation, 139, 144, 165
punishments, 114, 129, 144, 147-148, 150, 159, 167, 197, 200, 228
Puolo Wai, 174
purges, xxxi, 60, 78, 96, 105, 112, 120, 135, 137, 141, 158, 179, 187, 215, 220, 226-227, 255-256, 267, 271

R
rationality, xxi, 132, 144, 164, 180
realism (IR theory of), xvi, xx, xxi-xxvi
    defensive realism, xxi, xxv

offensive realism, xxv, xxvi
rebuilding, 31, 37, 200-201
reconciliation, 138, 178, 186, 200, 204, 211
Red Cross, 121, 146, 276
refugees (camps), 118, 121, 136-137, 142, 146, 161, 171, 173, 198, 211, 223, 255-256
religious conversions of former KR, 225
religious minorities of Cambodia, 160, 177, 216, 222
religious persecution, 114, 129, 135, 141, 148, 150, 160, 222, 246, 248
revisionism (also see apologists), xxxvi, 47, 106, 177, 199, 222-224, 253, 269
rice, 5, 64, 69, 72, 75, 81-83, 92, 118-119, 129, 145-147, 167, 178, 199, 201, 235, 271
Roosevelt, Franklin Delano, 31-32
Royal Cambodian Armed Forces, 214, 276
rump state, xix, xxxvi, 130, 165, 185-204, 209, 220, 225-226, 260, 272

S

S-21, 157-159, 222, 224-226, 249-252
Sak Sutsakhan, 120-121
Saloth Sar, viii, 11, 47, 170
Salvation Front, 200
Saukham Koy, 121
Second Indochina War, xxxiv, 34, 36, 52, 57-66, 68, 70, 236, 267
Secrecy, 18, 50, 70, 78, 101, 111, 114, 129, 132, 136, 161, 170, 178, 266-267
Siam (also see Thailand), 4-6
Sihanouk, Norodom (see topical entries)
Sihanoukville, 72-73, 92
Sino-Soviet relations, xxix, 44, 202, 239
Sino-Soviet split, xiv, xvii, xxiv, 44, 51, 239
Sino-Vietnamese relations (border war), 195-198, 202, 203, 259, 271
Sirik Matak, 139
So Phim, 78
Son Ngoc Minh, 49
Son Ngoc Thanh, 15, 22

INDEX

Son Sen, 19, 220-221
South Korea (see Korea, South)
South Vietnam, 42, 49, 58-59, 68, 78, 103, 109, 186, 244
    IR/relations with Cambodia, 38, 51, 59-61, 68-70, 82, 101-102, 110, 266-267, 269
    military, 50-51, 60, 66-67, 71-72, 74, 81, 92, 97, 100, 102-106, 108, 115, 162, 235-237, 239, 241, 242-243, 269
Soviet Union, 38, 40, 68, 80, 129-131, 134, 136, 169, 175-176, 191, 194, 276
    Cambodia relations, 24, 51-52, 61, 68-69, 93, 110, 112, 143, 170, 173, 201-202, 266, 272
    China relations, xix, xxv, xxix, 31-32, 195-196, 202
    Vietnamese relations, xxiii, 9-10, 40-41, 48, 59-60, 72, 121, 134, 185-186, 191, 194-196, 271-272
Stalin, Joseph, xviii, xix, 17, 132, 135, 141, 238
starvation (see famine/food insecurity)
State of Cambodia, 192, 199, 228, 272
"Super Great Leap Forward", 134, 270

T

Tay Ninh Massacre, 78, 178
territorial disputes, (see border disputes)
Tet Offensive, 70
Thailand
    IR/foreign relations, 6-7, 12, 16, 22-23, 35, 51, 104, 169, 172, 190, 195
    military, 12, 171-172, 190
    relations with Cambodia, xvii, 4-5, 12, 20, 69, 101, 130, 161, 168, 171-172, 177, 189-190, 194-195, 198-199
Thai Communist Party/insurgency, 20, 172, 190-191, 194
theory (in international relations), xx-xxxiii
Tito, Josep Braz, xiii, xvii, 135
Tonle Sap Lake, 7
Torture, 114, 130, 150-151, 157-158, 161, 164-167, 225, 229, 247-248, 250-253, 267
Tou Samouth, 48, 112

training camps, 15-17, 49-50, 67, 84, 241, 243
Transparency International, 230
tribunals (see Extraordinary Chambers in the Courts of Cambodia)
Tuol Sleng Prison (see S-21)

U

UNICEF, 146, 276
United Nations, 118, 211-212, 217-218
    peacekeepers/observers, 190, 192, 211-212
    positions/policies, 60, 121, 162, 191, 194, 204, 220, 222, 272-273
    Secretary General, 191, 210
United Nations Transitional Authority Cambodia (UNTAC), 204, 209-212, 228
United States (see topical entries)
USS Mayaguez, 174, 244, 245
USSR (see Soviet Union)

V

Vichy (French regime), 12-14, 32-33, 264-265
Viet Cong, viii, xxxiv, 51-52, 67, 69-70, 78, 81, 85, 92, 94-95, 98, 100-102, 108, 237, 239, 241, 243, 266-267
Viet Minh, 14-22, 24, 30, 33-45, 48, 60, 265-266
Vietnam (see topical entries)
Vietnam-US War (see Second Indochina War)
Vietnamese (ethnic minority in Cambodia), xvii, xxii, xxxvi, 5, 8-10, 13, 16-17, 20, 29-30, 45, 50, 67, 92, 95, 109-110, 130, 178, 180, 194, 201, 212-213, 216, 222, 257, 263-264, 266, 270
Vietnamese Workers' Party, 265
Vong Sarendy, 139

W

war communism, 130-134, 152
war crimes (also see ECCC), xxxvi, 142, 157, 161, 163, 177, 209, 216-227
Wendt, Alexander, xxviii
WikiLeaks, xxviii

INDEX

withdrawal of Vietnamese forces, 40, 44-45, 49, 105-106, 112, 120, 174-175, 191, 193, 200, 202-204, 210, 268, 271-272
Workers Party of Kampuchea, 46, 78
World War II, xxix, xxxii, 12-15, 31-34, 37, 63, 74, 101, 196, 235, 265

X

xenophobia, xiii-xviii, xxix, xxxv, 1, 6, 29, 30, 94, 106, 109, 133, 142, 148, 160, 180, 213, 227, 259

Y

"Year Zero", 148, 246, 270
youth/background of Khmer Rouge fighters, 140-143, 151, 179, 252
Yugoslavia, xiii, xvii, xix, 62, 134-135, 145, 168

Z

Zhou Enlai, 40

#

1977-78 Vietnamese incursion into Cambodia, 172, 174, 177-179, 186, 196, 270-271
1981 UN International Conference on Kampuchea, 191, 287
1993 Cambodian elections, 212-215, 228, 272

About the Author

B.D. Mowell has taught in higher education for over 30 years, serving on the full-time or adjunct faculty of multiple colleges and universities. He has taught a variety of courses related to international studies including Introduction to International Relations, Comparative Government/Politics, International Organizations, Human Geography, and Geography of the Eastern World at the undergraduate level. Mowell has also taught a range of courses at the graduate level including International Political Systems, International Relations Theory, International Security Issues, Nationalism and Identity, Politics and War, and Strategic Geography and Geopolitics. Over his career, he has received numerous forms of recognition for his teaching including two endowed teaching chair awards, classroom research award and having been named Professor of the Year at his institution and a semi-finalist for state professor of the year by the Association of Florida Colleges.

The author holds ten academic degrees: undergraduate degrees in behavioral science and geography; five master's degrees in comparative religion, geography/history, marketing, nonprofit management/public administration, and political science. He completed a specialist degree in curriculum and instruction from the University of Tennessee and a doctorate in social science education from the University of Georgia. His PhD is in political science from Florida International University (the state university in Miami) with concentrations in international and comparative politics. Mowell completed doctoral work in international studies at the University of Miami and post-doctoral work via Harvard University's Summer/Extension College from which he obtained a graduate certificate in international security.

His research interests in recent years have focused upon international/national security issues, international organizations and political extremism. To date he has over 100 publications including books, book chapters in edited volumes, and articles in peer-reviewed academic journals. Recent book chapters include: "Xenophobia Unleashed: Anti-German Attitudes and Policies During WWI" in *U.S. Security Issues During World War I* (University of North Georgia Press 2023); "Cambodian Religious Communities and the Khmer Rouge Genocide" in *Routledge Handbook on Religion and Genocide* (Routledge 2022); "The LTTE and Prospects for Renewal of the Sri Lankan Insurgency" in *Emerging Conflicts and Regional Security in South Asia* (Routledge 2019); "U.S. Nuclear Weapons Policy and Strategy" in *The Future of U.S. Warfare* (Taylor and Francis 2017); "Domestic and Transnational Dimensions of Narcoterrorism and Countermeasures in Mexico" and "Comparative Analysis of Counterterrorism Issues, Policies and Institutions in Northern Europe and the Baltic States" in *Palgrave Handbook of Global Counterterrorism Studies* (Palgrave 2016).

Examples of recent journal articles include: "The Nature and Degree of NGO Interactions with the United Nations within the ECOSOC Framework" in *Estudios Internacionales* (2025); "Macro-Regional Patterns of Transnational CSO Affiliation/Participation within the UN-Civil-Society Framework: The Underrepresentation of Africa, Asia and the Developing World" in *Estudos Internacionais: Journal of International Relations* (2023); "Barriers to UN-Civil Society Collaborations: An Exploratory Study of CSOs within the UN-ECOSOC Consultative Status Program" in *International Studies* (2021); "Patterns of Representation in UN-Affiliated NGOs Related to Millennium Development Goals/Monterrey Areas and Regional Parity" in *Journal of Global South Studies* (2018); "Women in UN Peacekeeping Roles: Historical and Contemporary Patterns" in *E-International Relations* (2018); and "Pluralism and Proportionality in the Representation of European Transnational Civil Society within the UN Framework: A Sub-Regional Comparison" in *Journal of European Politics and Society* (2017).

Dr. Mowell has had a range of organizational affiliations throughout his career including serving a Fellow of the Royal (British) Geographical Society and a member of the Royal International Affairs Society (Chatham House), Consular Corps College, Foreign Policy Research Institute, World Affairs Council, and the National Council for Geographic Education—for which

ABOUT THE AUTHOR

he edited multiple books. He is a Founding Member of the Remembrance Society of the Victims of Communism Foundation/Museum. He has served as an Honorary Consul of the Republic of Latvia and as the United Nations Representative for multiple NGOs. Mowell has also served on the boards of directors of numerous governmental bodies and non-profit organizations.

www.ingramcontent.com/pod-product-compliance
Lightning Source LLC
Chambersburg PA
CBHW070750230426
43665CB00017B/2318